AF394521

Portrait of Britain
Vol 2

Portrait of Britain Vol 2

First edition

Sequence by Daniele Roa
Text edited by Gemma Padley
and Faith McAllister
Production by Anna De Pascale
Repro by Touch Digital
Cover image by Digby Oldridge

Images shortlisted from Portrait of Britain
2019, created by *British Journal of
Photography*

With thanks to Shaz Madani for initial
series design and Héloise Winstone for
production support

A CIP catalogue record for this book
is available from the British Library

ISBN 978-1-910566-54-1

First published in the United Kingdom
in 2019 by Hoxton Mini Press

Printed and bound by Livonia, Latvia

To order books, collector's editions
and signed prints please go to:
www.hoxtonminipress.com

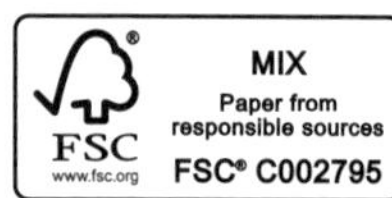

Portrait of Britain

Vol 2

HOXTON MINI PRESS

BJP x HMP

When we published the first *Portrait of Britain* volume in 2018 (the one with the man clad in a Union Jack wrestling costume on the front, looking either resigned or hopeful, you decide), we weren't surprised it sold out rather quickly. The whole notion of Britishness was very much up for grabs and the idea that a book containing a series of photographs could capture its essence was both preposterous and provocative. The images were seen up and down the country on billboards through a competition organised by the *British Journal of Photography*. We were worried, however, that come this year, when this annual collaboration with the *BJP* returned, the theme would be less prescient. We would have severed ties with the EU and be somewhere mid-Atlantic, drinking tea and fending off sharks with scones.

But here we are, still tethered, still confused, still angry, still screaming. The child on the front having a tantrum stuck in her tiny plastic chair probably knows nothing of Brexit. But something tells me she's well-versed in its drama and quite possibly knows more than both you and I about its outcome.

And what can I say of the pictures in this book? It goes without saying that it's unlikely they provide a coherent, simple portrait of what it is to be British. Sorry. But they are, each of them, arresting and original and remind us not only of the diversity of individuals in this country but also the diversity of how we view those individuals. I've always thought portrait photographs show as much of the photographer as they do their subject, and the many faces in here show the many ways of seeing ourselves. There is no one lens through which to view this country – as much as the politicians may persuade us there can be. And surely that kaleidoscopic picture is the portrait we are looking for: multifaceted, forever changing, full of different hopes and emotions. Long may that continue. But please, let's stop screaming.

Martin Usborne
Co-founder
Hoxton Mini Press

Introduction

In 1946, *How to Be an Alien* by George Mikes first appeared in print. Mikes was a Hungarian journalist who had left Nazi-occupied Europe for Britain at the start of World War Two. Presenting itself as a survival guide for emigrants, his book offered a satirical portrait of the author's new homeland. Mikes praised British 'virtues' such as 'patience, tolerance, cool-headedness, wry humour, courtesy'. And he also mocked our 'national passion' for queuing, discussing the weather and imbibing tea at any conceivable opportunity.

Over 70 years later *How to be an Alien* is still in print and has sold hundreds of thousands of copies. It's a classic in the genre of writings on national identity that stretches from George Orwell's 1941 essay, *England Your England* (that's the one about 'old maids biking to Holy Communion through the mists of the autumn morning') to, more recently, bestsellers like Bill Bryson's *Notes from a Small Island*.

The collective picture that emerges from these works is of a country whose customs and tastes and values have gone essentially unchanged for generations. Britain was, and will ever be, in Bryson's description, 'a green and kindly island' where people say 'Mustn't grumble', and 'Ooh lovely' at the sight of a plate of biscuits, and tune in devotedly to the *Shipping Forecast* and *Gardeners' Question Time*.

In movies, media and the popular imagination at large, it's this image of Britain that looms large as the true, authentic picture of the nation. What is the Brexit Leave vote if not an angry rejection of the complexity of globalised modernity in favour of the simplicities and certainties of an inviolable island condition. More tea, anyone?

The trouble is we do ourselves a disservice as a nation if we imagine this as the only real version of Britishness. The portraits in this book offer a different view of who we are. Here, we see not an idea of national identity defined by a set of homogenous traits. But something less prescriptive. We see a country unscripted, revealed page by page, in all its joy, its sorrows and anxieties, its accidental beauty.

A boy with freckles leans pensive over
the handlebars of his bike (p.285).
A woman in a yellow 'Girl Power'
t-shirt, stands in a field, untroubled by
the ominous clouds gathered behind her
(p.191). A group of teenage girls in mini
skirts cluster together, gloriously young
and unstoppable (p.291). There are drag
queens and the copiously tattooed,
the queer, the camp, the headscarfed,
the gimp masked. Men and women
with facial disfigurements, physical
disabilities and emotional fragilities
impossible to see from the outside.
And the young couple locked together
in a moment of harmony. Her eyes are
closed and she's resting her head on her
partner's shoulder. And watching them,
all you can think is how beautiful
they look, as if nothing of the world's
carelessness has yet to visit them (p.295).

Turning from face to face, I'm reminded
of another tradition of Britishness by
which we can know this country.
A way of life that's more vigorous
but no less valid than that described
by Mikes or Bryson. That's the Britain
of housing estates and illegal raves;
of drill, grime and dubstep; of ancient
and frankly rather weird folk festivals
in rural towns; of sticking two fingers
up to pompous officials.

As it happens, it was Orwell who was
one of the first to describe this more
discrepant strain in our national culture.
In the same essay that he waxes bucolic
about bicycling old maids, he falters
for a moment and, in a voice suddenly
uncertain, he seems to be glimpsing a
changing Britain coming into view.
'Are we not 46 million individuals,
all different? And the diversity of it,
the chaos! The clatter of clogs in the
Lancashire mill towns, the to-and-fro
of the lorries on the Great North Road,
the queues outside the Labour Exchanges...
How can one make a pattern out of
this muddle?'

Perhaps Orwell didn't need to worry.
Perhaps the way to make best sense
of Britishness is to acknowledge that
the muddle is the pattern. By that I
mean that the truth of Britain doesn't
necessarily lie in the countryside or
in the city. It's not about modernity vs
tradition or Remain vs Leave. There is
not a finite amount of national identity
to go around. That's what the portraits
in this book remind us of so eloquently.
There's no mystery to being British.
You just have to be yourself.

Ekow Eshun
London, 2019

Portraits

MABEL
by Dan Sully
London

My beautiful daughter, Mabel, at seven months.
I usually encourage her to smile when I take photos
of her but this time I captured her natural,
quizzical look.

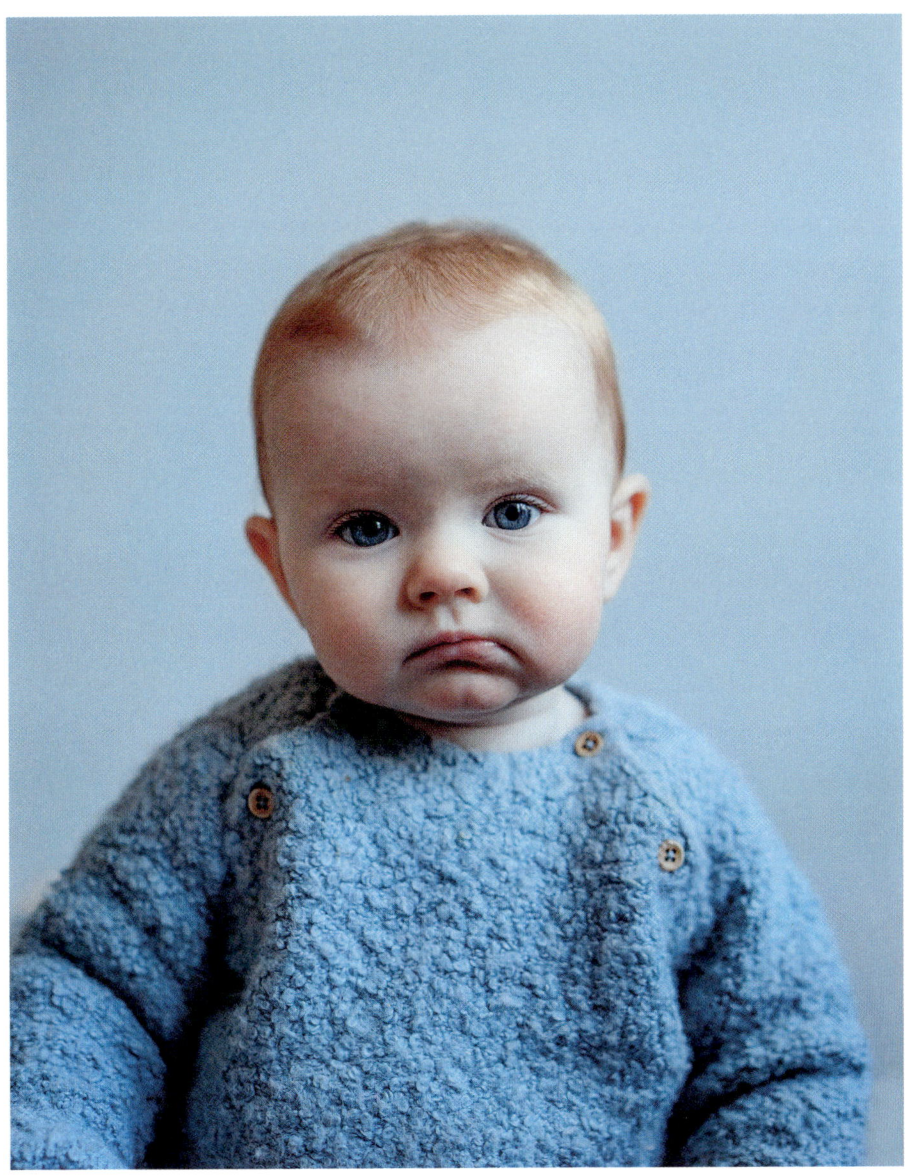

JACK HILL WITH HIS DAUGHTER
by Antonina Mamzenko
London

This is award-winning photojournalist Jack Hill with
his daughter during the People's Vote march in October
2018. I've attended as many marches as possible in
2018 and 2019 and have been moved by the sight
of so many families taking part.

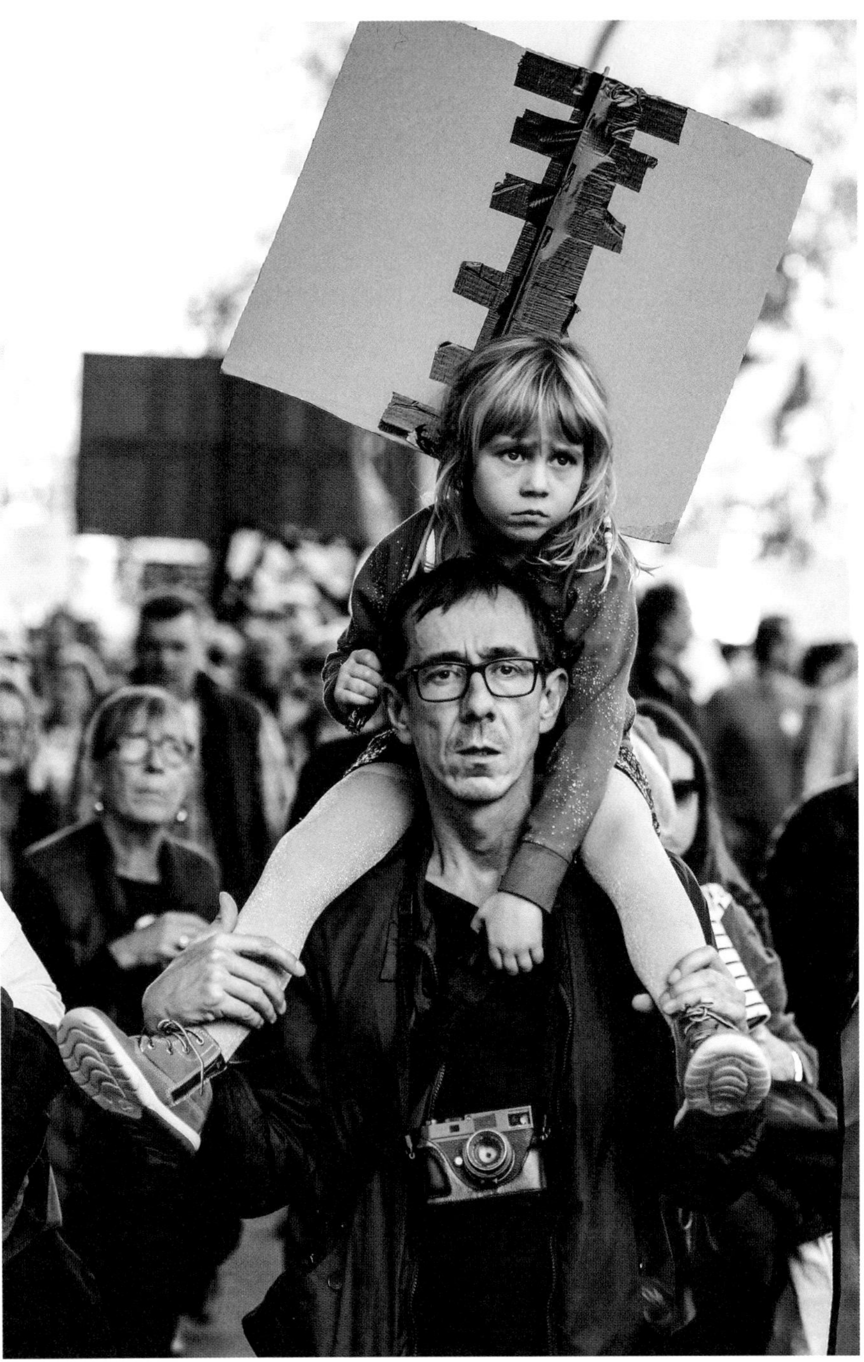

FLORENCE
by Matilda Hill-Jenkins
London

Florence is my younger sister by three years.
We were extremely close. I started photographing her
religiously six years ago. Our dad died in September 2018
and I fell out with her and my mum a few months later.
We've not spoken since. I miss her every day.

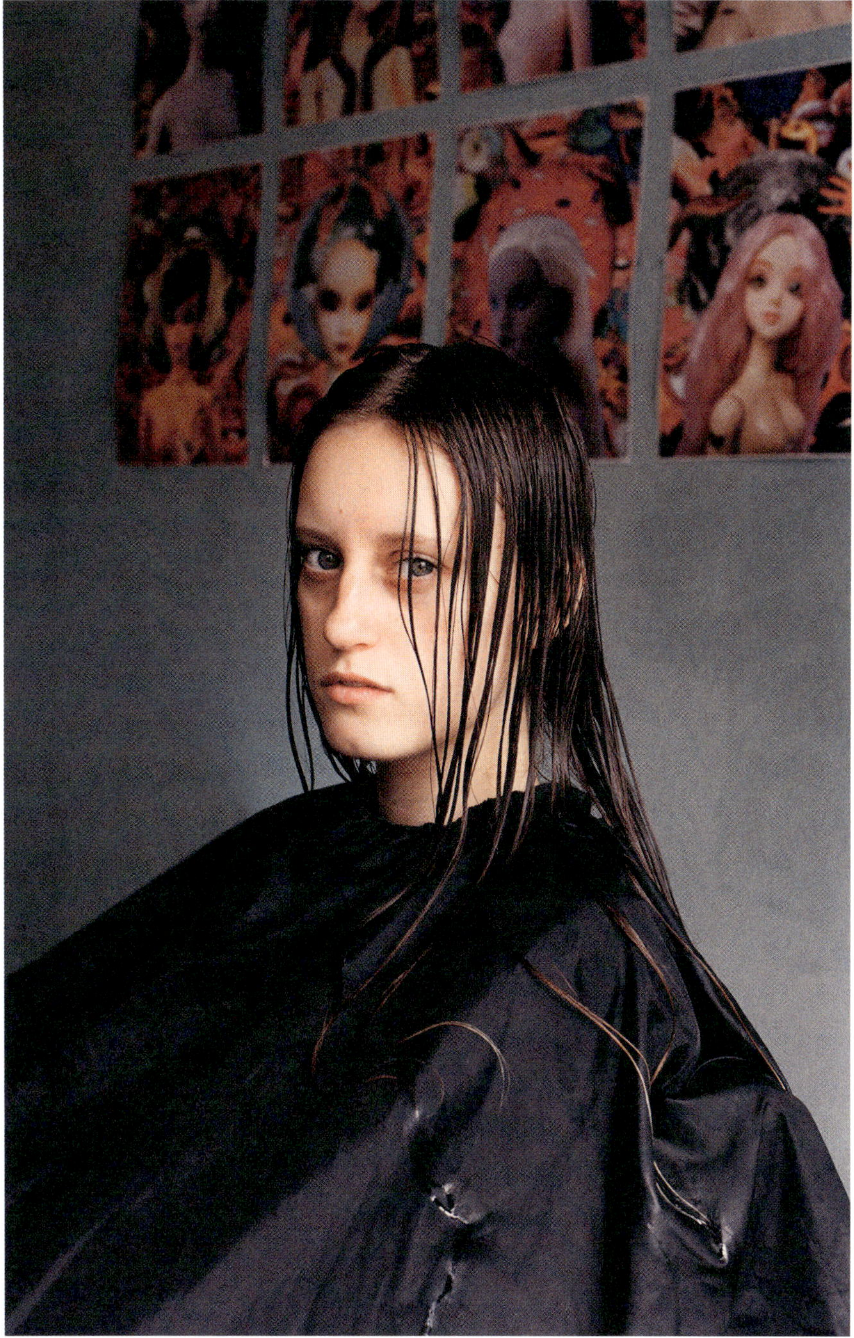

KENNINGTON'S ETON SCHOLAR
by Tristan Bejawn
London

Sharp, well spoken and easy-going, Joshua attended
a state school before earning a place at Eton College
on a full scholarship. He has since been offered
a place at the University of Cambridge.

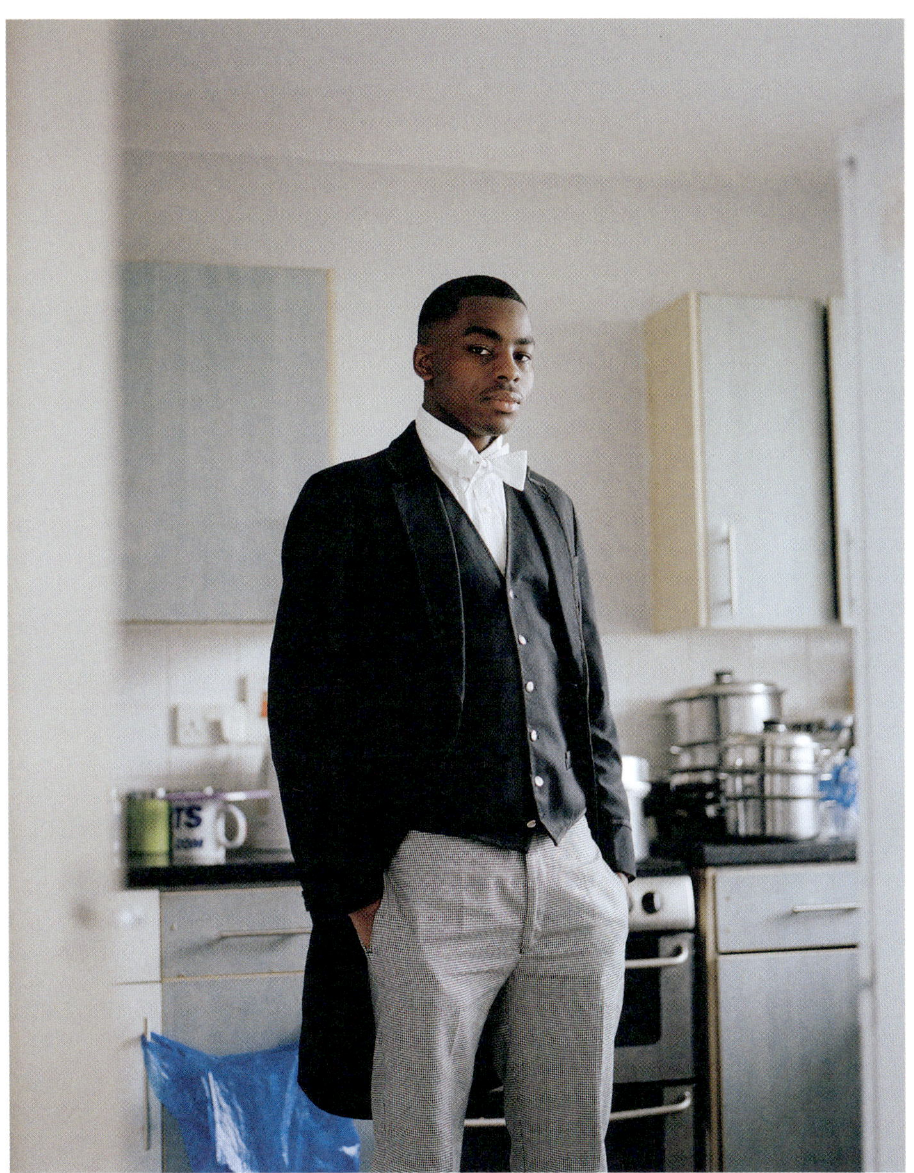

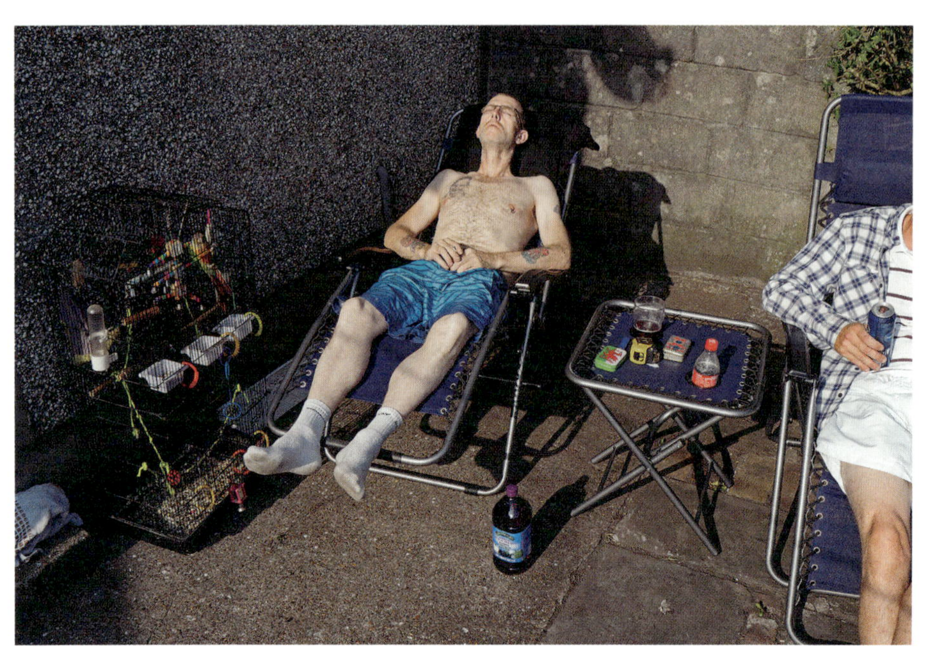

DARREN IN HIS BACK GARDEN
by Nik Roche
Swansea, West Glamorgan

In summer, my friend Darren often takes his pet bird
Marley outside with him to enjoy the sunshine.

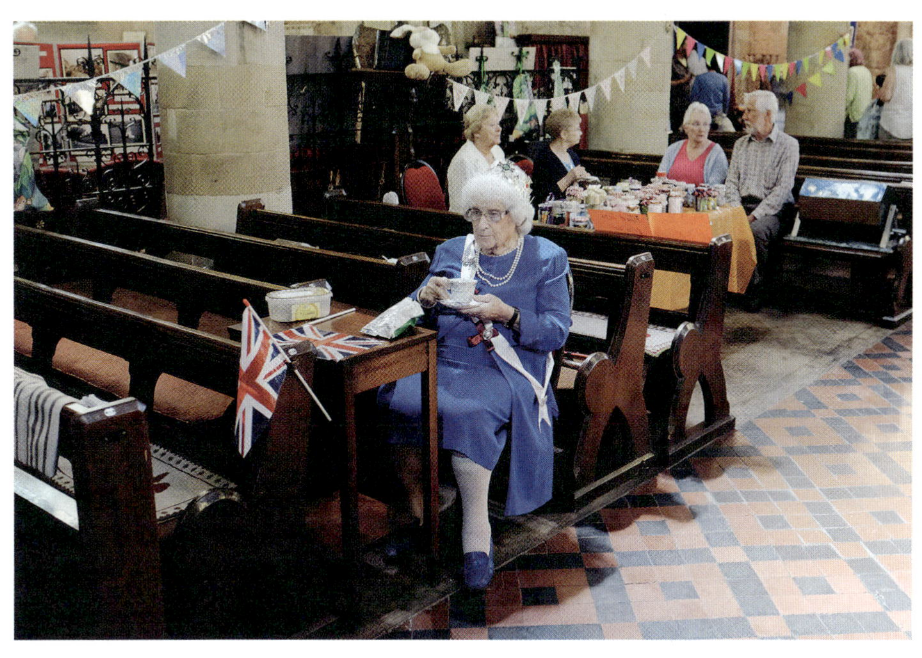

ROYAL WEDDING DAY
by Jon Nicholls
Alveley, Shropshire

On the day of Prince Harry and Meghan Markle's
wedding, I saw this lady, a local resident, enjoying
the festivities. The wedding was being shown on a big
screen and she had dressed up for the occasion.

RODDY
by Orlando Gili
Glyndebourne, East Sussex

Dedicated opera fan Roddy has been a visitor
at Glyndebourne, famous for its annual opera festival,
for more than 70 years. He met his wife there when
he was 19 and the couple went every year until
her death in 2018.

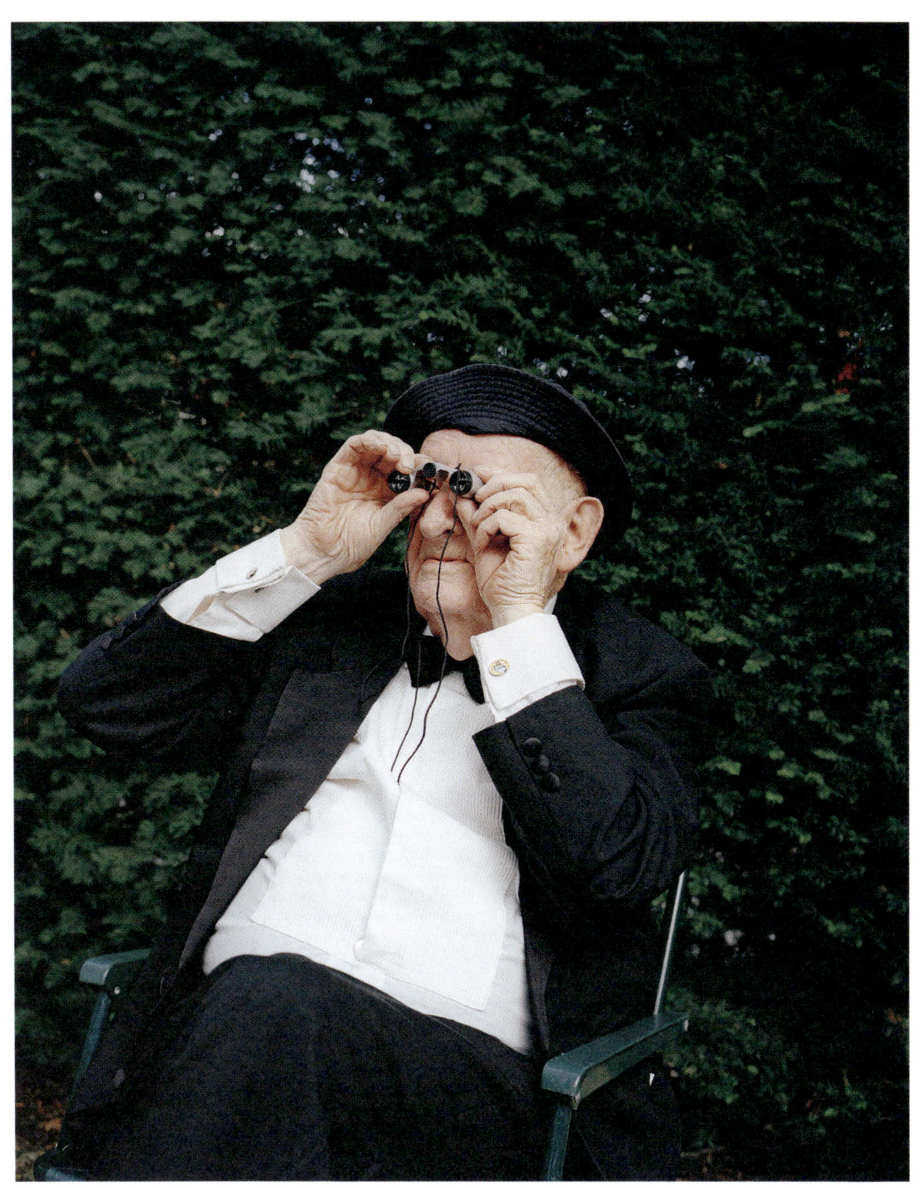

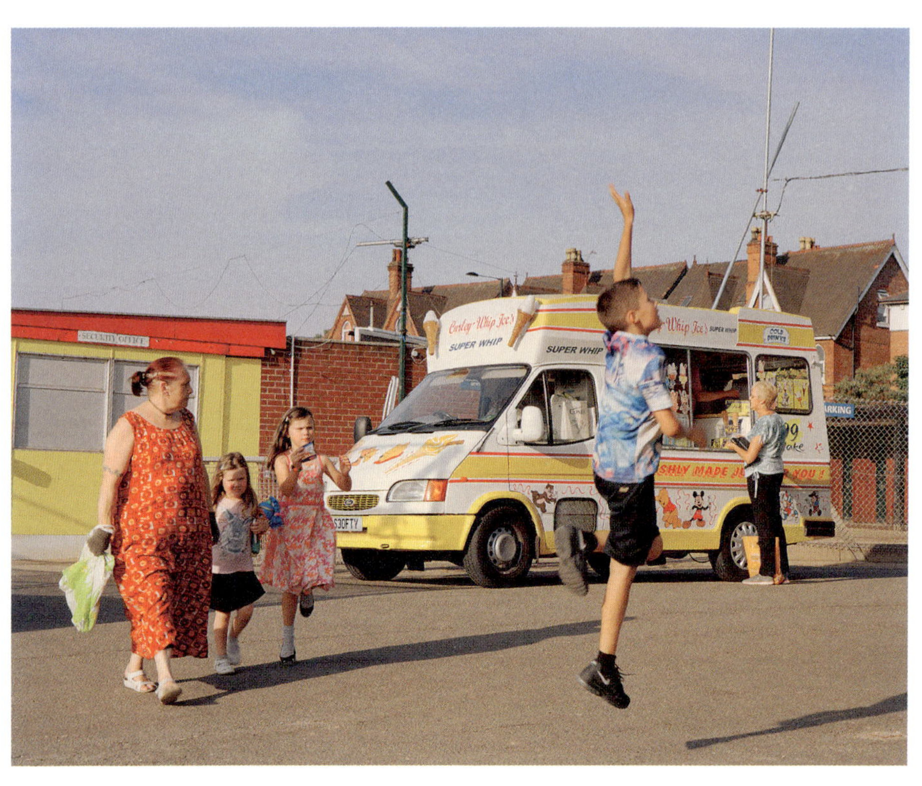

ICE CREAM VAN
by Sam Wright
Birmingham, West Midlands

I took this image at Perry Barr stadium where speedway
racing takes place. The image sparks memories of family
days out and the joy of getting an ice cream on
a scorching hot summer's day.

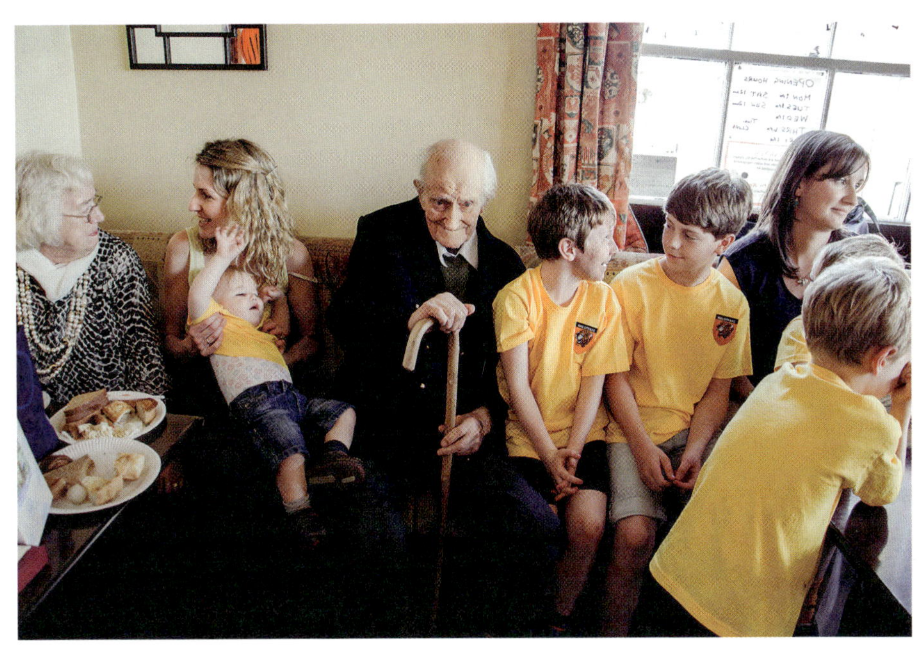

DENIS
by Michele McIlvenny
Beverley, East Yorkshire

My grandad, a former footballer, at his 90th birthday
party with some of his great grandsons. Overwhelmed by
the attention, he cried. The only other time I've seen him
cry was the day the love of his life died suddenly aged 67.

MUMMY ON CHRISTMAS DAY
by Nicola Morley
Longridge, Lancashire

My 87-year-old mother is a blogger, businesswoman,
widow and grandmother who doesn't like being told what
to do. Her blog is called *Telling Tales*, which she set up
so that old people could share their stories online.

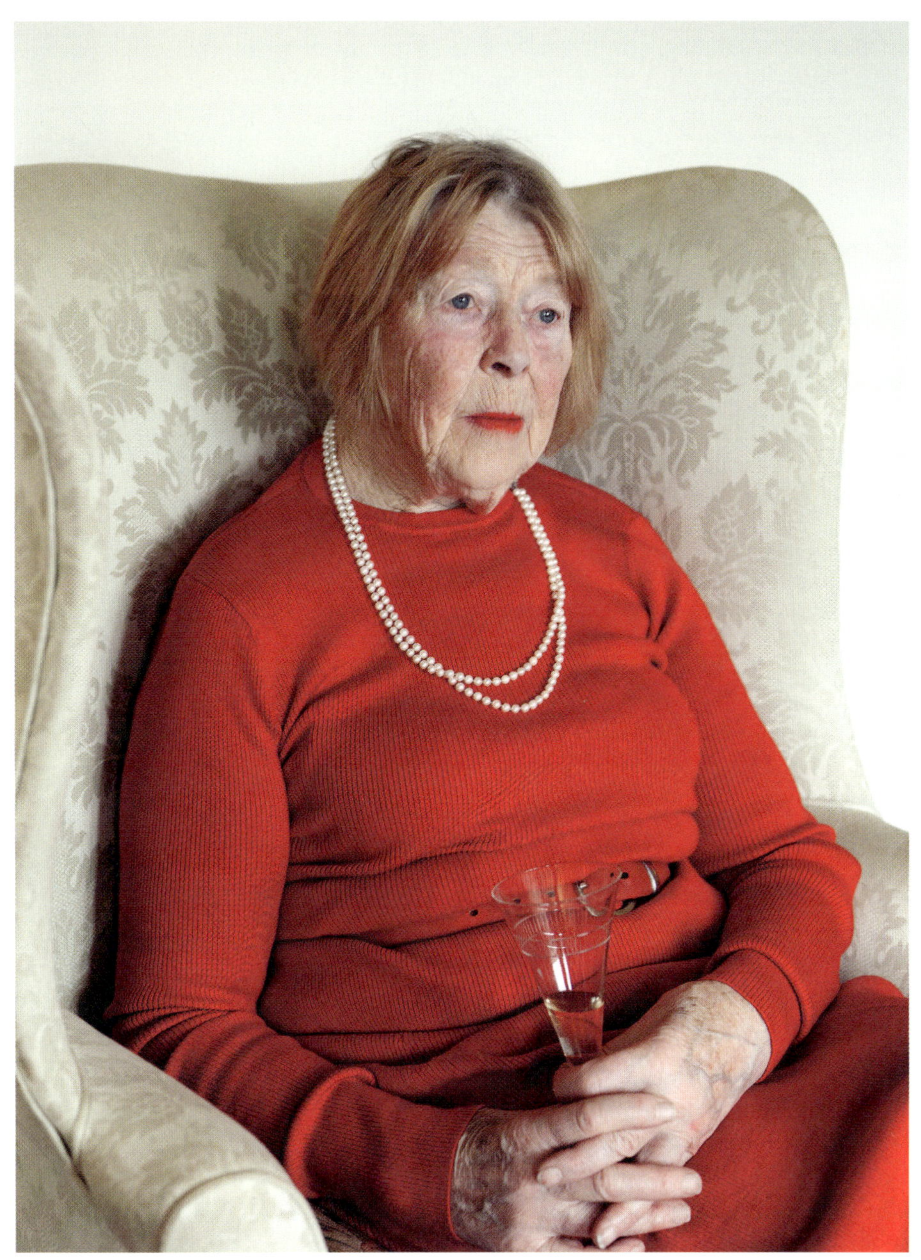

YASODHARA
by Gavin Li
London

Yasodhara is a Sri Lankan artist who specialises
in painting flowers. She is also a domestic violence
survivor and single mother.

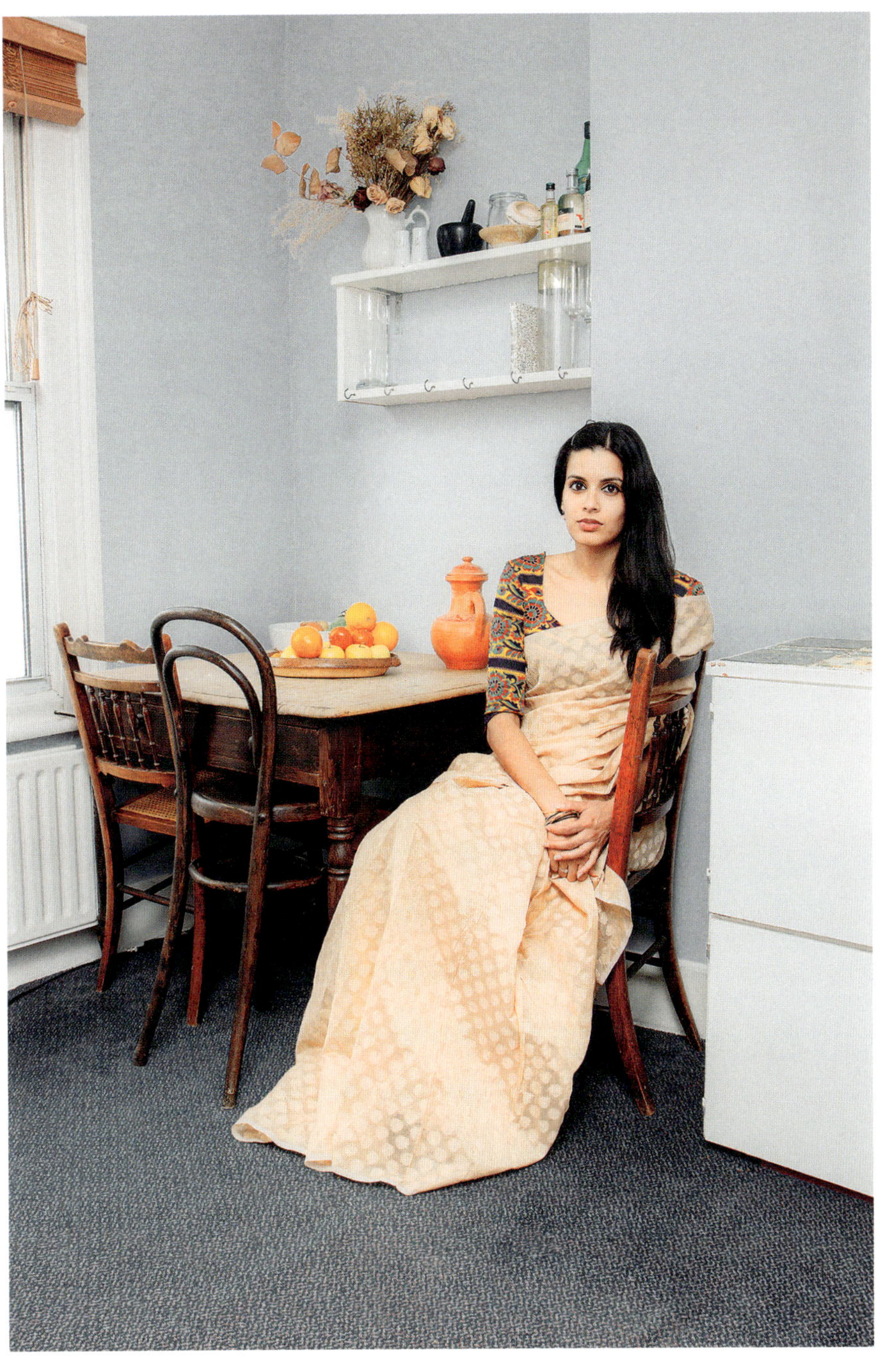

PORTIA AND NGAIRE
by Vicky Grout
London

Portia is a good friend of mine. She was very close to her due date and we really wanted to capture her last few moments of pregnancy before she and her boyfriend Honé welcomed Ngaire into the world.

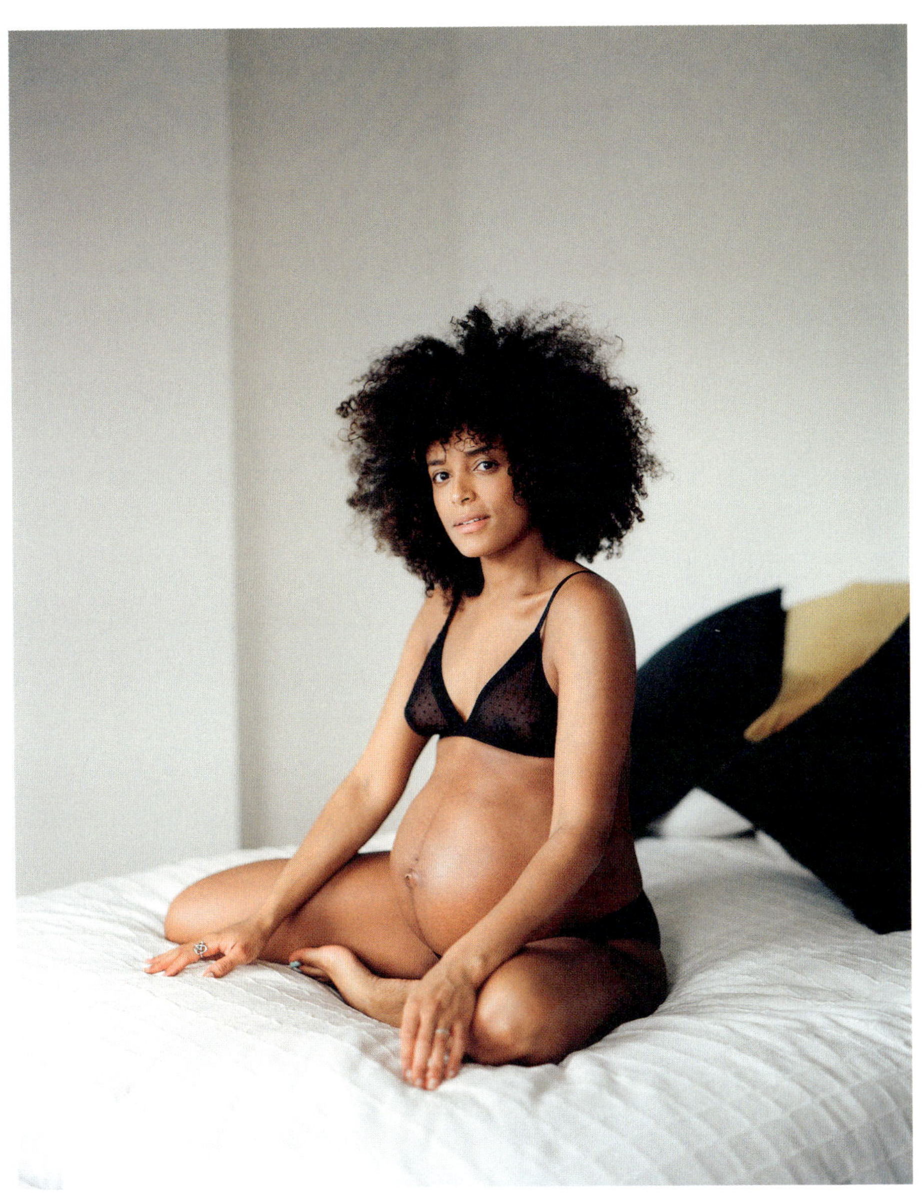

VALERIE
by Amanda Fordyce
London

I noticed Valerie as she was walking down the street
carrying groceries. I thought she looked beautiful and
very stylish. We had a little chat and she kindly agreed
to walk to a purple garage door I'd just passed.

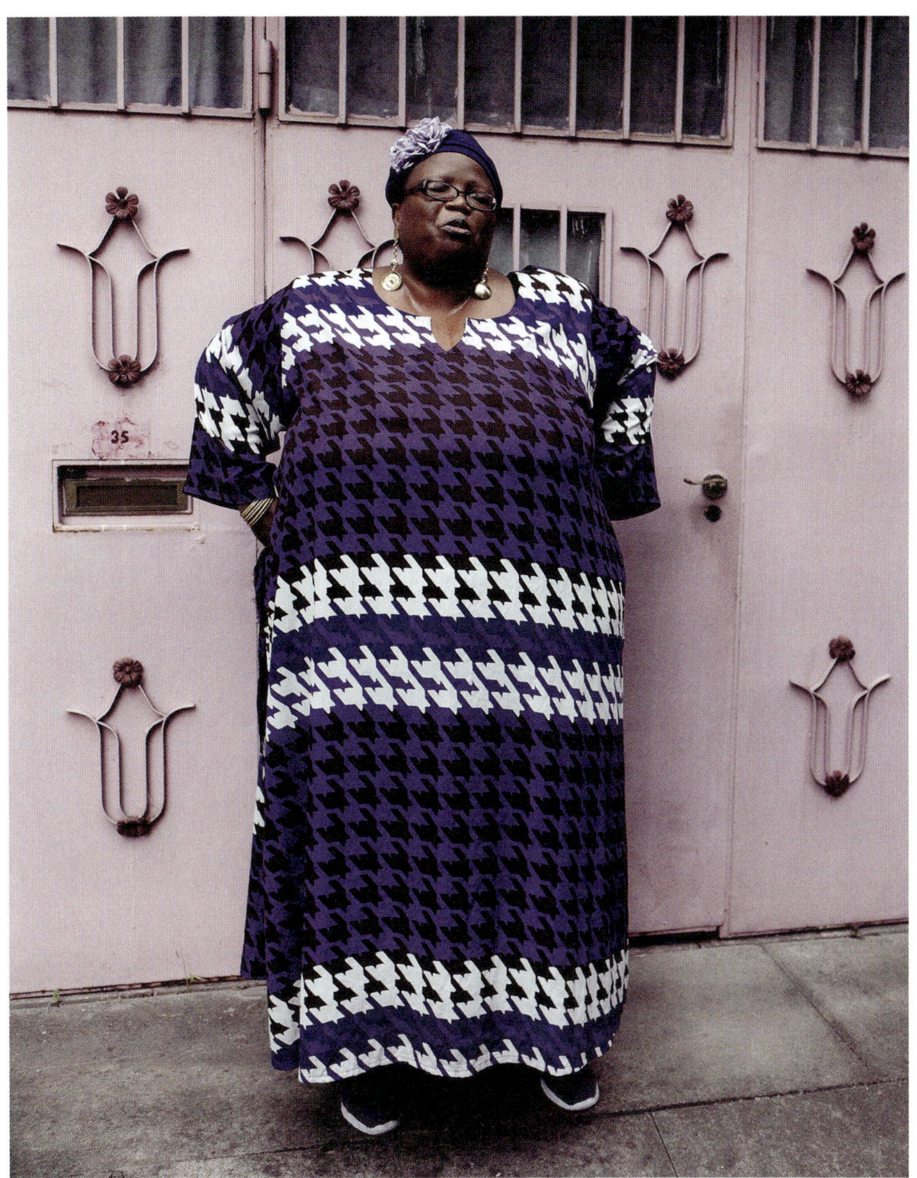

ANTI-TRUMP PROTESTER
by Katie Waggett
London

In July 2018, tens of thousands of people marched
through London to protest Donald Trump's UK visit.
With many parallels to be drawn between 'post-Trump
victory' and 'post-EU referendum', I feel this portrait
captures the mood of the nation.

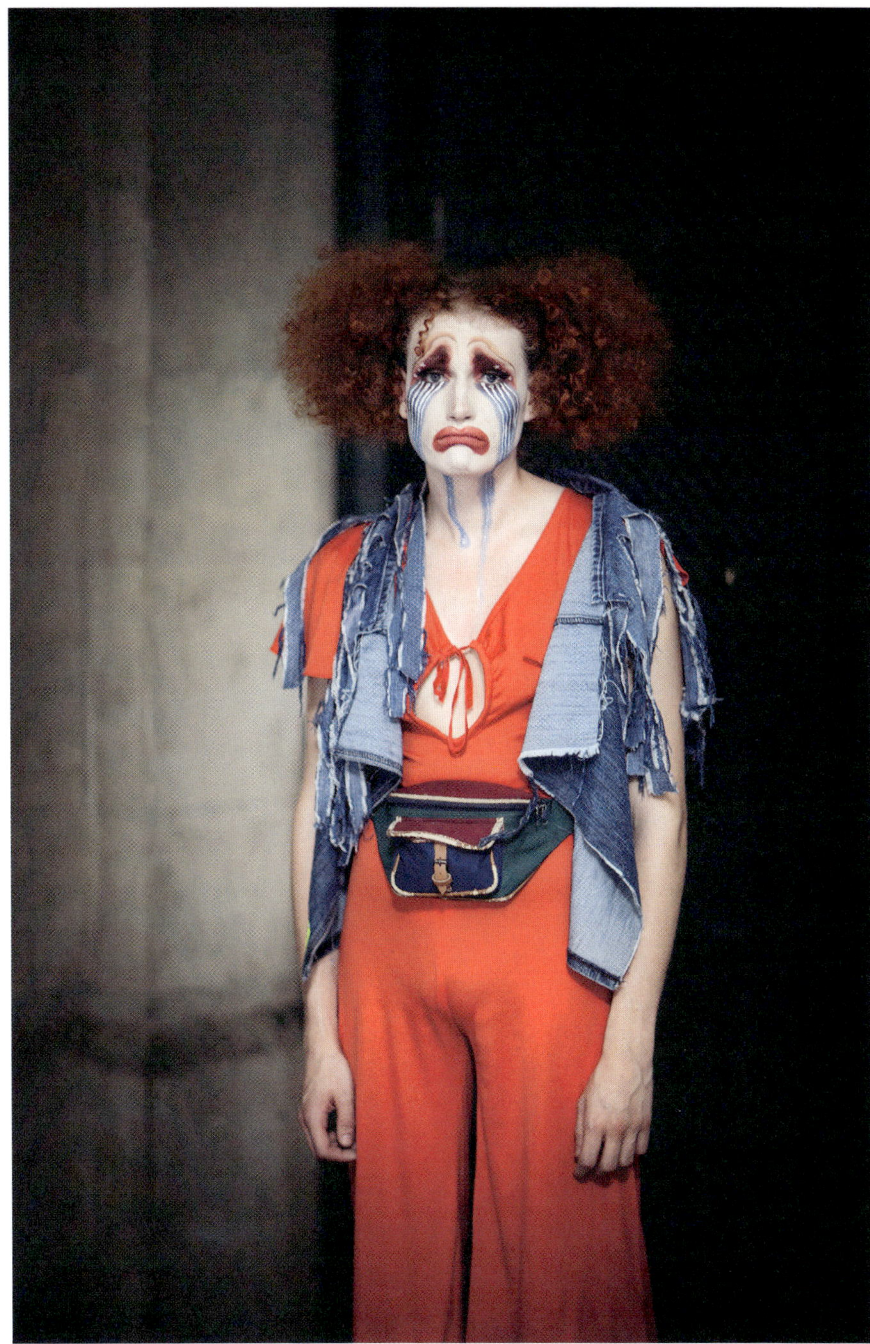

BILATERAL
by Amy Cassidy
Chesham, Buckinghamshire

In September 2018, my friend Sam was diagnosed
with breast cancer. She was 35 at the time. Sam chose not
to have reconstructive surgery after a bilateral mastectomy
and hopes to provide support and empowerment to other
women who might be going through similar experiences.

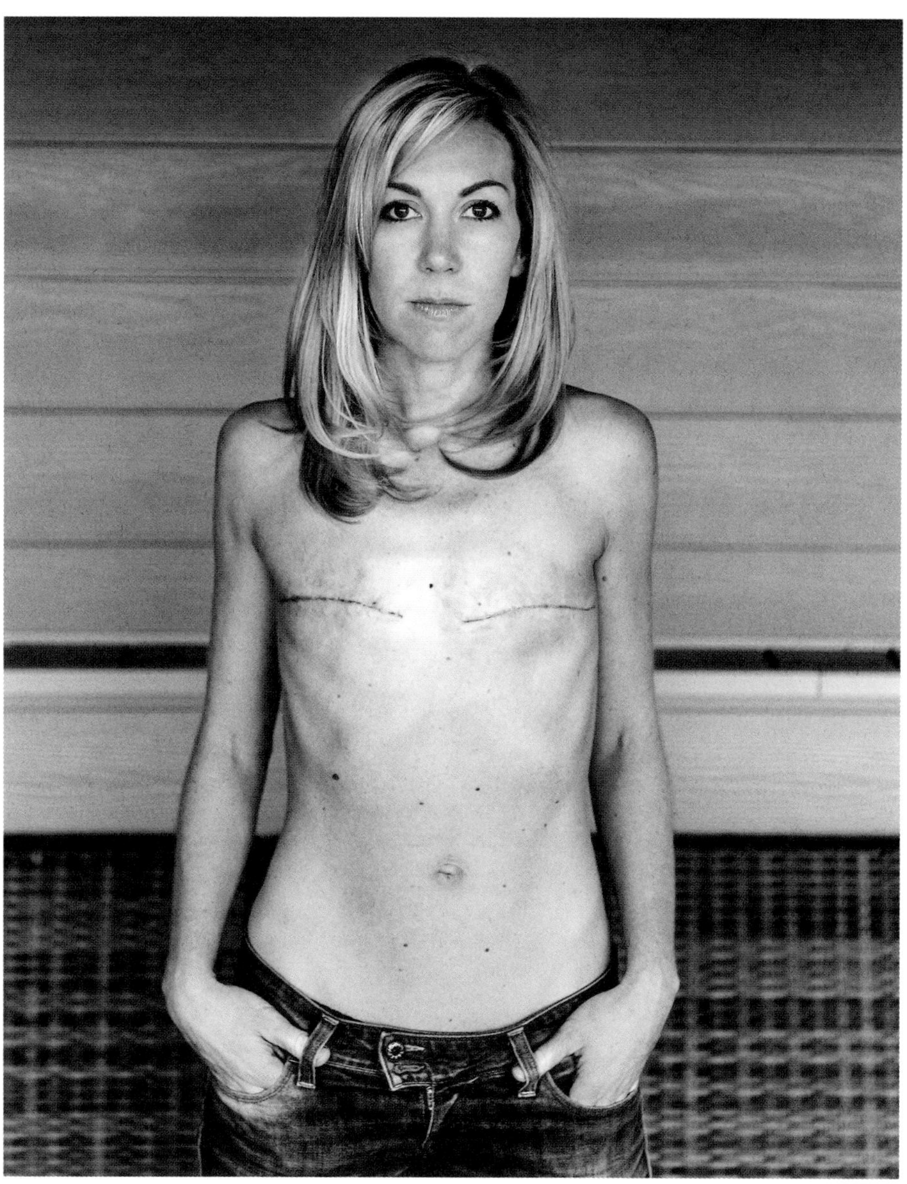

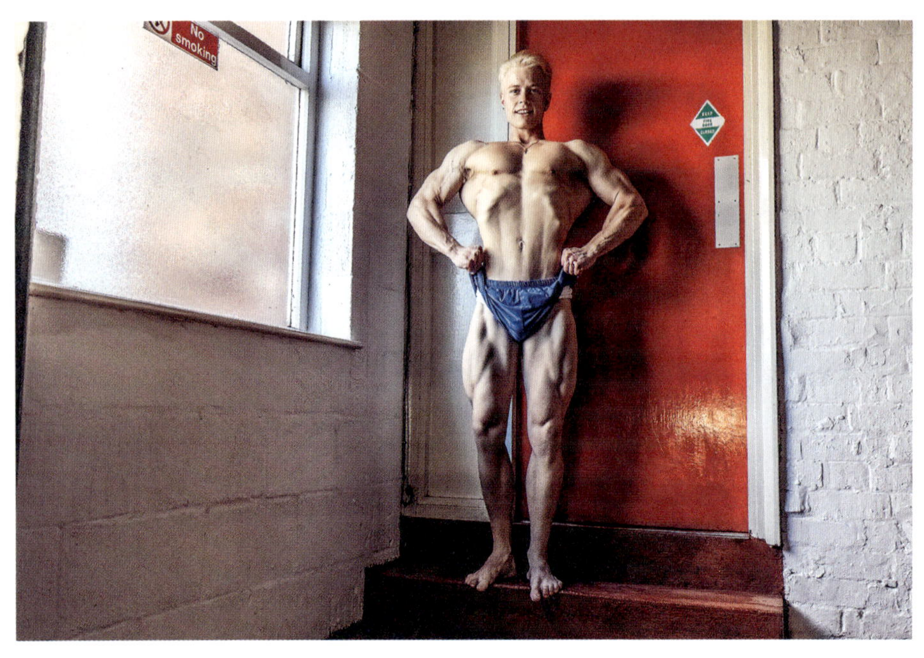

KYLE IN THE GYM CORRIDOR
by Tero Puha
London

'I've always had a thing for superheroes: Spider-Man, Thor,
Hulk. As a kid you want to be that guy with a six-pack and
pecs flexing. It gives you a sense of empowerment.' – Kyle

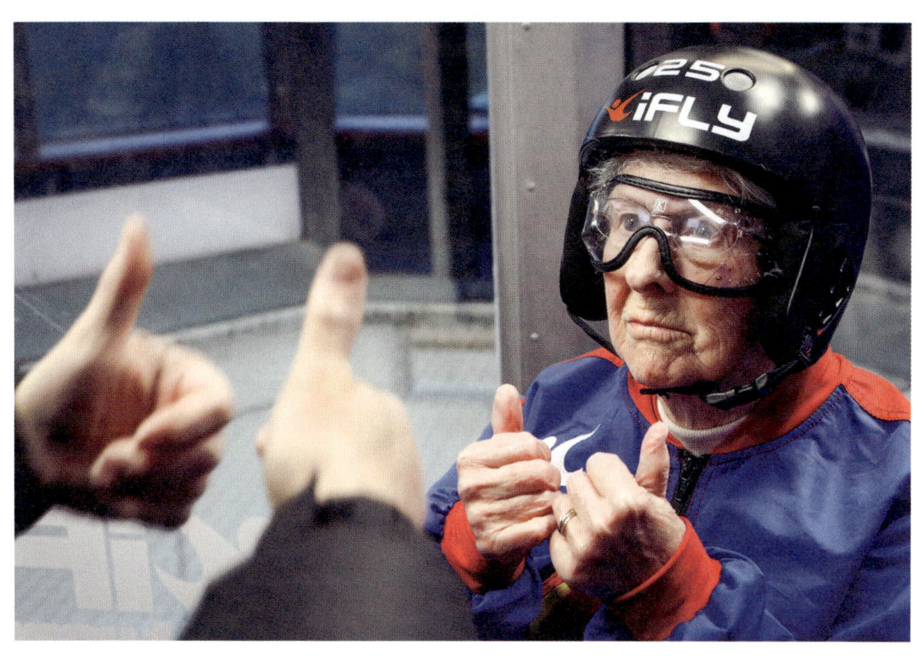

SUPER GRAN! A-OK
by Celia Bartlett
Milton Keynes, Buckinghamshire

'I don't want to spend my 90th birthday with the old
people in my sheltered housing block!' And so she didn't.
A quick kit check and thumbs up and my mother-in-law
was good to go for her indoor skydive.

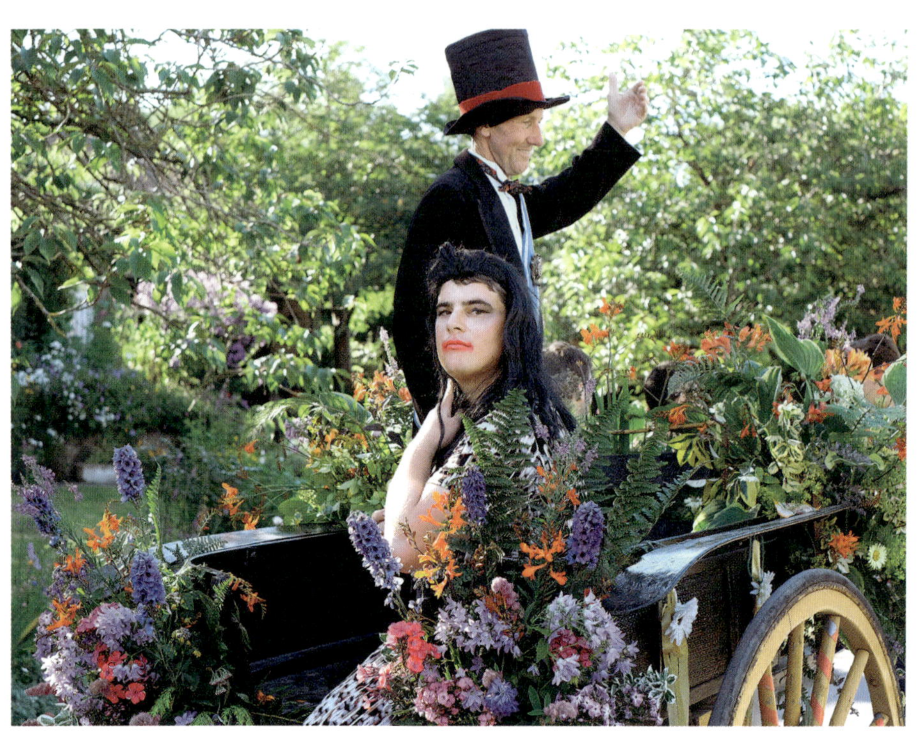

THE LORD MAYOR'S PARADE
by Tessa Bunney
Kilburn, North Yorkshire

Part of the annual Kilburn Feast (a festival that dates back
hundreds of years), The Lord Mayor's Parade sees a mock
Mayor and Mayoress appointed for a day. They tour
the village and get up to all kinds of shenanigans.

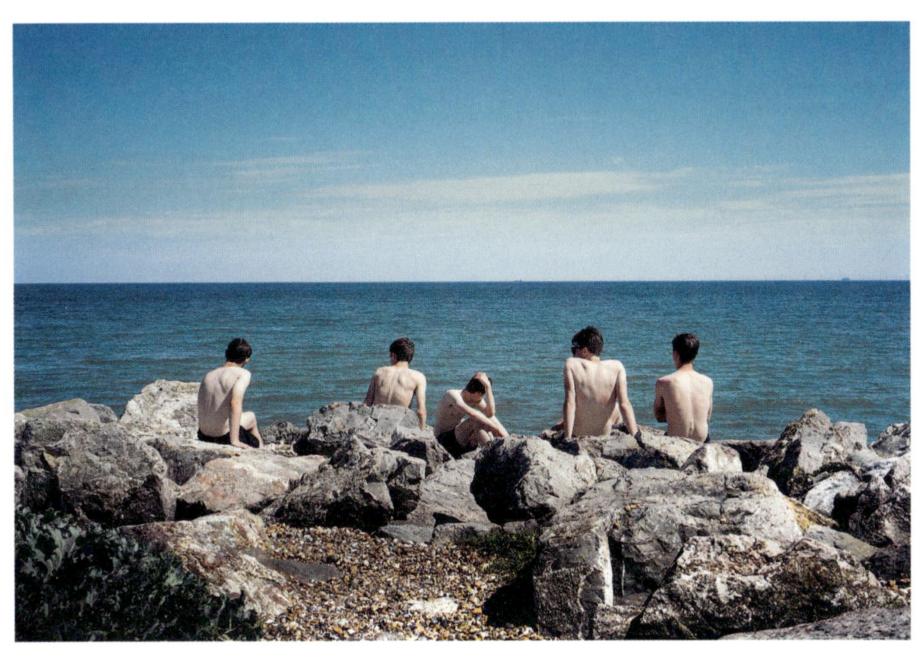

UNTITLED
by John Fowler
Worthing, West Sussex

CHARLIE DRESSED FOR THE PROCESSION
OF BOATS
by Simon Roberts
Eton, Berkshire

Eton College's famous 4th June celebrations include
the Procession of Boats where boys dress in naval uniform
and elaborate floral hats. The first procession took place
in 1793 on the birthday of King George III,
the school's greatest patron.

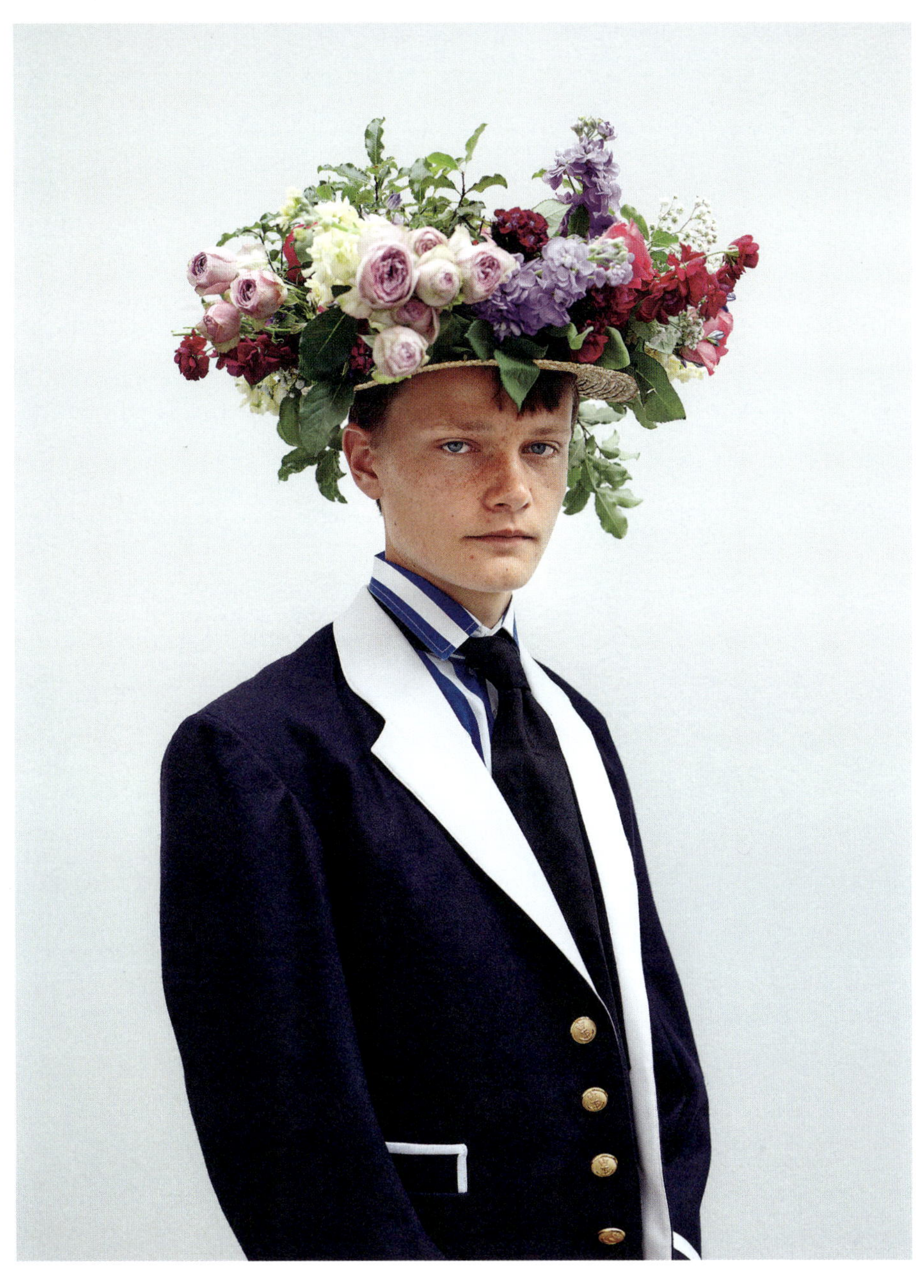

ELIZABETH TRUSS
by Sophie Ellen Lachowycz
Hockwold cum Wilton, Norfolk

It was an honour to photograph the Rt Hon Elizabeth
Truss MP for South West Norfolk at Hockwold Hall.
I photographed her for *209 Women*, a project that brought
together 209 female photographers and 209 female MPs
to champion women in politics and the arts.

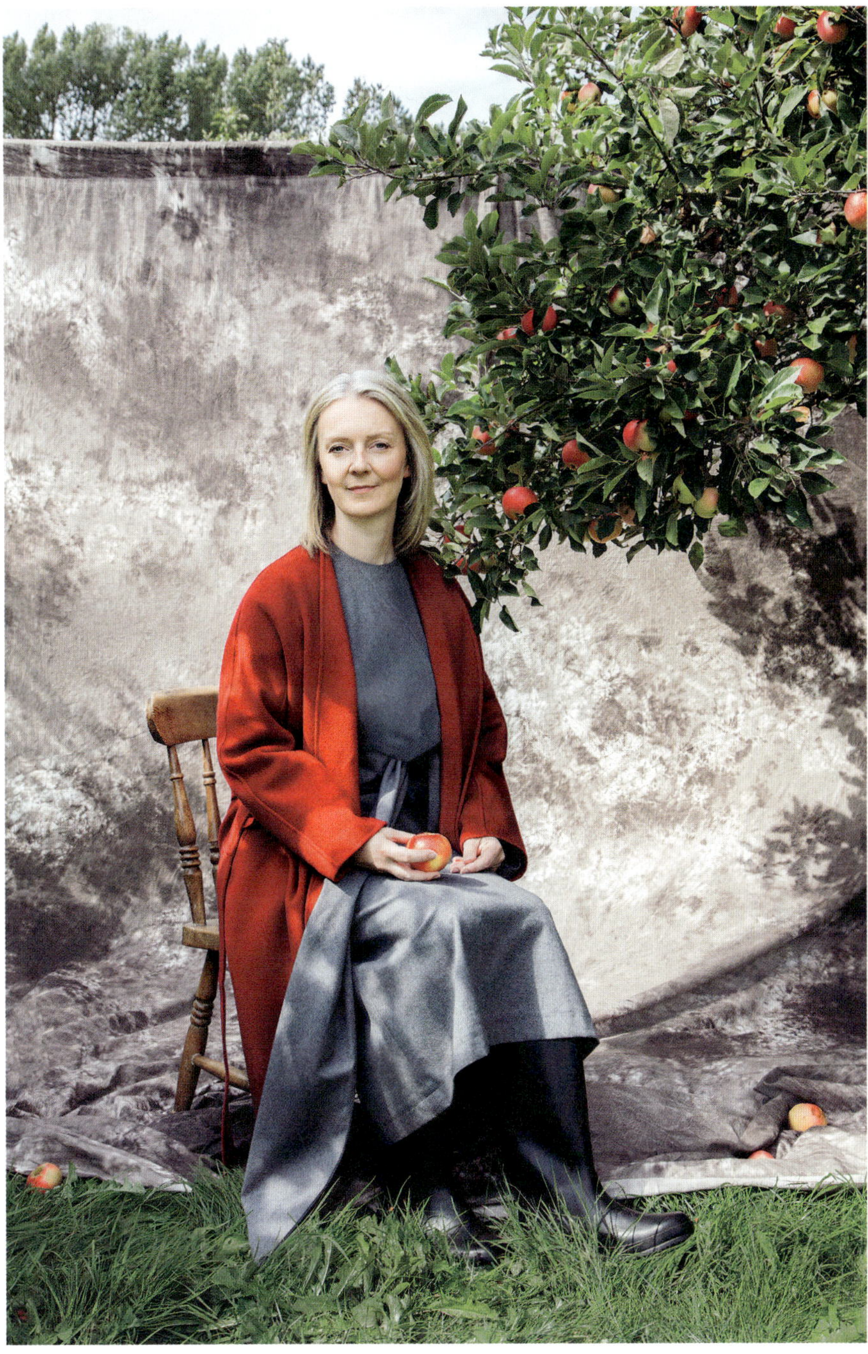

JUDITH KERR
by Neil Spence
London

Acclaimed writer and illustrator Judith Kerr wrote many
much-loved children's books including *The Tiger Who
Came to Tea*. I wanted to ask her to imitate the tiger and
found the courage to do so for the last shot of the sitting.

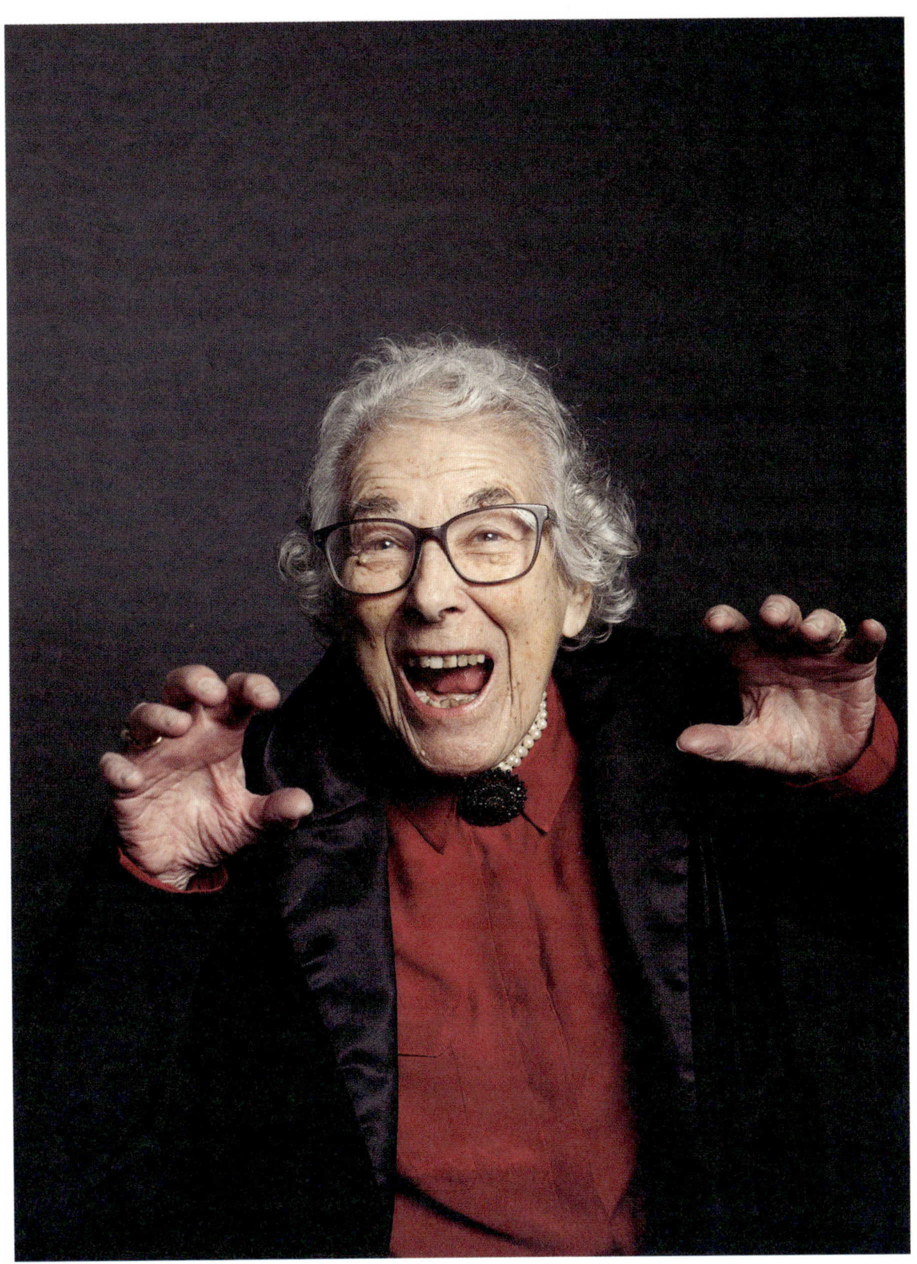

MCDONALD'S DRAG QUEEN
AT LEEDS PRIDE
by Jonathan Straight
Leeds, West Yorkshire

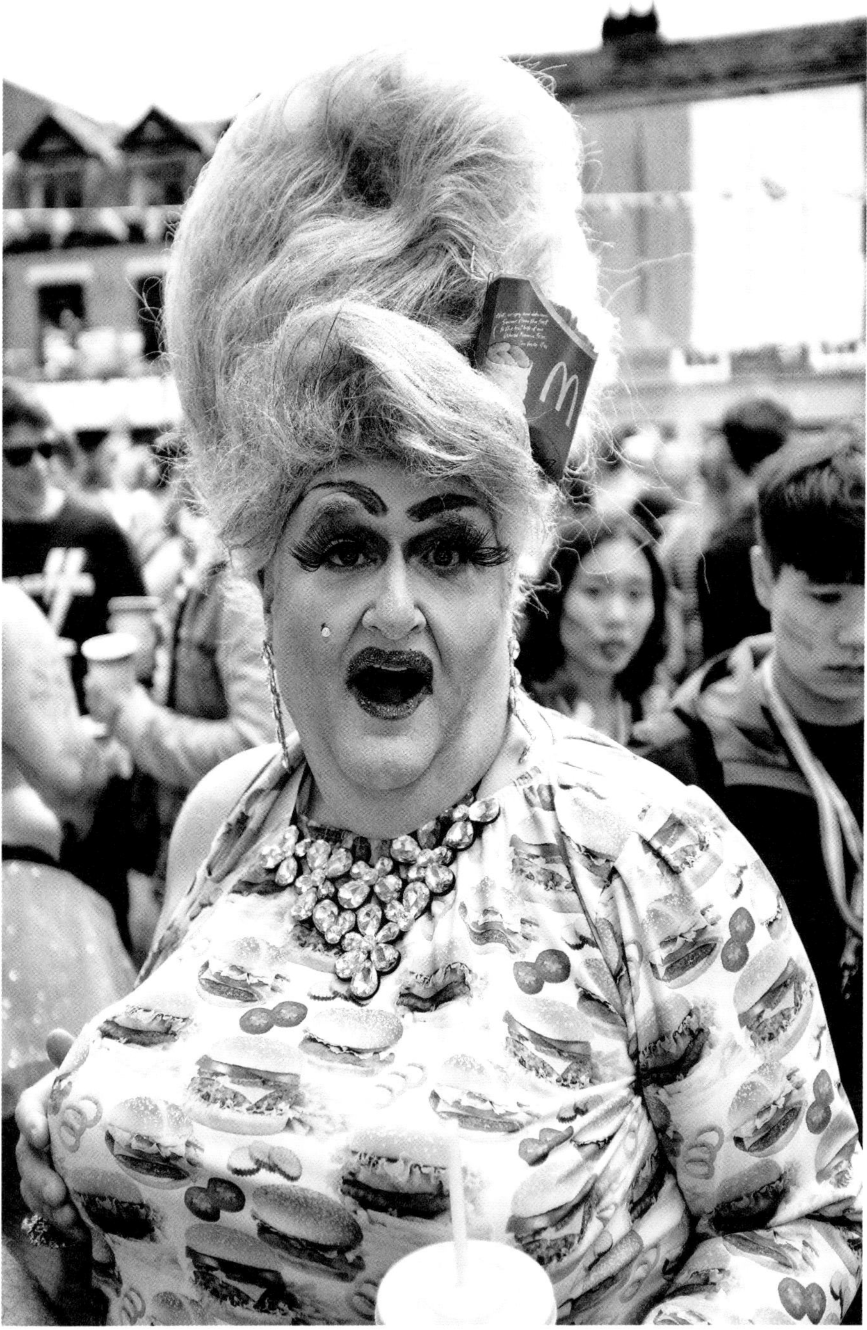

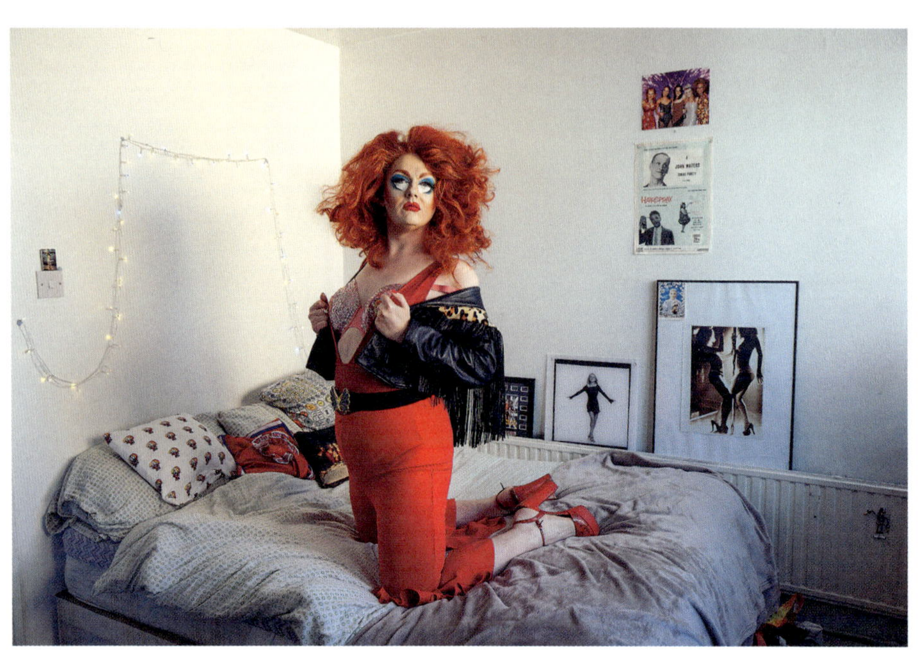

JUST MAY – WHO DO YOU THINK YOU ARE?
by Claudia Rocha
London

Just May is a drag queen who is inspired by pop icon
Geri Halliwell. 'When I was six years old I saw the
Spice Girls on TV for the first time and said to myself:
"That's what I want to be when I grow up."' – Just May

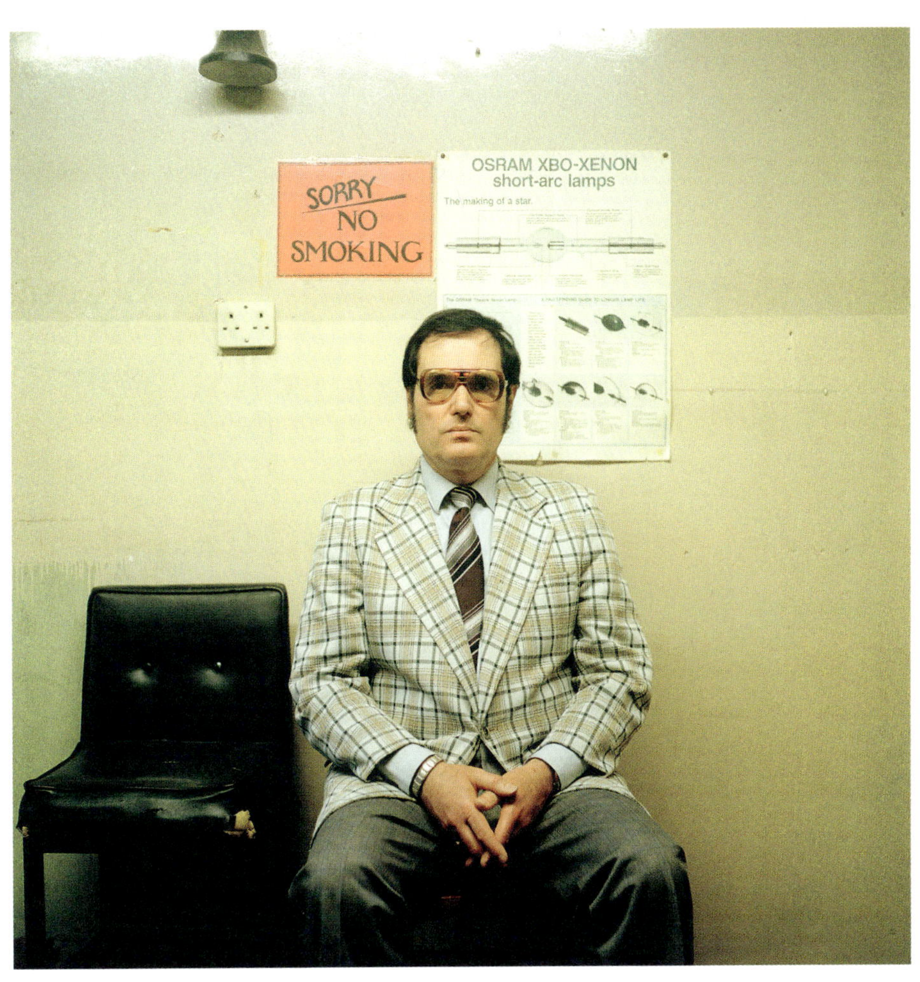

THE CINEMA MAN
by Emmalouise Smith
Norwich, Norfolk

This is Simon, 'The Cinema Man', in the former projection
room of Hollywood Cinema which has since closed down.
Inspired by the movie stars and films of yesteryear,
Simon paints film posters for a living.

LEO
by Jade Danielle Smith
London

'I am here in support of Extinction Rebellion.
To change everything, we need everyone.
This is our rebellion.' – Leo

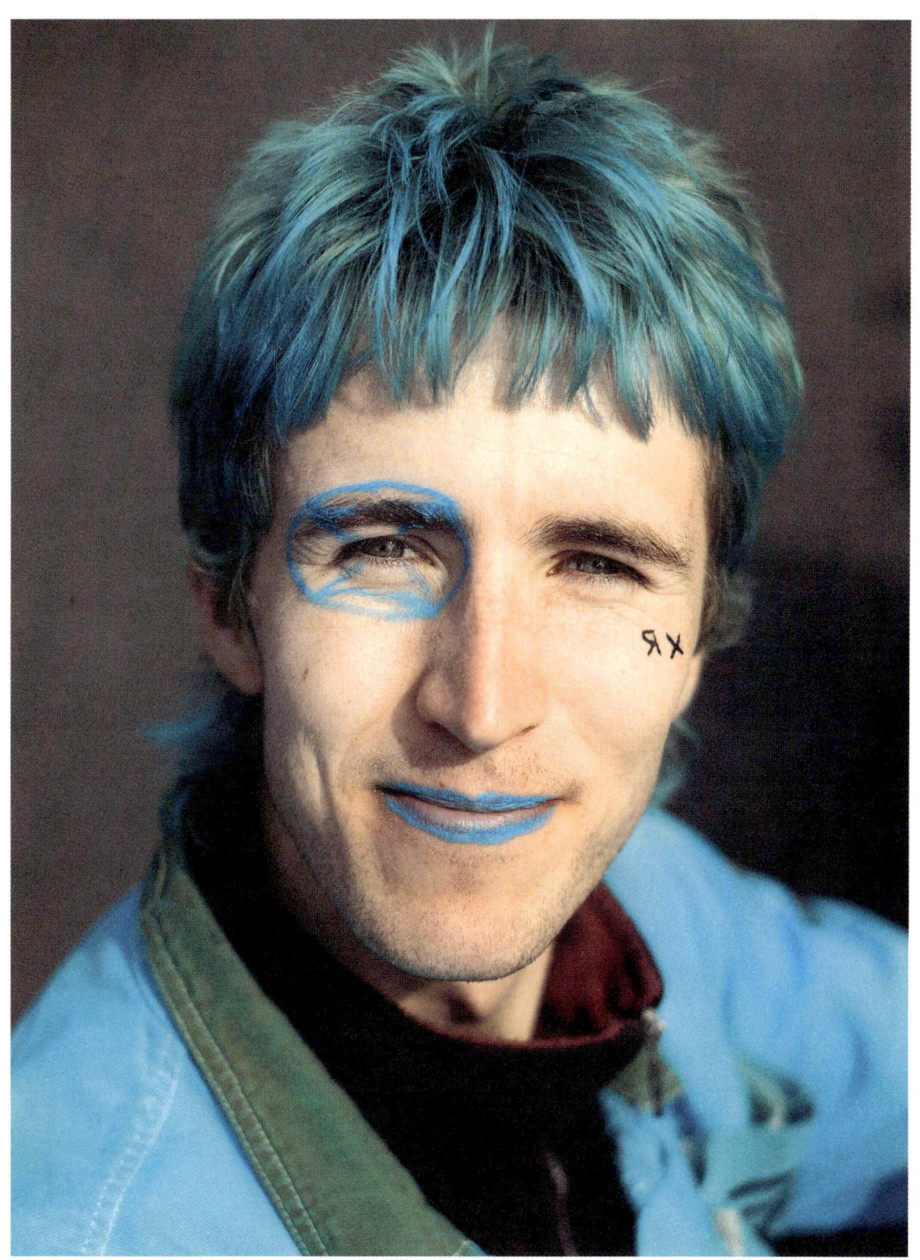

HOLLIE
by Louise Honée
Easington Colliery, County Durham

I met Hollie in the former mining town of Easington
Colliery, where toughness and tenderness collide.

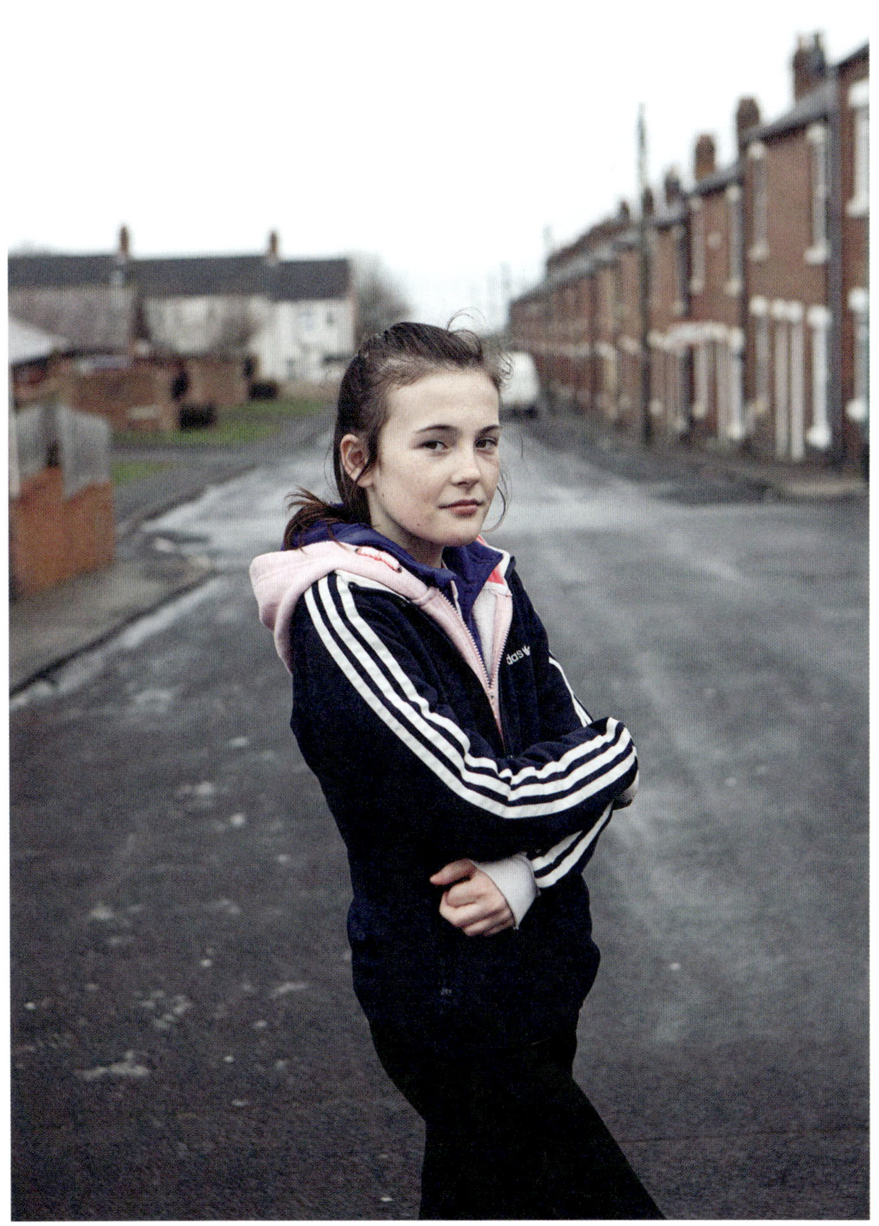

JOHN
by Kathleen Dipper
London

John lives next door to my uncle who has multiple
sclerosis. He is a kind, warm-hearted soul. John and
his family help out if ever my uncle is in need.

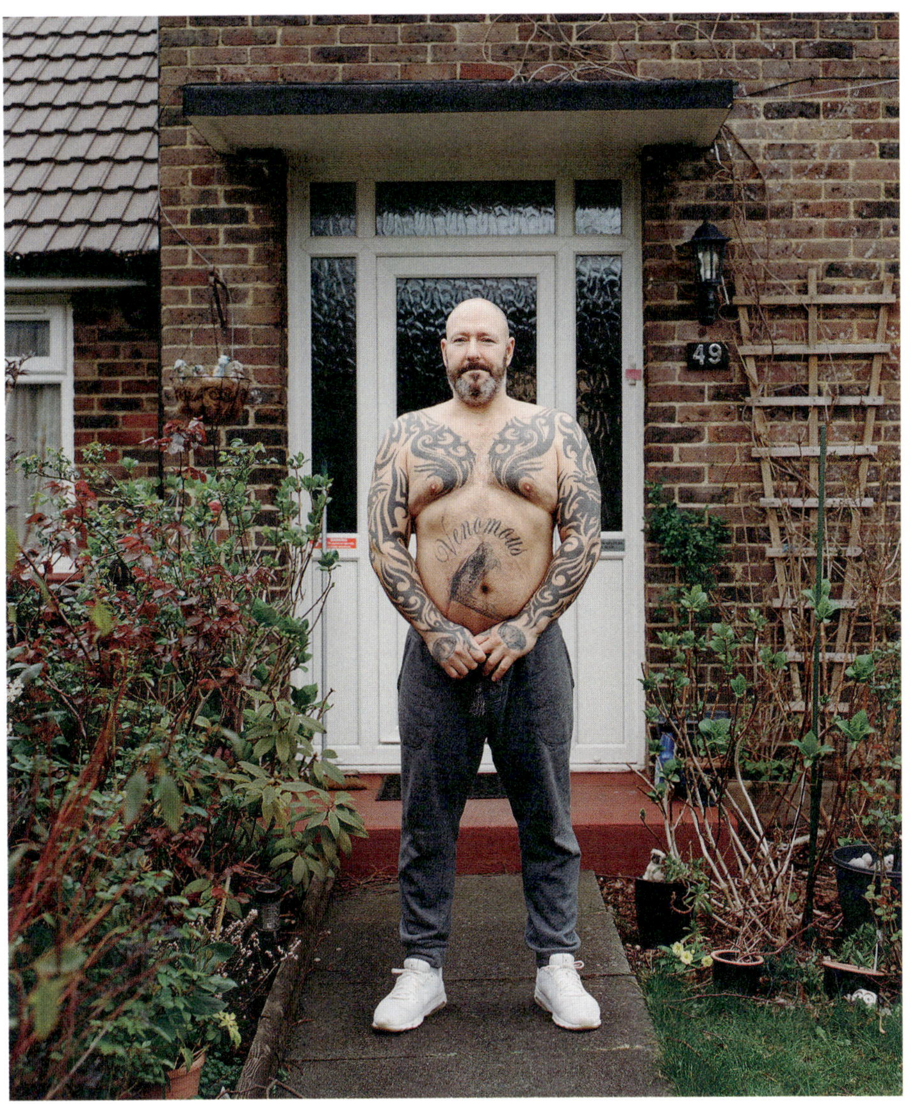

STEPHEN
by Daniel Harrington
London

Stephen owns a bookshop in Highbury in north London,
an area that is becoming increasingly gentrified.
He reminisces about the disappearance of shops
and how the local area is changing.

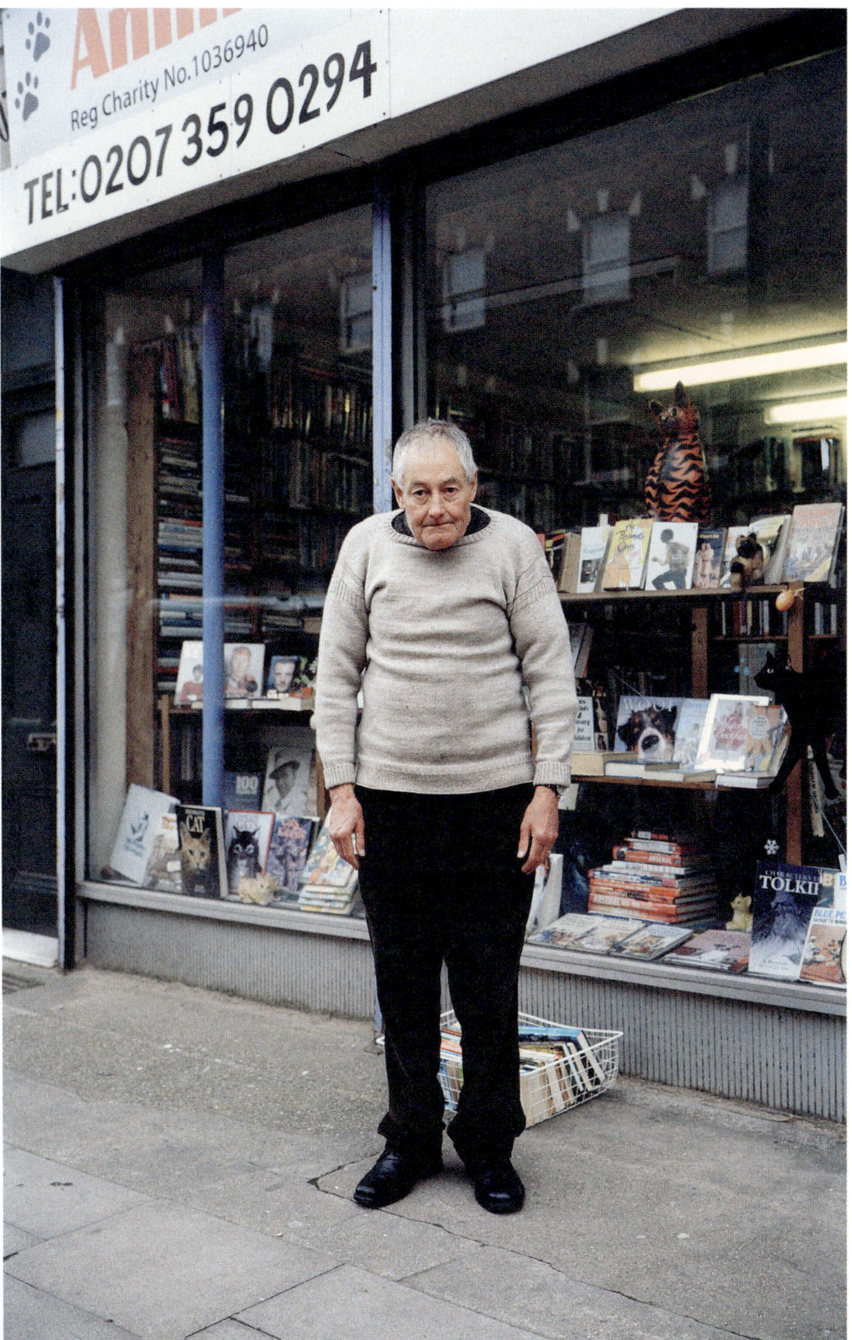

Reg Charity No.1036940
TEL:0207 359 0294

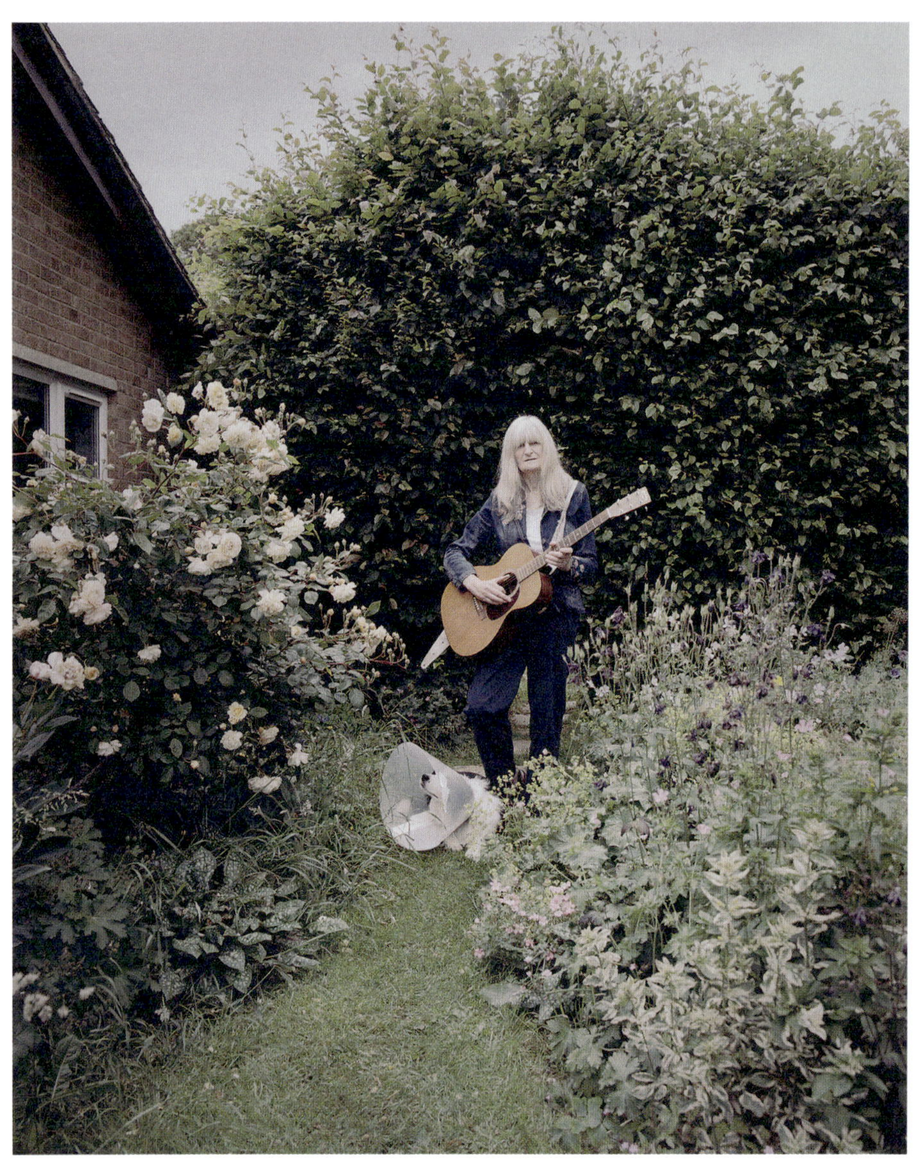

MAEVE
by Kensington Leverne
Beckley, Oxfordshire

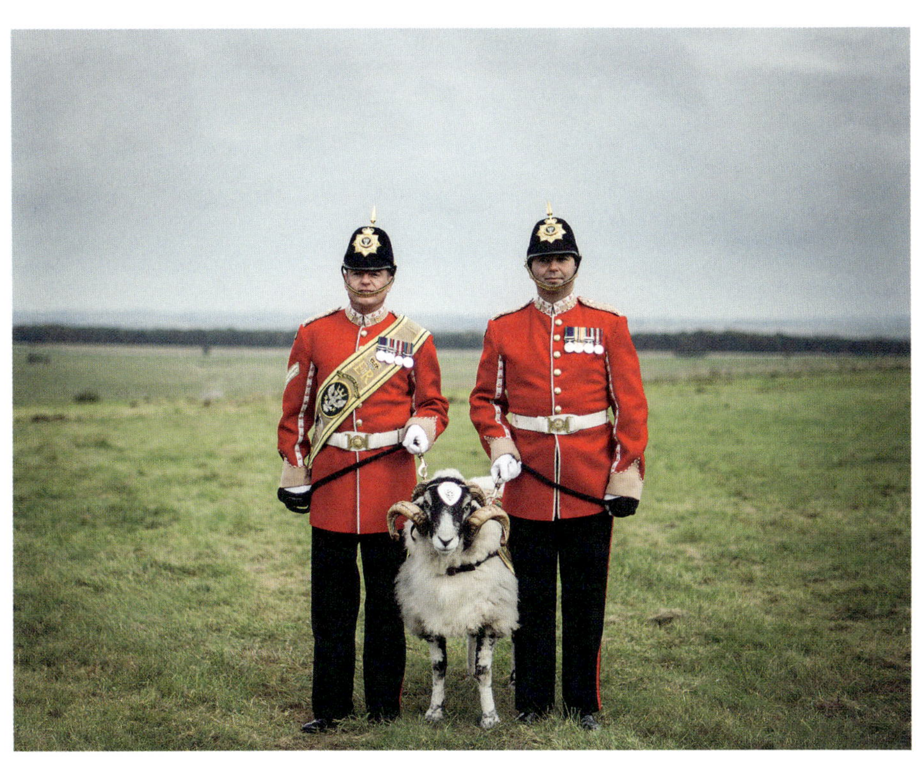

PRIVATE DERBY
by Eddie Mulholland
Salisbury Plain, Wiltshire

I came across Ram Major Coporal Phillip Thornton
and Ram Orderly Stuart McLean with mascot Private
Derby XXXl during a British Army demonstration.
Sadly, the animal passed away in 2017.

STREET CULTURE IN SUBURBIA
by Lee Hooper
Folkestone, Kent

Wearing the right kind of clothes is important to
most young people who are eager to belong. In that sense
Juqaj and Alex are no different and to me they represent
a snapshot of Kent's modern male tribes.

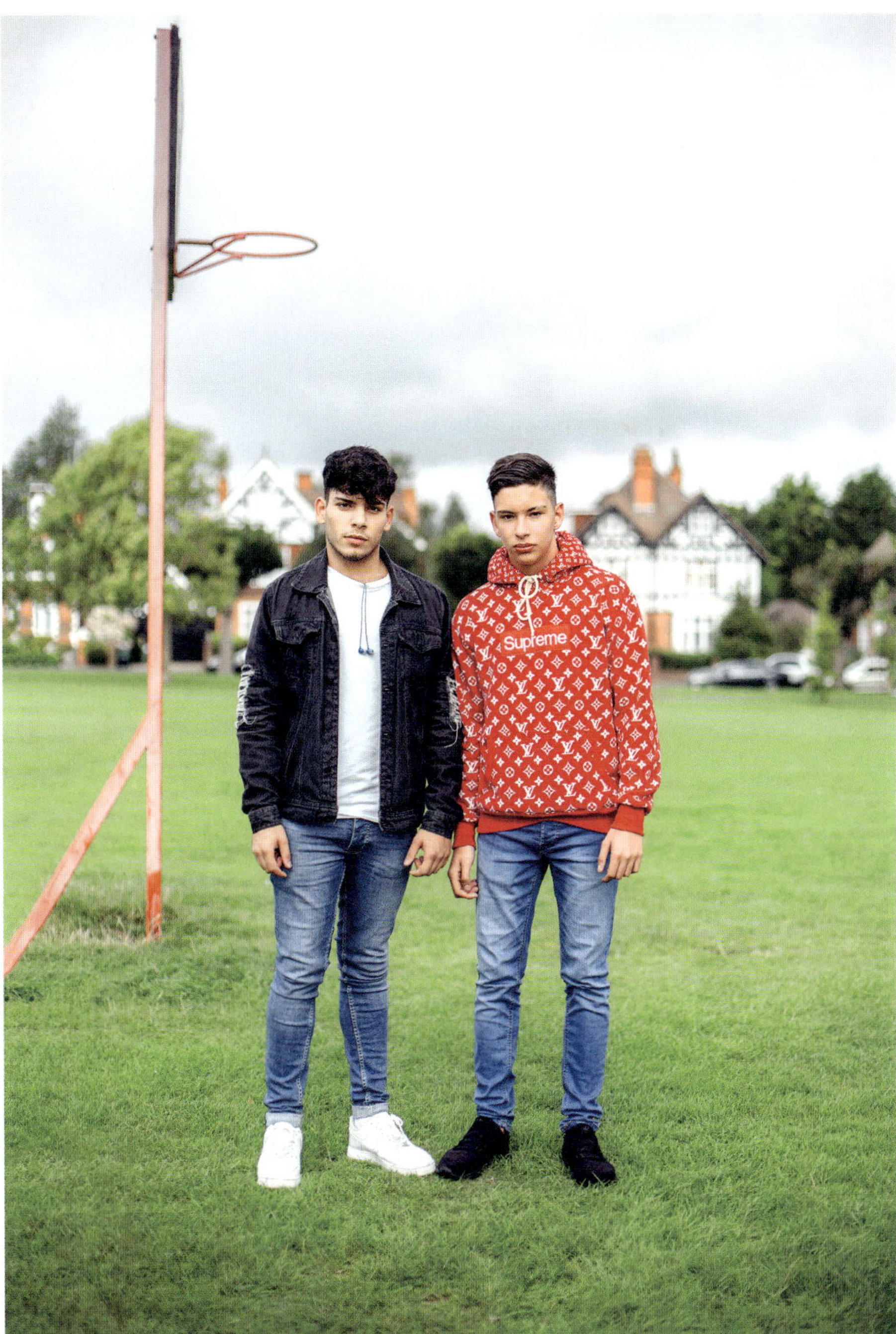

WILLIAM WITH HIS MEDAL
by Tom Willis
London

It was a privilege to photograph Charlton Upbeats
Down's Syndrome football team. The bonds the Upbeats
share with each other and the love they have for
football was incredibly touching to see.

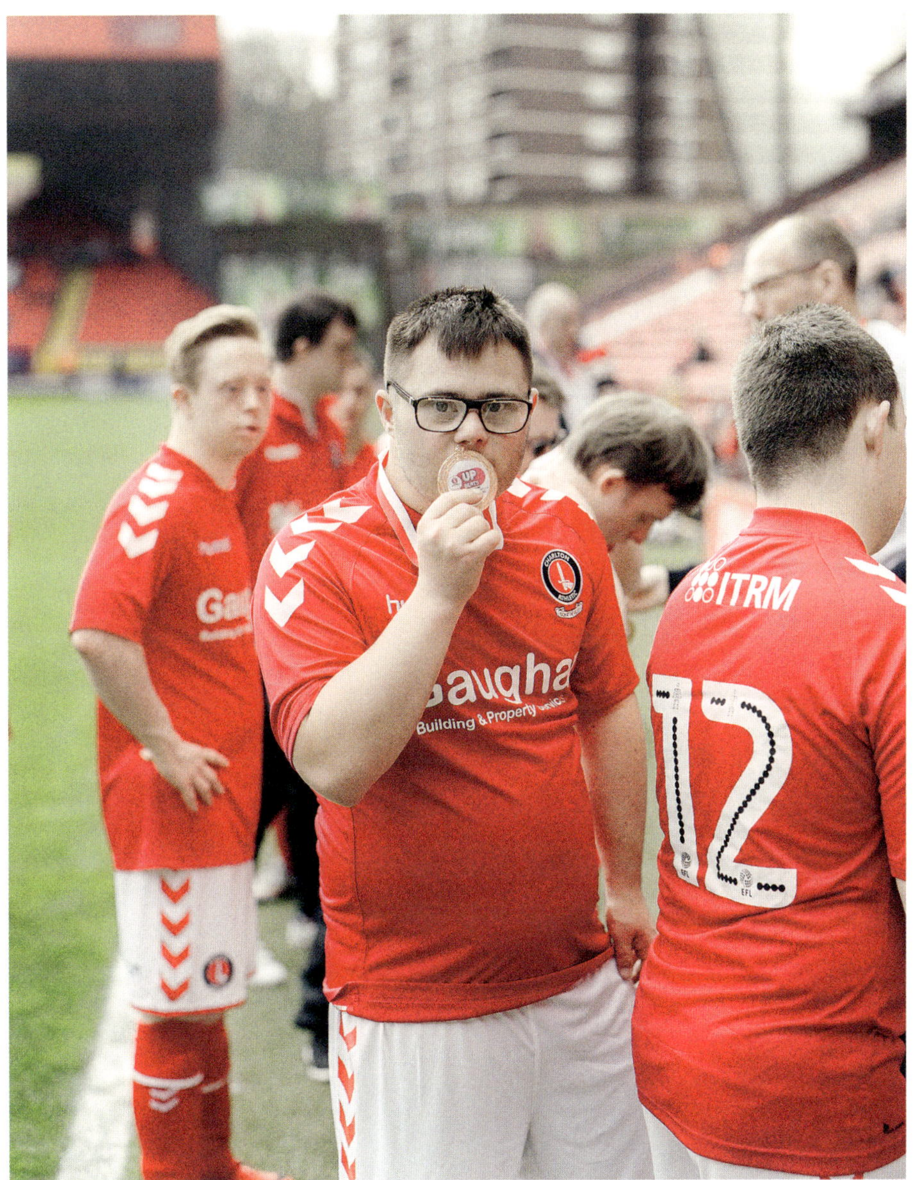

CHRIS AND JEANIE
by Rebecca Sunflower Thomas
Cardiff, South Glamorgan

Jeanie (right) is an eccentric woman who loves
all things vintage. Chris is Jeanie's sister-in-law.
They're both fashionistas and have known
each other for years.

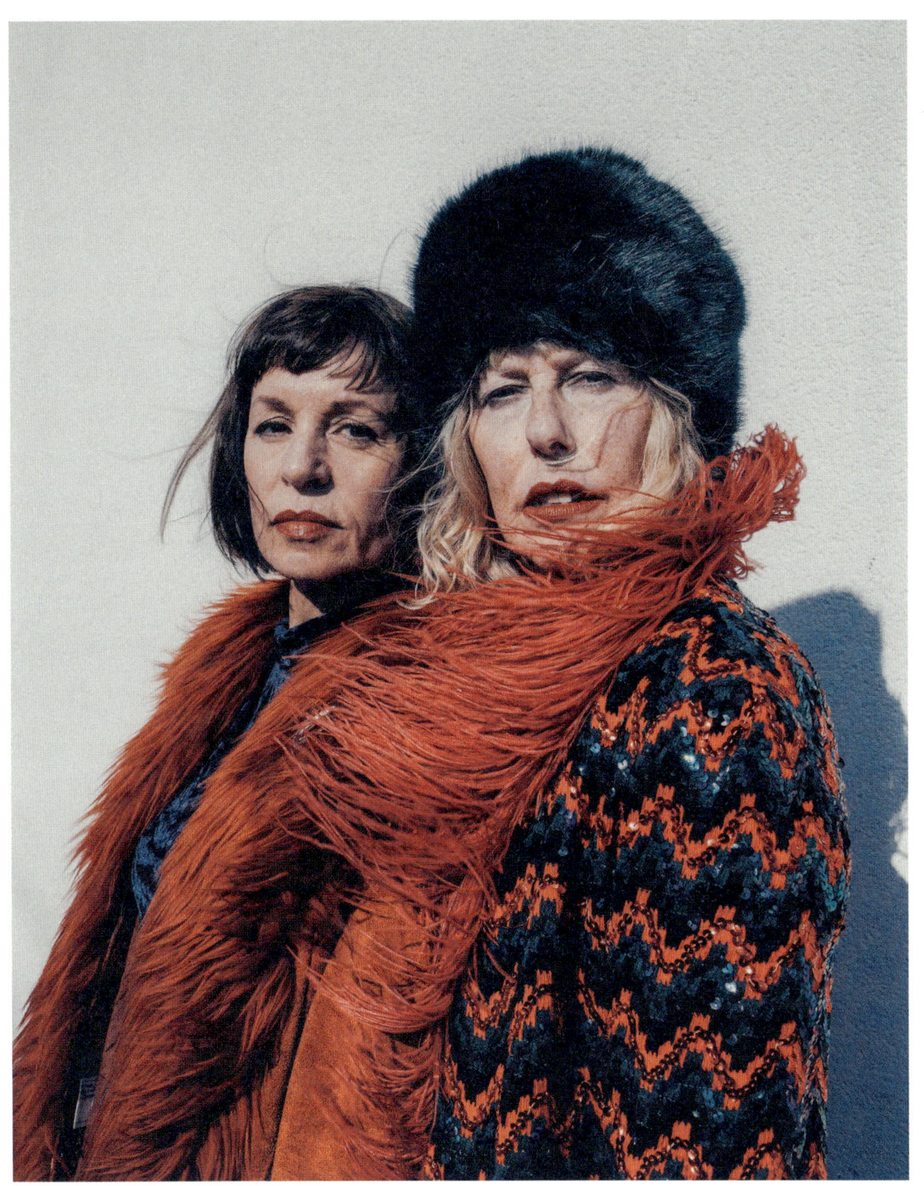

SOHO GEORGE
by Theo McInnes
London

George Skeggs is a former Teddy Boy and full-time
Soho ambassador. In his mid-80s, George is one
of the most outgoing and charismatic people
you will ever meet.

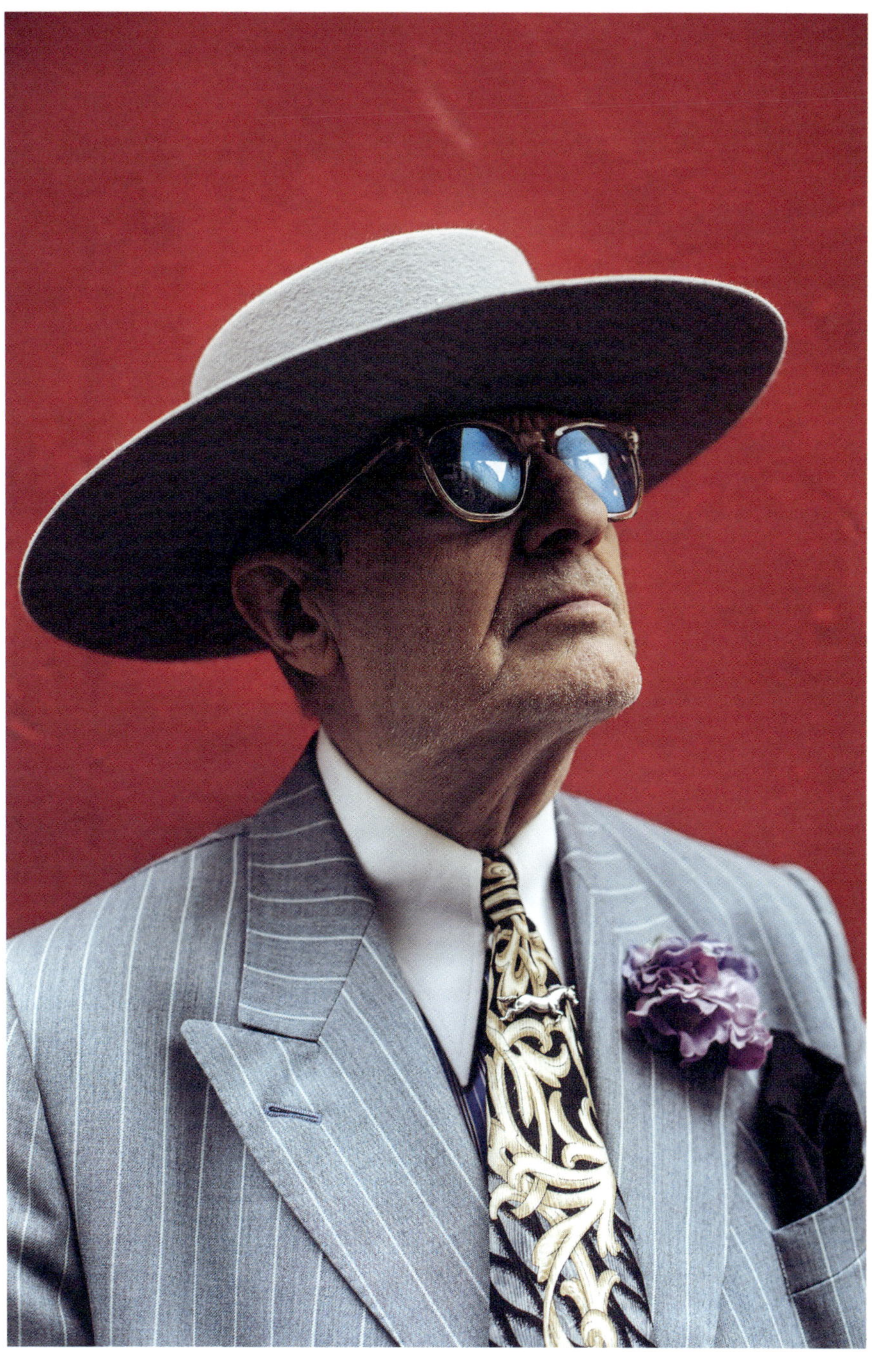

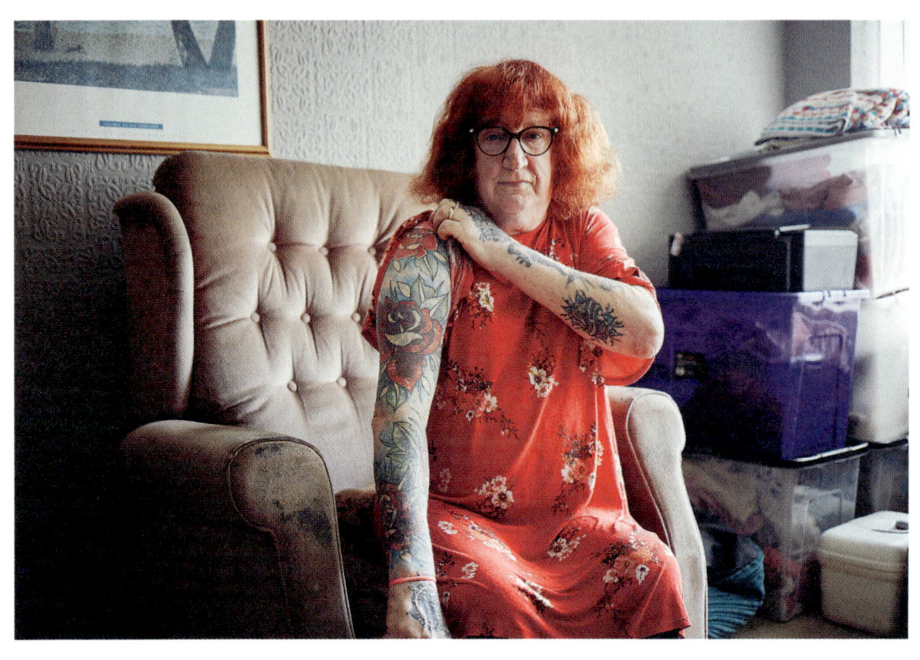

SARAH
by Kate Abbey
Harrogate, North Yorkshire

Sarah went out in public dressed in ladies' clothing
for the first time four years ago. At first she walked with
her head down but now she strides with confidence.

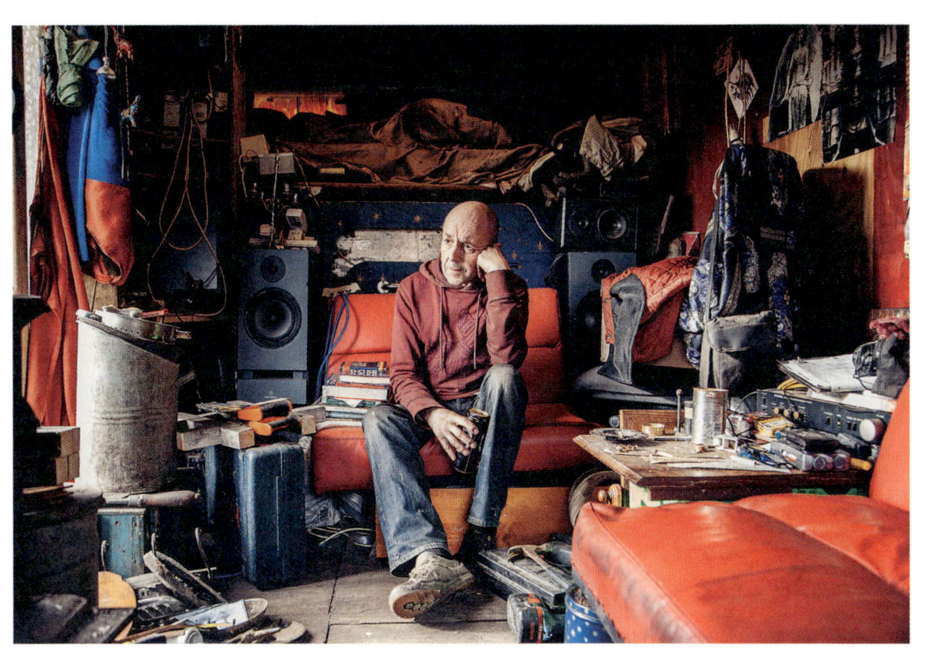

TIM
by Lee Brown
Sheffield, South Yorkshire

Tim lives on a Traveller site in Sheffield. He has spent
a lot of time working on his home and built a decking area
outside where he and his friends sit and talk for hours.

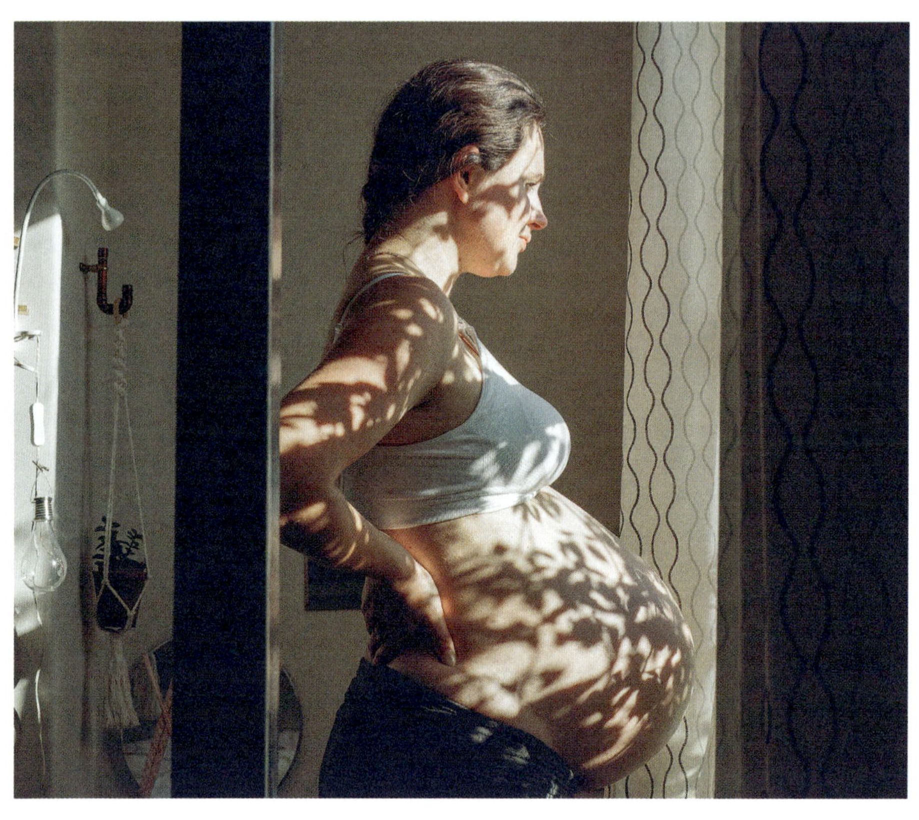

JESS AND THEO
by Poppy French
Guildford, Surrey

Jess and I have known each other since we were children.
She is the first of my school friends to have a baby.

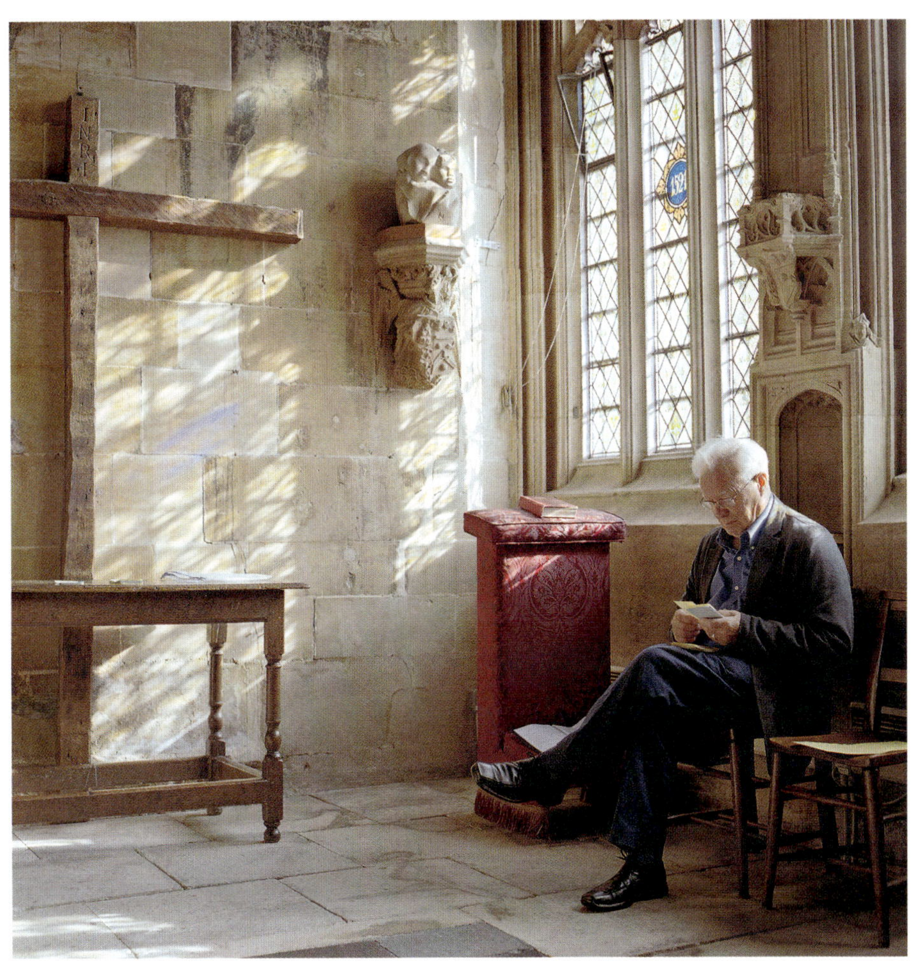

QUIET REFLECTION
by Jamie Harriss
Lincoln, Lincolnshire

This was my first visit to Lincoln Cathedral;
I was captivated by the building's beautiful architecture.
I love the combination of dappled light and this
gentleman's quiet concentration.

BISHOP LIBBY LANE
by Peter Kindersley
Chester, Cheshire

'I always want things to be better, but I want to make
them better by getting stuck in. And the way of making
the church better was by doing it from within.'
– Libby Lane, the Church of England's
first female bishop

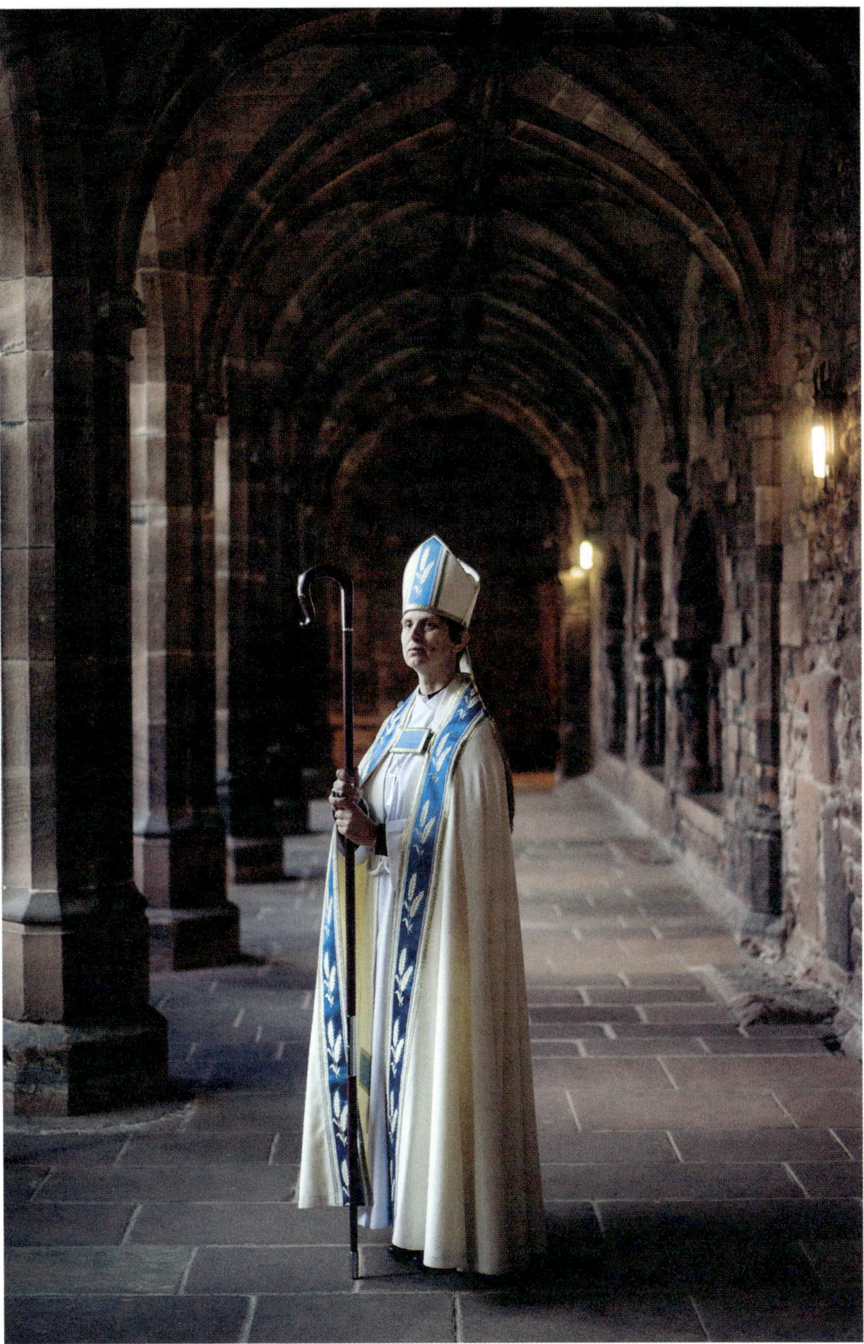

SISTERS MAUREEN AND AILEEN
by Paul Wenham-Clarke
Edinburgh

Aileen has Down's syndrome and lost her hair when
her mother died. She had always lived with her mother.
Aileen's sister Maureen now looks after Aileen.

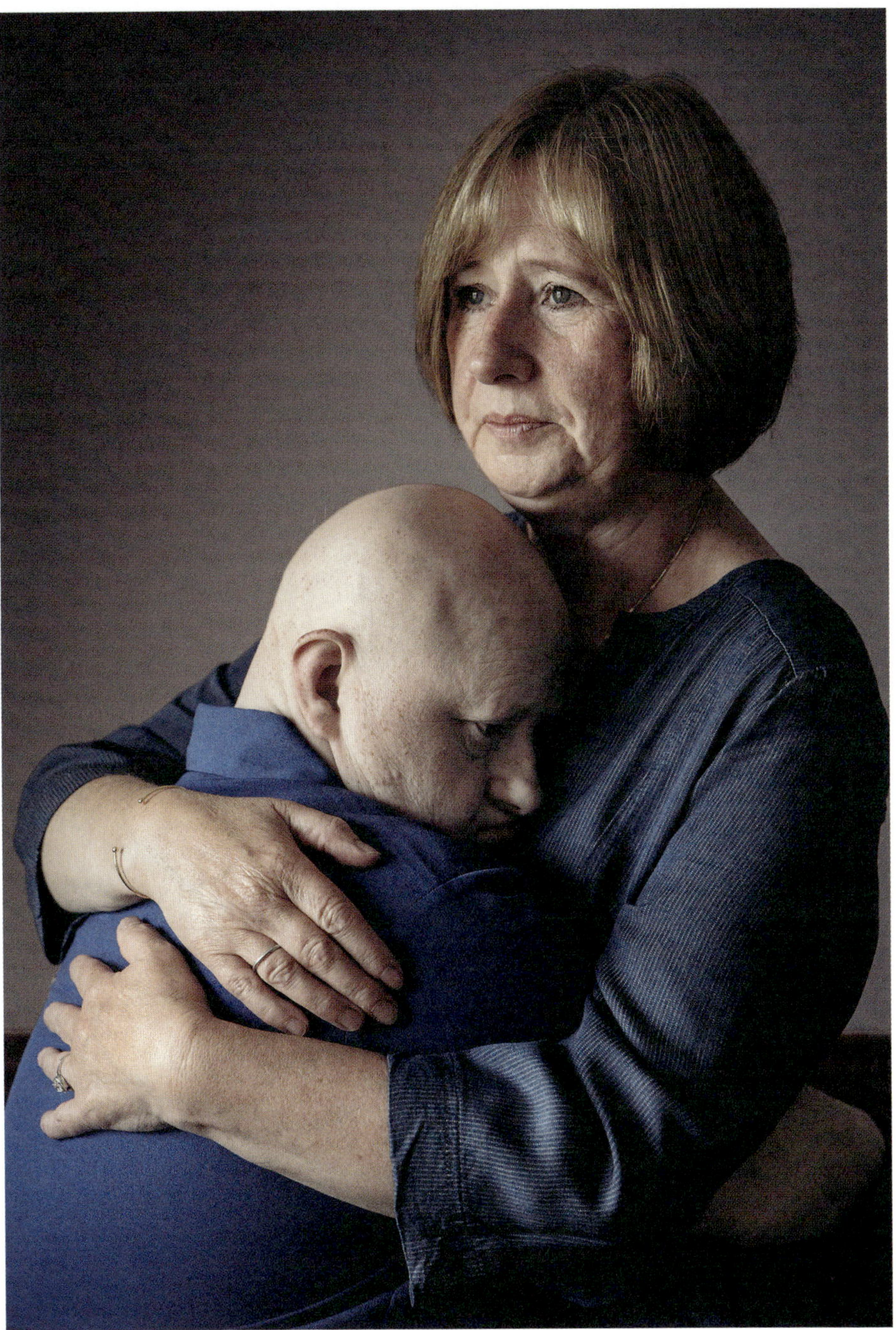

BARBICAN
by Maya Wanelik
London

I love London's brutalist architecture and wanted
to echo the shapes of the building in Ella's poses.
I see the portrait as a metaphorical representation
of my feelings regarding Brexit.

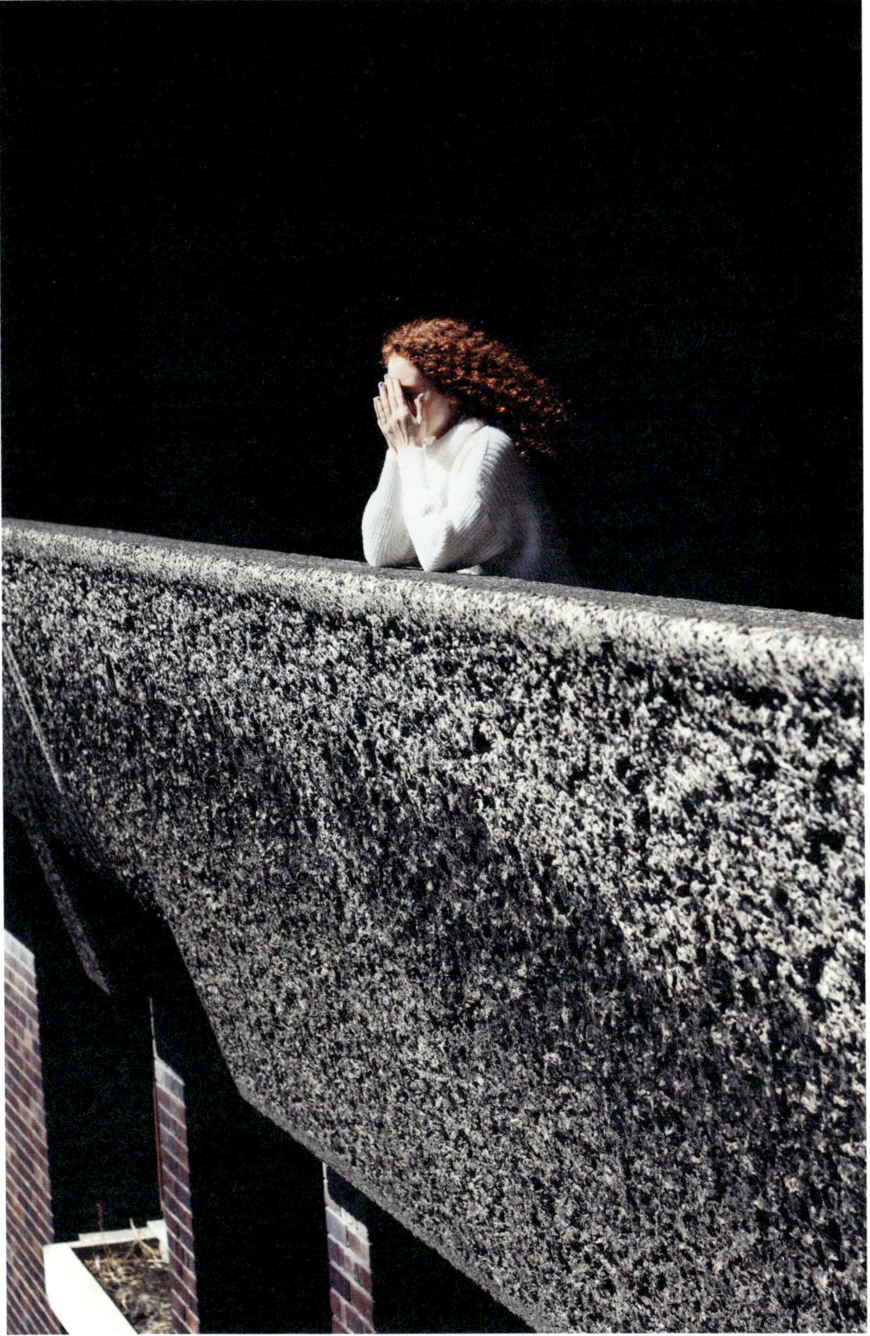

BABIRYE
by Myah Jeffers
Halland, East Sussex

Babirye Bukilwa is an actor, poet, playwright and force
of nature. As the sun began to set on the penultimate day
of Brainchild festival, someone whispered a joke into
Babirye's ear and she let out a warm, infectious laugh.

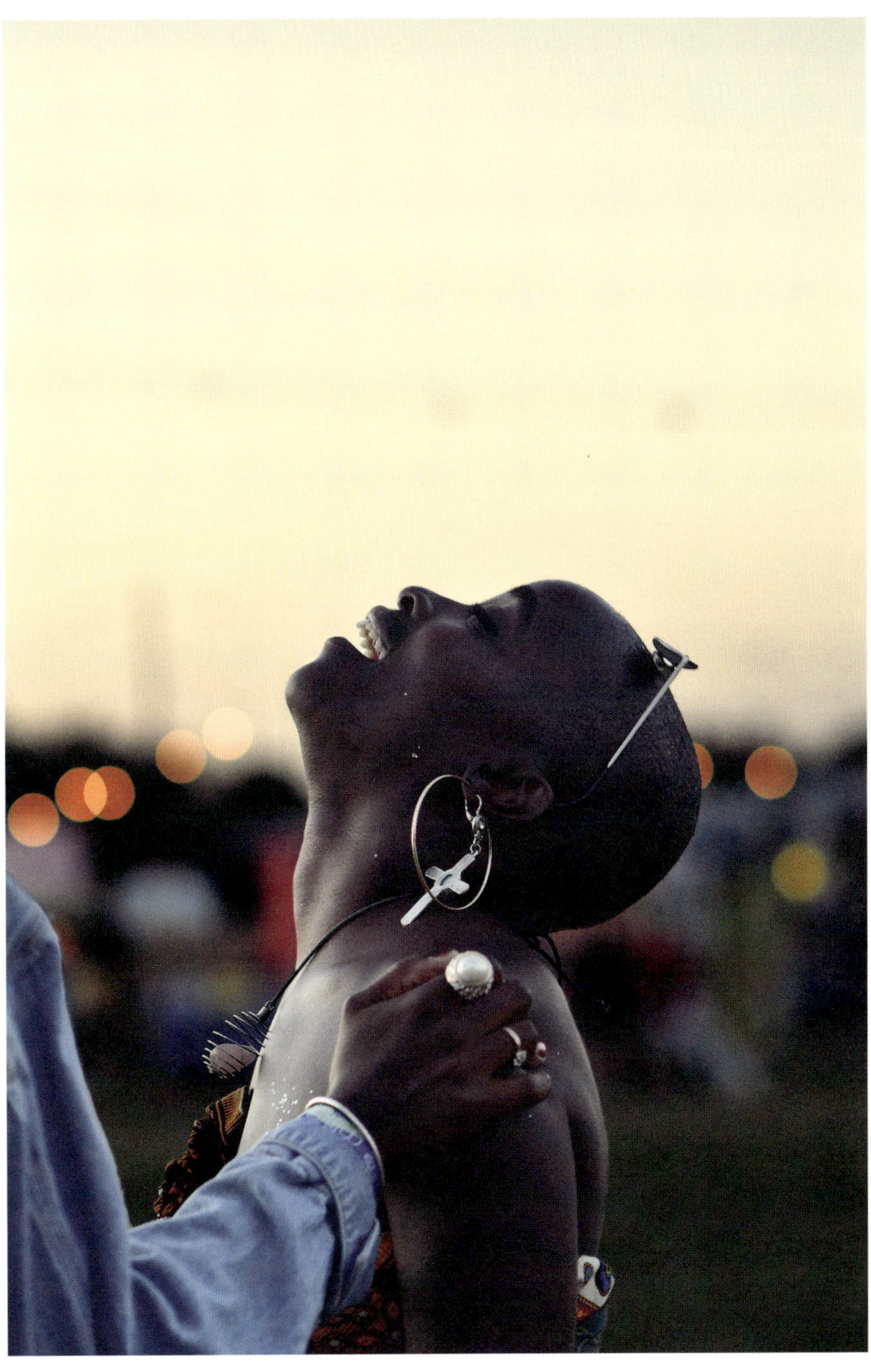

MELISSA IN THE RED ROOM
by Sapphire Stewart
Farnham, Surrey

My sister Melissa was recently diagnosed with
multiple sclerosis. I wanted to show her raw beauty
and strength as well as allude to the difficult journey
she and our family have undergone. Melissa has taught
me how life is meant to be lived.

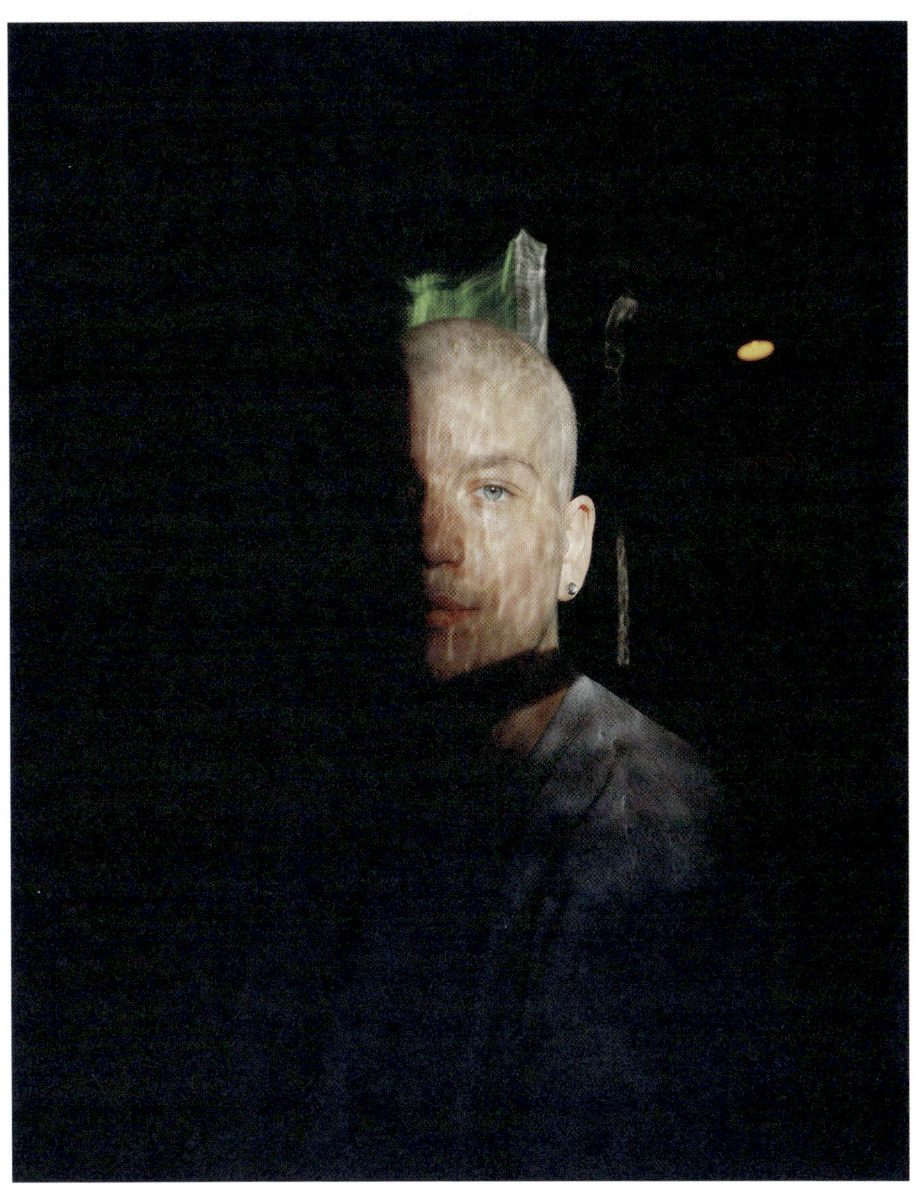

MADE IN THE BLACK COUNTRY
by JJ Jordan
Kingswinford, West Midlands

Chris has worked for the same furniture company
in the heart of the Black Country for over 20 years.
Chris, like everyone I met at the factory, was extremely
friendly, warm and engaging.

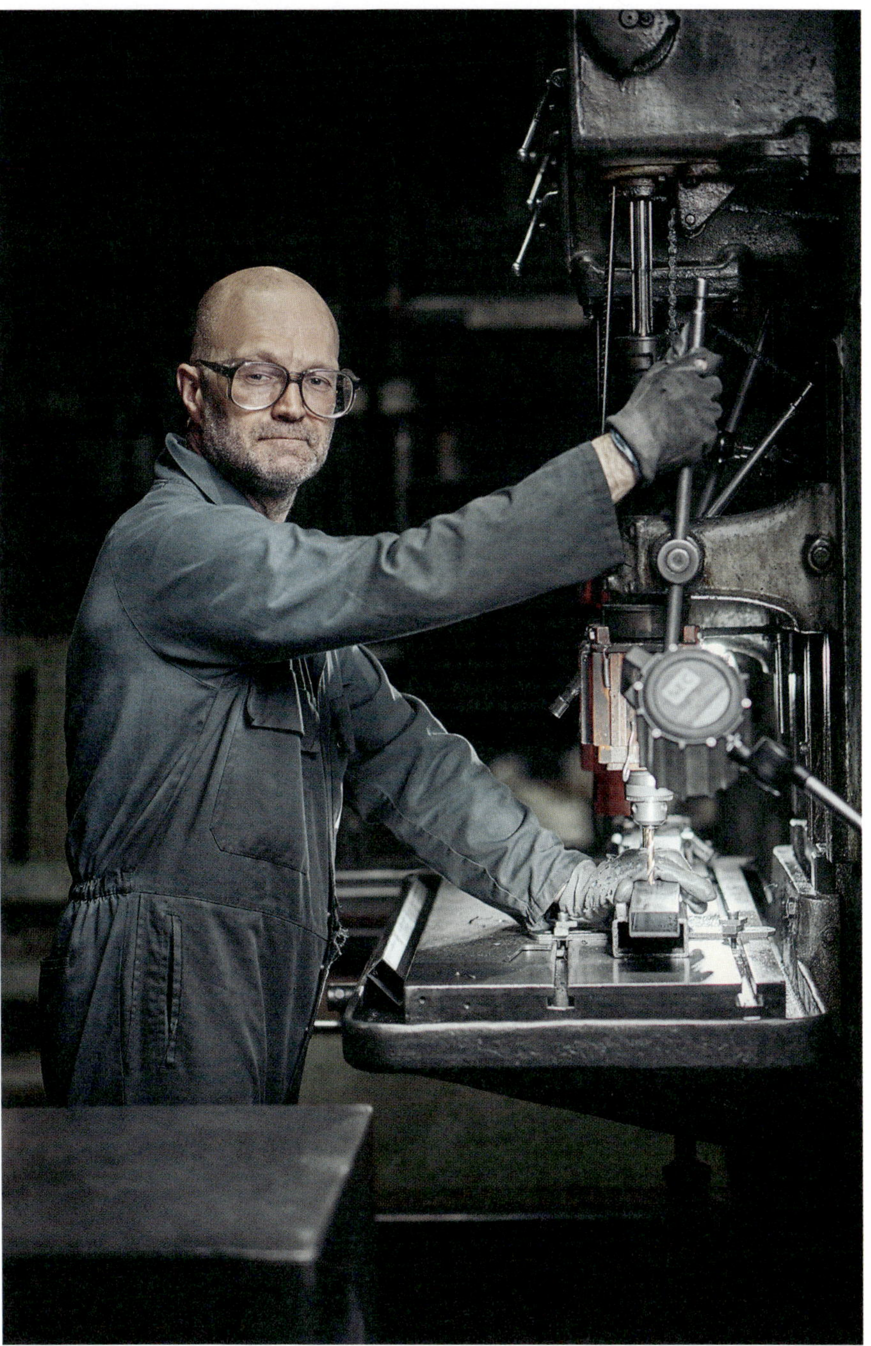

GOSIA
by Rebecca Sunflower Thomas
Merthyr Tydfil, Mid Glamorgan

I met Gosia four years ago during a photoshoot. She left
Poland in 2005 and has been in the UK ever since.

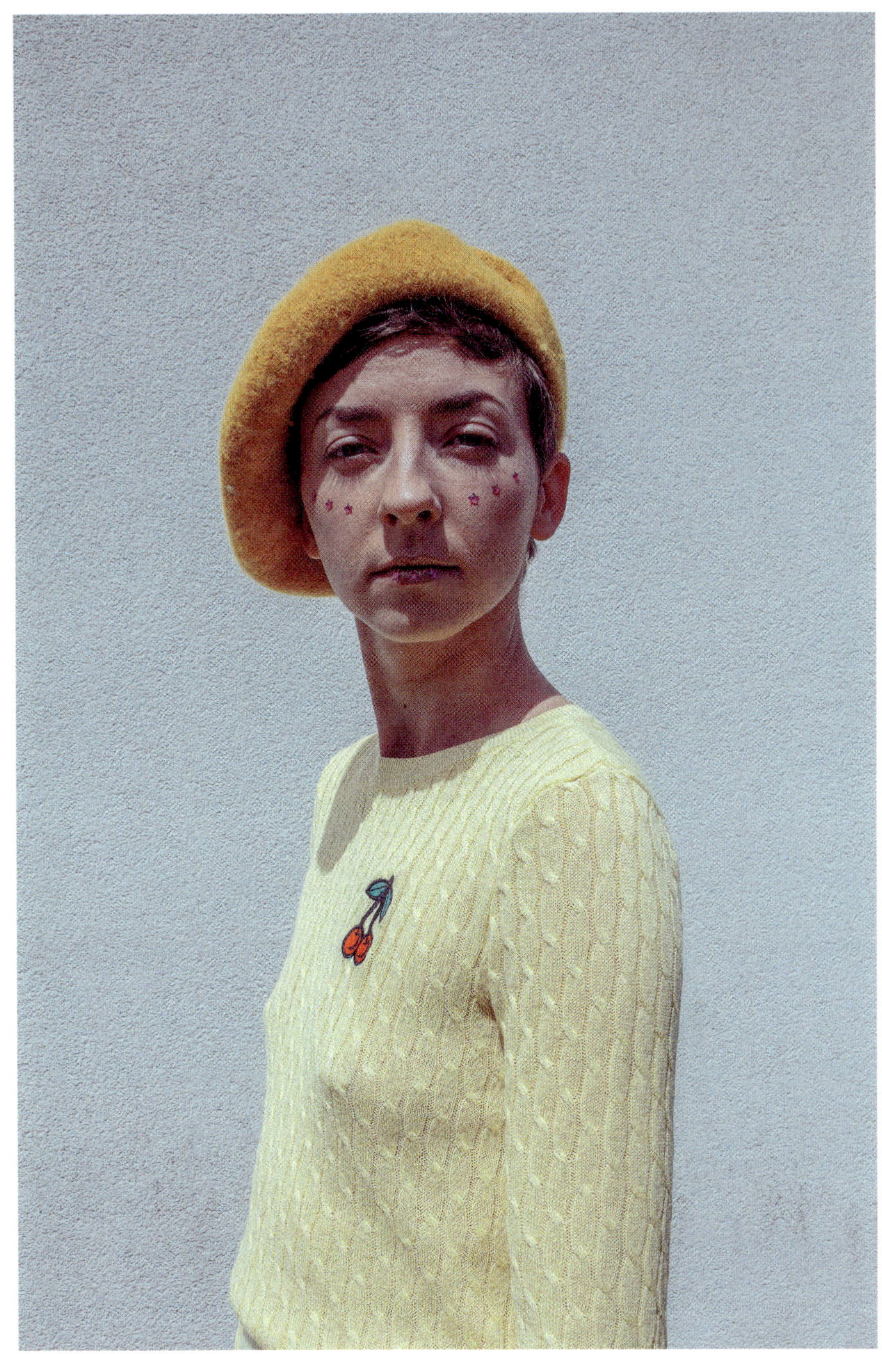

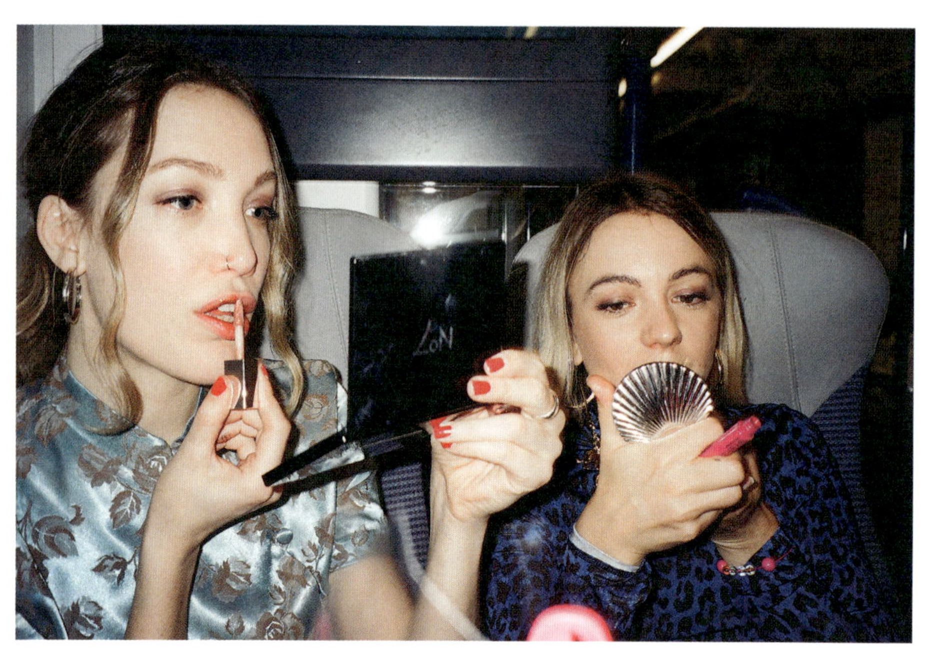

GOING OUT
by John Earnshaw
On a train between Manchester and Yorkshire

These are my two best friends, Megan and Tuesday, who
are both fashion designers. We were travelling to Yorkshire
together to spend New Year's Eve with a group of friends.

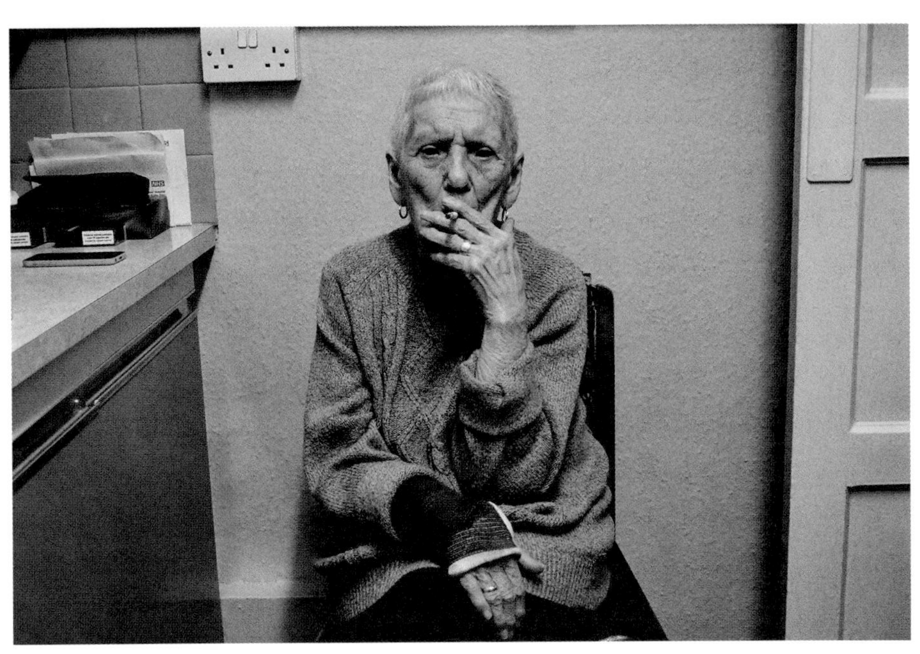

NAN WITH BROKEN ARM
by Sam Wainwright
London

My nan, who was 88 when this picture was taken,
had recently broken her arm. As a result, she lost a lot
of confidence but her defiance still shines through.

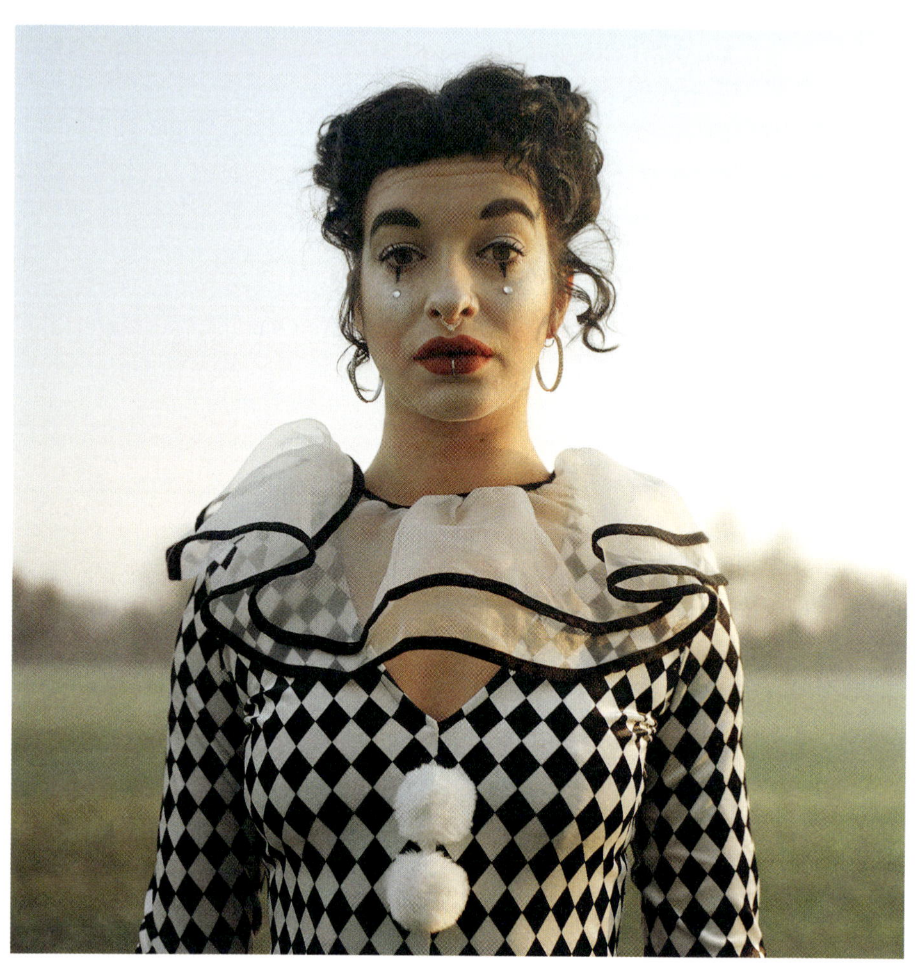

BETHANY BUTTON
by Eva Watkins
Bristol

'I'm in love with performing. Being in the circus is like
being surrounded by a talented, supportive and insane
family. I've never felt love like it.' – Bethany

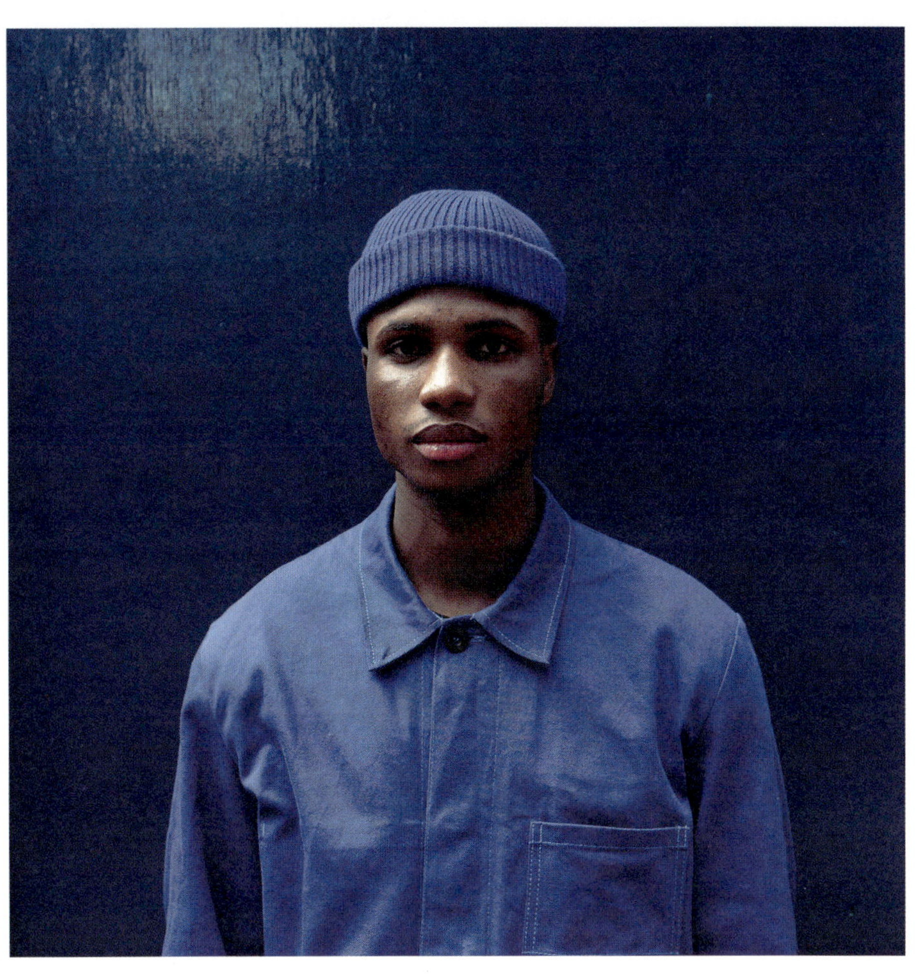

BLUE
by Robert Huggins
London

I spotted this man in the crowd. Dressed all in blue,
he cut a distinctive figure. We struck up a rapport and
he agreed to stand for a portrait. Something about
his eyes and expression hints at his inner self.

GRACE
by Allie Crewe
Manchester, Greater Manchester

I have been working on a series of portraits of trans people in the UK for two years. Grace is a junior doctor. I love the rawness of her gaze.

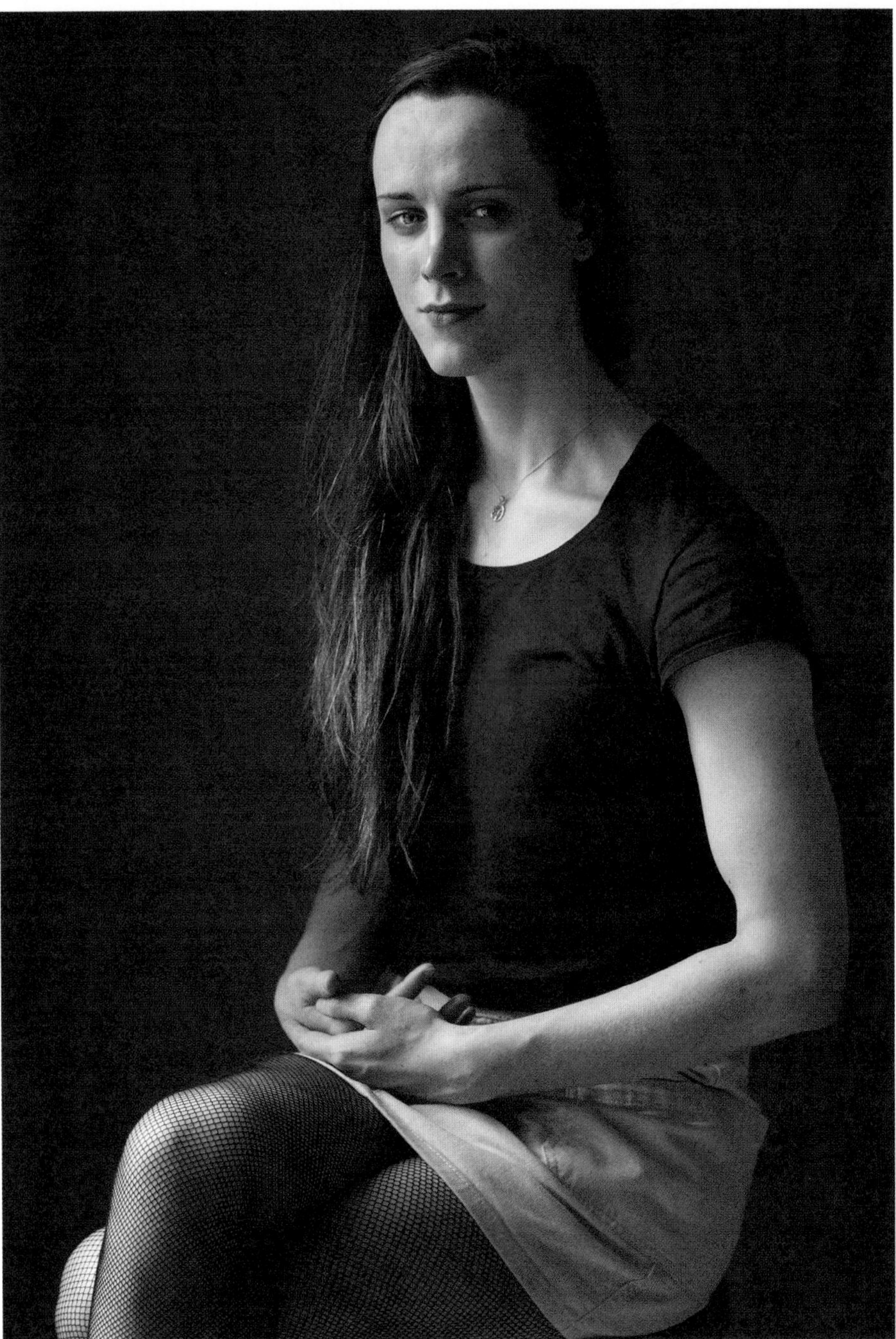

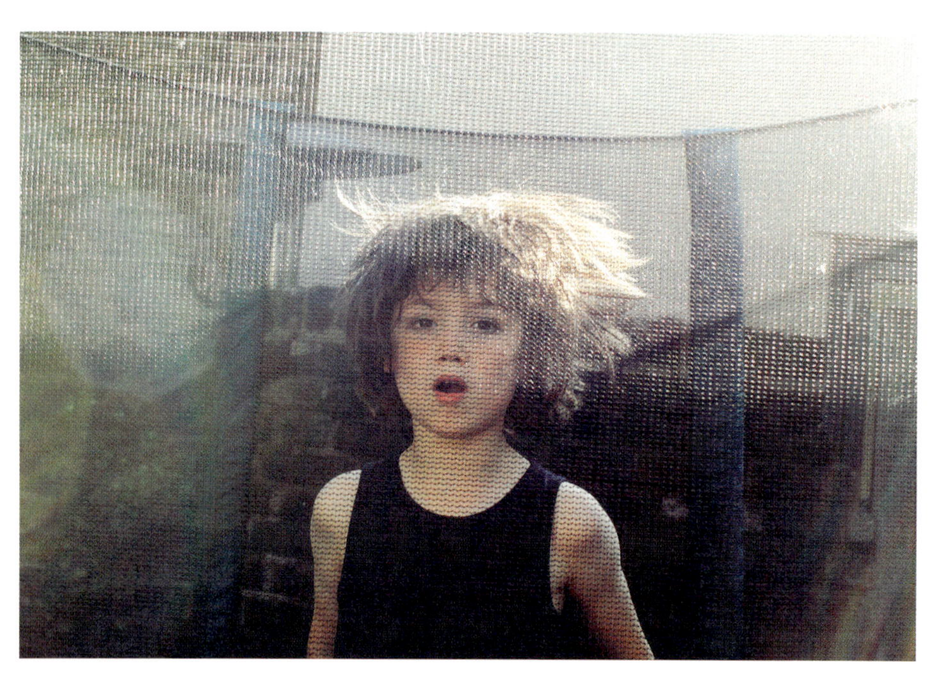

OLIVER AND THE TRAMPOLINE
by Wayne Hanson
London

Countless gardens and backyards across the nation have
trampolines. Many hours and a great deal of energy are
spent jumping on them by children, my son included.

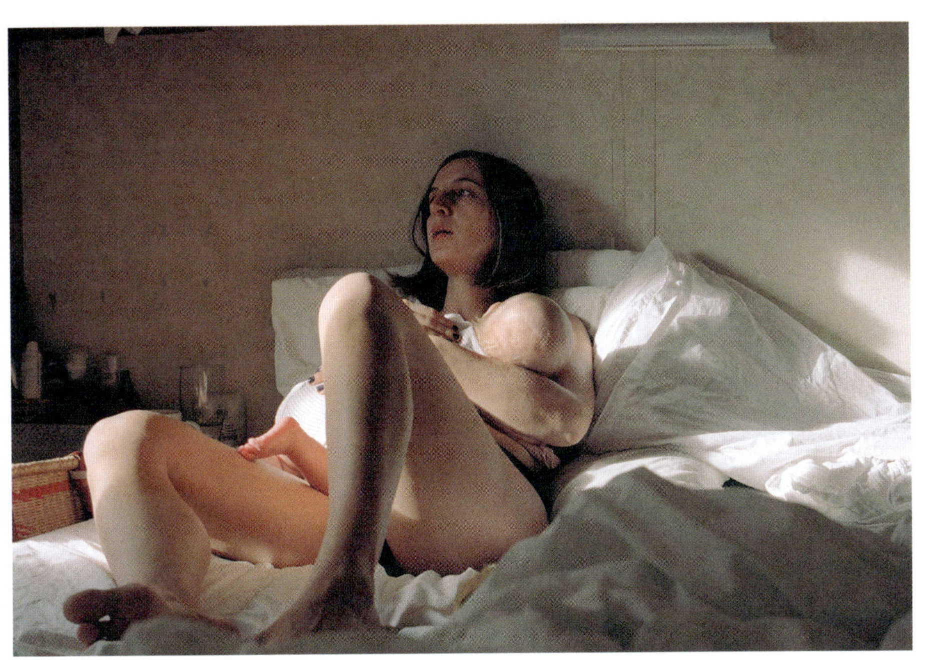

CLUSTER FEEDING
by Naomi Wood
Frome, Somerset

This is me, feeding my nine-week-old son at home in
our static caravan. My husband and I are saving to buy
a house. The early days of breastfeeding are hard and no
one tells you you'll be stuck in the same spot for hours.

ARIANNA
by Paolina Stadler
London

Arianna is nine. I took this picture at her brother's
christening. It was all pretty hectic with lots of kids
running around but I love this moment of quiet.

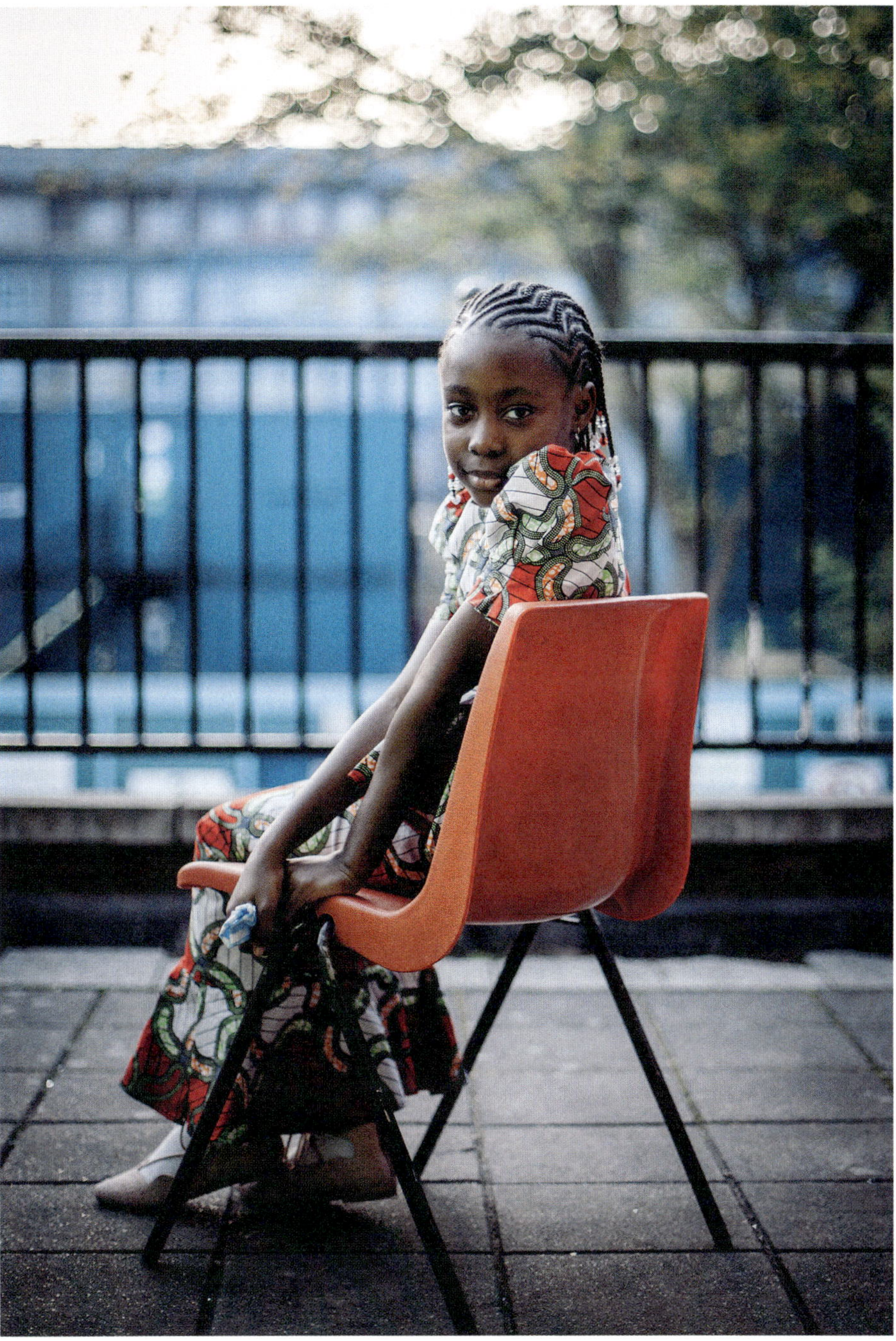

THE WRESTLER
by Claudia Agati
London

Claire is a professional wrestler. She is part of
Lucha Britannia, an English lucha libre-style (freestyle)
wrestling promotion based in Bethnal Green, east London.
Claire fights not only with her opponent but against
a standardised ideal of femininity, claiming the right
for women to be strong, loud and fearless.

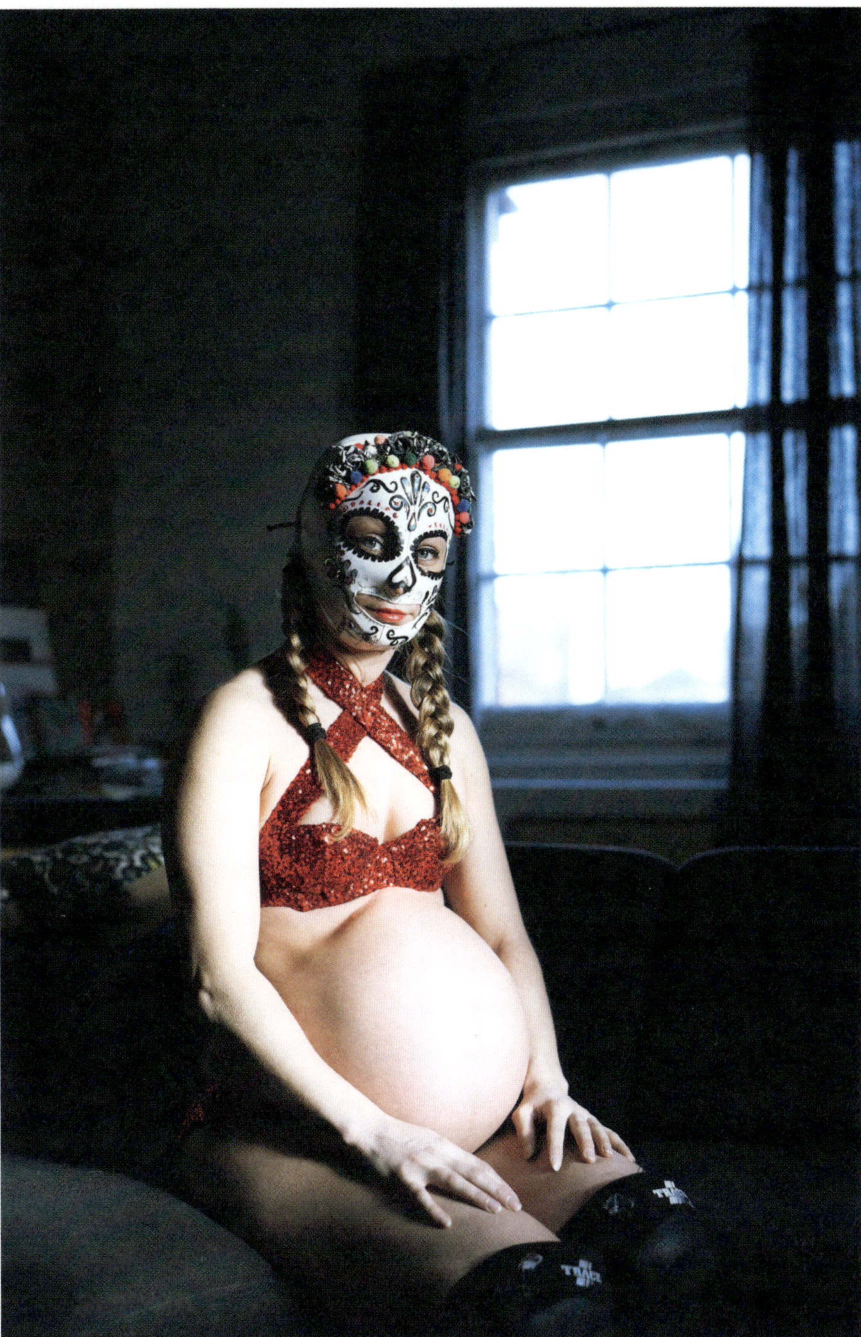

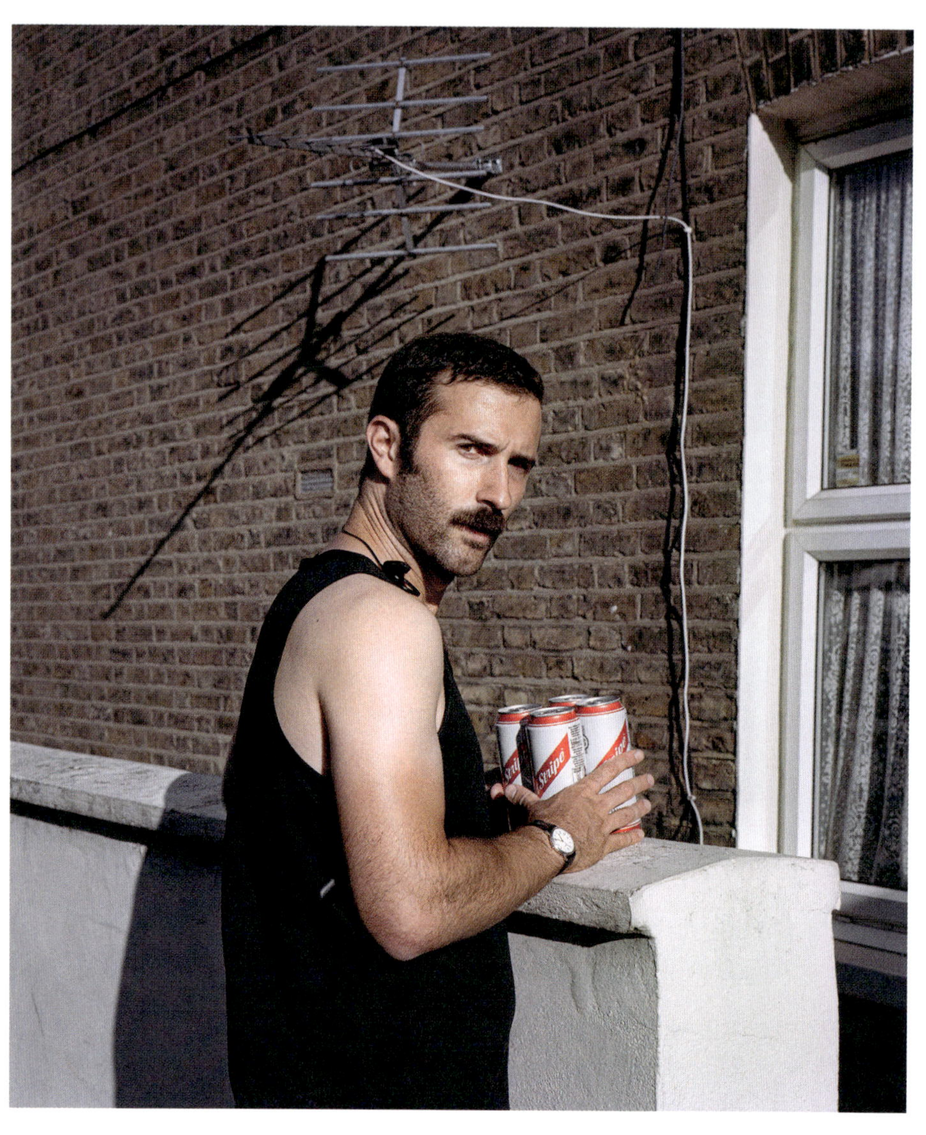

LOUIS
by Le Massi
London

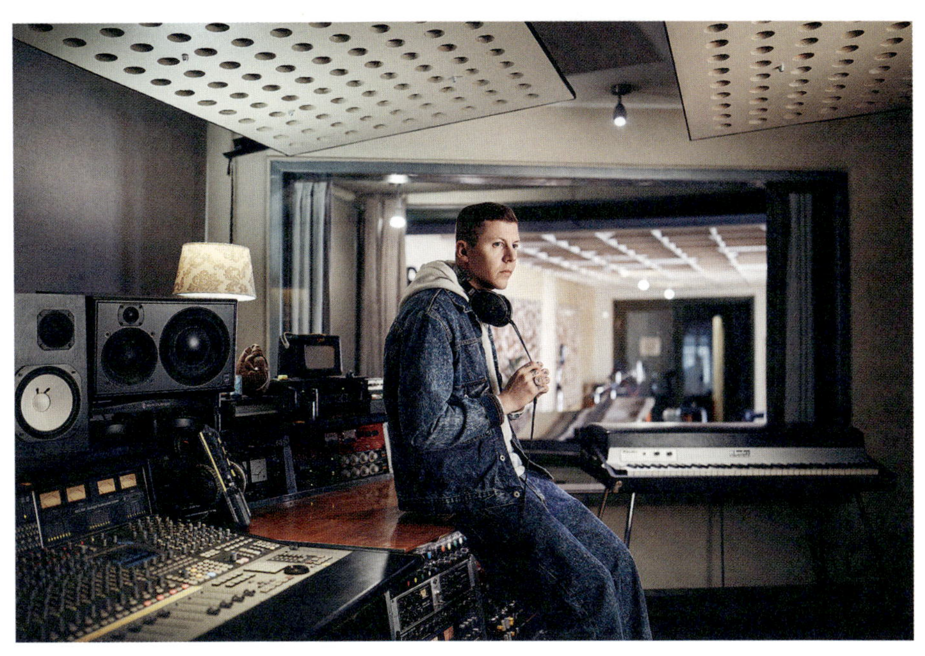

PROFESSOR GREEN
by Jon Attenborough
London

I photographed British musician Stephen Manderson
aka Professor Green when he was recording a podcast.
I've shot him a few times and he's great at making the
photographer relax; usually it's the other way round.

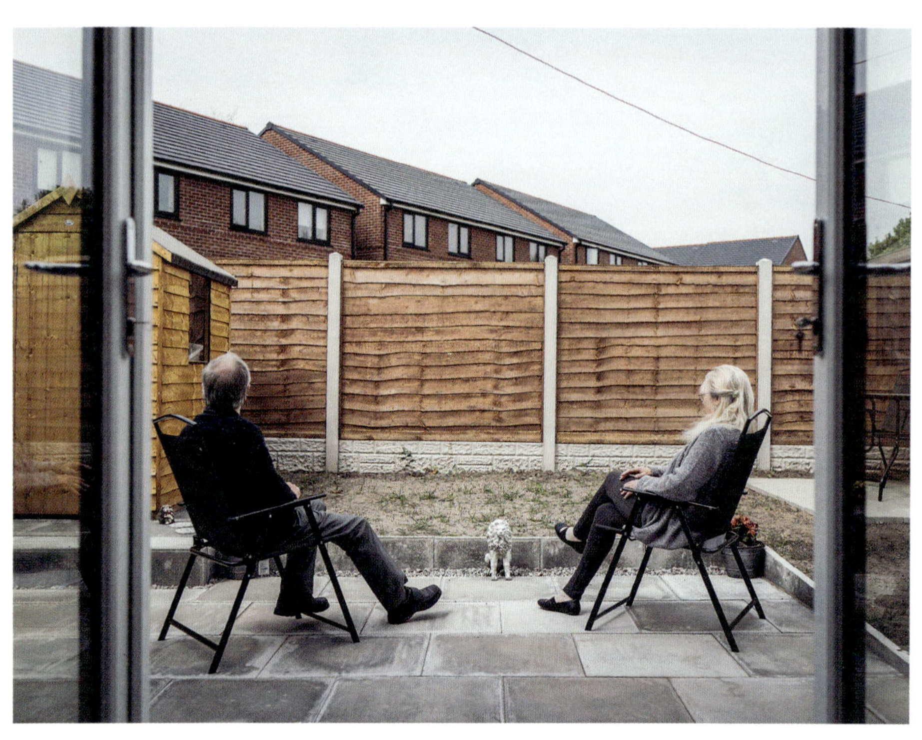

MR AND MRS BARTON
by Sebastian Wells
Wigan, Greater Manchester

I met this couple one Sunday morning. We had some tea
and they showed me their house and garden. Wigan was
made famous by George Orwell's *The Road to Wigan Pier*,
a sociological study of working class life. Eight decades
on and in light of the EU referendum in which almost
64% of voters in Wigan voted to leave, Orwell's work
seems alarmingly prescient.

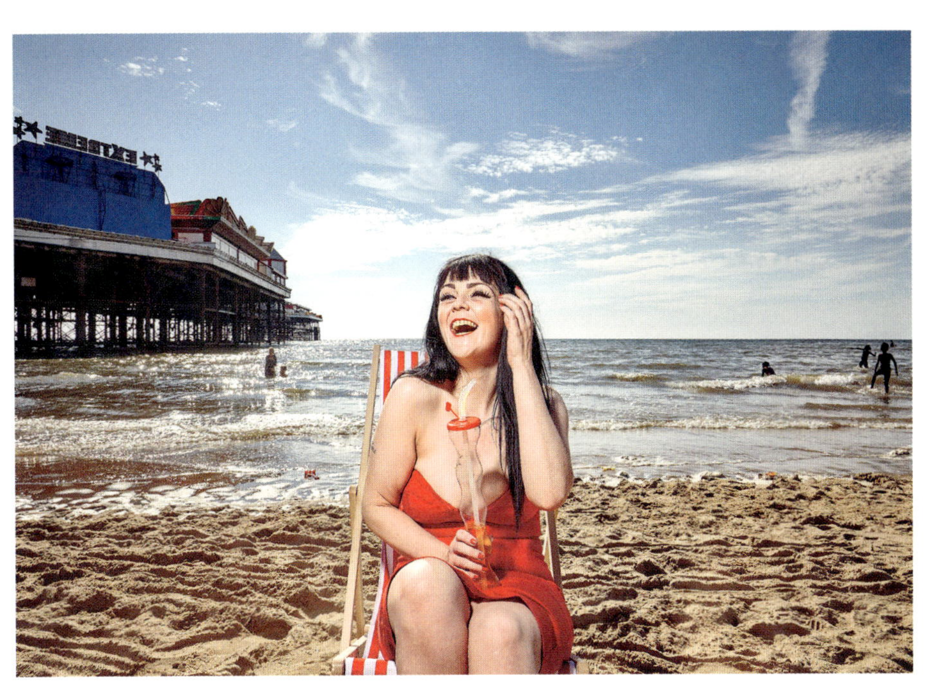

BLACKPOOL BEACH
by Matt Davis
Blackpool, Lancashire

I photographed Emma for a series about holidaymakers
enjoying the Great British summer on Britain's beaches.

AISHA
by Christian Cassiel
London

I would always see Aisha, who is of Caribbean and
Irish heritage, on nights out. Aisha told me she was initially
unsure about this image but realised it's an honest
depiction of who she is.

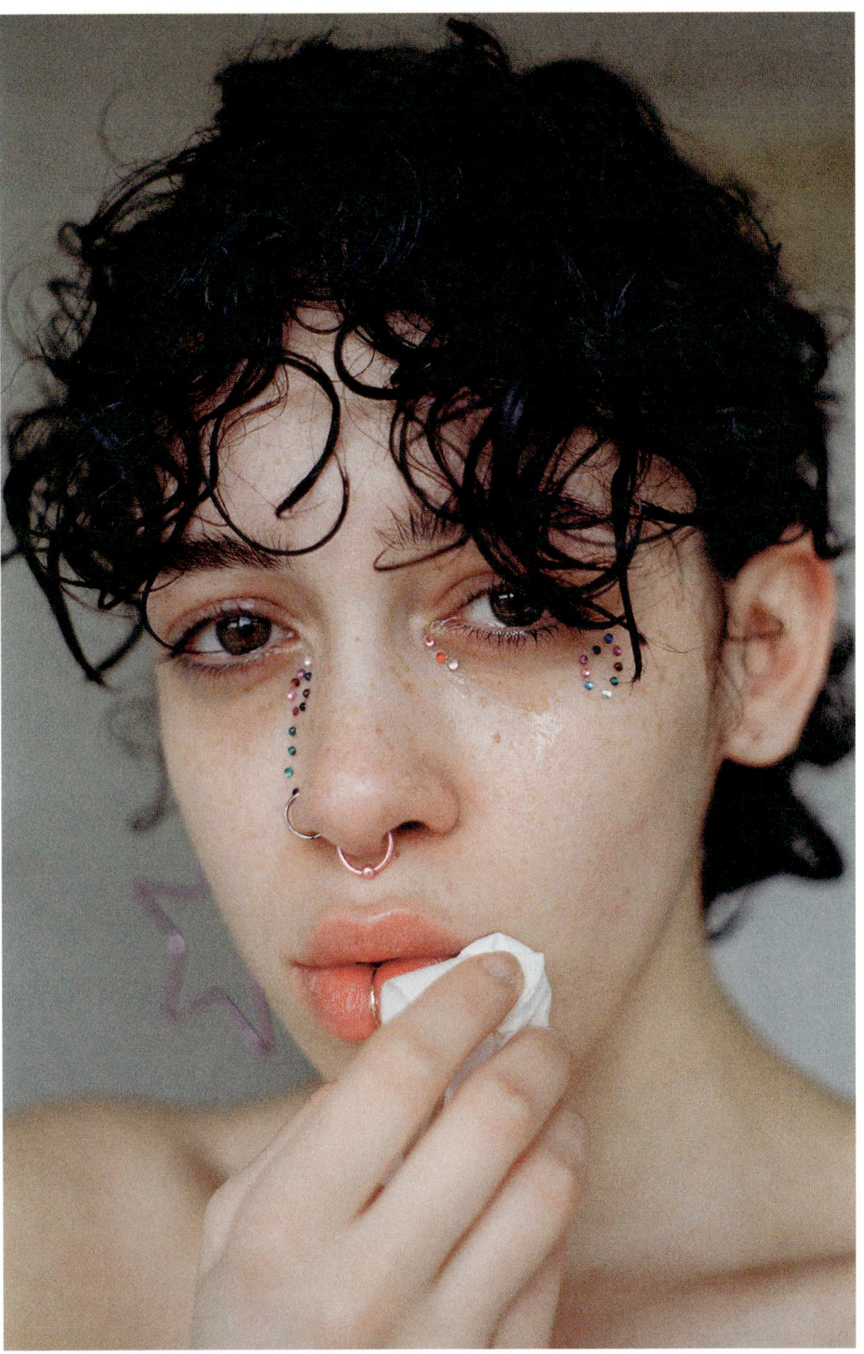

MARY
by Dylan Collard
London

Mary has sickle cell disease and receives regular
blood transfusions. A talented singer, she has performed
at the Music of Black Origin (MOBO) Awards and sings
with a choir at events around the country. I photographed
Mary for an NHS campaign to encourage
people to give blood.

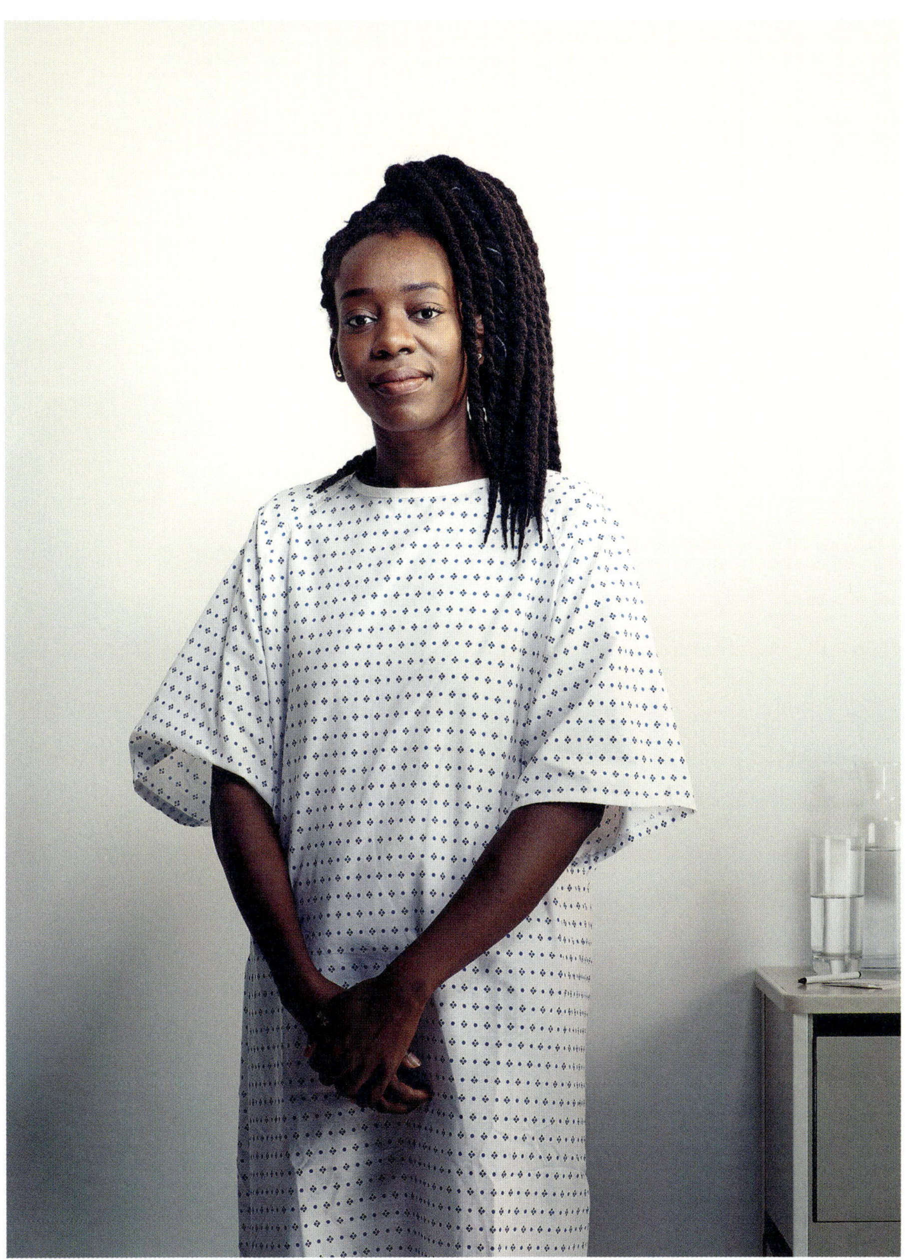

I AM BETHAN NOW
by Fabio De Paola
Coventry, West Midlands

Bethan Henshaw was born a man and at the age of 57
will undergo gender reassignment surgery to become
female. She has always known that she is transgender
but forced herself to live a man's life.

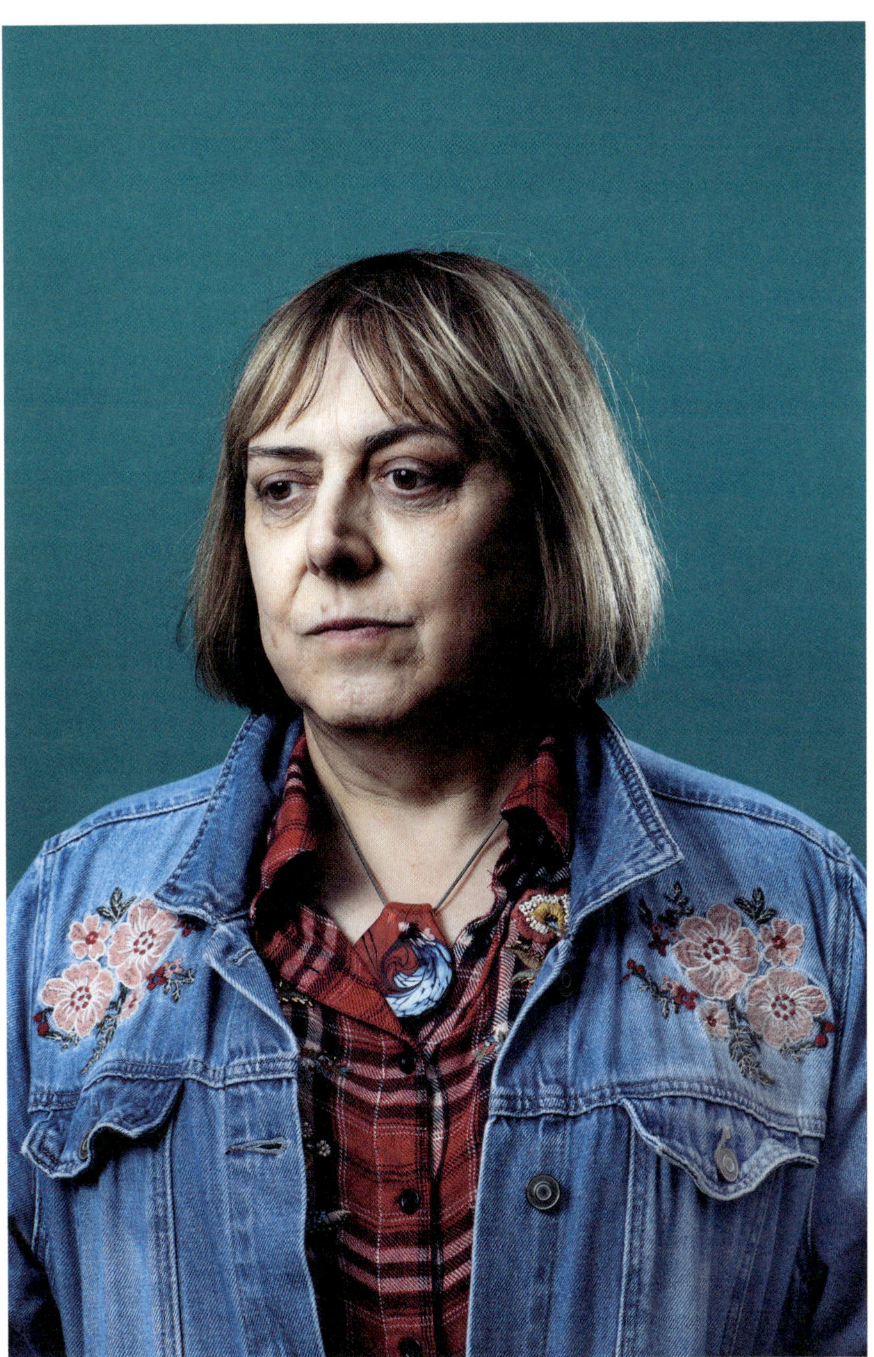

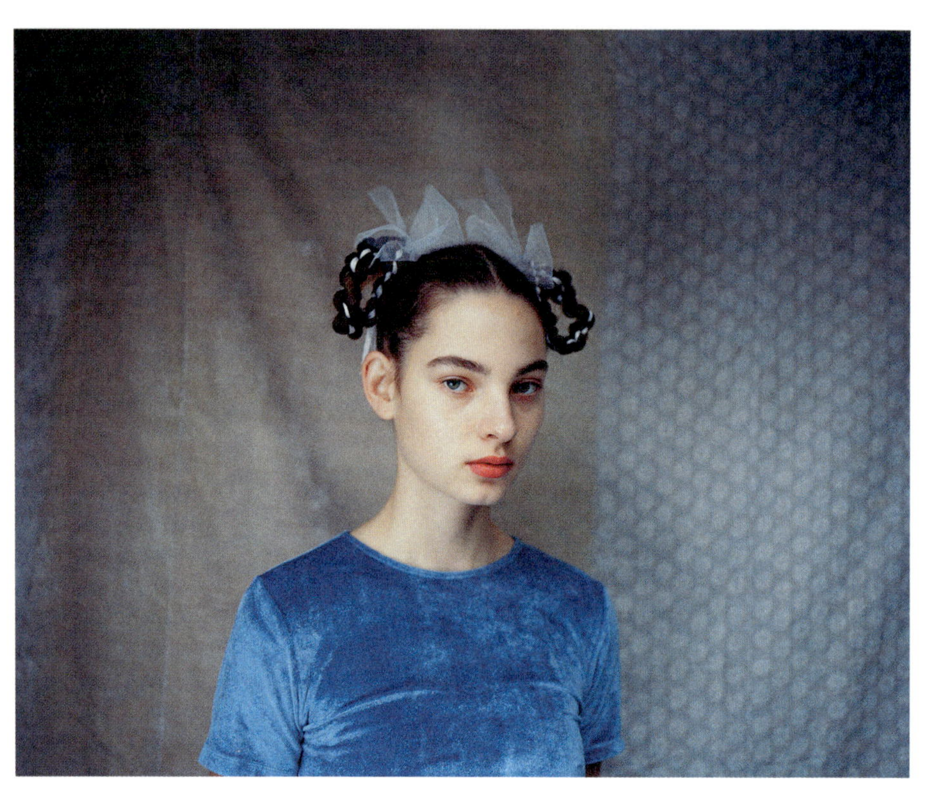

ZHENYA MIGOVYCH
by Josie Gealer-Ng
London

Zhenya is a young Ukrainian model. She hadn't been
in London long when the photograph was taken
but she was full of confidence.

108

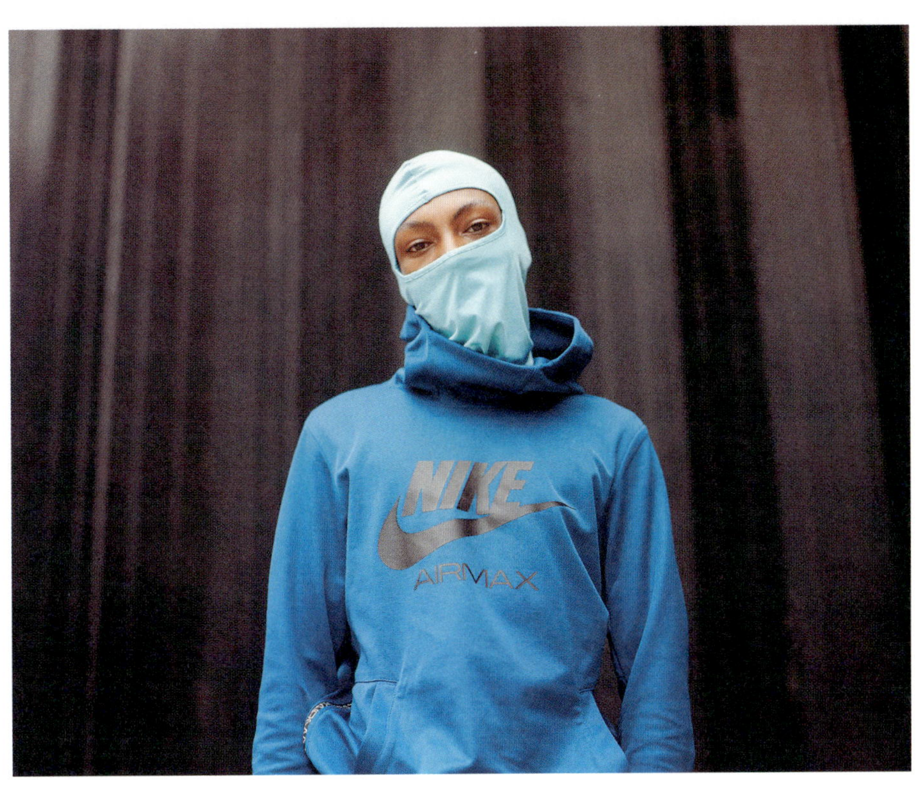

SL
by Vicky Grout
London

This is UK drill artist SL who never shows his face.
Over the years, urban music has often been blamed for
youth violence. Drill music, which originated in Chicago's
South Side, is the latest genre to be scapegoated.

CARA
by Heather Glazzard
Manchester, Greater Manchester

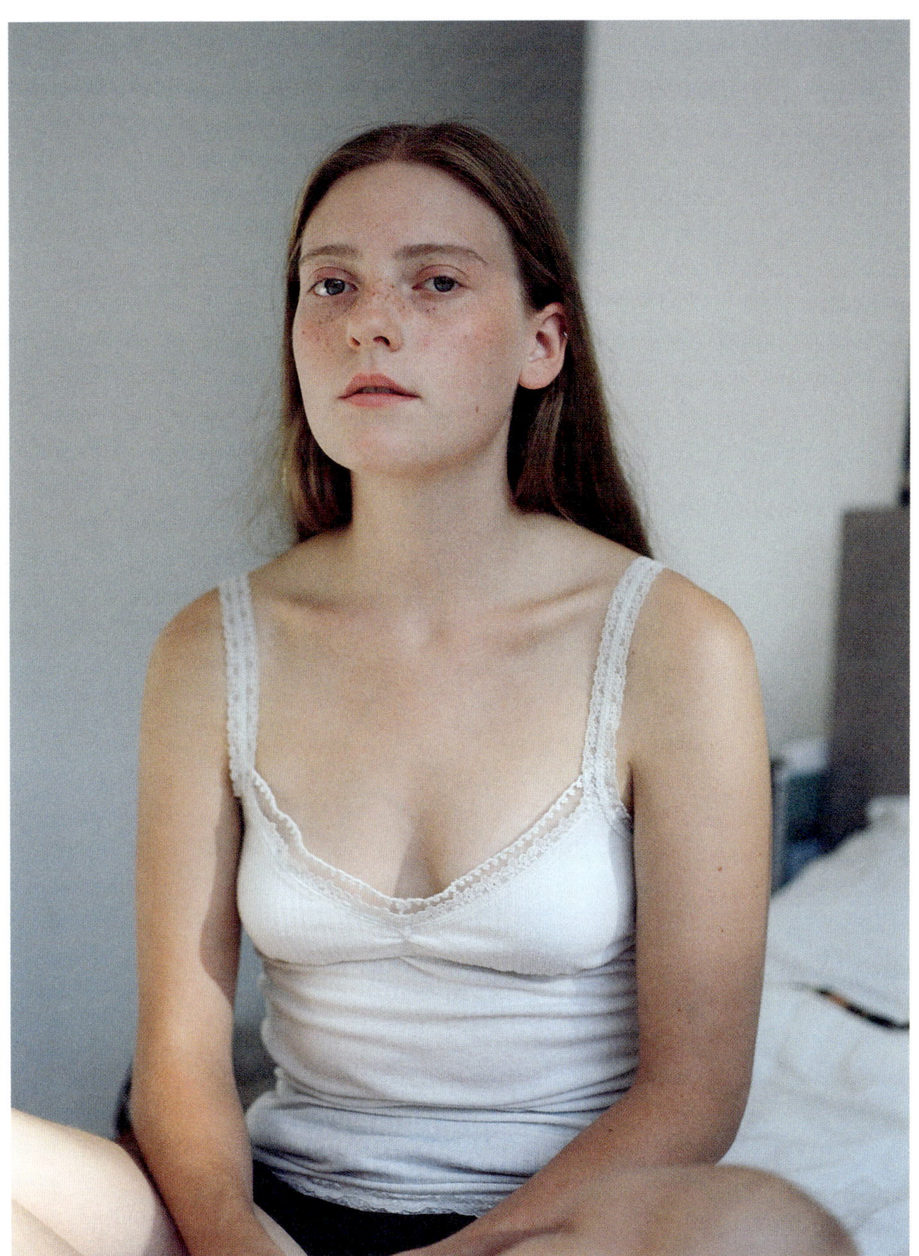

DEALING WITH DISTANCE
by Renee Osubu
London

Nicholas and Michael are identical twins who share
life's highs and lows. They have experienced distance
for the first time as one is attending university out of
London while the other pursues a career in the capital.
Meeting the brothers has opened my mind to the
importance of companionship among men.

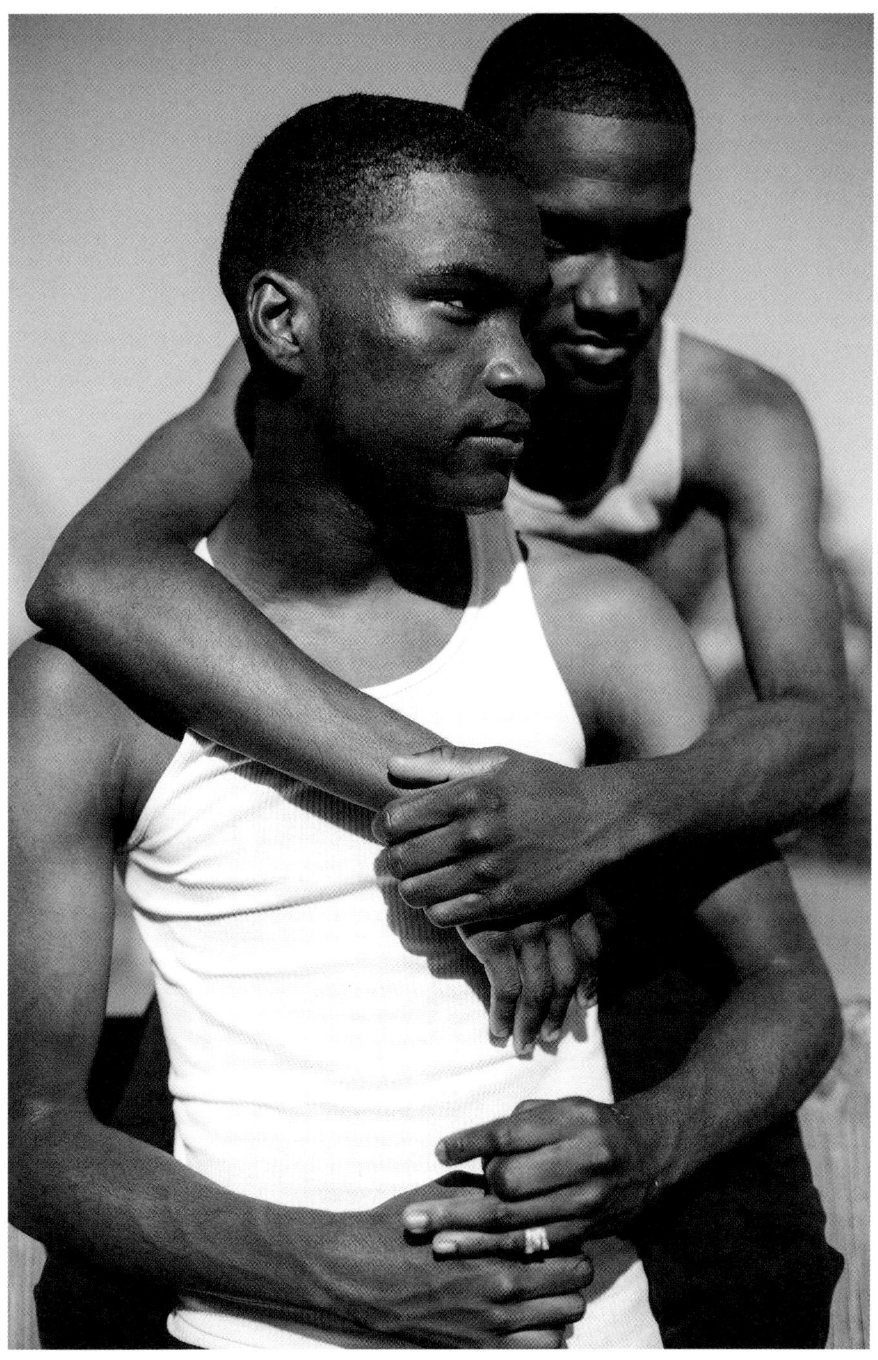

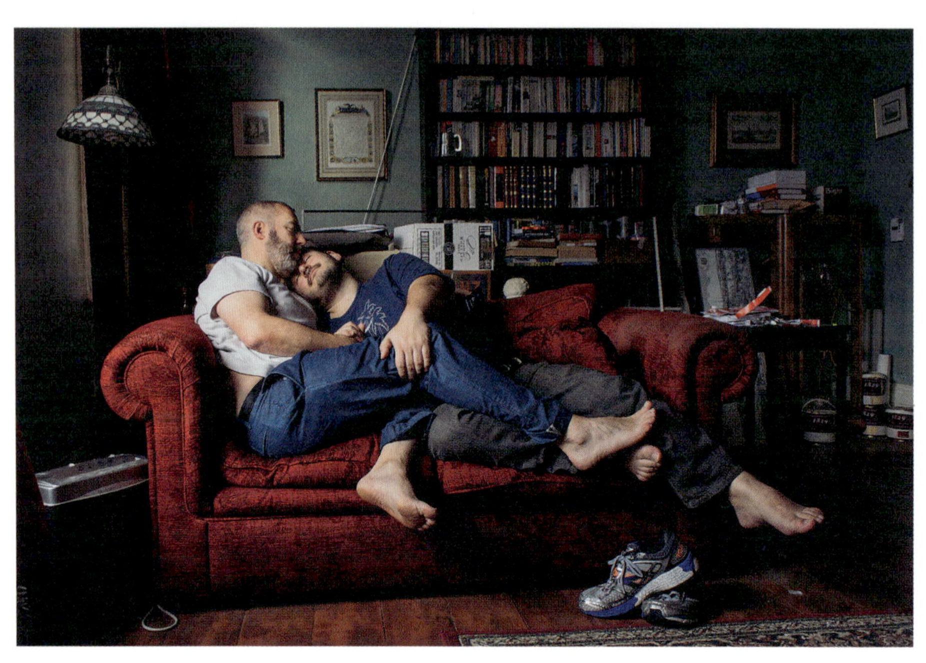

SNUGGLE
by Scott Hamilton
London

I met Alex in late 2015 and fell in love with him
very quickly. He is one of the kindest, most loving
people I have ever met.

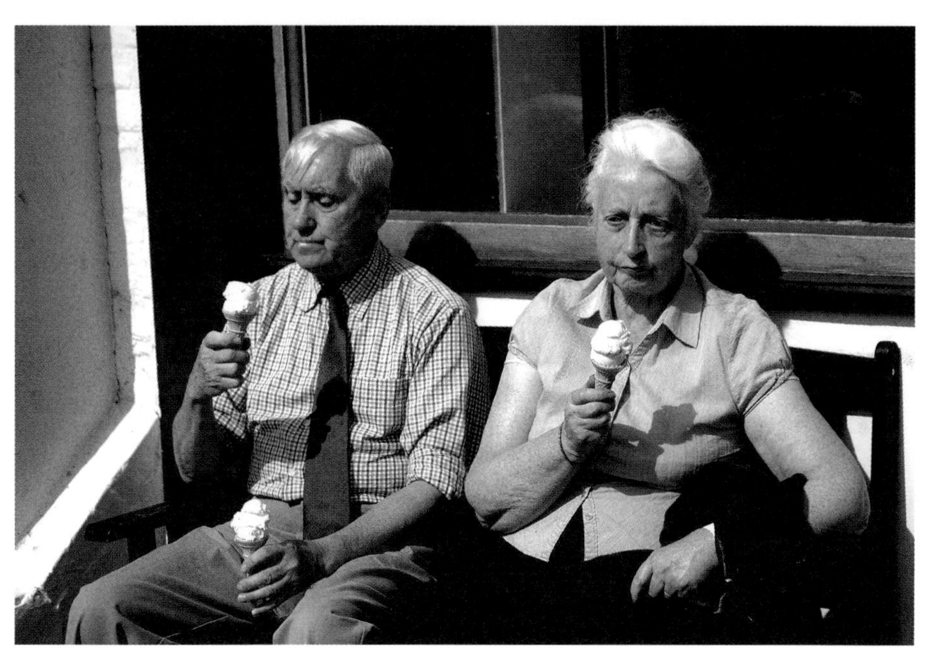

ENJOYMENT
by Mairi Turner
Ironbridge, Shropshire

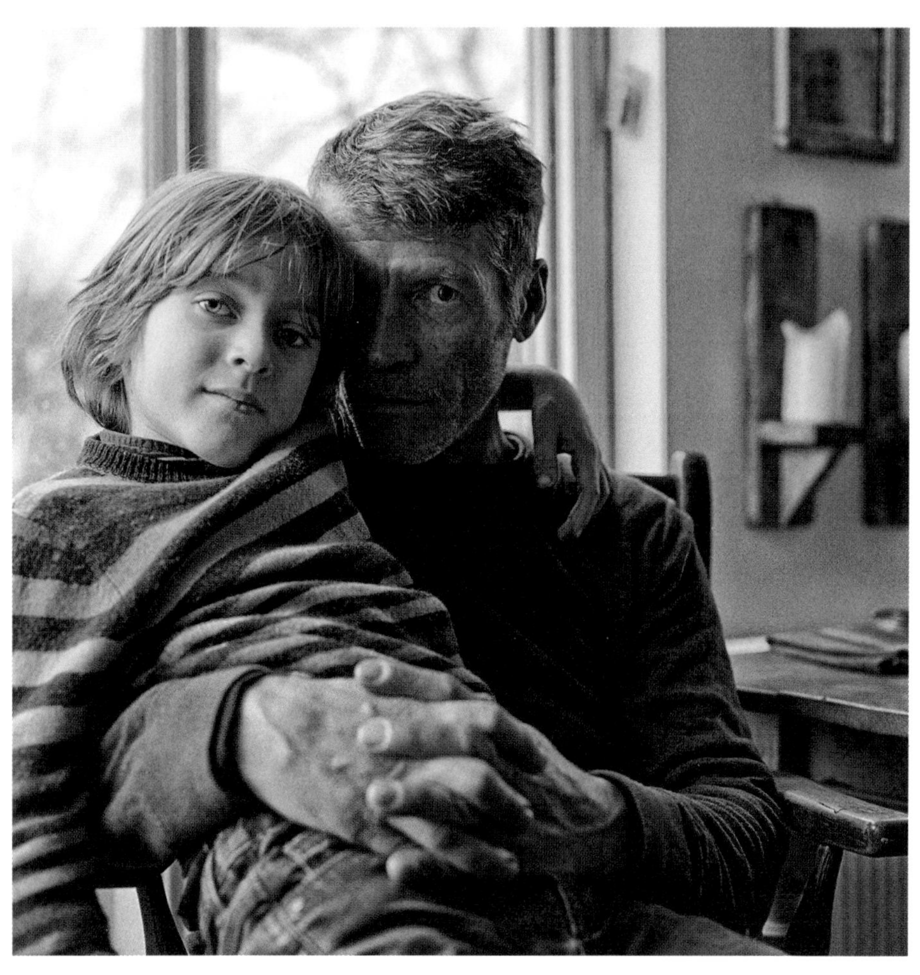

RONNIE AND YANNIC
by Peter Tainsh
London

Ronnie and I studied together at Edinburgh Napier
University in the 1980s. We met again for the first time
in over 25 years on the day of this portrait. He was
in London briefly with family.

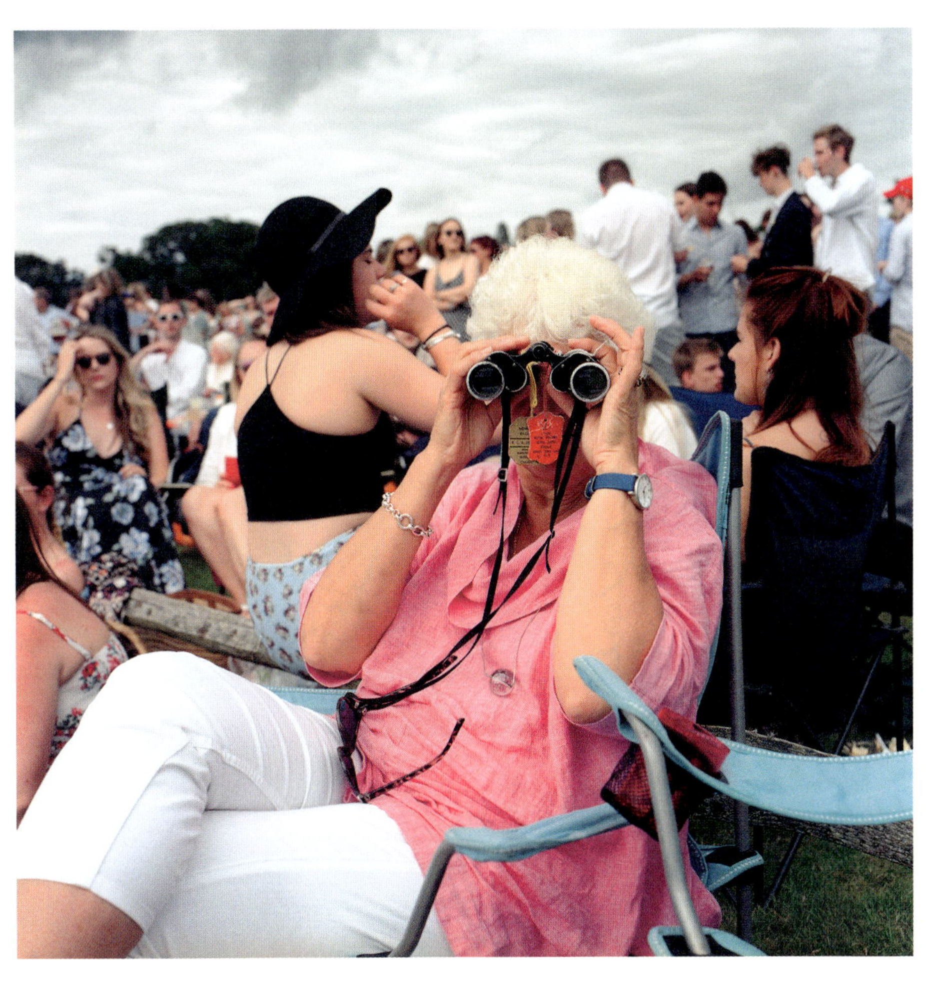

POLO SPECTATOR
by Hannah Burton
Midhurst, West Sussex

DAN BALDWIN
by Alun Callender
Storrington, West Sussex

Dan Baldwin is an artist who creates kaleidoscopic
paintings and ceramics. I wanted the portrait to reflect
Dan's style and the edginess of his work.

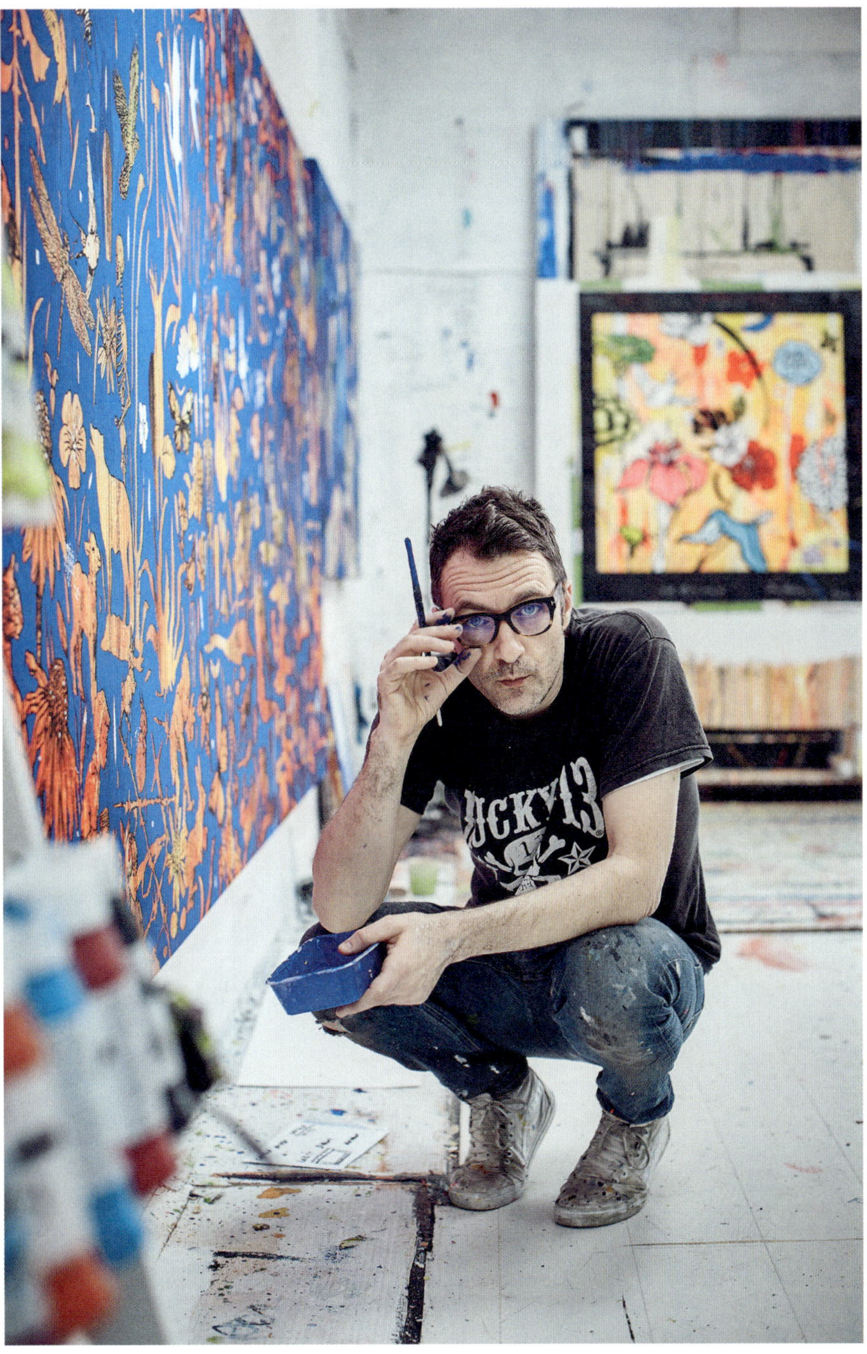

GRAN
by Slater King
London

I saw this lady on the streets of Dalston, east London.
She whirled around to take the spotlight, posing with
glee. One minute she was blowing a kiss, the next she was
serious and focused. I remember watching her
walk away jauntily.

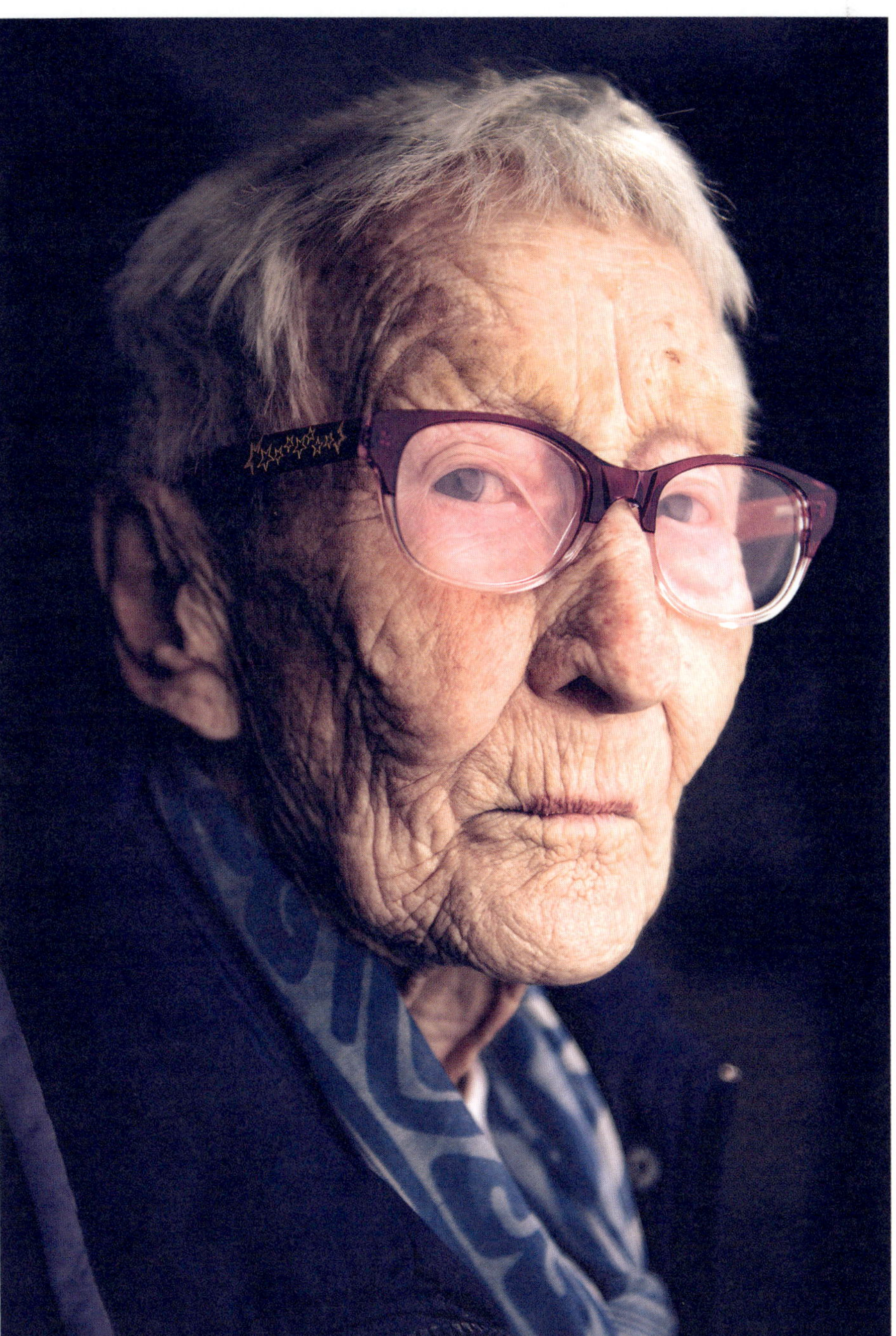

ERNIE IN A CHILD'S CHAIR
by Adam Deakin
Coningsby, Lincolnshire

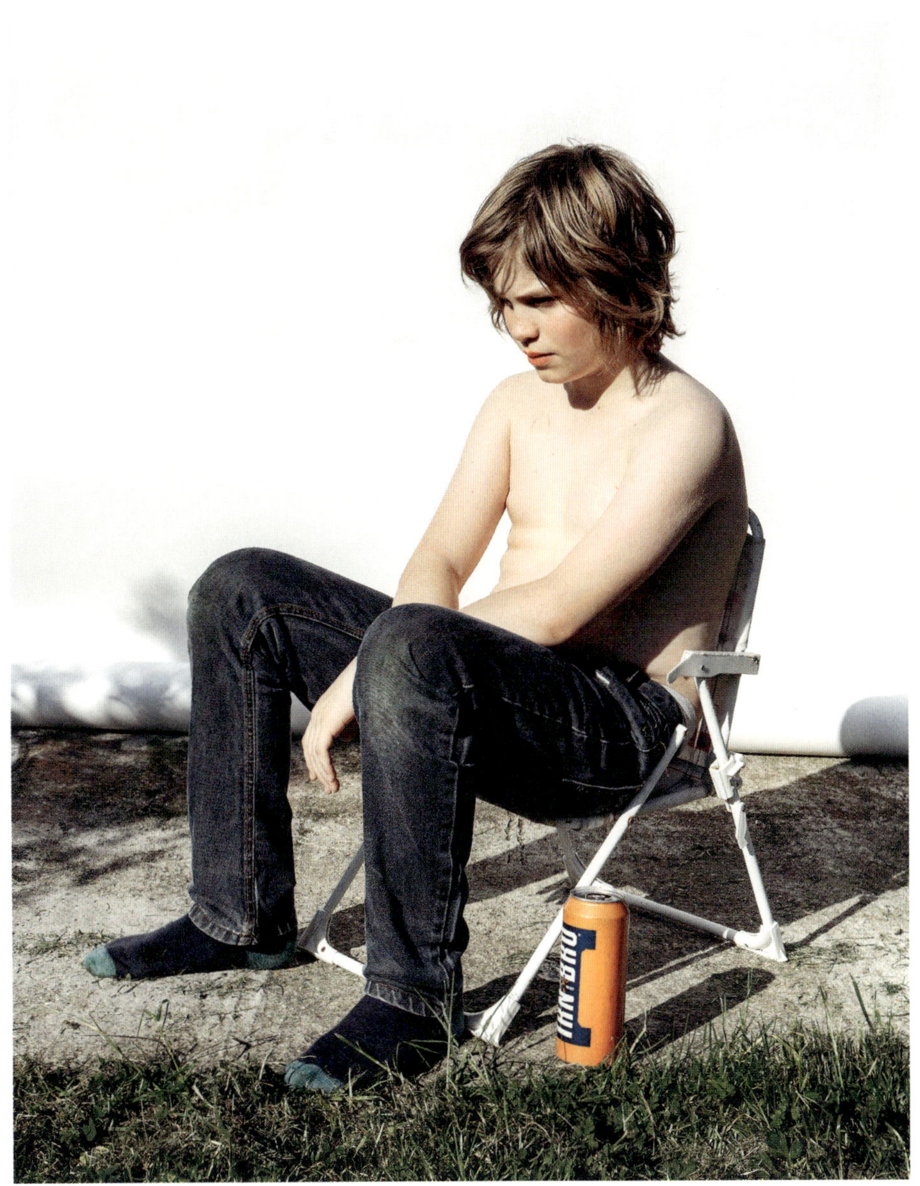

WILD BOY
by Samuel Fradley
Exeter, Devon

Tavis makes musical steel pans for a guy in the city.
That's his version of a job. Perhaps we need more
free-spirited people like Tavis.

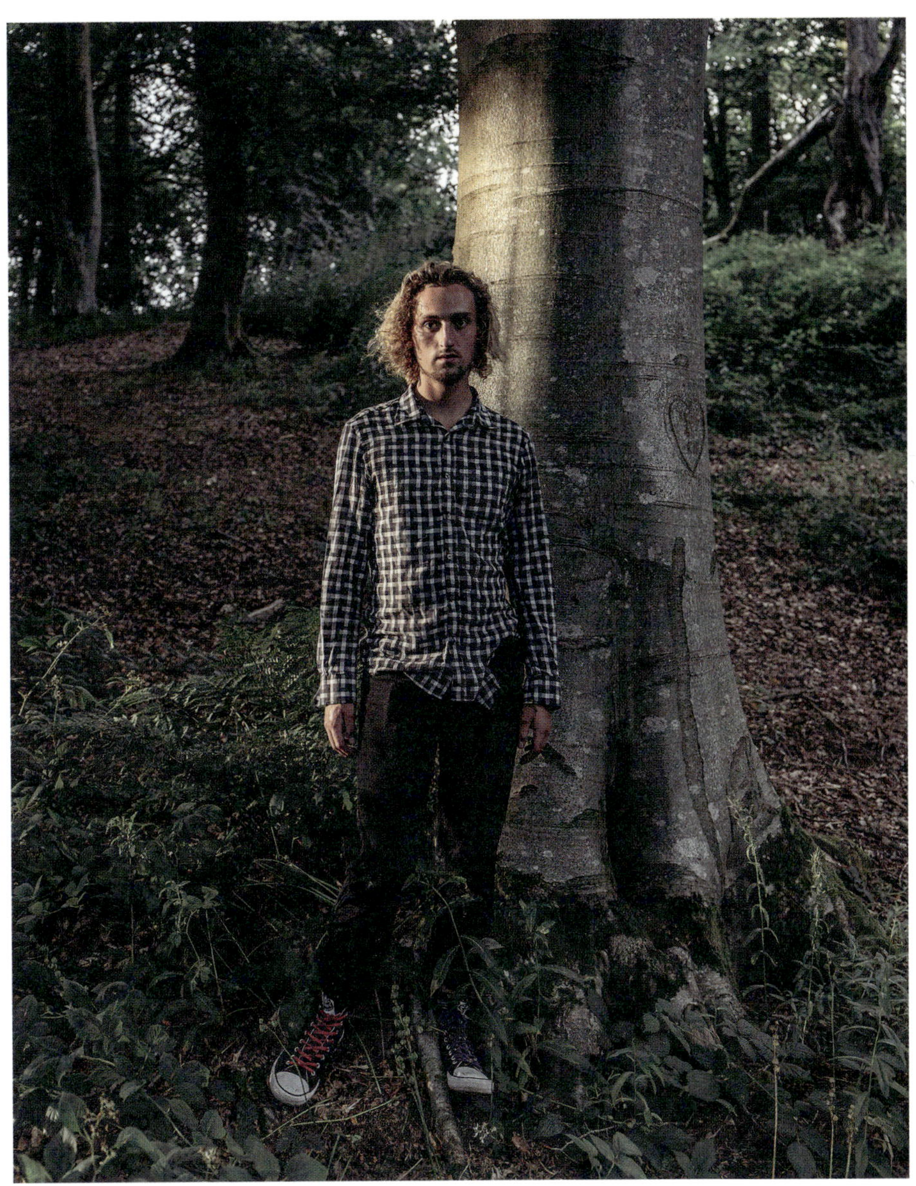

MERRYN
by Liam Arthur
Penzance, Cornwall

'When I skate, I put my headphones in and leave all
my problems at the door. Now that I've started I never
want to stop. It's become my answer to most things. I have
experienced some hatred because I am a girl skating but
you're going to get that whatever you do. I won't let
that stop me from doing what I love.' – Merryn

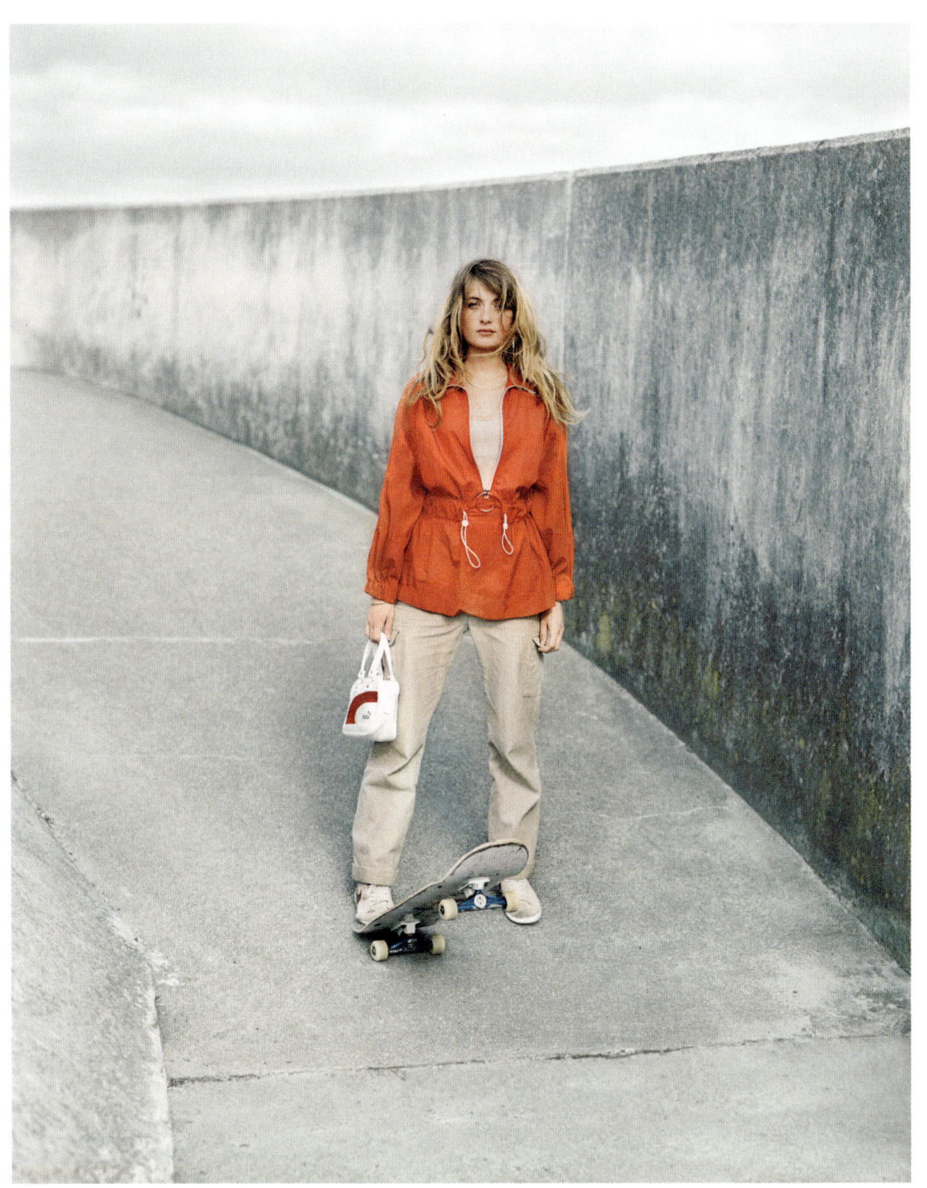

KRYSTOF WITOLD
by Thom Corbishley
London

I made this portrait of Krystof, who is studying
fashion design, last summer. He had made a suit entirely
from National Rail tickets, which he said represented
his transient and mobile upbringing.

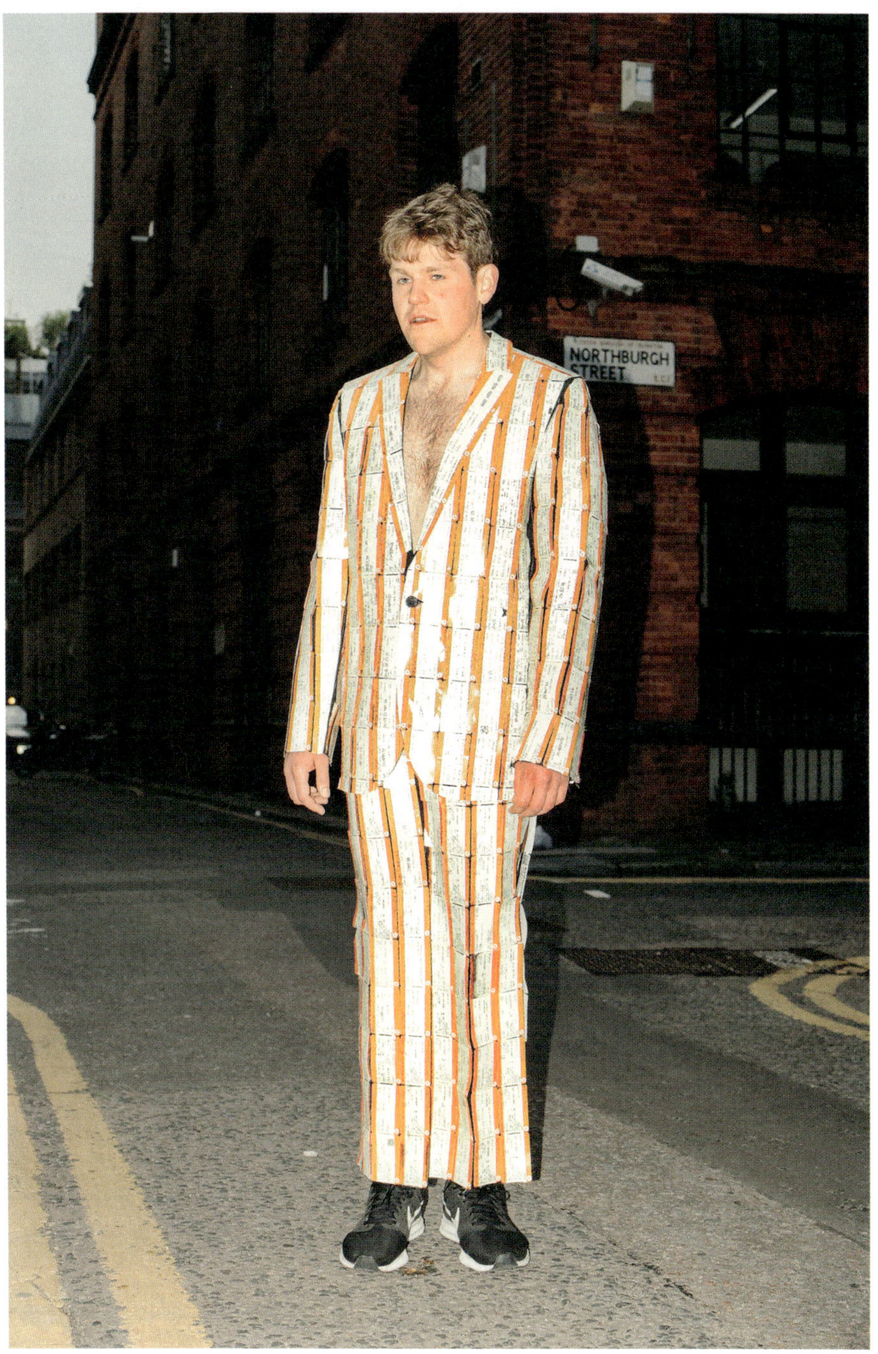

NORTHBURGH
STREET

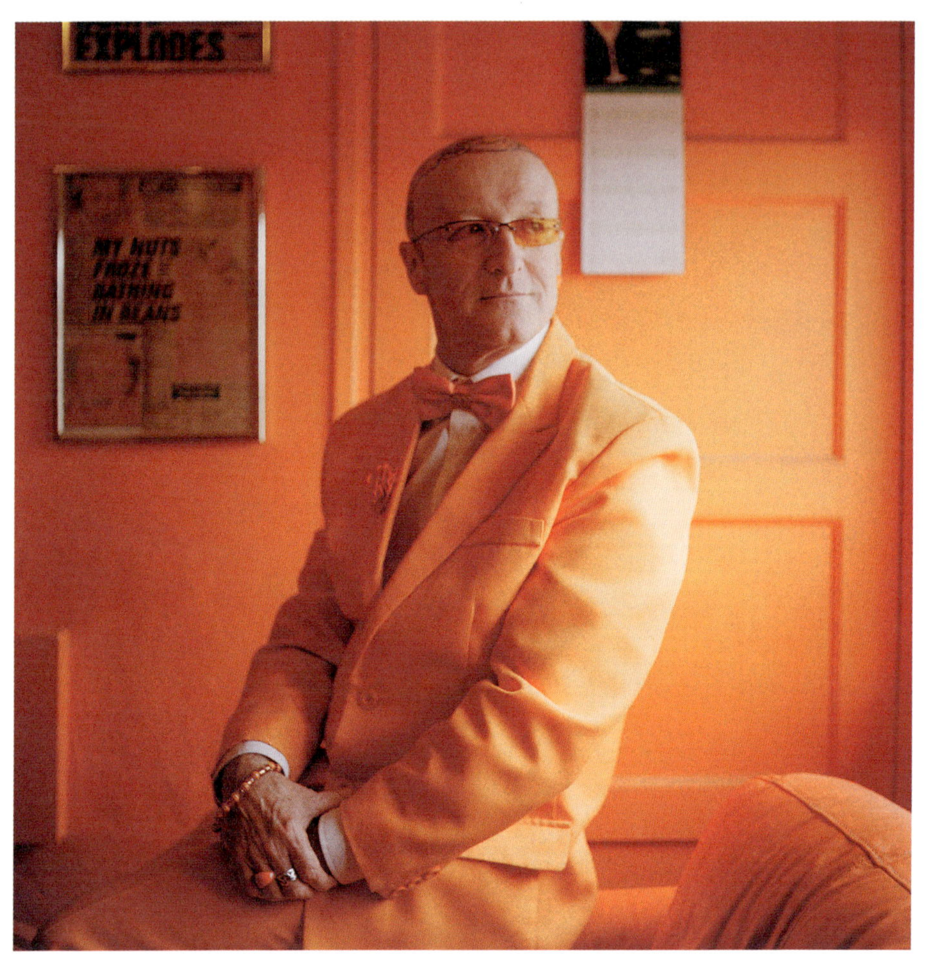

CAPTAIN BEANY
by Alecio Ferrari
Port Talbot, West Glamorgan

Captain Beany changed his name from Barry Kirk
by deed poll in May 1991. A much-loved local character,
he is a fundraising superhero who has raised thousands
of pounds for good causes.

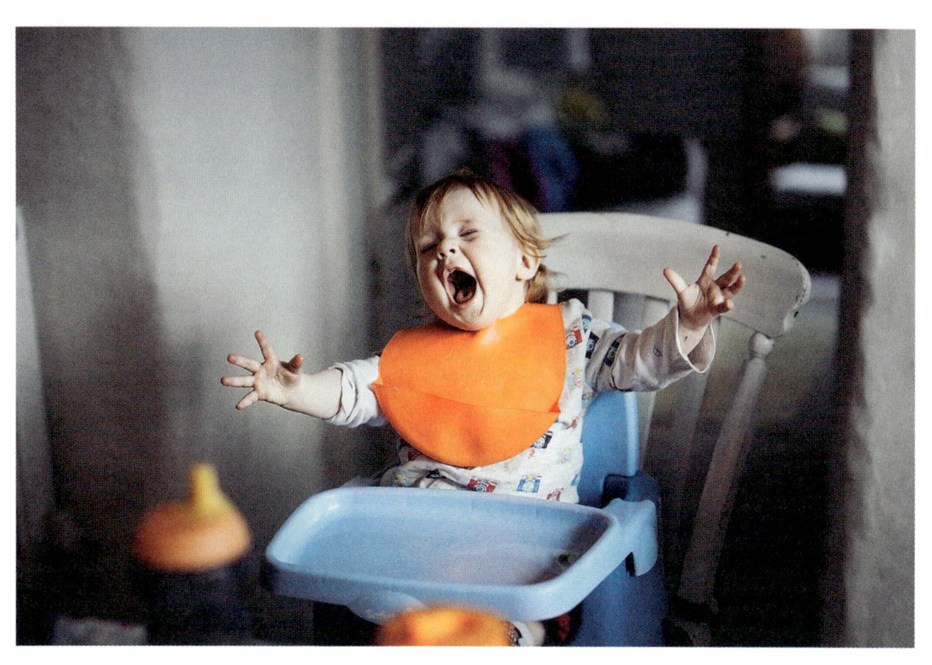

MAI WAITING FOR SUPPER
by Digby Oldridge
Longcot, Oxfordshire

This is one-year-old Mai at suppertime,
waiting for her pasta meal.

TOBI KYEREMATENG
by Louise Haywood-Schiefer
London

Tobi is the founder of Black Ticket Project,
an initiative that gives young black people free access
to the theatre in London. I took the image for *Stylist*'s
2019 Remarkable Women Awards. Tobi won the
'Inspiration of the Year' award.

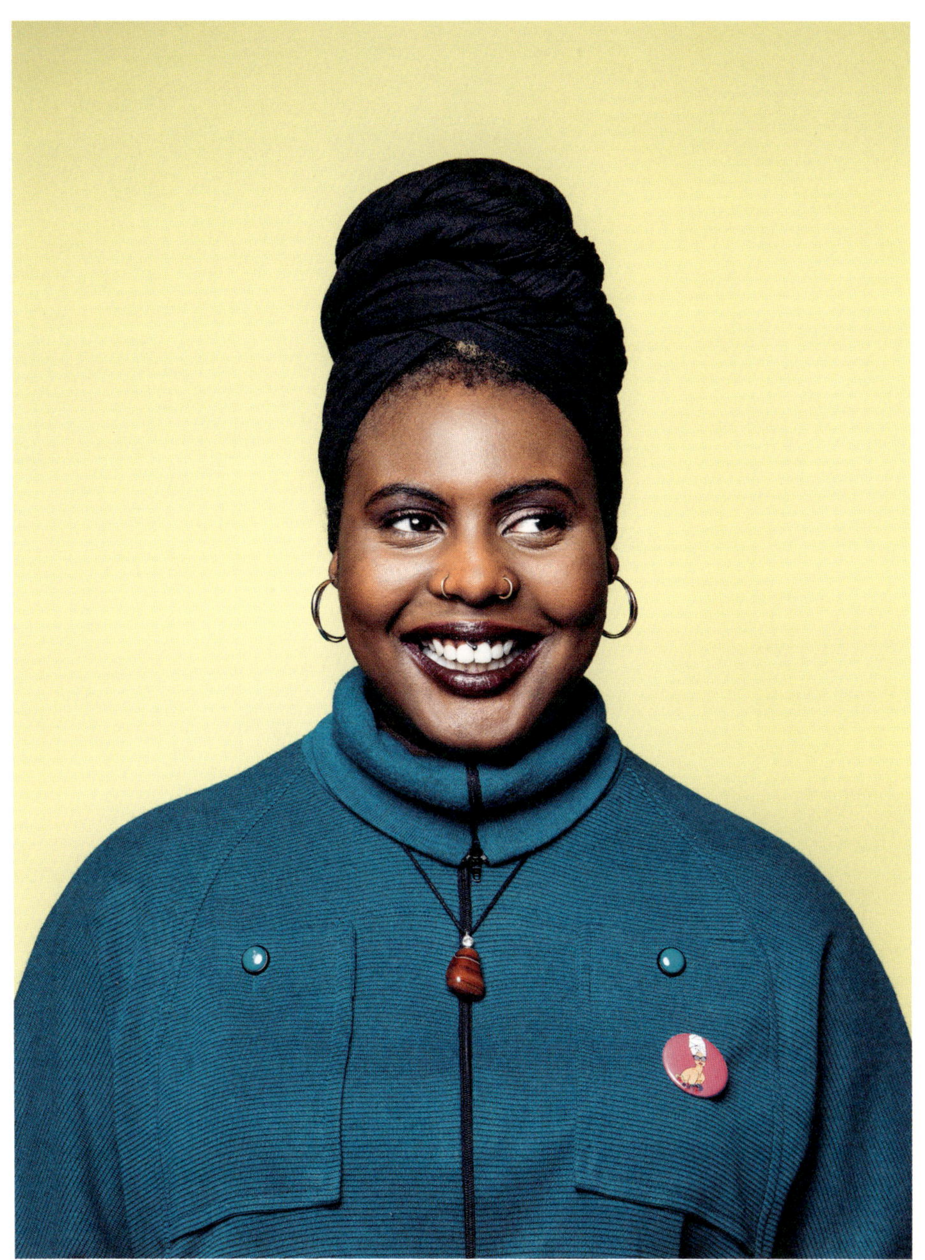

CHRIS WITH PRESENTS FOR HIS GIRLFRIEND
by Murray Ballard
Brighton, East Sussex

I spotted Chris across a supermarket car park.
He told me the flowers and cupcakes were for
his girlfriend who had had a tough week.

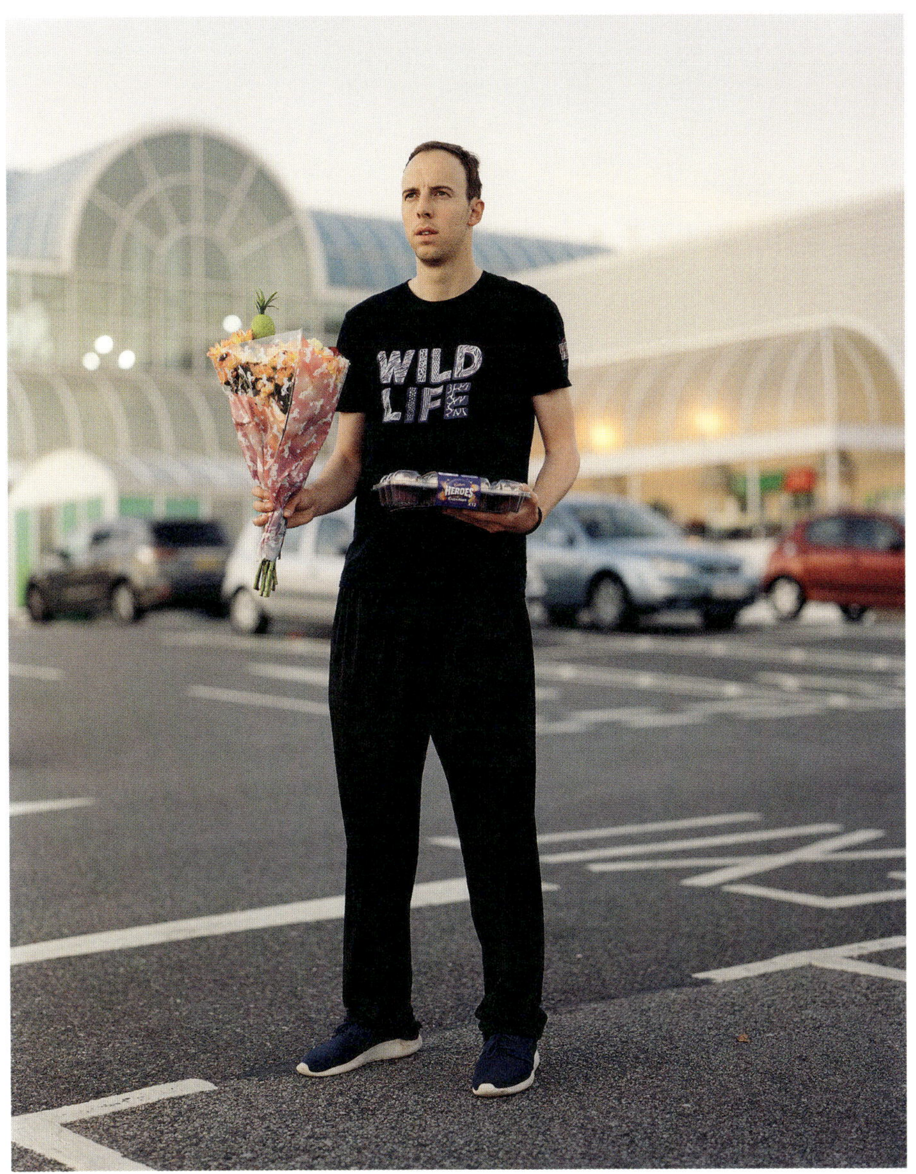

MEGAN
by Robbie Boyd
Glasgow

Megan overcame her anxiety, caused by alopecia,
by performing burlesque.

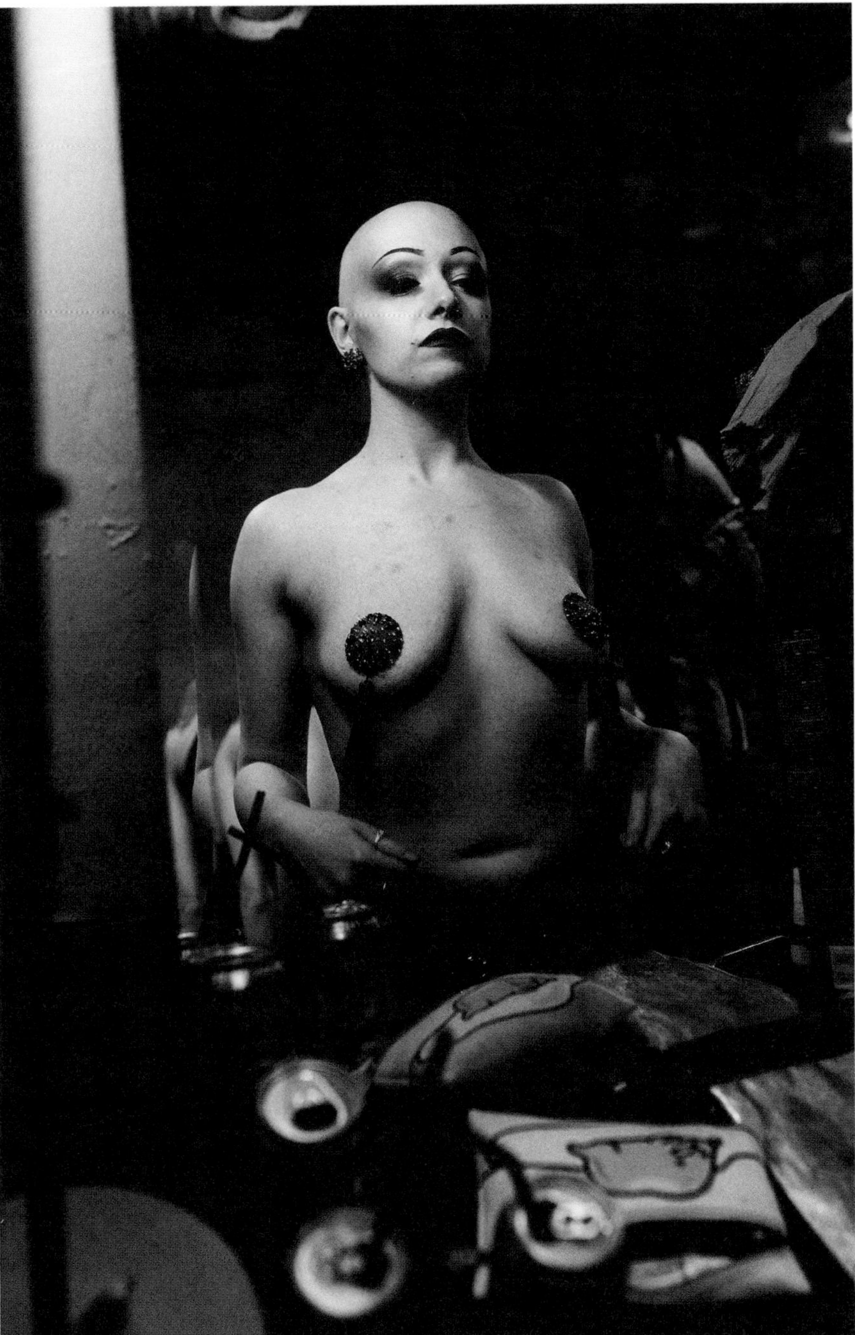

MY BROTHER PAUL
by David Pickens
Stratford-upon-Avon, West Midlands

My brother's Port Wine Stain affects his hearing
and sight on one side of his face, but it's never held
him back. He leads a full and active life.

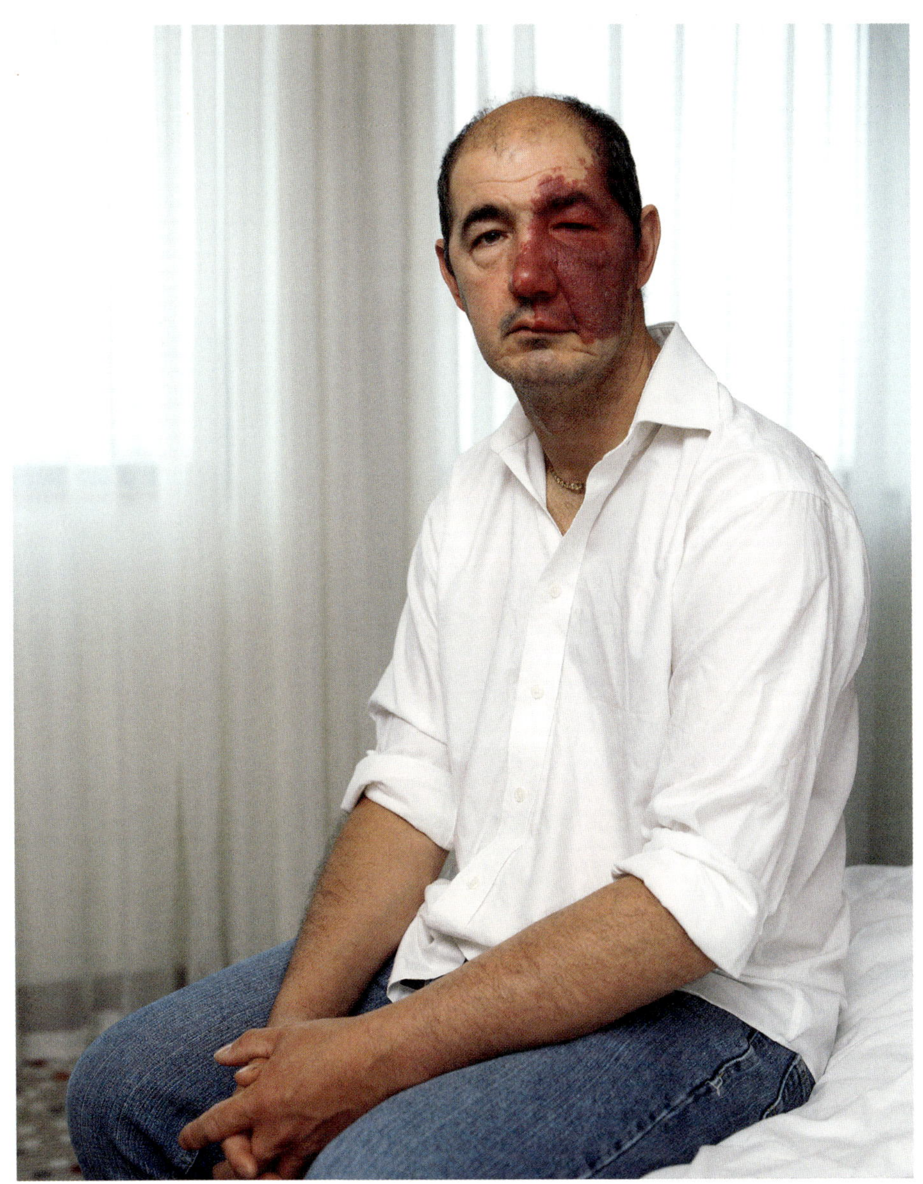

DERBHLE
by Kristina Sälgvik
London

Derbhle Crotty is an Irish actress. At the time of
the shoot she was starring in a touring production
of Richard III. Derbhle came to my studio for a couple
of hours and towards the end of the session
she suggested pinning up her hair.

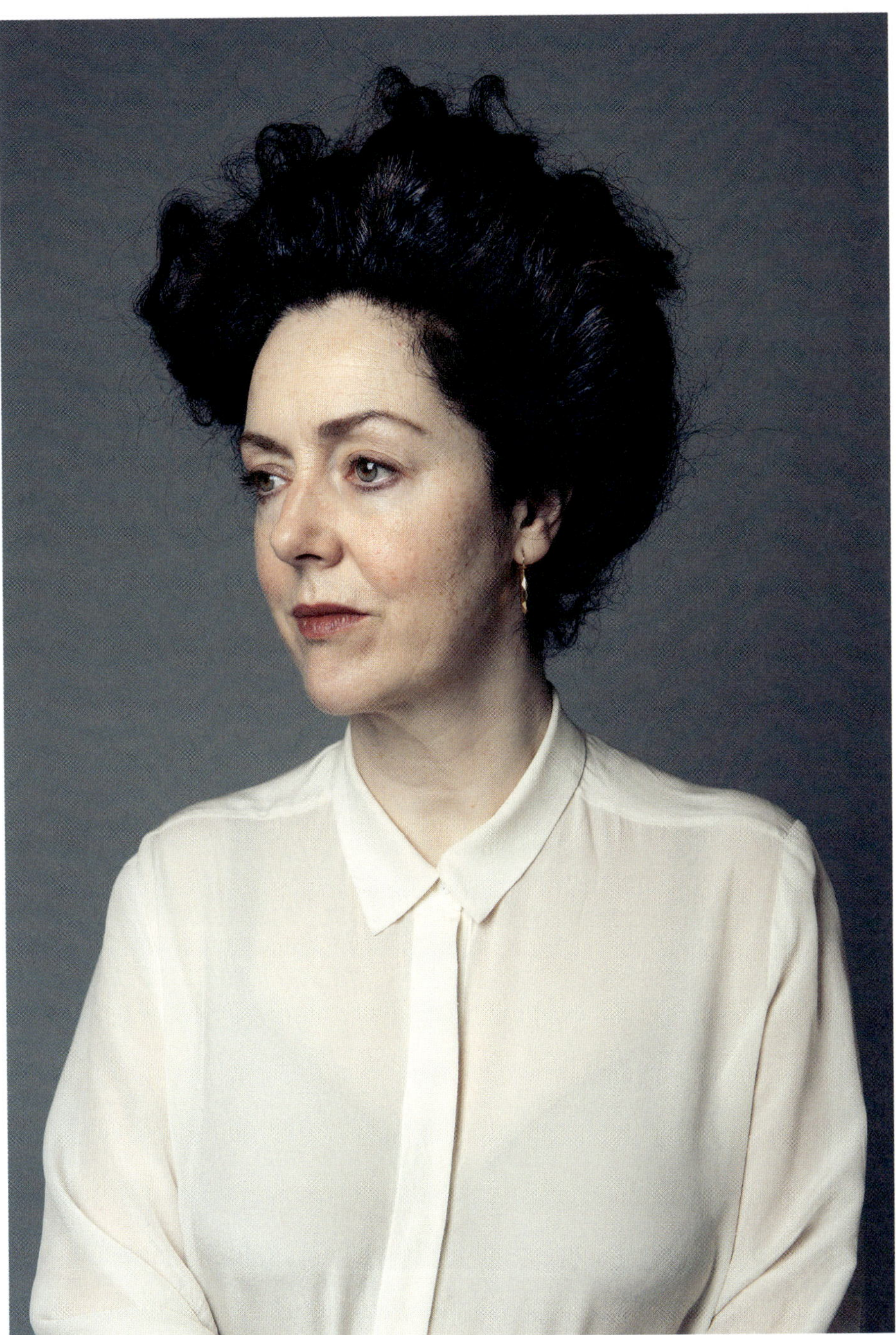

COUPLE AND BABY
by Claire Lawrie
London

I captured this young couple leaving The Whittington
Hospital with their second child. They were so calm
and open to being photographed.

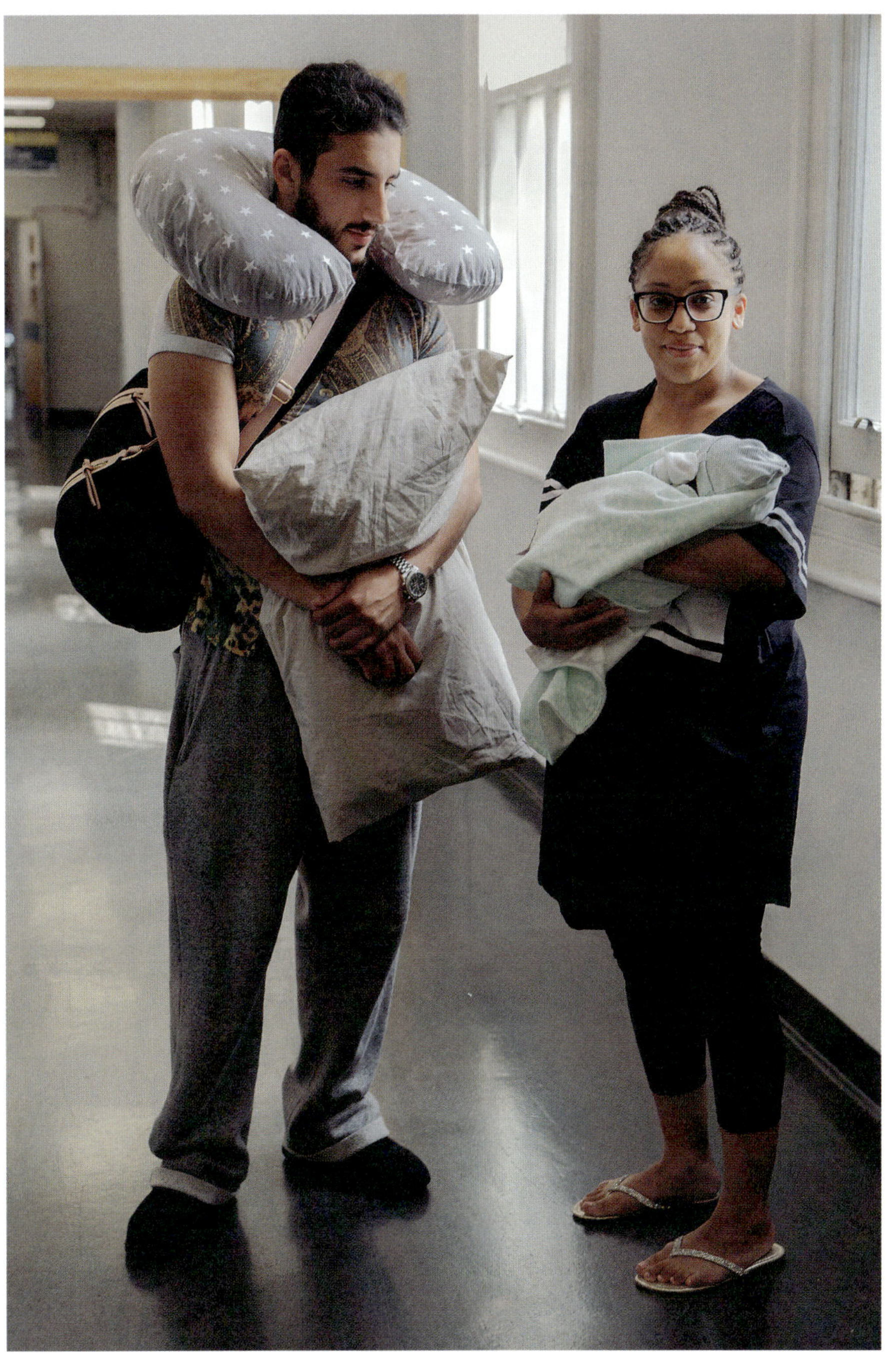

VIRAM
by Leigh Anderson
London

Viram Khunti is a paint line operator at a furniture
factory. He has been working for the company since 1979
and recently had a chair designed and named after him
in honour of his loyal service.

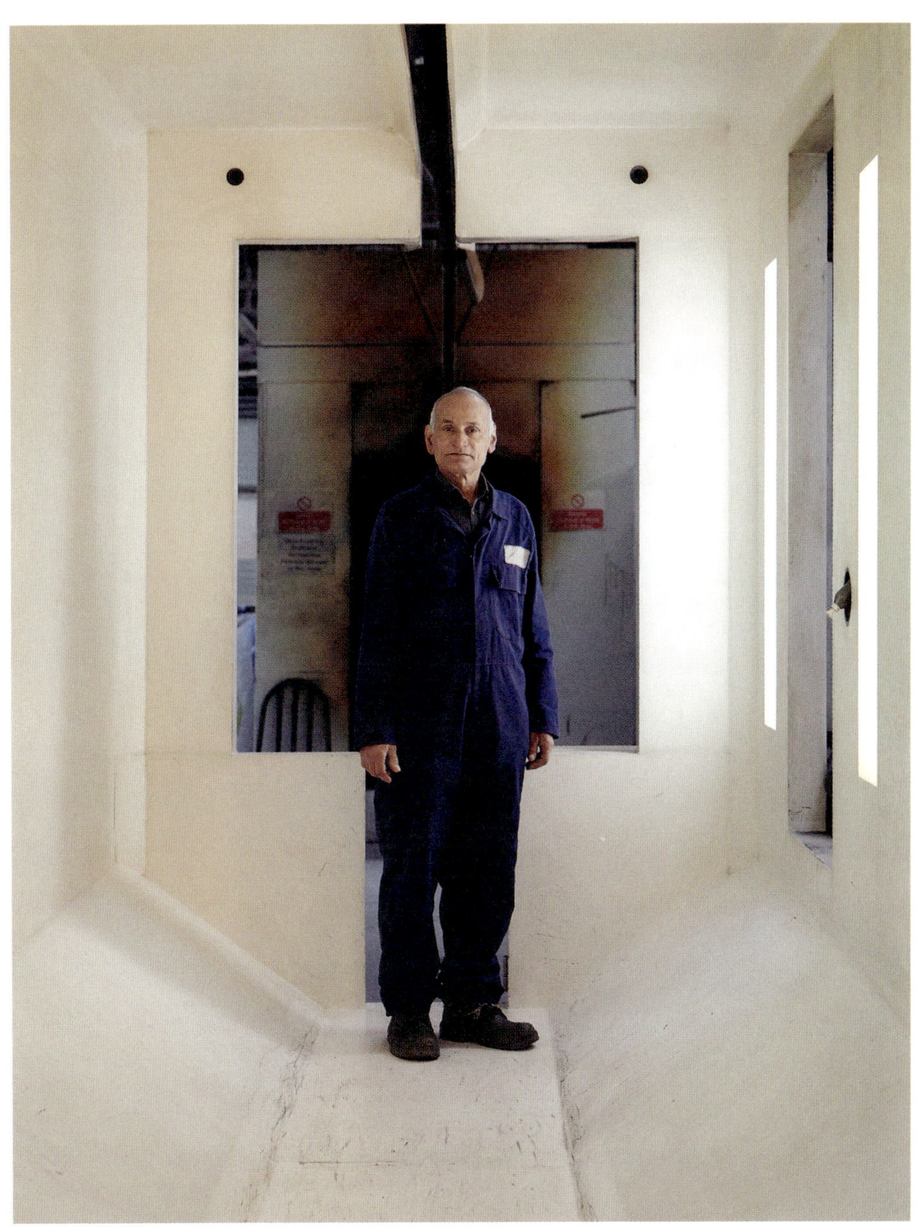

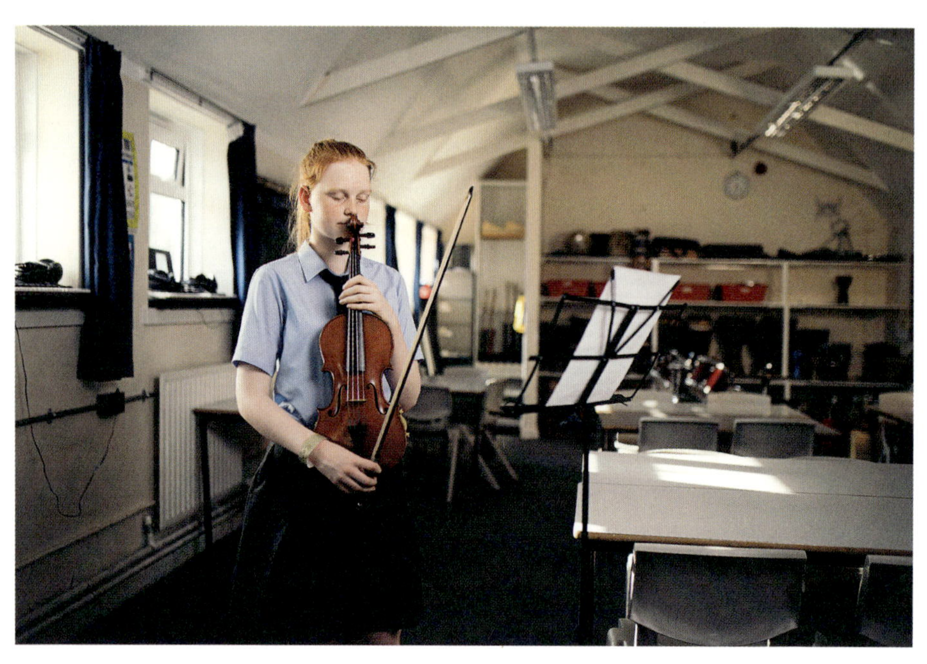

STELLA
by Kelvin Murray
London

'Music is a really big part of my life. It's important to me
because it enables me to be creative. I can play by myself
or with other people, which I really enjoy.' – Stella

146

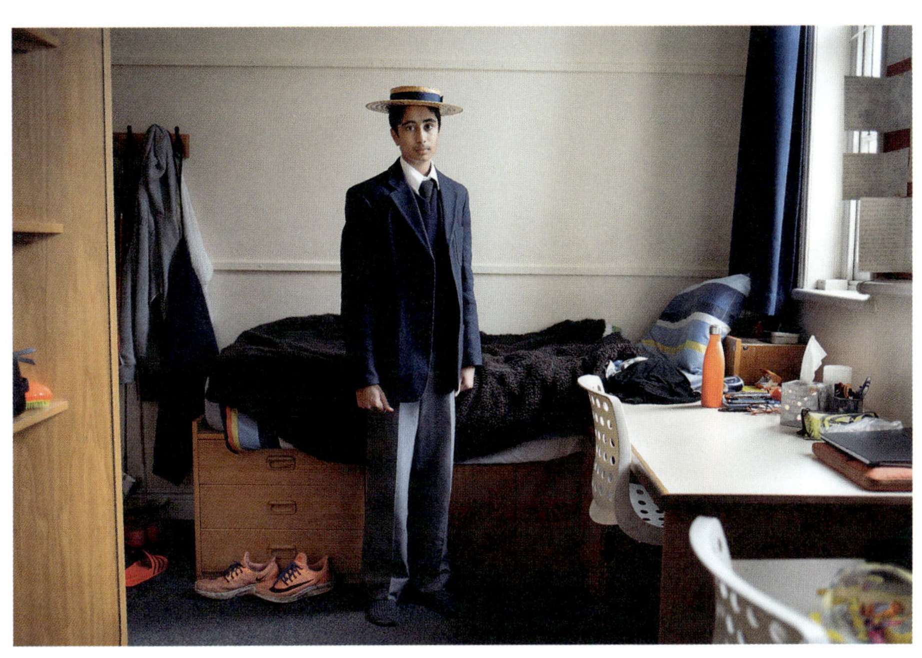

BOY, HARROW SCHOOL
by Madeleine Waller
London

When I began a photographer-in-residence post at one
of the country's elite boys' boarding schools I initially felt
intimidated by the formality of life at the school. I set out
to capture a sense of the individuals who give it meaning.

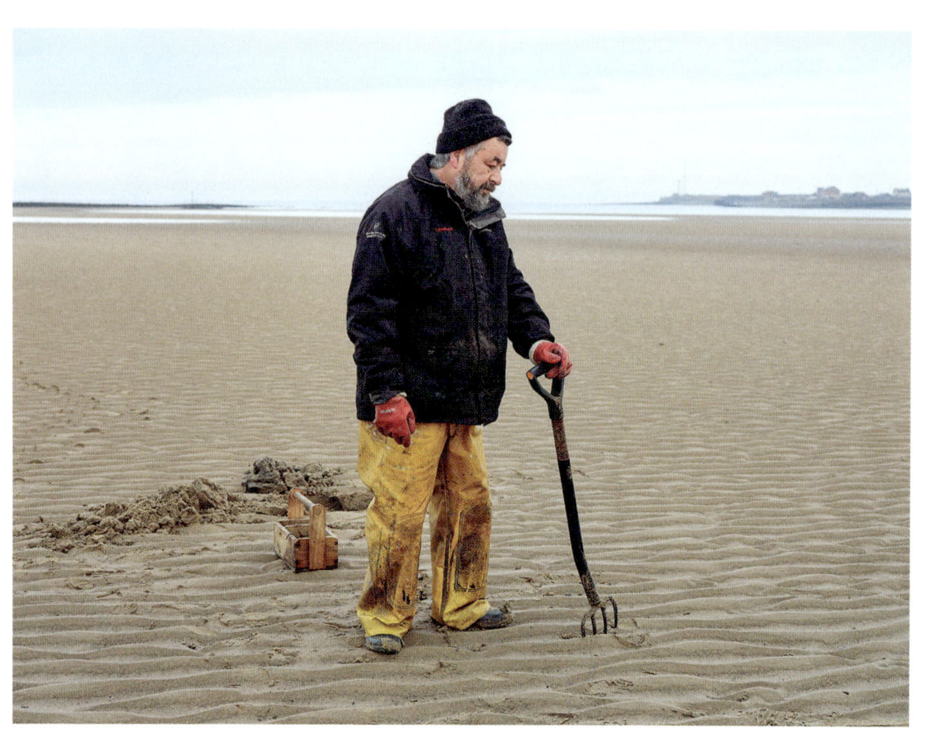

DIGGING FOR LUGWORMS
by Tessa Bunney
Bran Sands, Cleveland

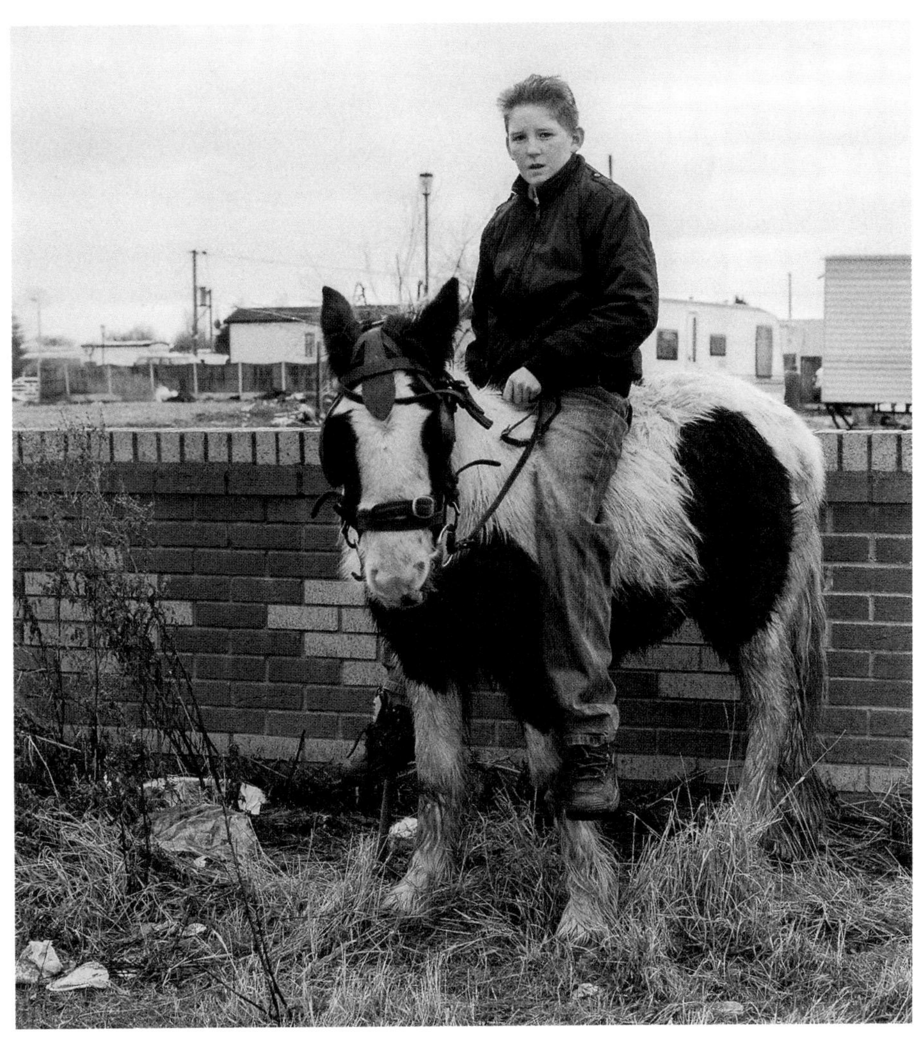

JIMMY
by Mary Humphrey
Cottenham, Cambridgeshire

Jimmy belongs to a Gypsy-Traveller community. I was
delighted to include his pony in the photograph since
horses are an integral part of Jimmy's way of life.

ZAIN
by Matt MacPake
London

I'd been photographing in the area for a few hours
when I saw Zain. He looked amazing and I asked
if I could take his picture. Behind him is the iconic
Alexandra and Ainsworth Estate in north London,
which has been used as a film set on several occasions.

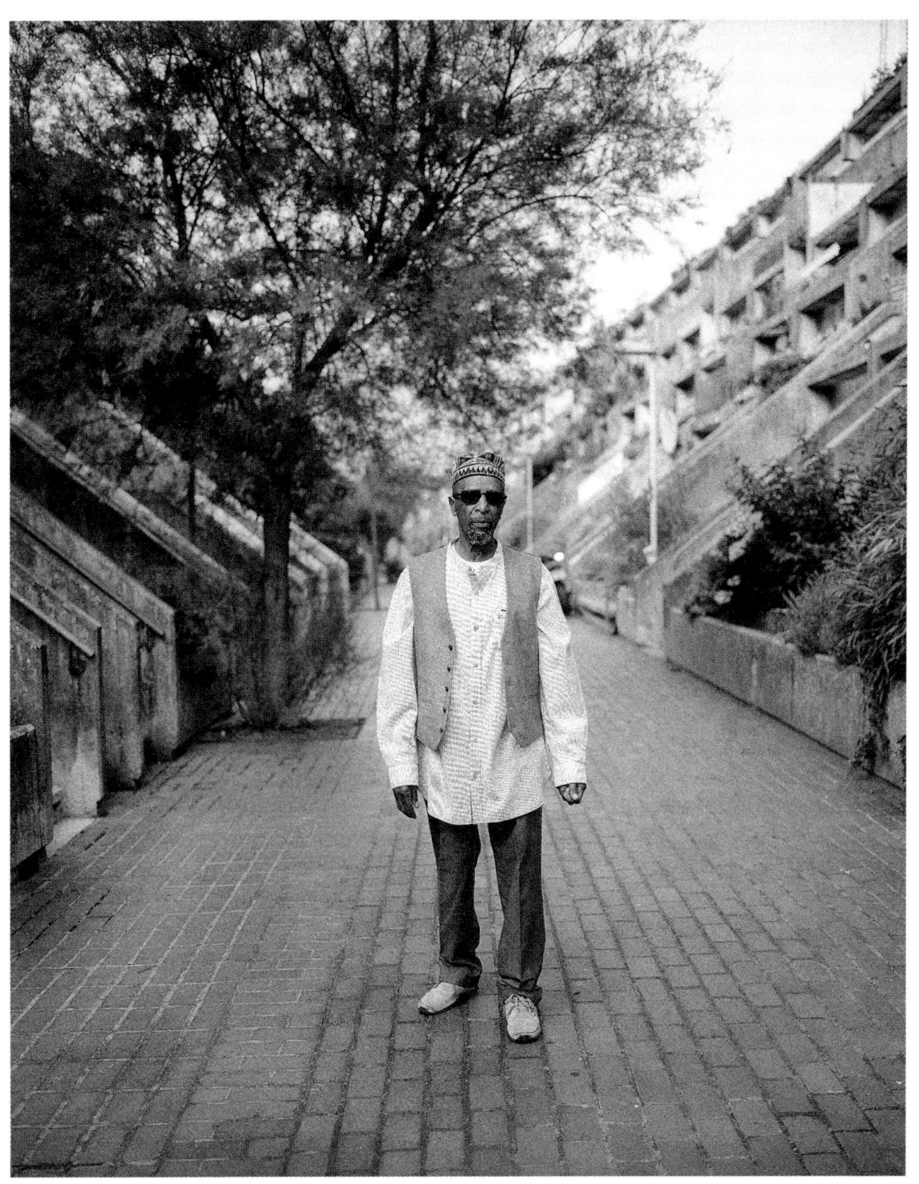

BRENDAN
by Garrod Kirkwood
Aberdeen

Brendan swims in the sea all year round. He and other
hardcore sea swimmers brave all kinds of conditions on
a daily basis in a bid to get close to nature.

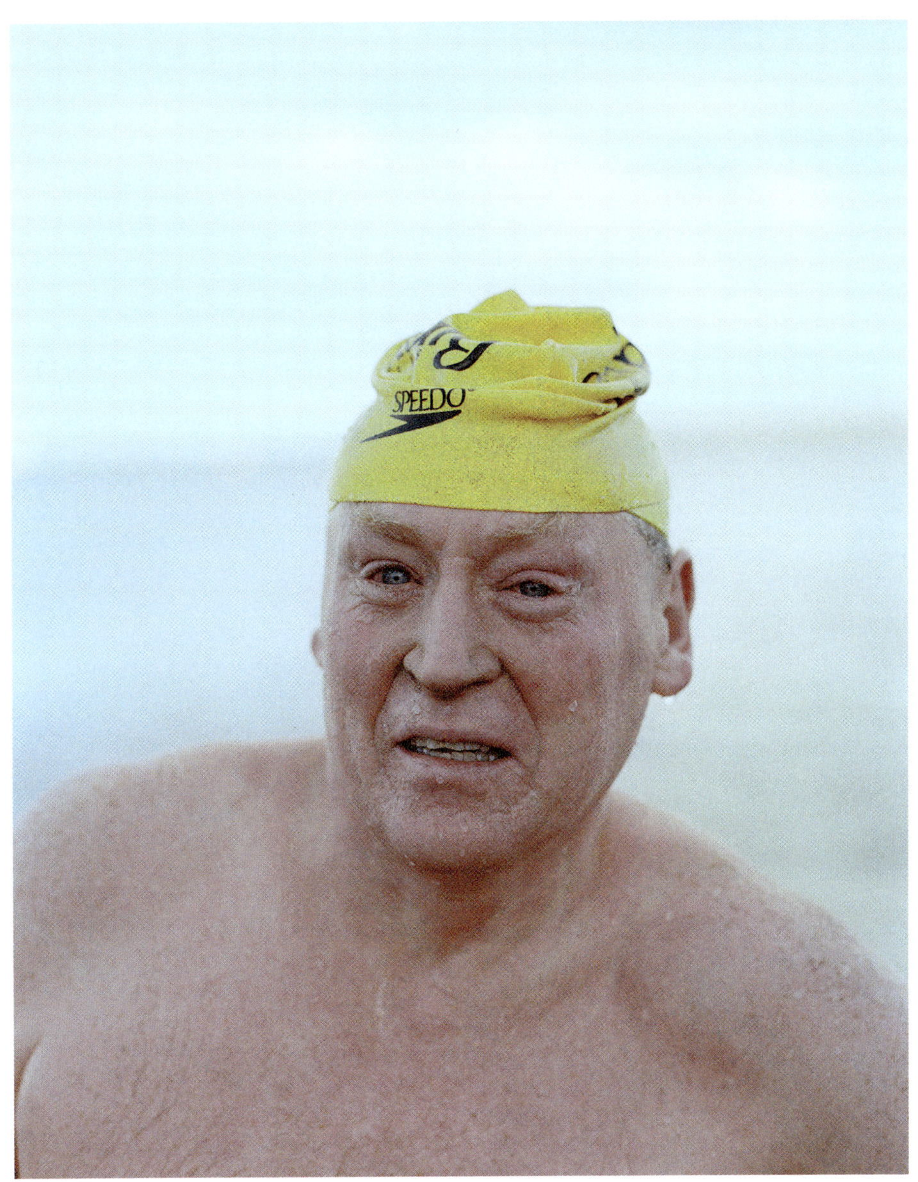
SPEEDO

JENDER ON THE DLR
by Jender Anomie
London

My ex-girlfriend and I used to make portraits together
to document our life. I remember feeling particularly
rough this day because I hadn't been able to style
my hair or put on a face. Even so, it's still me,
just without any of the usual trimmings.

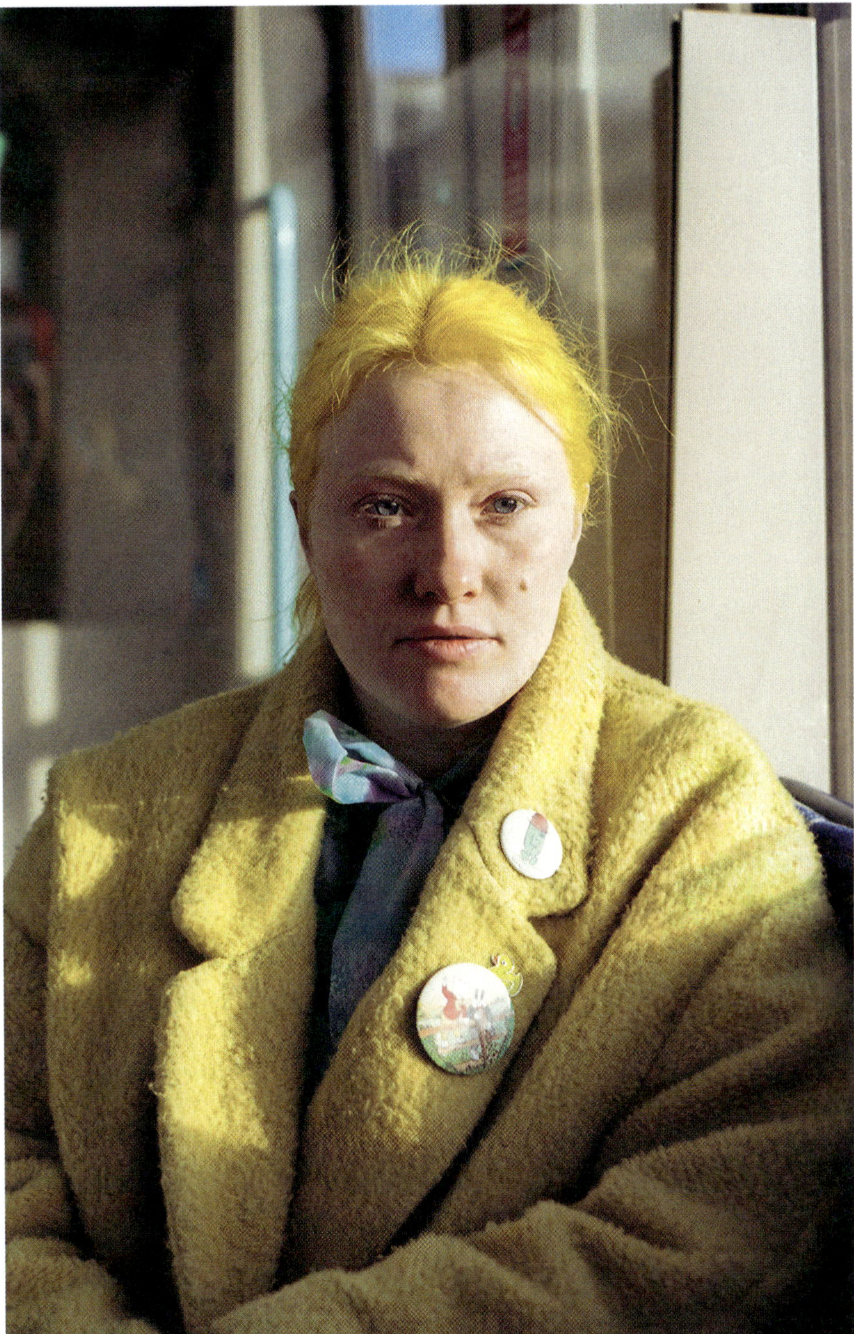

ANNE
by Richard McCullagh
Chorley, Lancashire

This is my grandma, Anne, who came to the UK
from Ireland in the 1950s. I've shot a series of images
in my home town and it made sense to photograph my
grandmother who has witnessed its gradual decline.

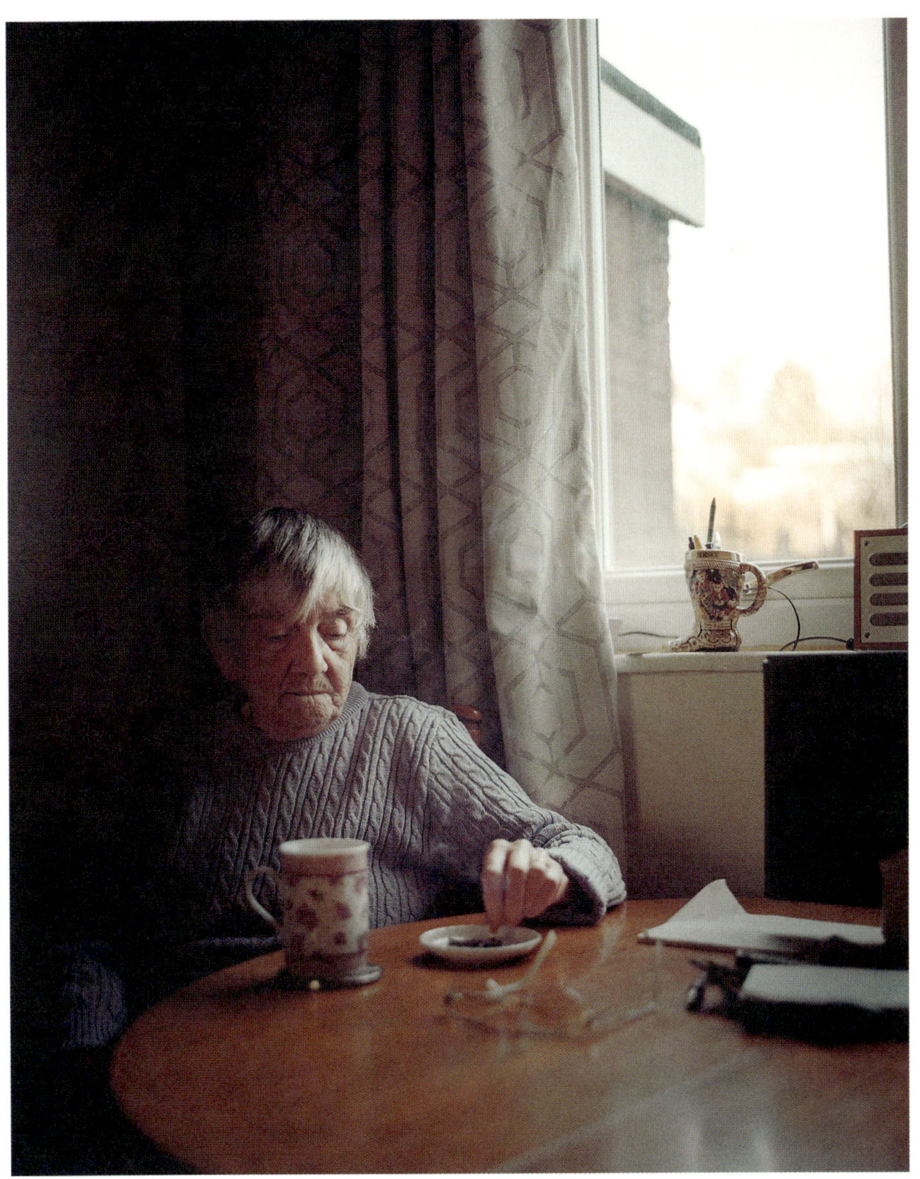

TWO WOMEN AND A DOG
by Dav Stewart
London

Two of the many characters who are part of the diverse
community of Roman Road in east London.

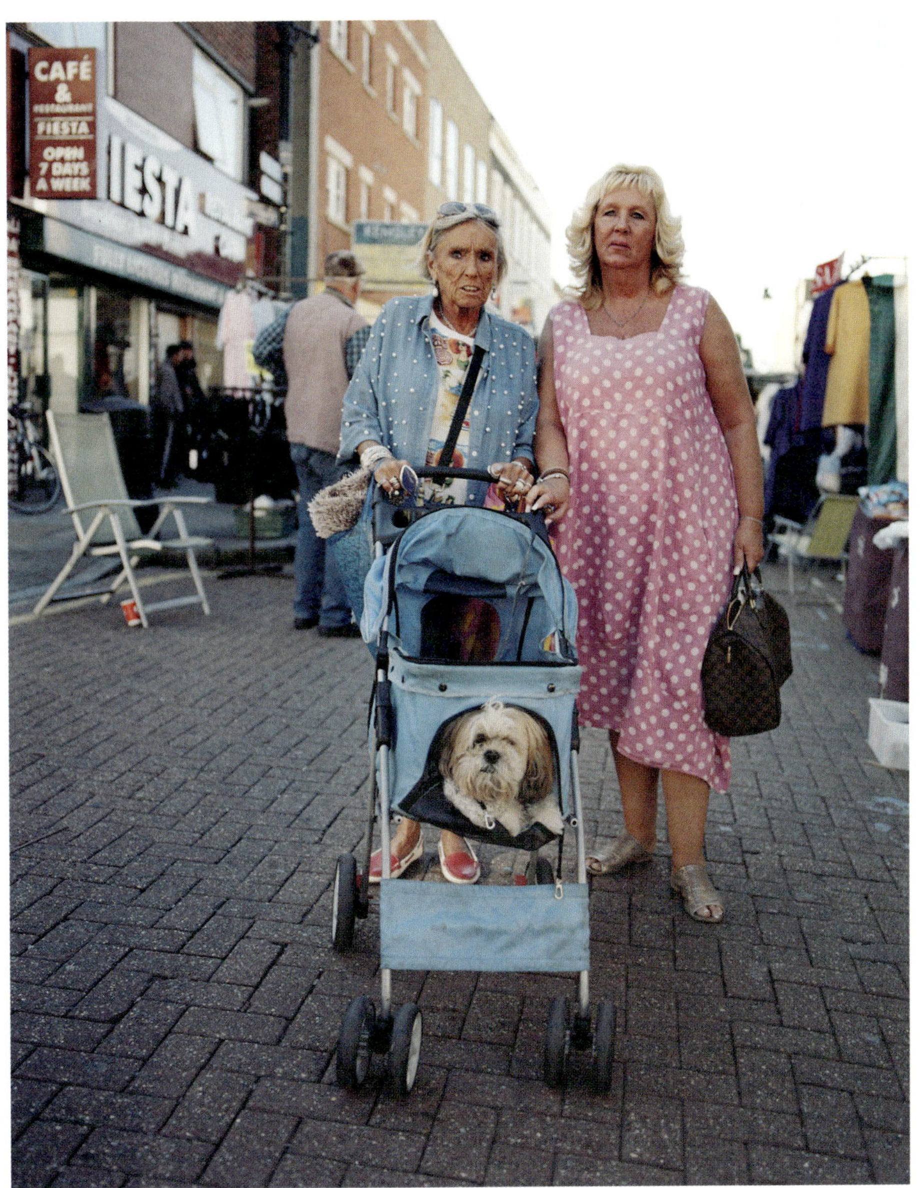

CAFÉ
&
RESTAURANT
FIESTA
OPEN
7 DAYS
A WEEK
FIESTA

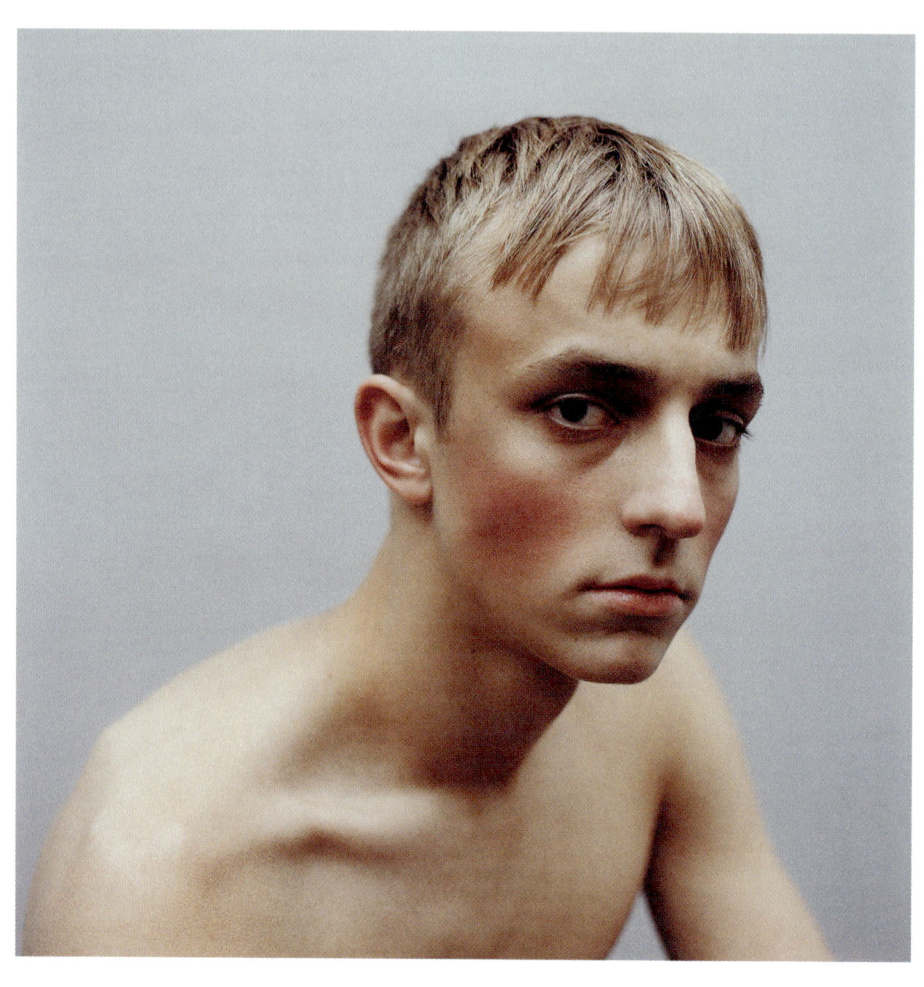

JACK
by Holly Whittaker
London

It was the first time Jack had sat for a photographer.
To me, he seemed older and wiser than his 17 years.
He was calm and at ease with himself.

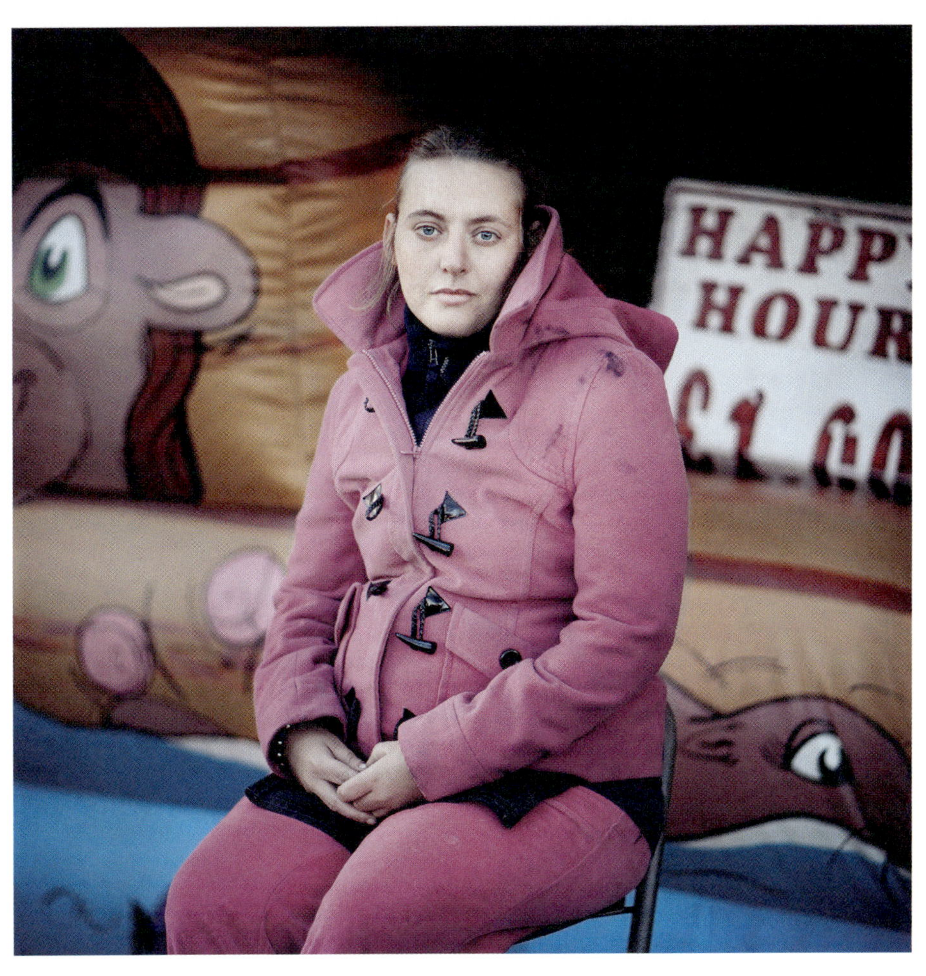

STACEY
by Fraser Wright
Doncaster, South Yorkshire

I spotted Stacey at a fair attraction she was managing
at Doncaster Racecourse. Her pink outfit caught
my attention.

MARIA SIGMA
by Alun Callender
London

Textile designer and weaver Maria says her work is
inspired by the colour palette of the British landscape.
Using British wool and drawing on her Greek heritage,
she creates minimal, contemporary pieces.

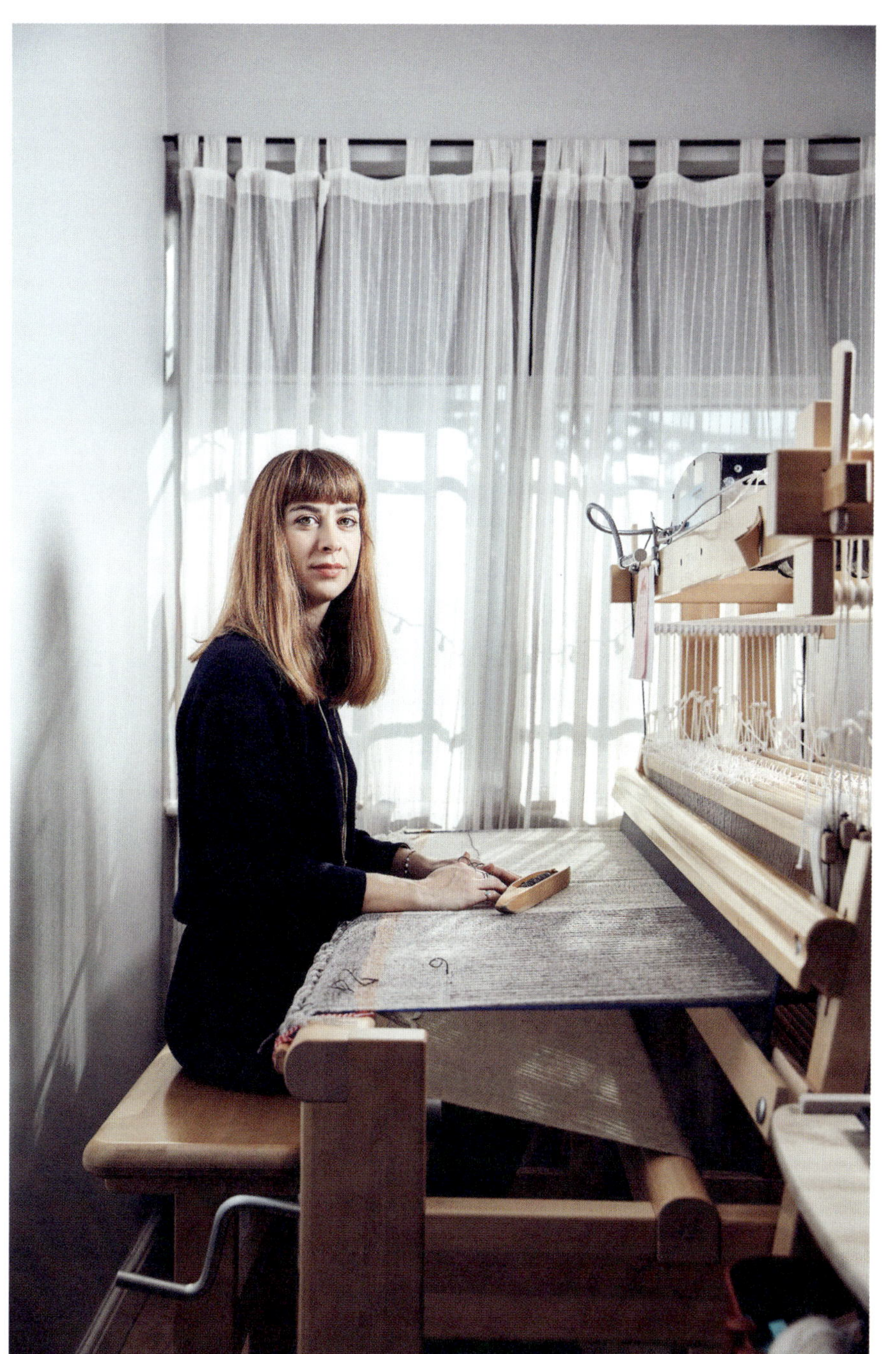

LIVESTOCK AUCTION
by Jonathan Browning
Taunton, Somerset

A young worker pauses while administering a drug
to lambs at a livestock auction.

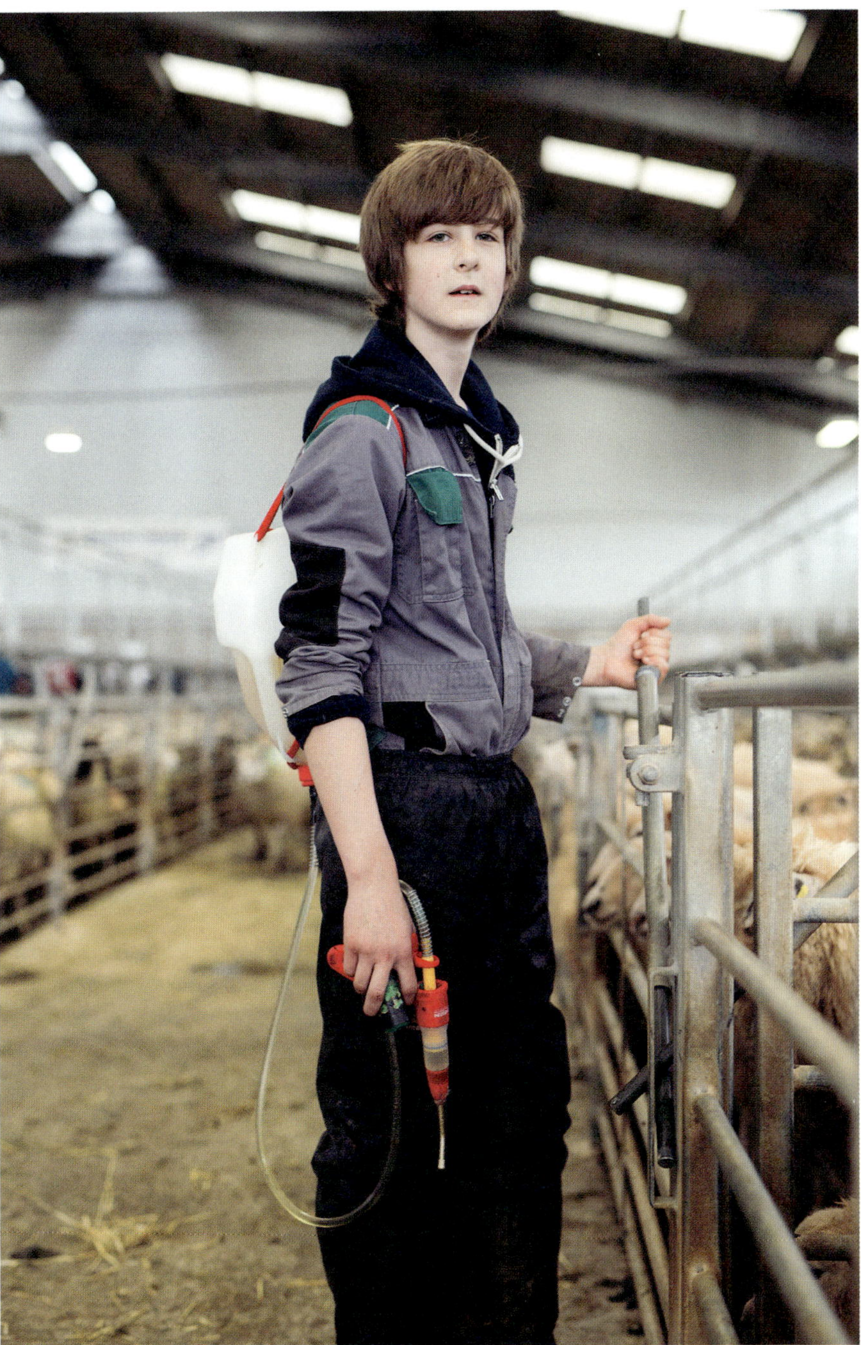

LOYLE CARNER
by Phil Sharp
London

Benjamin Gerard Coyle-Larner, better known by
his stage name Loyle Carner, is an English hip hop artist
and actor. When we met for a magazine shoot,
he seemed to not take himself too seriously.

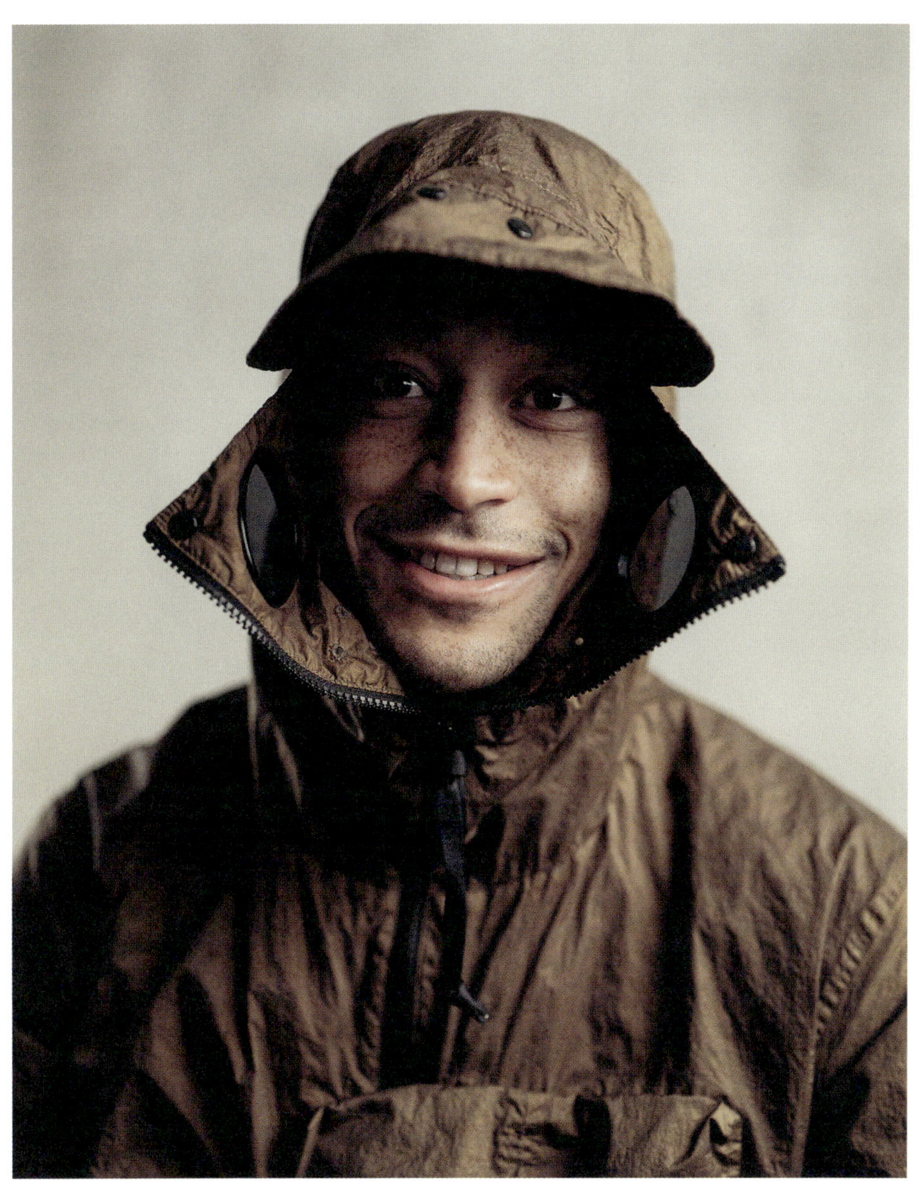

THE REENACTOR
by Olivia Symonds
Whittington, Shropshire

This young man belongs to an American Civil War
reenactment society based in the UK. I find the concept
of a British group reenacting a historical event that took
place thousands of miles away fascinating. The care and
commitment that goes into the reenactment is impressive.

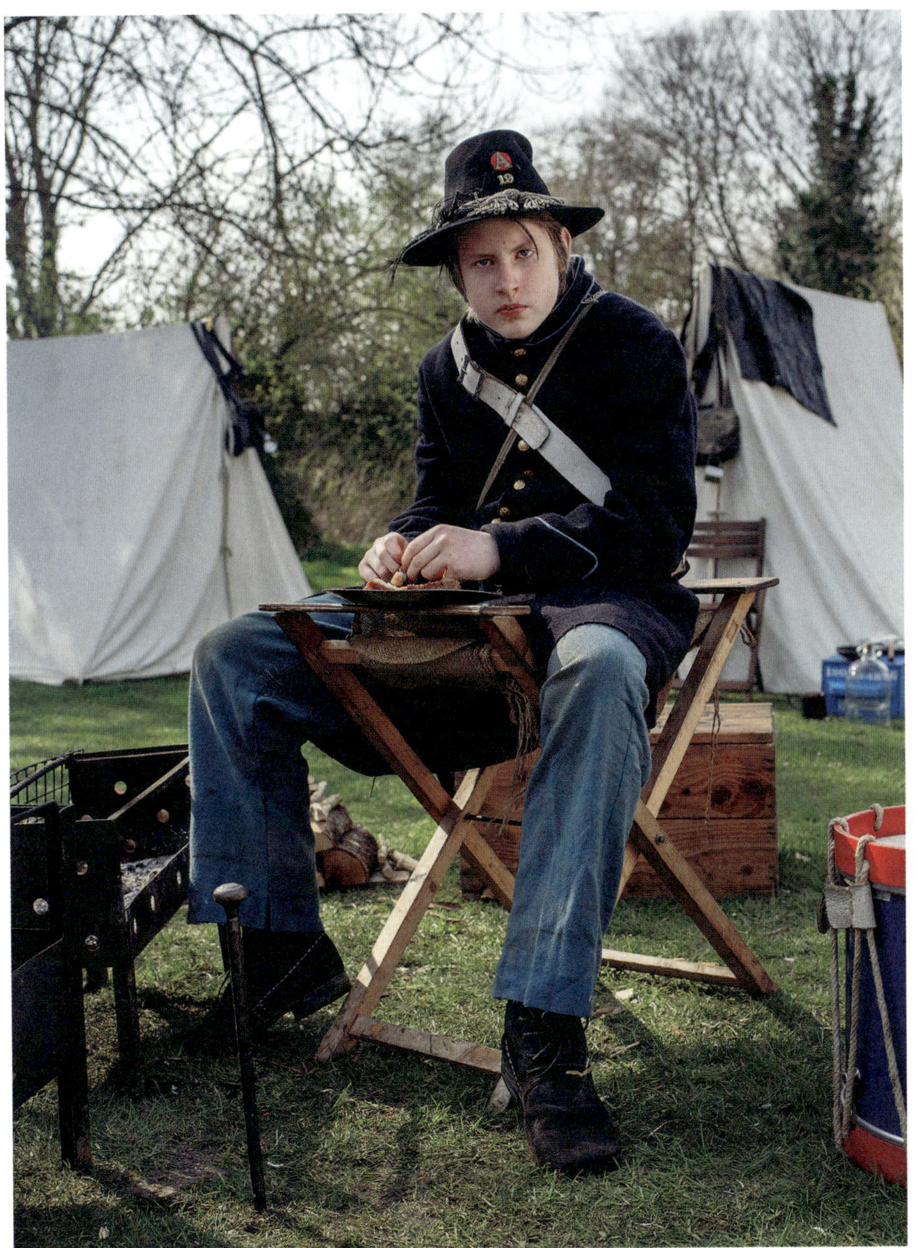

ONE-WOMAN PROTEST
by Oliver Woods
London

This lady was protesting alone outside the BBC in central
London over several days in October 2018. She was happy
for me to take her picture but didn't want to give her
name. 'I have to be anonymous because the cat lobby is
very powerful,' she said. There was something very British
about her protest that encompassed a love of wildlife, free
speech, politeness and a desire to back the underdog.

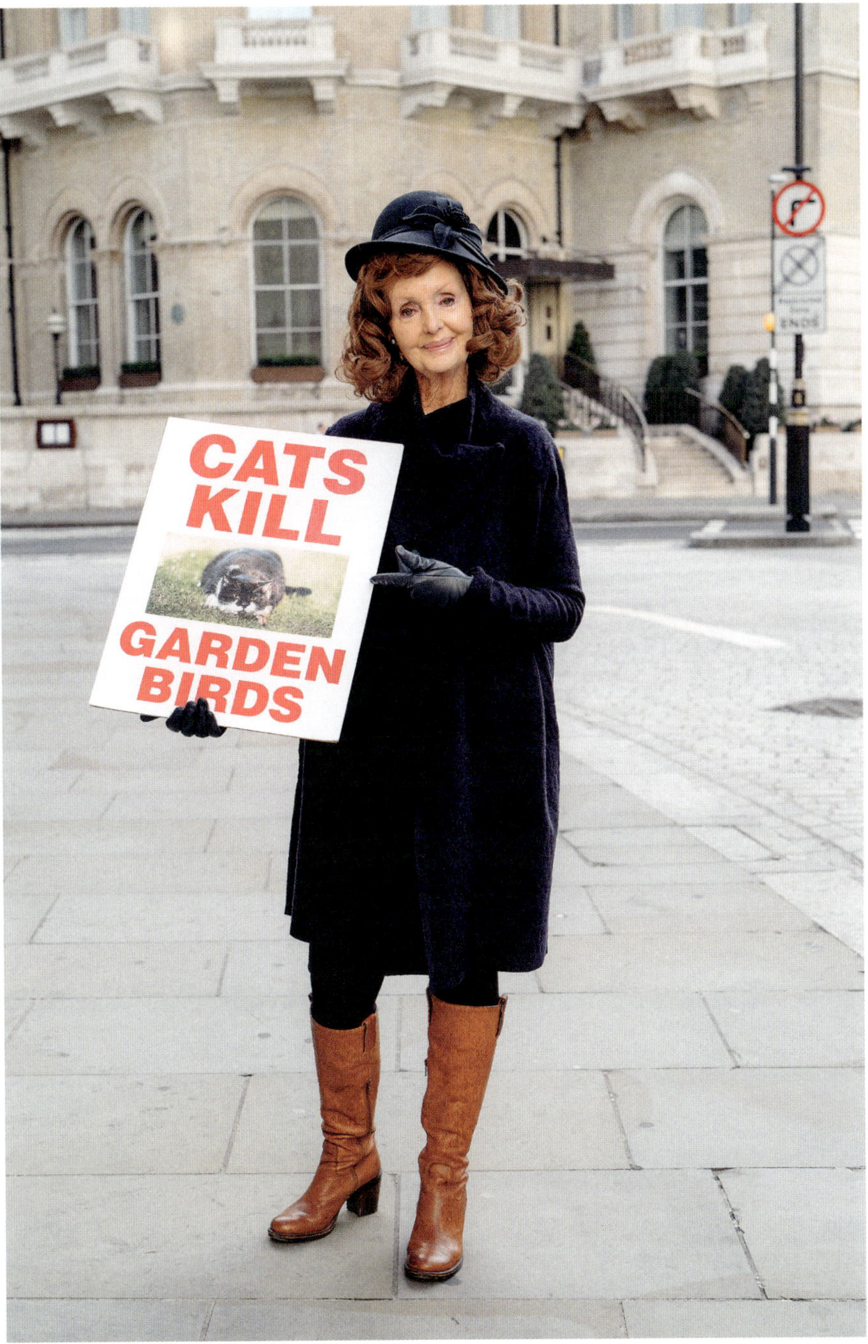
CATS
KILL
GARDEN
BIRDS

EMMA, POULTRY FARMER
by Nick Goring
Pilmoor, North Yorkshire

'I love the outdoors and farm life; I've been very lucky
to grow up with this. My family has always been involved
in farming and worked on different farms – arable, dairy,
poultry and game. For a few years I lived on a pig farm.
It's not a job, it's a lifestyle to me.' – Emma

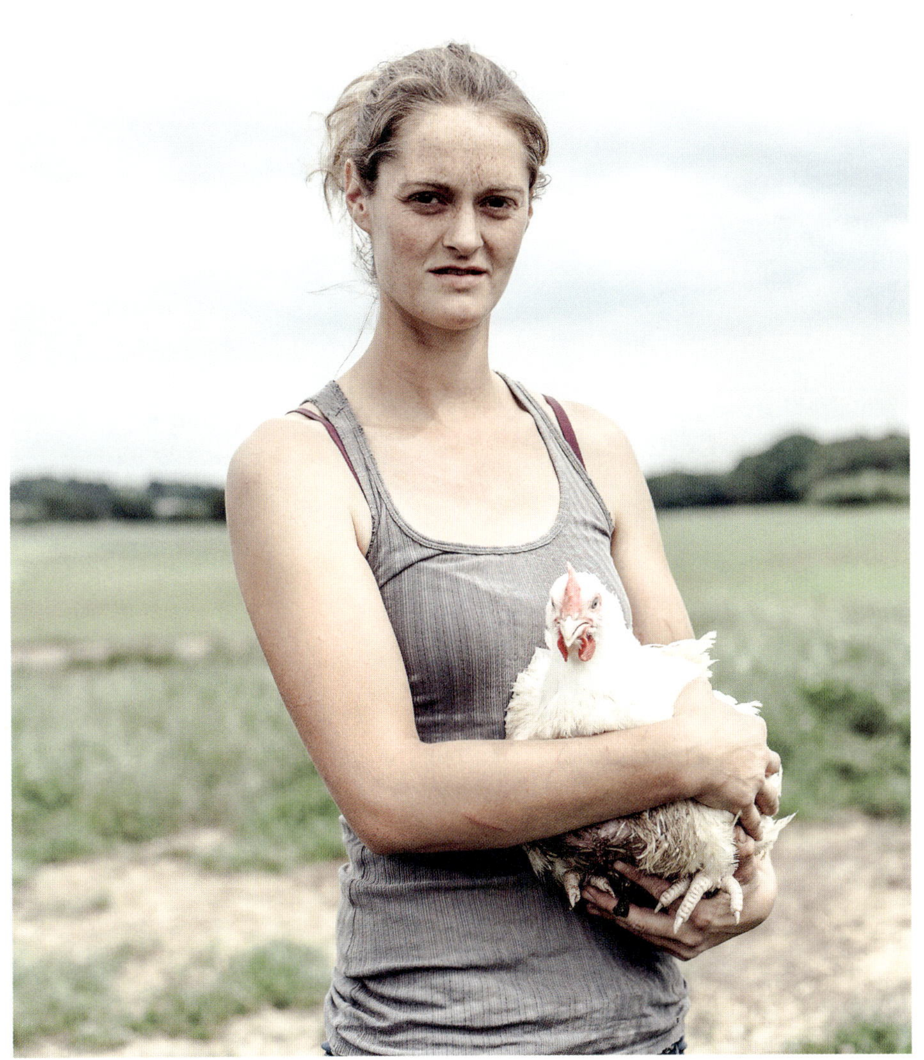

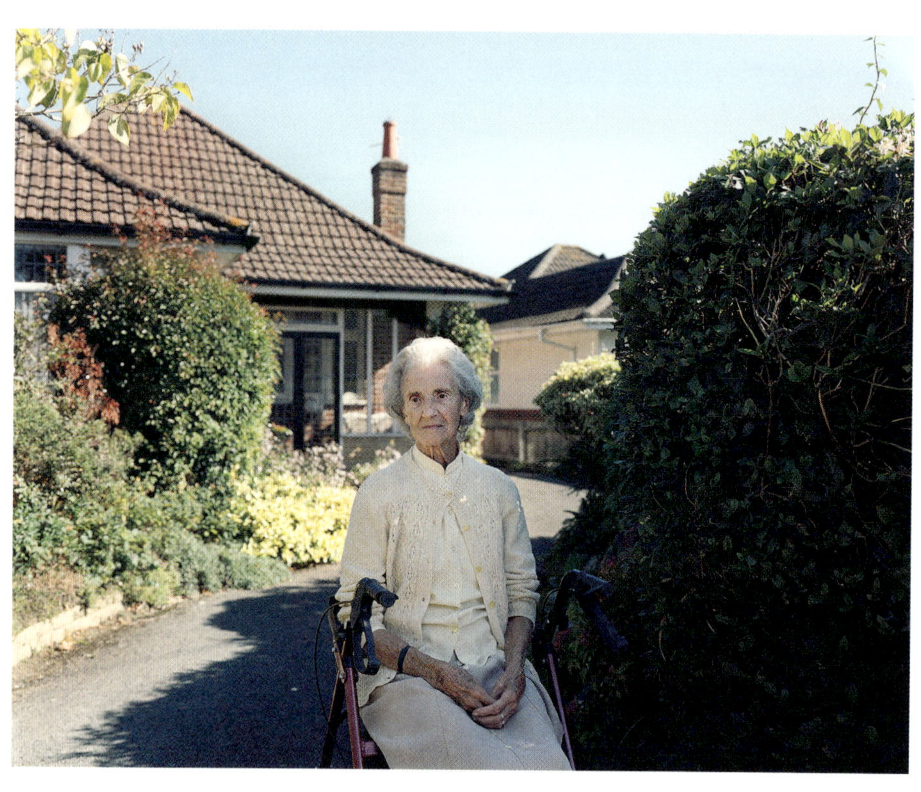

HILDA
by Garry Simpson
Christchurch, Dorset

I noticed Hilda sitting outside her house, immaculately
dressed. She told me she was moving soon to live with
her family after living in this house for many years.

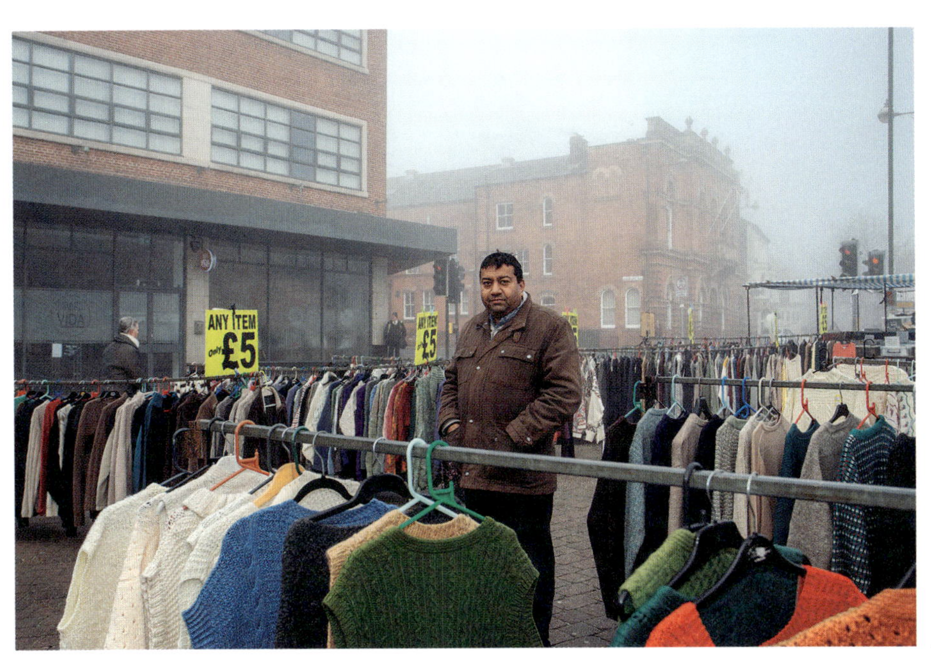

MARKET SELLER
by Jessica Pearson
Ilkeston, Derbyshire

Mr Horsley has been selling clothes at Ilkeston Market for
20 years. He sources most of what he sells from countries
in the EU. I wanted to explore how the uncertainty
of Brexit is affecting Britain's small market towns.

THE CLAIRVOYANT
by Chris Taylor
Brighton, East Sussex

When I happened upon Eva Petulengro, who is
a clairvoyant and astrologer, I knew nothing of her fame
or history. She has had many famous clients. The way
she was sitting in a relaxed and almost regal way
caught my attention.

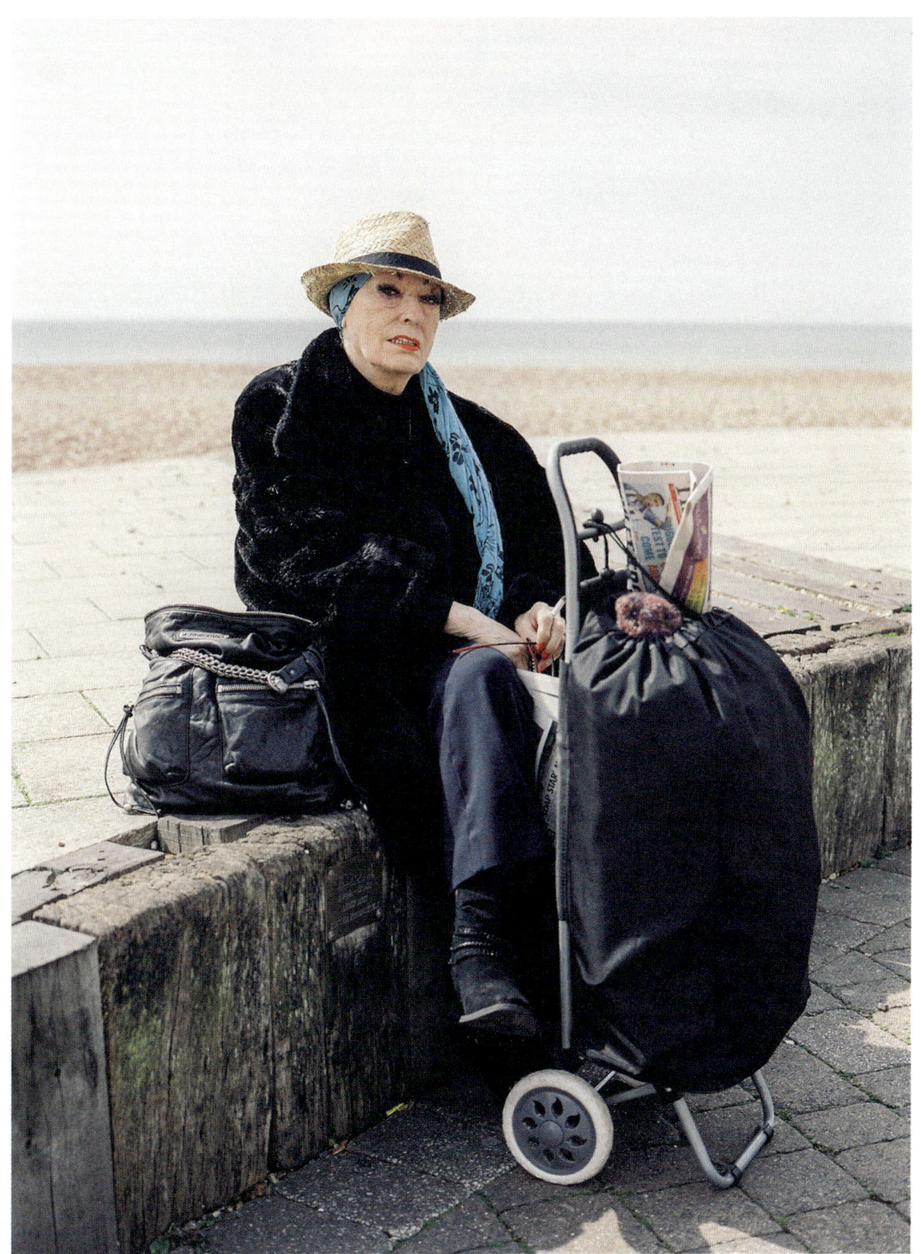

MICHAEL HOROVITZ OBE:
POET, EDITOR AND ARTIST
by Katharina Dubno
London

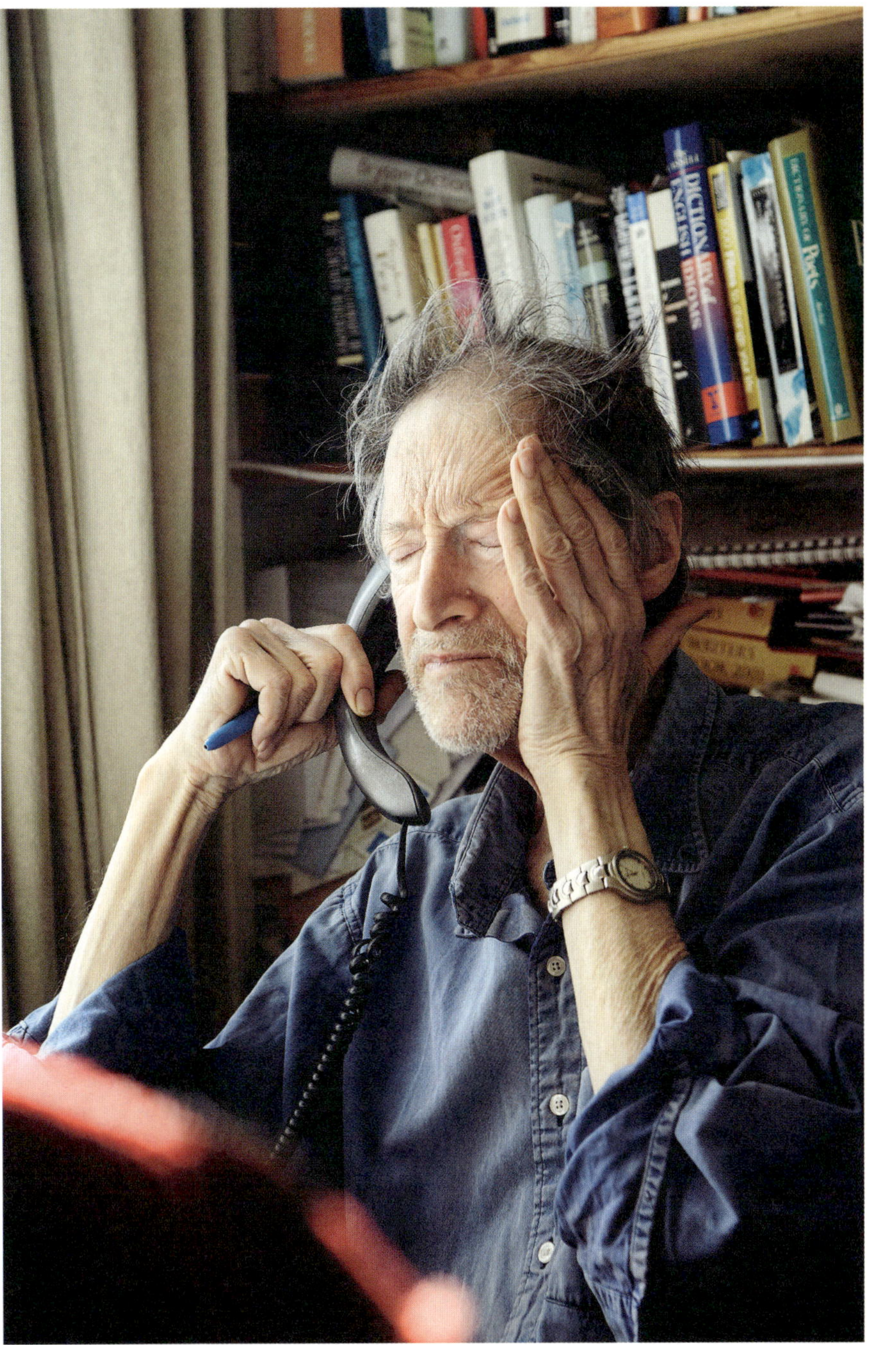

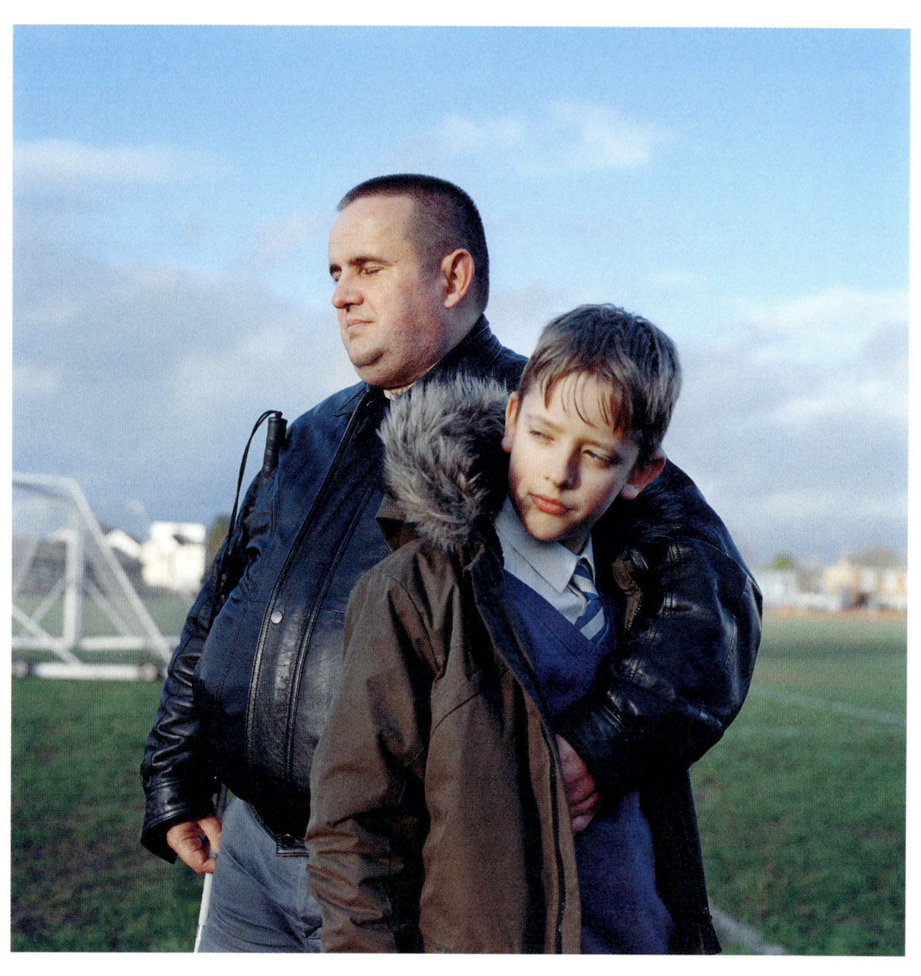

ADRIAN AND LUCA
by Gianluca Urdiroz Agati
Poole, Dorset

Adrian, who is blind, was born in Hungary and moved
to England with his wife some years ago. I noticed Adrian
and his son Luca out shopping one day and was moved
by the way Luca assisted his father.

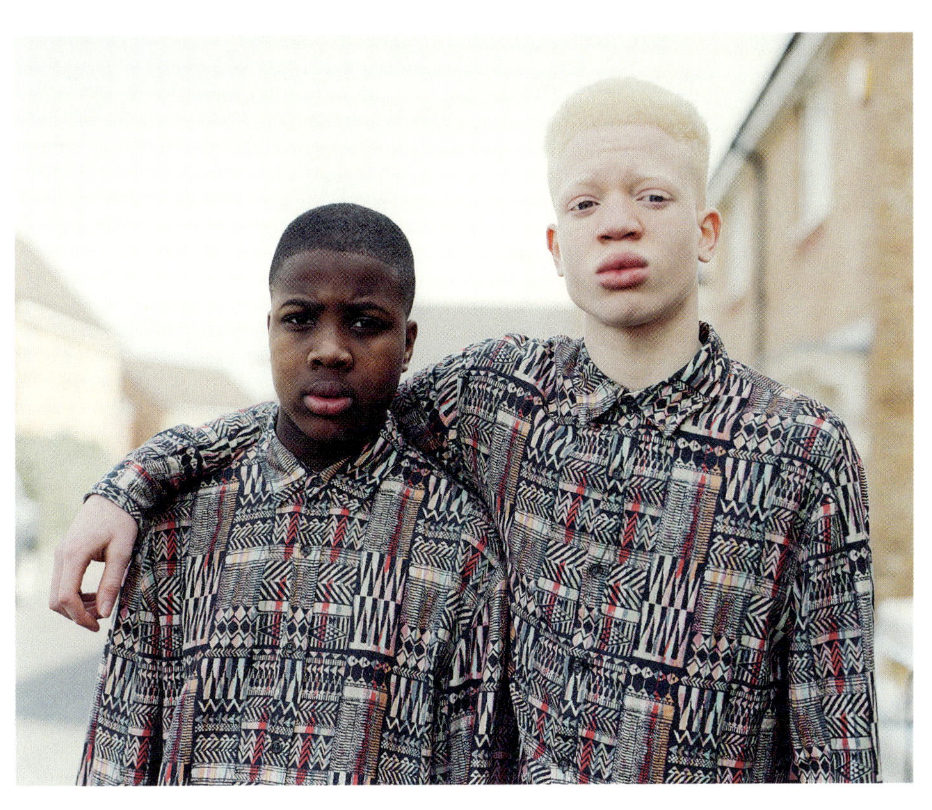

EZRA AND SHEM
by Josie Gealer-Ng
Manchester, Greater Manchester

Brothers Ezra and Shem, who are 12 and 14, had just been
signed to new, inclusive modelling agency, Zebedee.
They have a strong bond.

SURFER IN THE SNOW
by Tom Keen
Tynemouth, Tyne and Wear

After spending a couple of hours taking a series of portraits
of surfers in the snow, the light was fading. I had packed
up my kit and was walking along the beach when I saw
Simon. We had a brief chat and I asked him to pose.
It turned out to be the best portrait of the day.

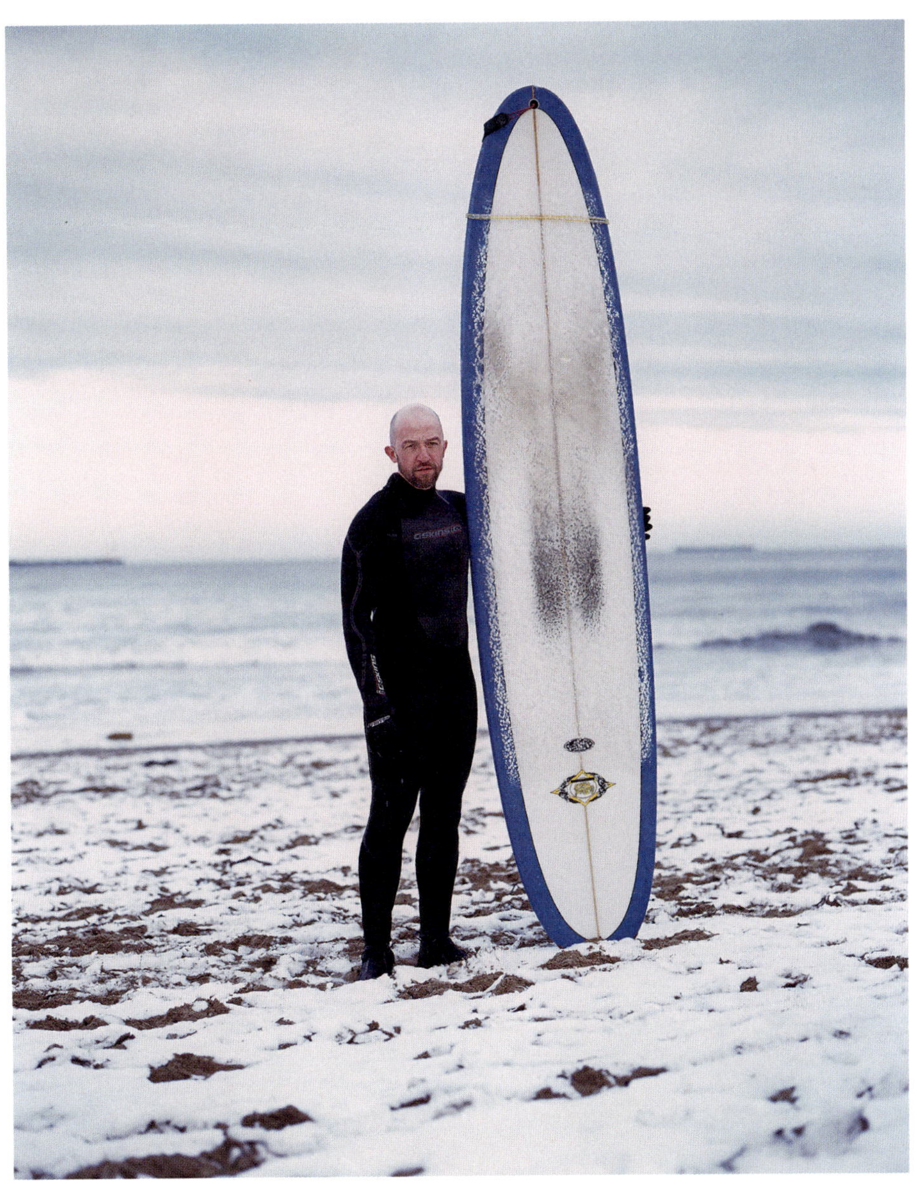

DANIEL
by Matt MacPake
London

I was at Stratford station when I saw Daniel sitting
on the ground. I liked that he was wearing a football shirt.
In the coming years, changes in fashion will date
the image – in a good way.

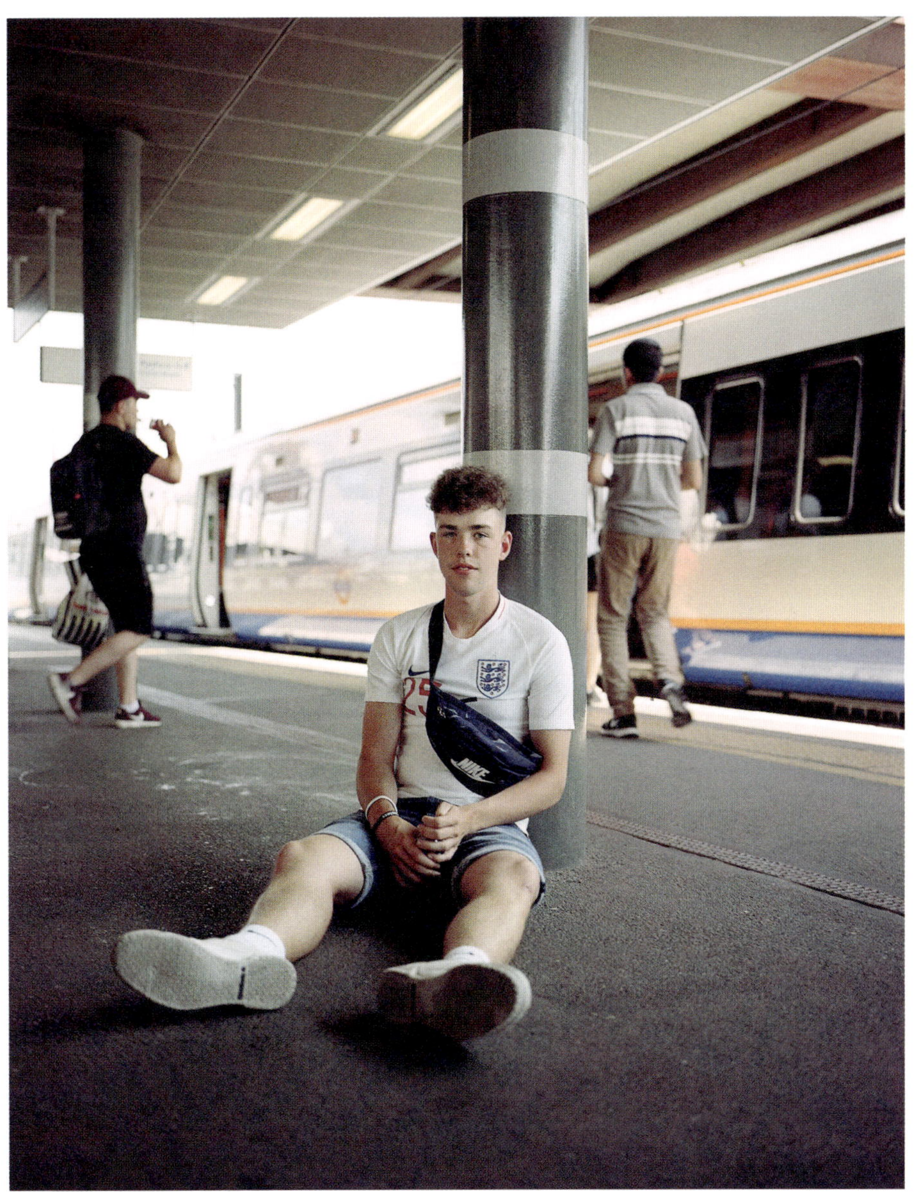

TEZ
by Ollie Grove
London

I met Tez through a charity called The Big House,
which supports young care leavers through theatre. To me
the image is reminiscent of those times when we share
our journeys with strangers and find ourselves asking
questions about the lives of our fellow travellers.

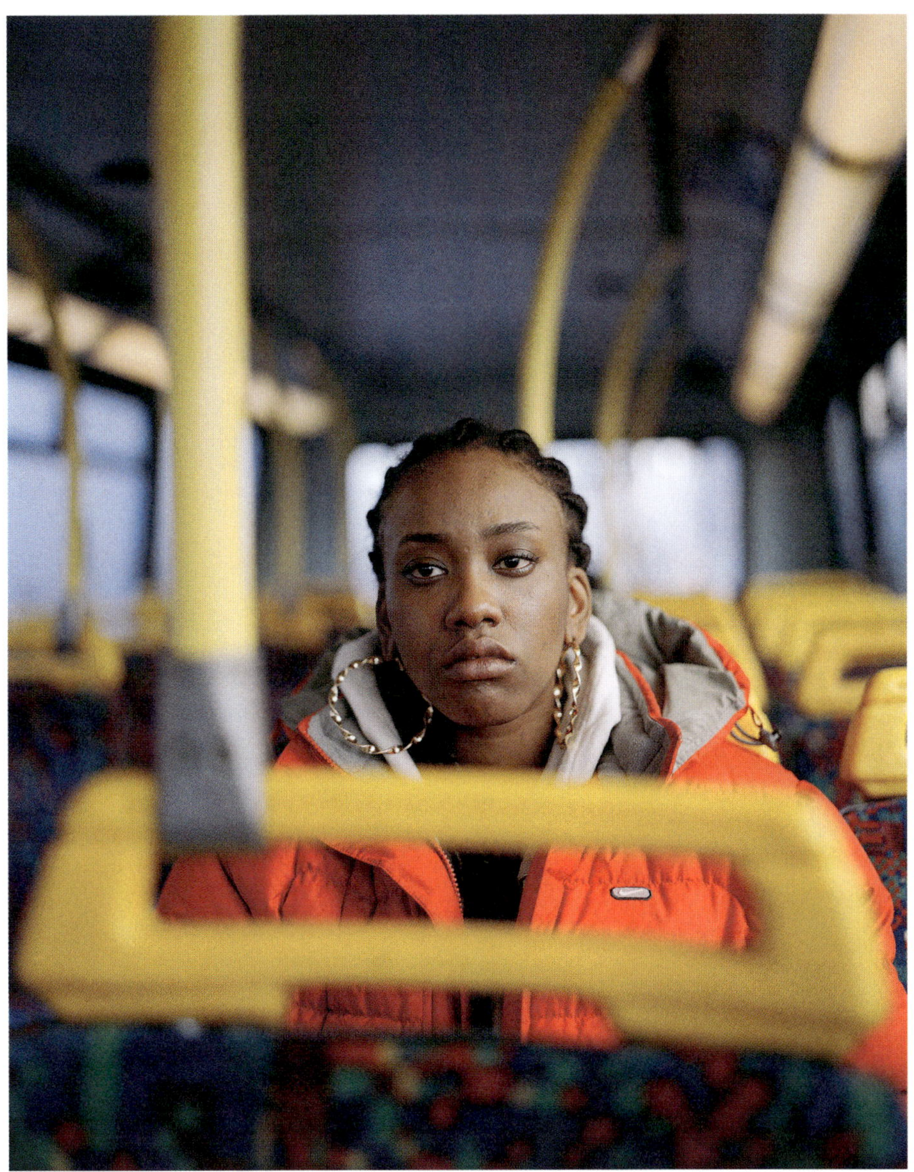

FRANKO-B
by James Tye
London

Franko-B is an Italian performance artist who lives
and works in London. He used to cut himself on stage
and the performance would be him bleeding in front
of the audience. His shows are less provocative now
but still fascinating.

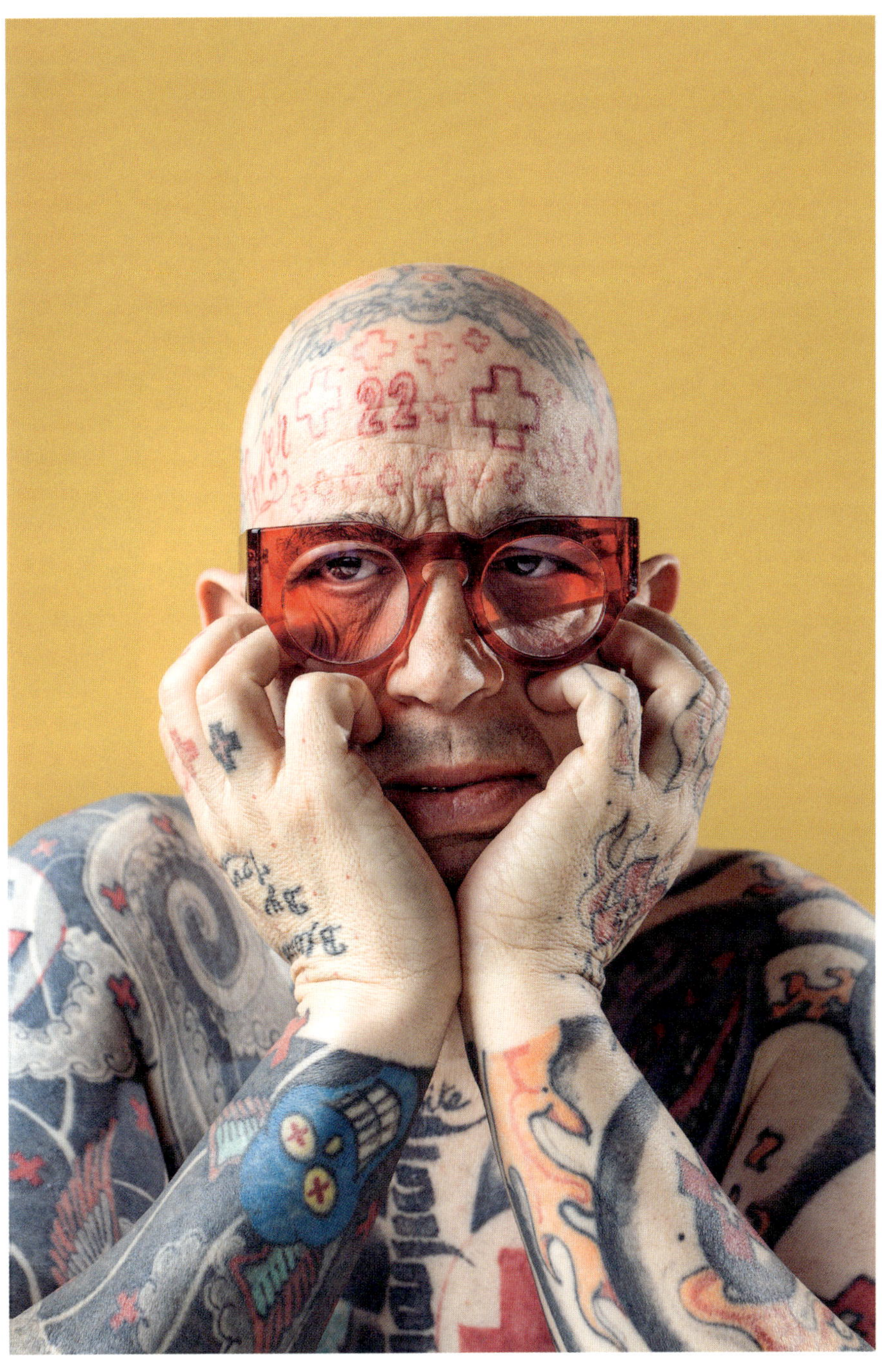

LOVEDAY
by Robert Darch
Sweetham, Devon

Loveday has just finished studying a baccalaureate at
college and, like a lot of young people, is trying to decide
what to do next in life. She is creative, outgoing and
at home in the natural world.

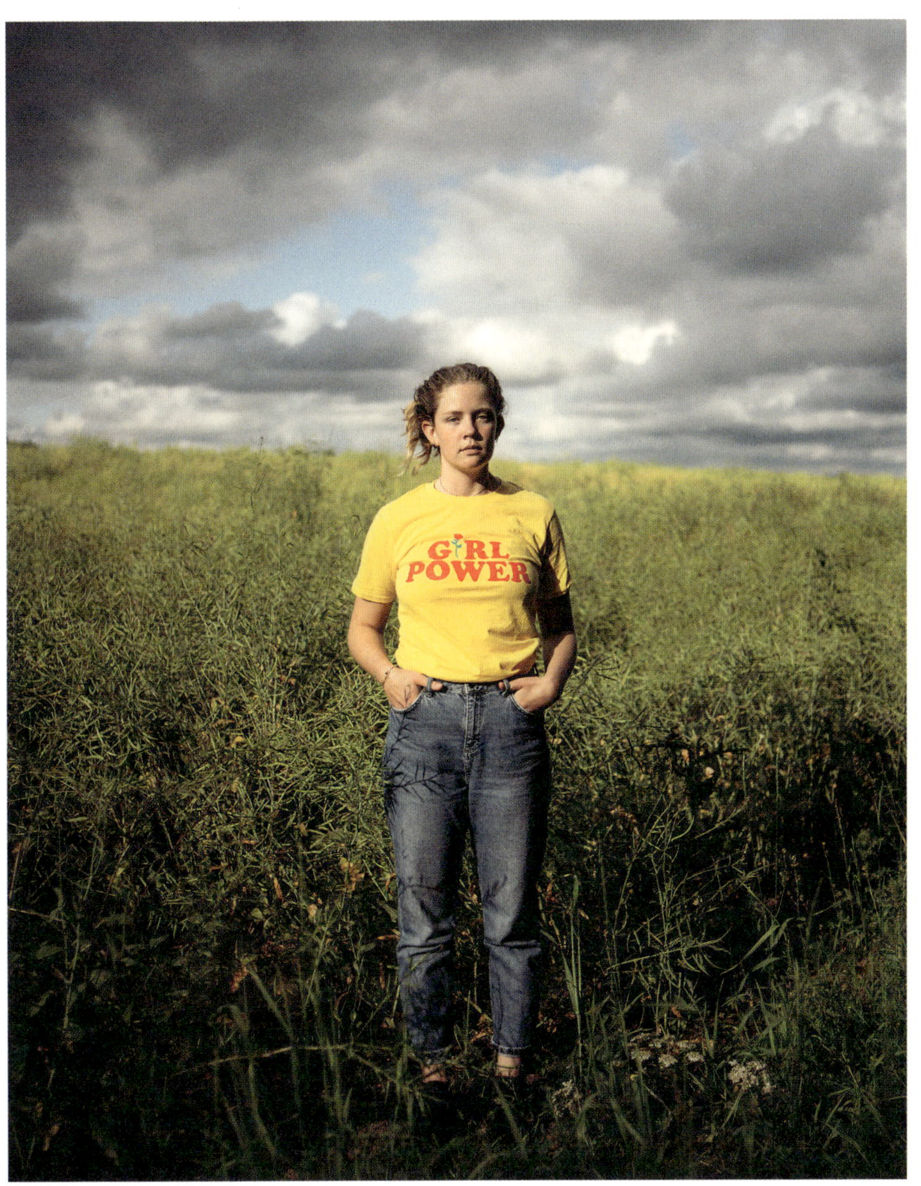

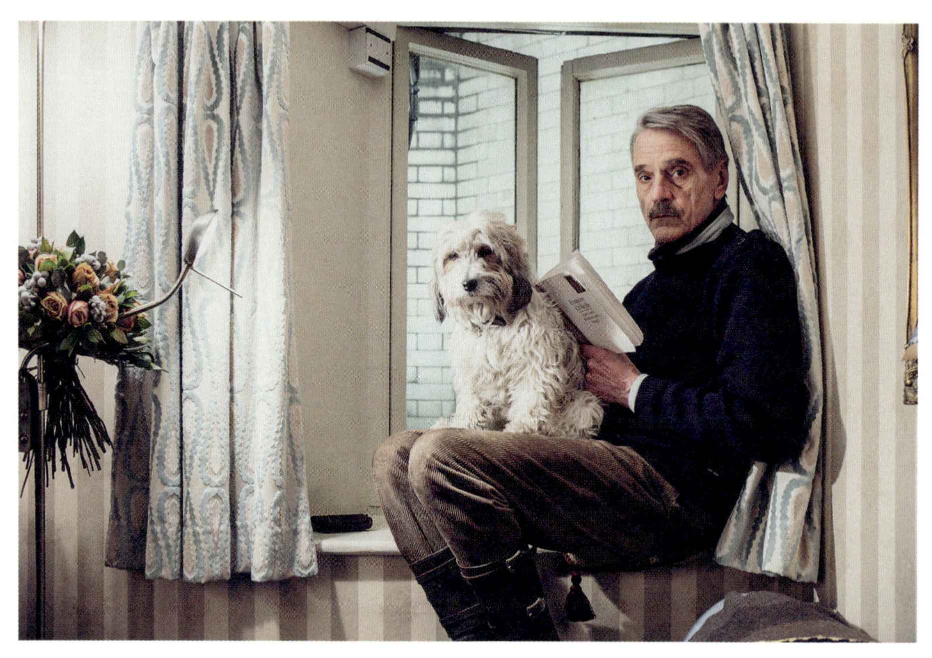

SMUDGE AND JEREMY
by Matt Humphrey
London

British actor Jeremy Irons with his dog Smudge before
a performance. Each actor uses a dressing room differently;
it becomes something of a home from home. This was
as much Smudge's space as it was Jeremy's.

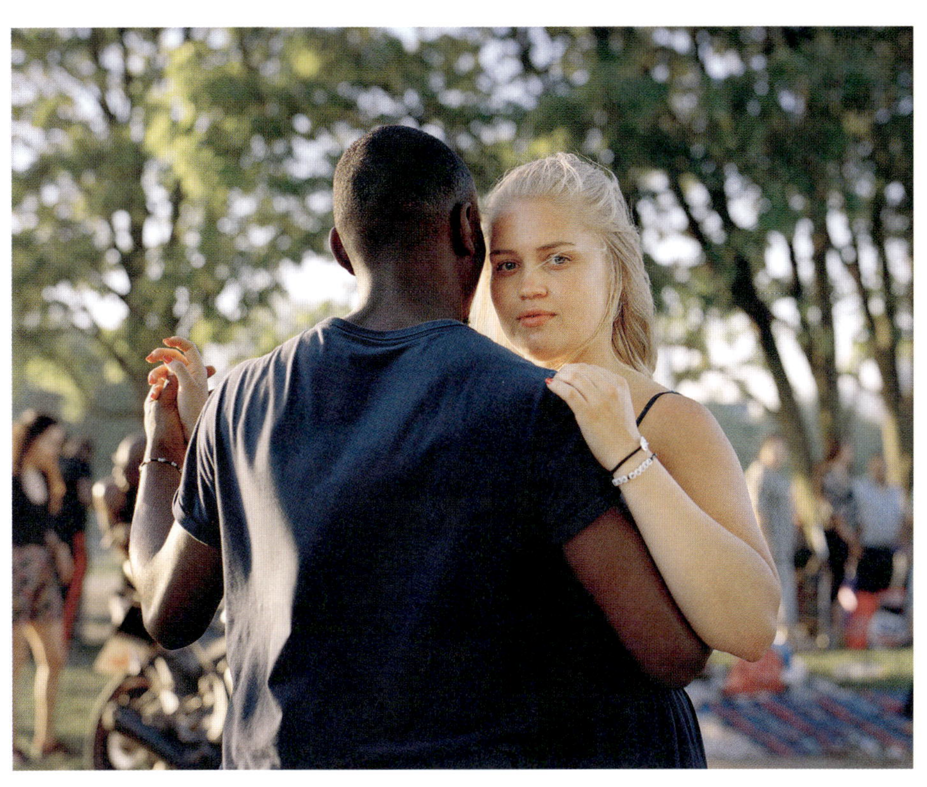

EBBA AND EDDIE
by Max Miechowski
London

I noticed a large group of people in Burgess Park who
had set up a sound system and were salsa dancing. I took
many photos but this intimate shot is my favourite.

RNLI CREW MEMBER
by Kate Wolstenholme
Cromer, Norfolk

The services provided by charities including the Royal
National Lifeboat Institution save many lives at sea.
The workers, most of who are volunteers, dedicate
their lives to helping others.

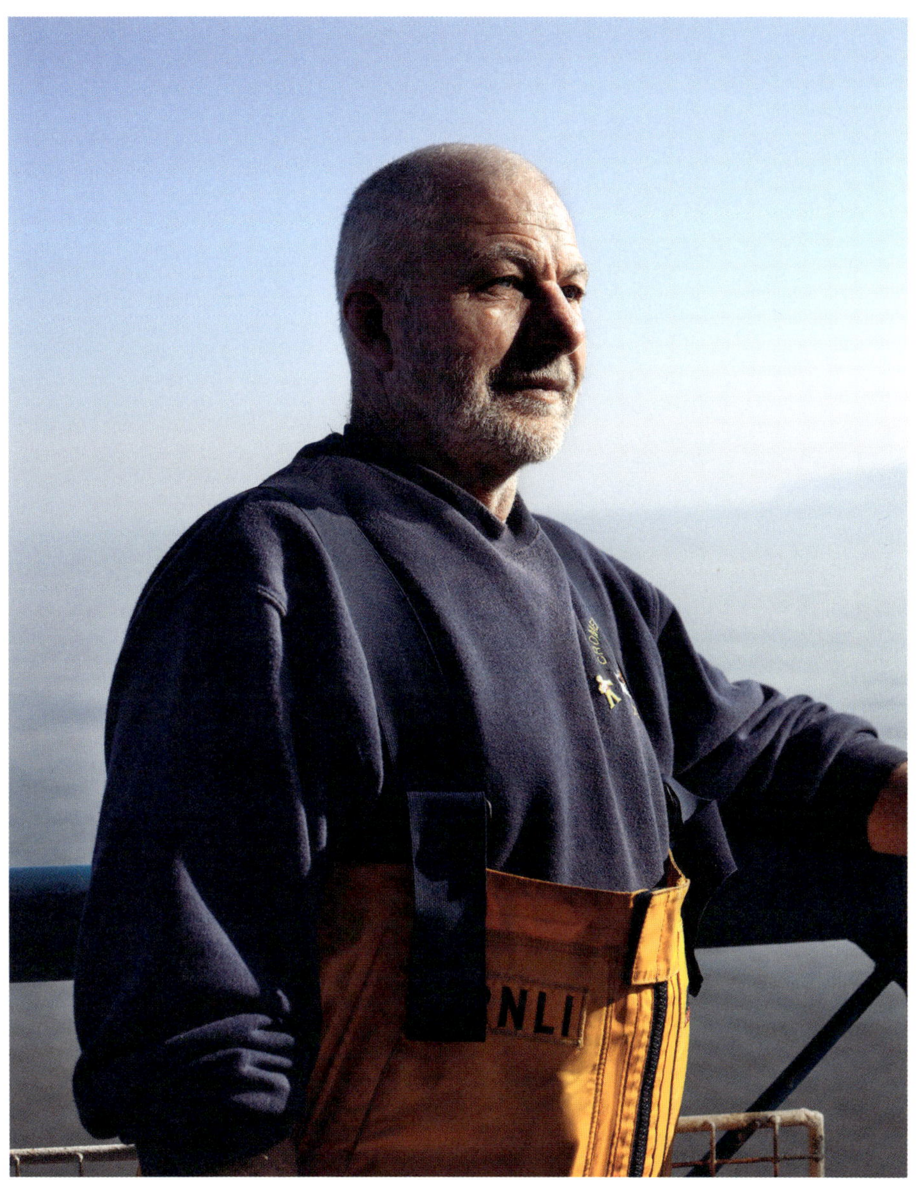

SEAFORD MOD
by Fabio De Paola
Seaford, East Sussex

Ruth Rose was born a man and at the age of 81
underwent gender reassignment surgery to fully become
a woman. Her greatest passion is wild swimming.
She swims every morning.

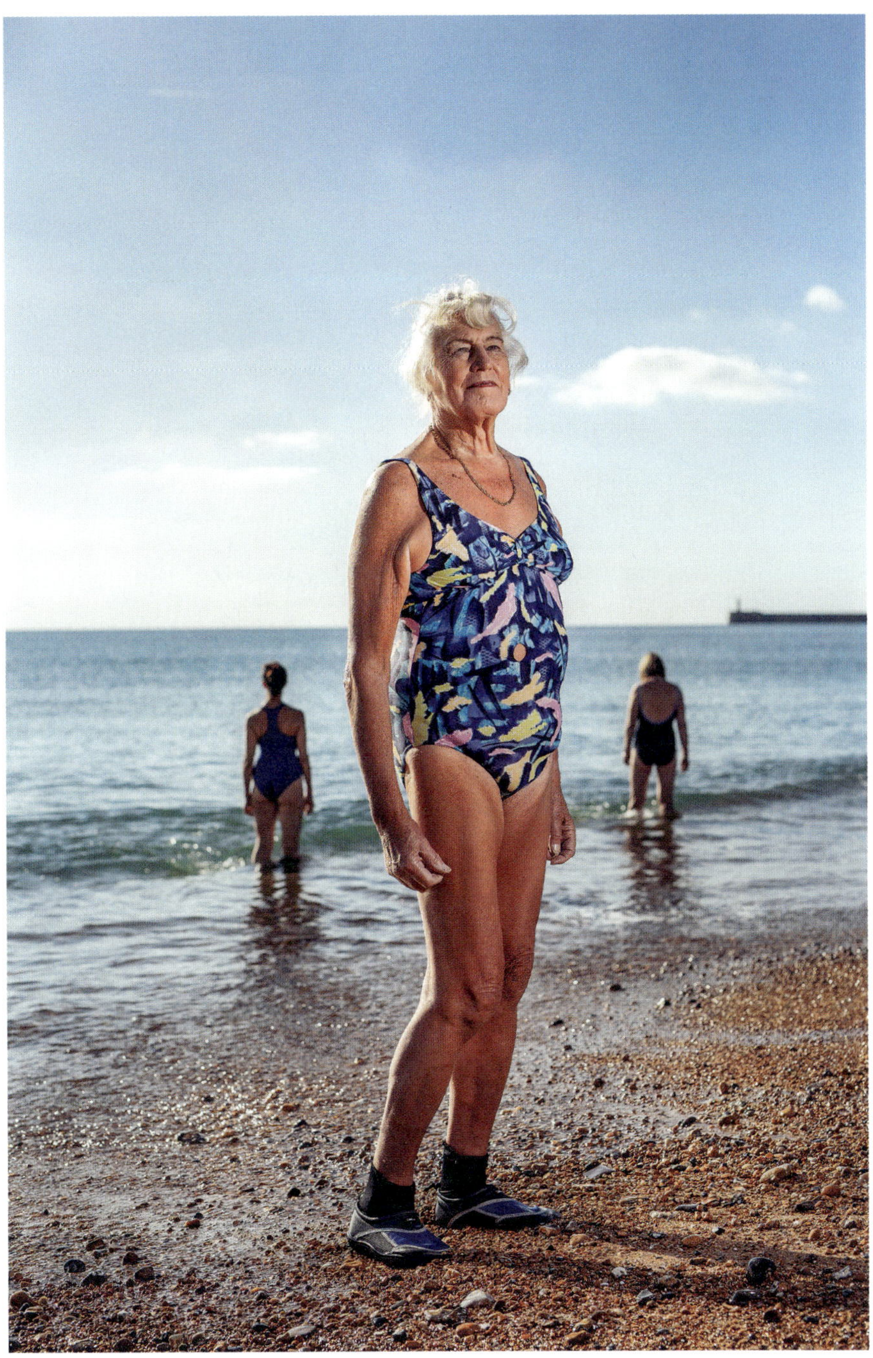

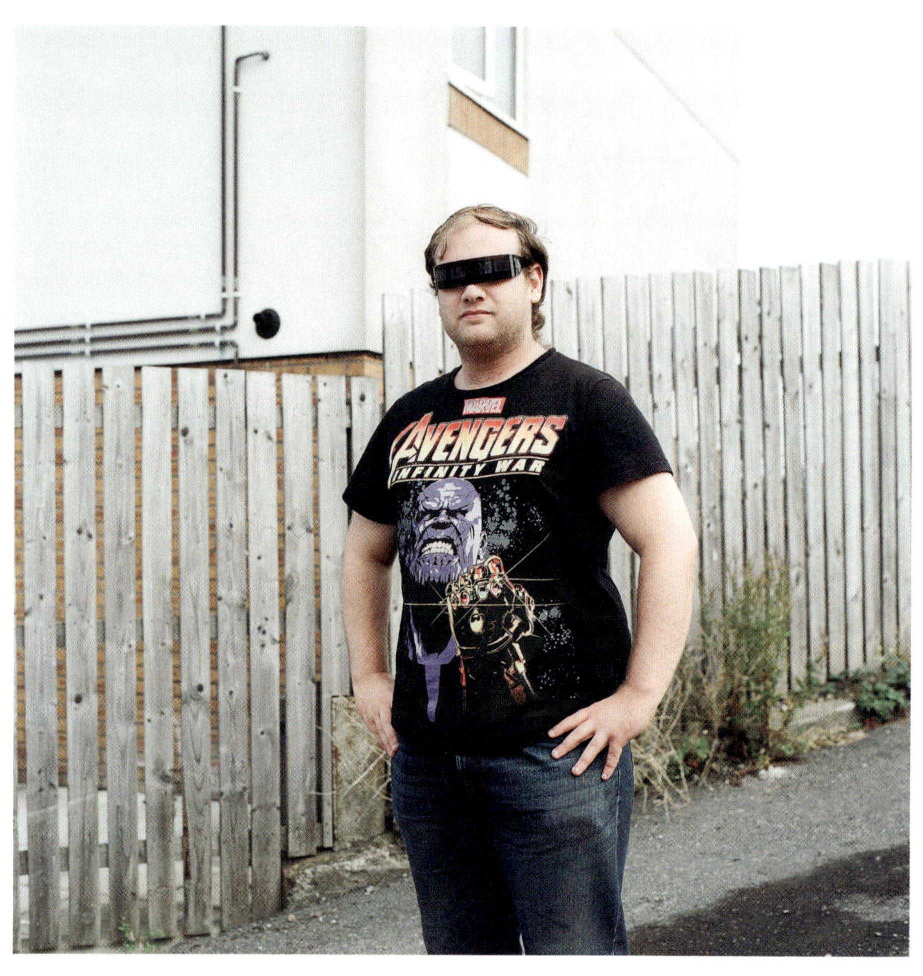

BEN SCOTT
by Robert Law
Holyhead, Anglesey

I met Ben while making a photography project about
the seaport town of Holyhead, a gateway to Ireland.
I asked about his modified sunglasses and Ben
explained they greatly help his autism.

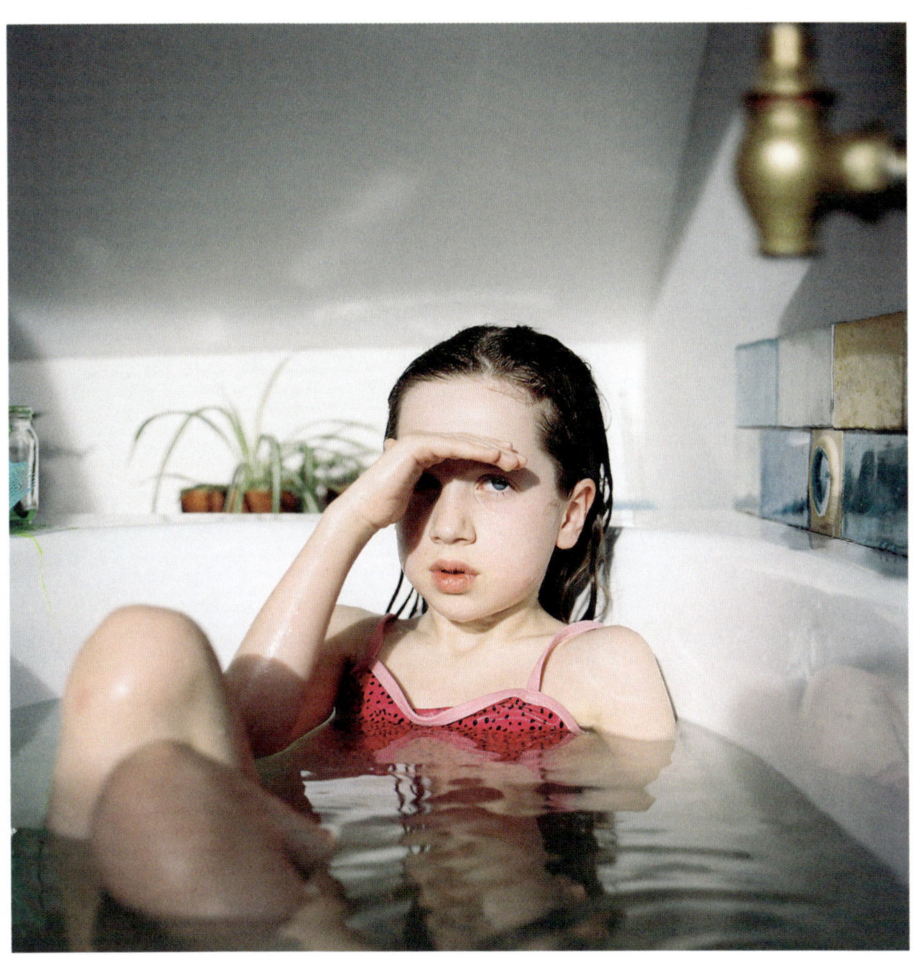

SWIMMING COSTUME
by Molly Matcham
Hallbankgate, Cumbria

Recently my daughter Bobby has decided she would like
to wear a swimming costume in the bath. Times are
changing, she's growing up. Kind, intense, funny
and creative, Bobby has taught me so much.

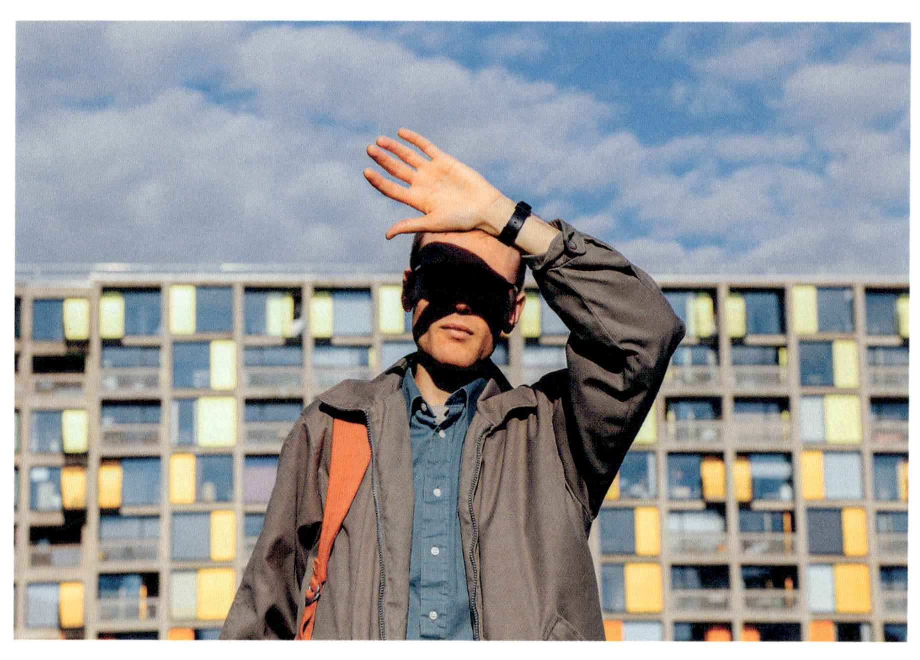

ROBBIE
by Joe Horner
Sheffield, South Yorkshire

Robbie is a singer-songwriter. I wanted a shot in front
of the iconic brutalist Park Hill because the values and
ideas of the estate are important to me: social change,
modernism, creativity, community, culture and hope.

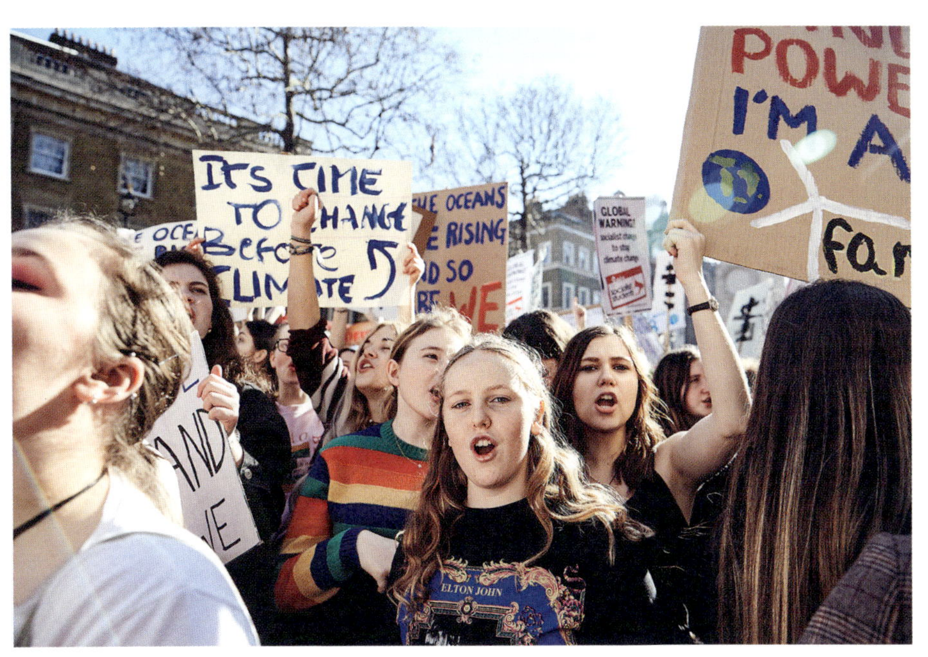

YOUNG HOPEFULS
by Julia Kennedy
London

The positive energy at the climate protests inspired
by young activist Greta Thunberg was almost tangible.
It was amazing to see so many young people coming
together to take action.

CHRIS KETTLE
by Tom Morgan
London

I was taking pictures of English flags on an estate
in south London and knocked on Chris' front door.
'What the hell are you doing taking pictures in my
garden!?' he said. I told him I was doing a project
about people with English flags outside their houses.
He invited me in and told me his life story.

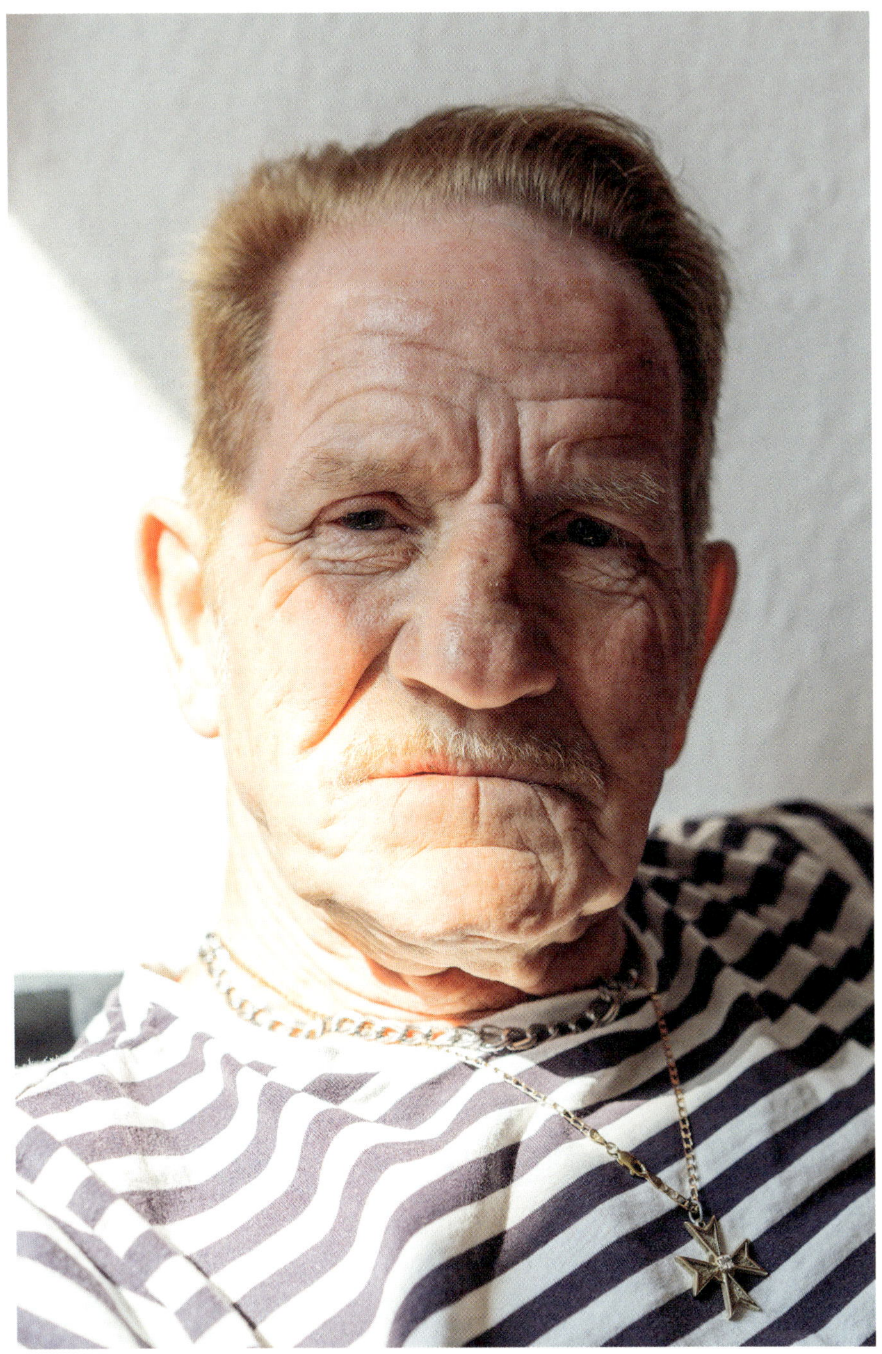

LUAR
by Vikram Kushwah
Burcot, Oxfordshire

Luar is a London-based Israeli photographer and
filmmaker. I photographed her for a series about
diversity and feminism within the fashion industry.
She said: 'My body is very feminine and I am incredibly
embarrassed by its shapes. When I was a teenager
I wanted to hide it. Fighting those thoughts
and feelings is a daily struggle.'

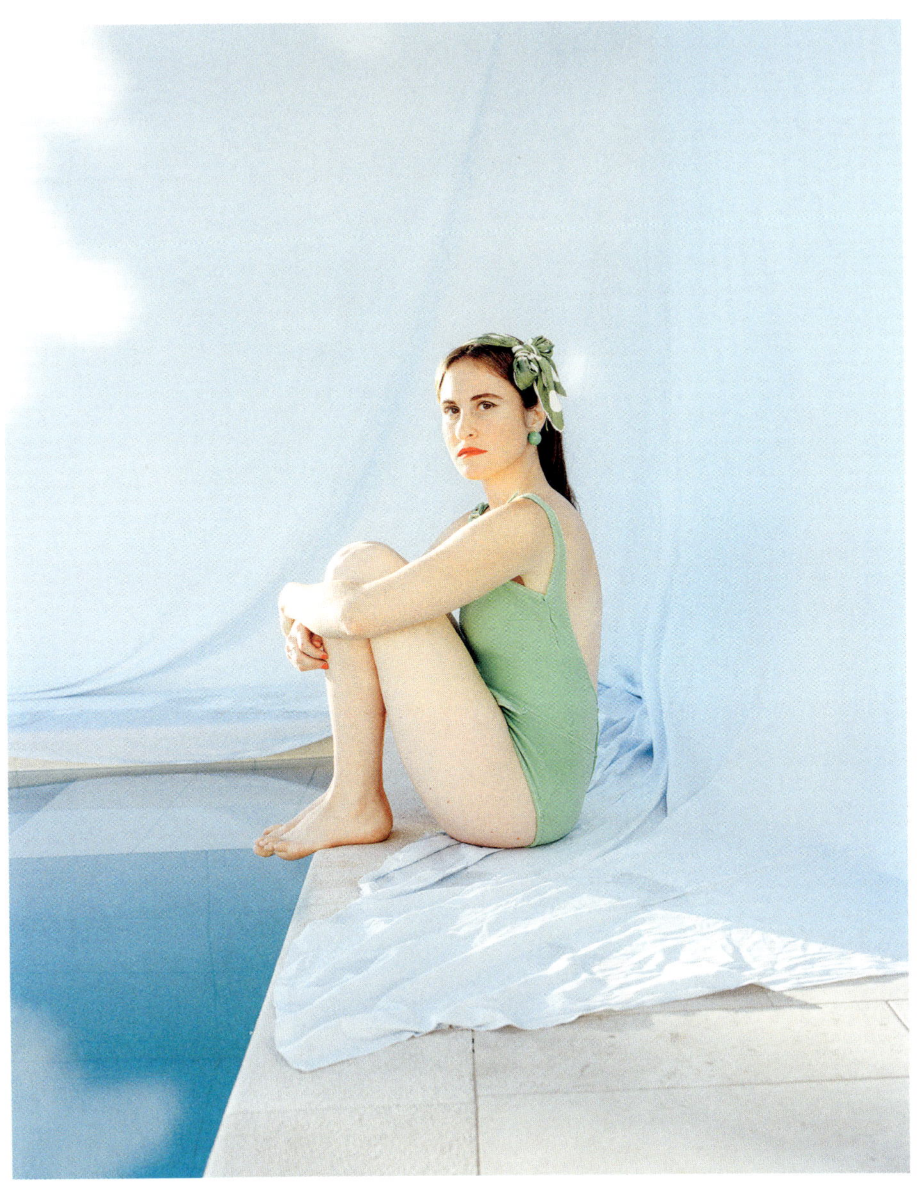

LADY AT SHUTTLEWORTH AIRSHOW
by Daniel Ciufo
Biggleswade, Bedfordshire

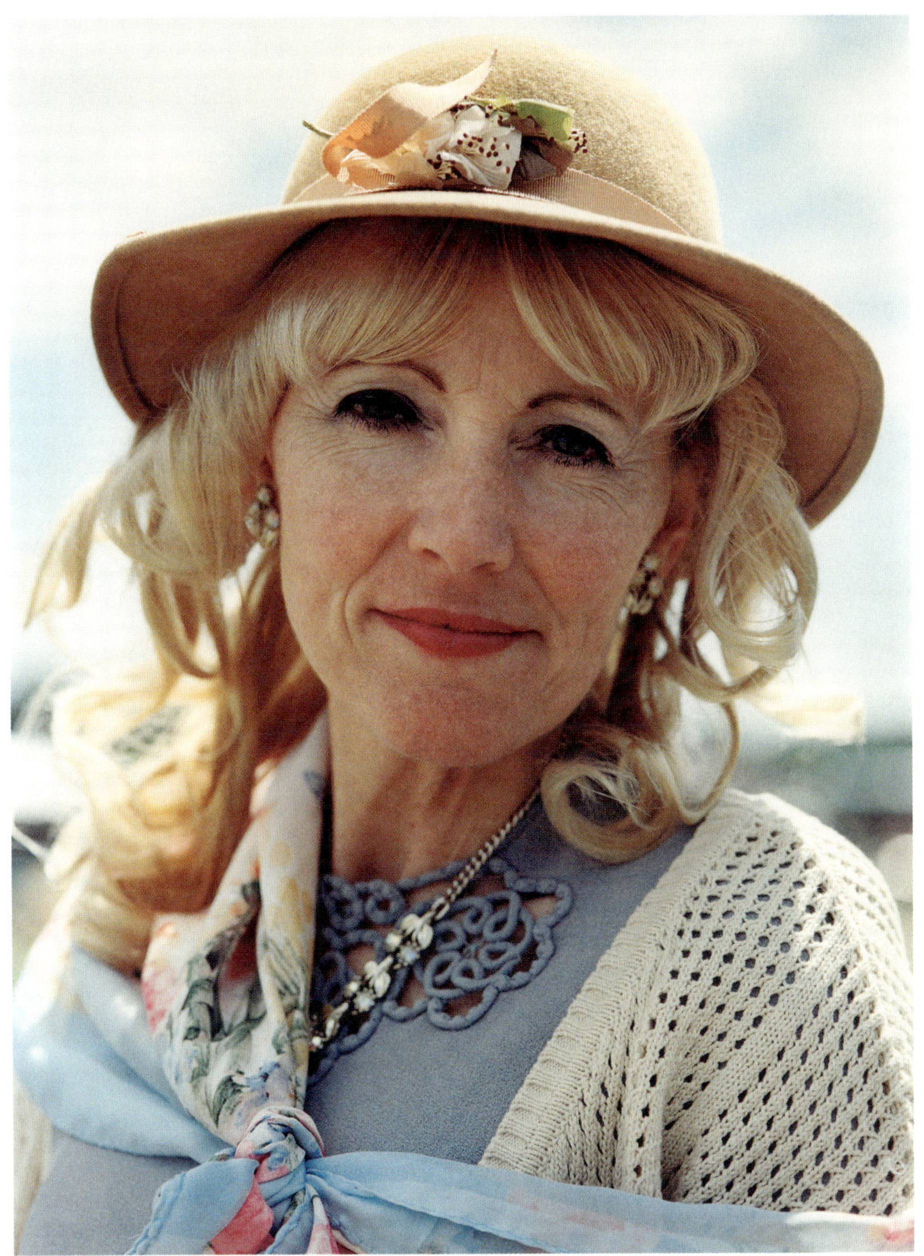

TONI, BALLROOM DANCE CLASS,
POSK CENTRE
by Lewis Khan
London

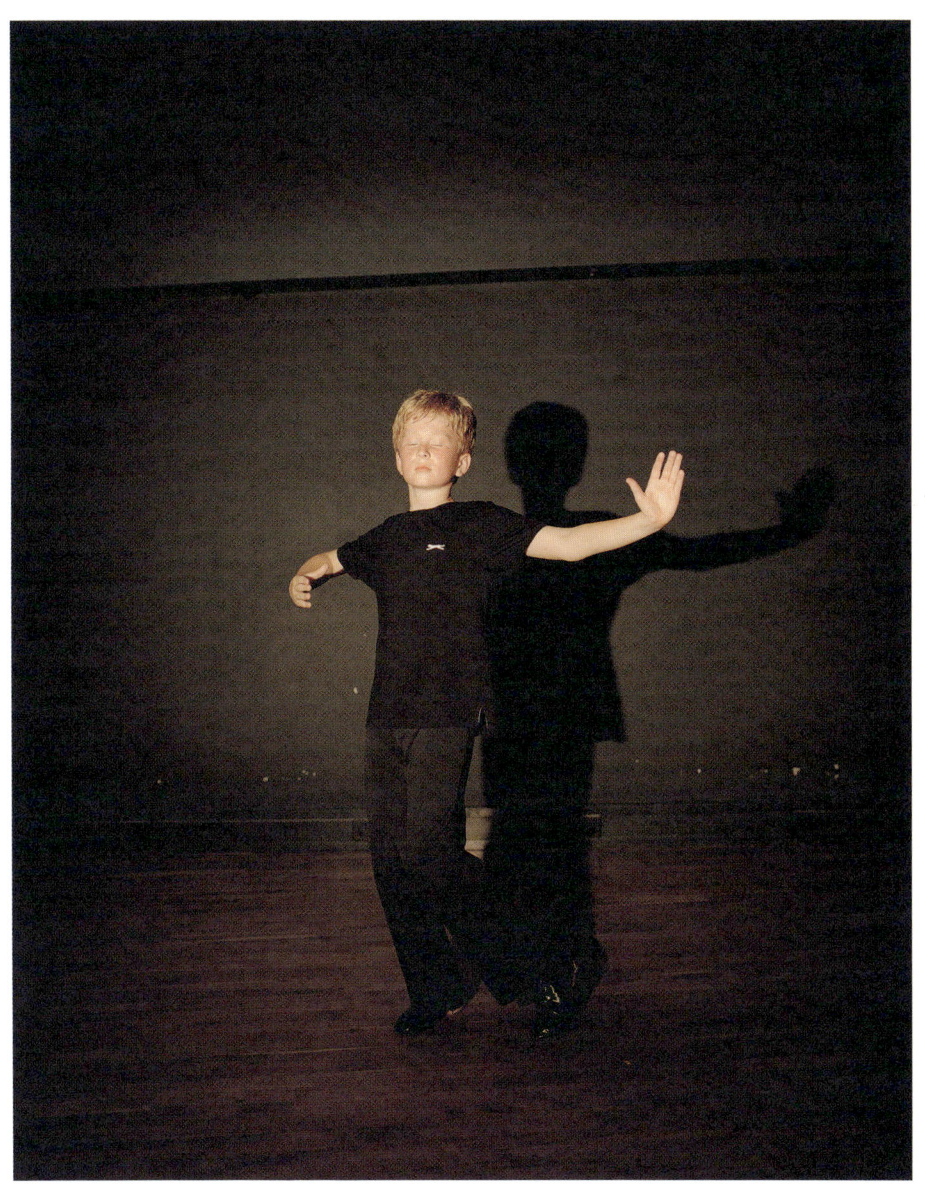

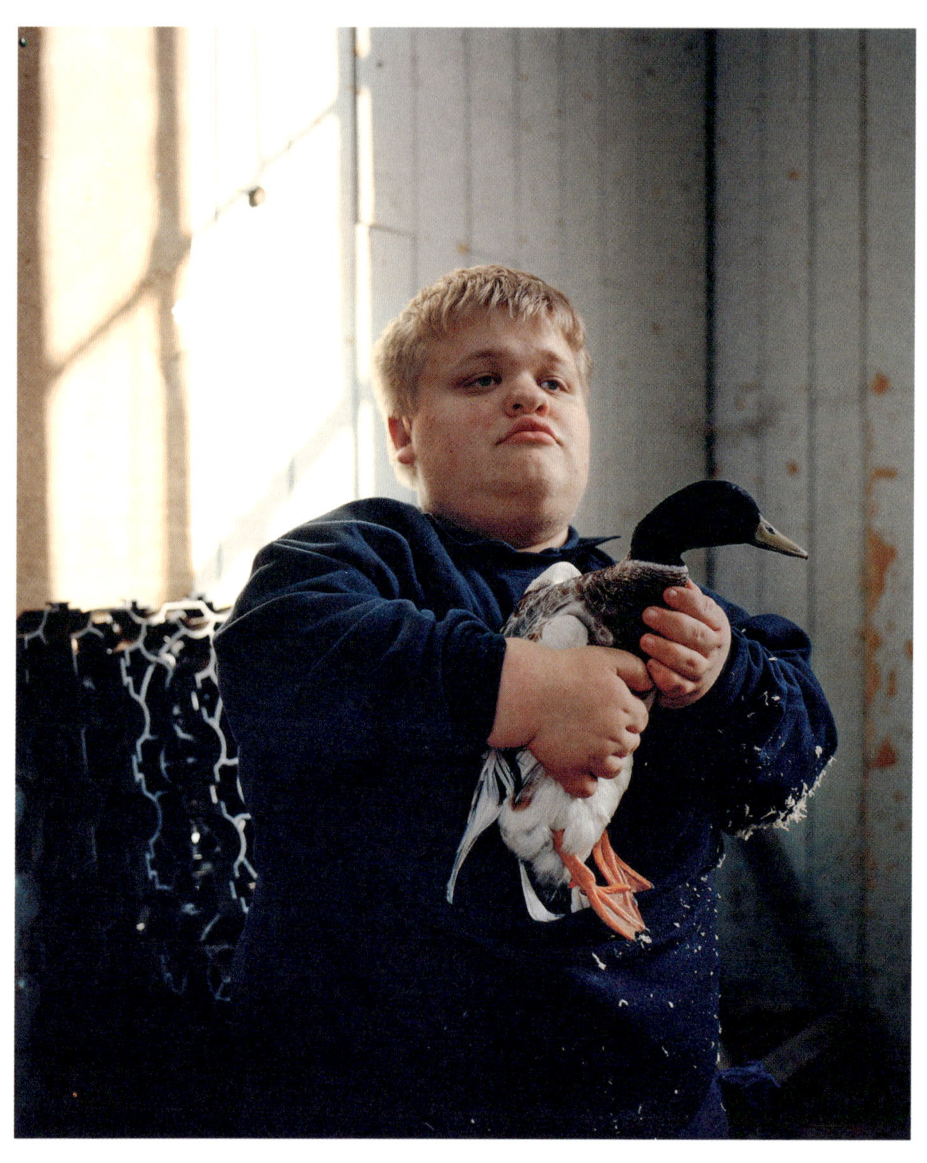

WILLIAM
by Jack Joyce
Oswestry, Shropshire

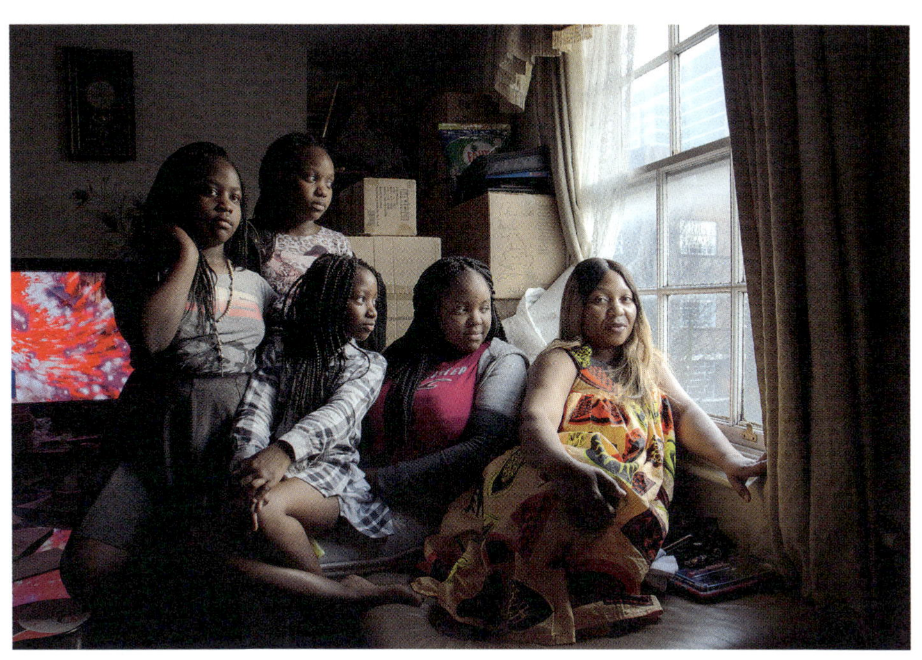

HARRIET AND HER GIRLS PACKING UP HOME
by Liz Hingley
London

Harriet Muhiza and her daughters are among the hundreds
of residents in London who are being rehoused to make
way for the new HS2 railway that will connect the north
and south of England. For families like Harriet's the process
of being displaced by major urban developments is
hugely disruptive and unsettling.

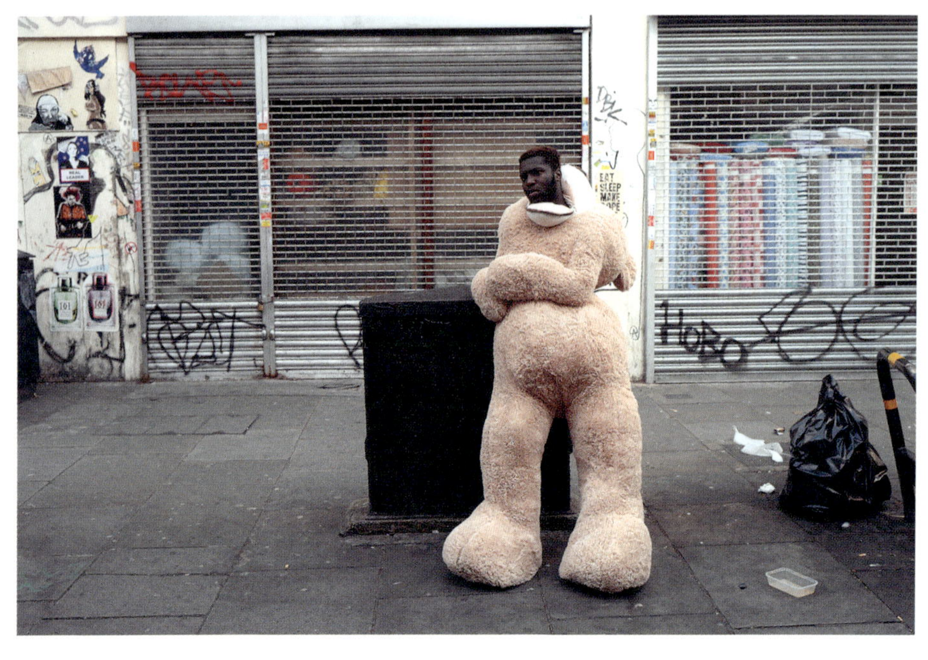

TEDDY
by Robert Huggins
London

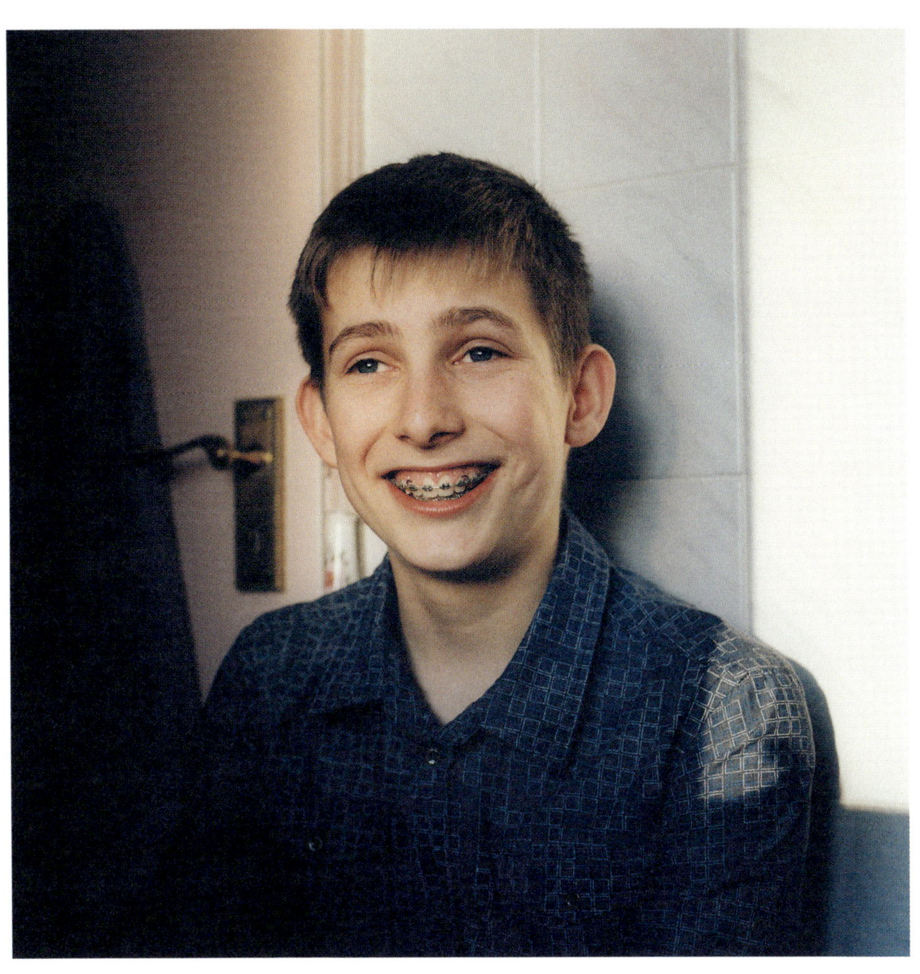

TRAIN TRACKS
by Kendal Noctor
Crokenhill, Kent

There is a 16-year age gap between my cousin and I.
Seeing him brings back feelings about my own teenage
years. I remember having braces; as soon as I got
them I wished they were gone.

GARY
by Simon Murphy
Glasgow

Gary has had a very difficult life – addiction, homelessness –
but has found strength in the lifestyle and music of Mod.

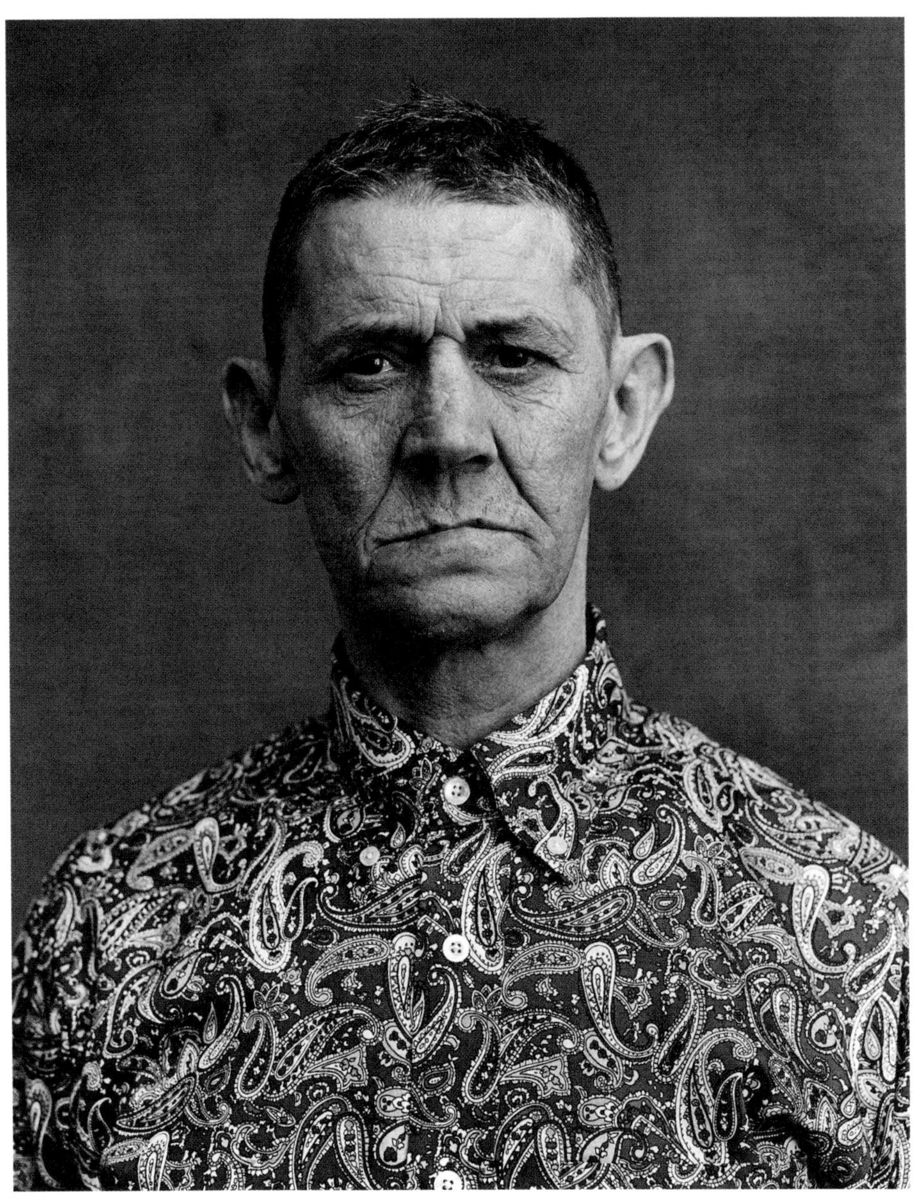

LEWIS
by Phillip Prokopiou
London

Lewis is an old friend who embodies unapologetic
queerness. A performer, artist and curator, Lewis is
someone who, through their art and appearance,
questions society's notions of gender and beauty.

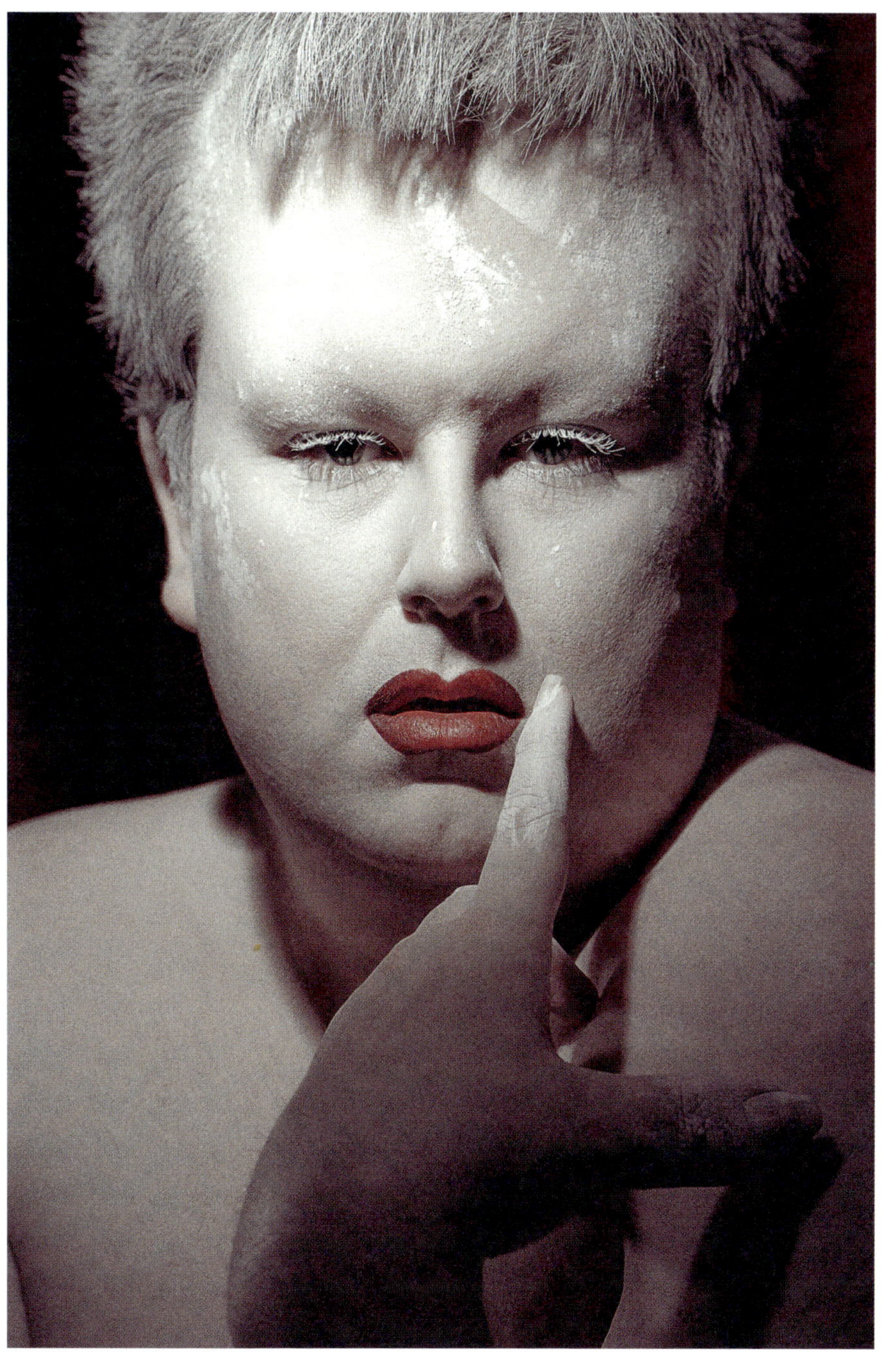

TARA

by Rebecca Sunflower Thomas
Cardiff, South Glamorgan

Tara was about to sit her A-levels when I took this portrait
of her. I wanted to capture the joys of youth and a sense
of endless possibilities.

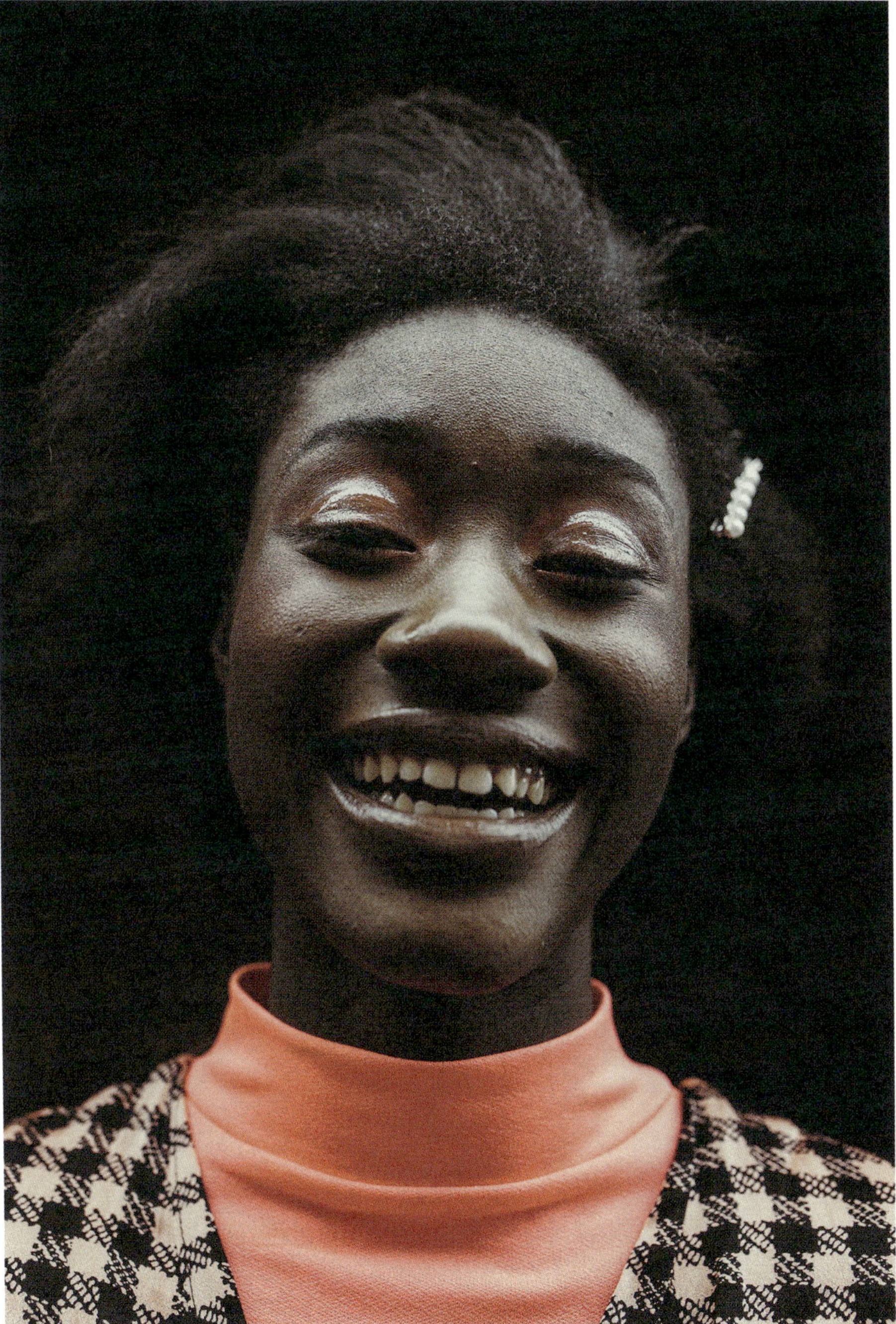

AMANDA
by Kristina Sälgvik
London

'The simplicity of this image is spot on. Many people
I know, including my mother, have commented on how the
image captures my personality and determination perfectly.'
−Amanda Milling, MP for Cannock Chase in Staffordshire

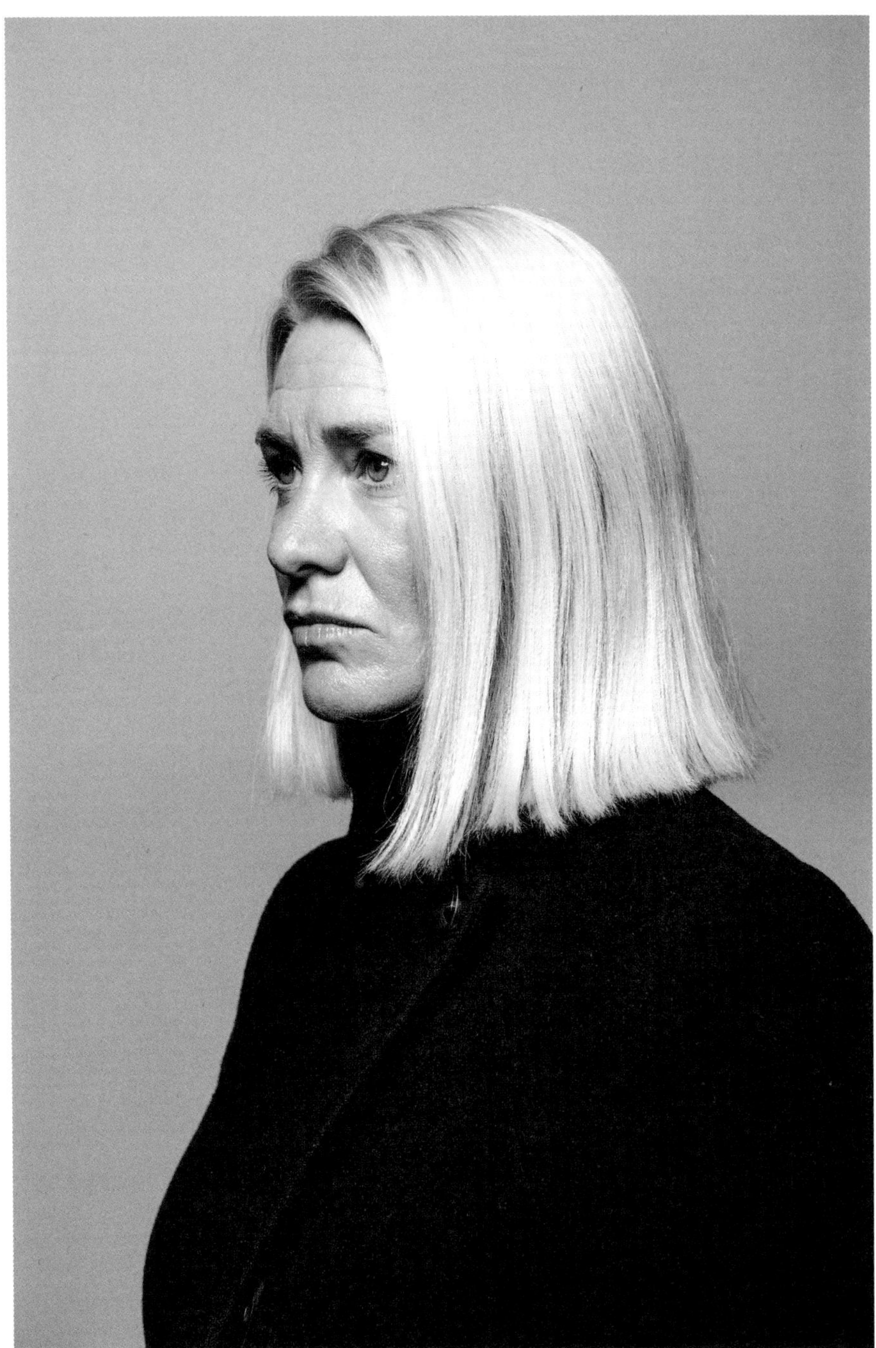

K'FIRST
by André Jacques
London

K'First is a friend of mine who I met through mutual
friends. He moved to London from Thailand 10 years ago.

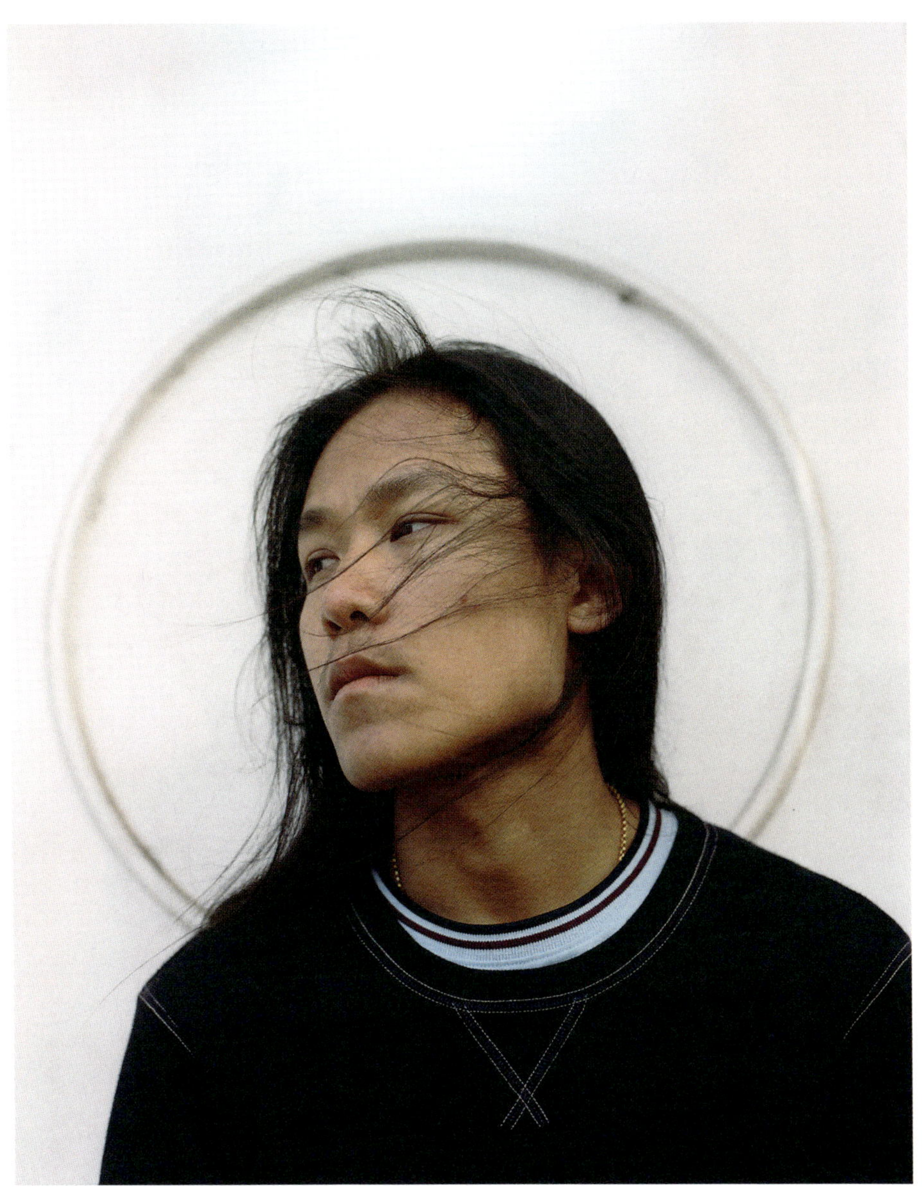

SORIANO
by Lewis Khan
London

To me this portrait has a sense of sincerity and tenderness.
I think of the camera as a tool to connect with strangers
and share in a creative process.

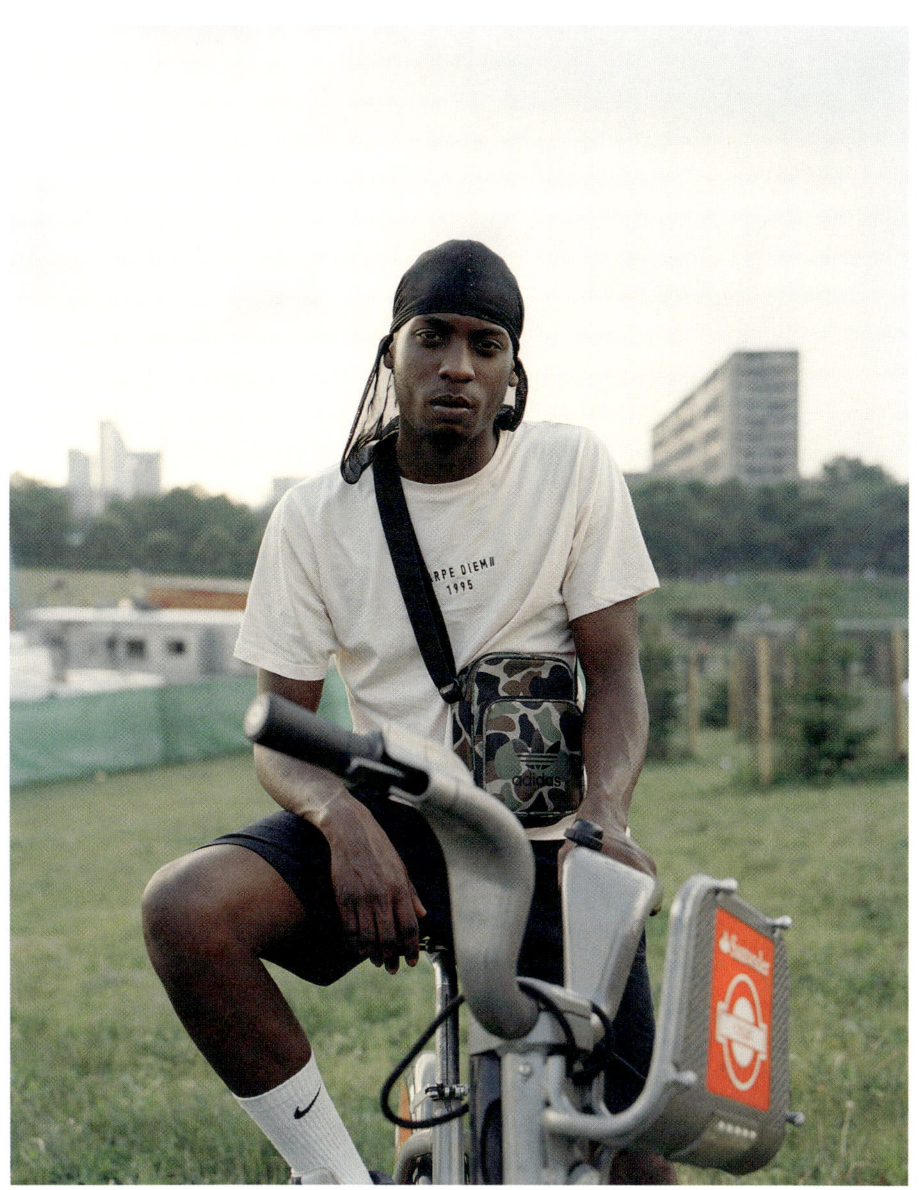

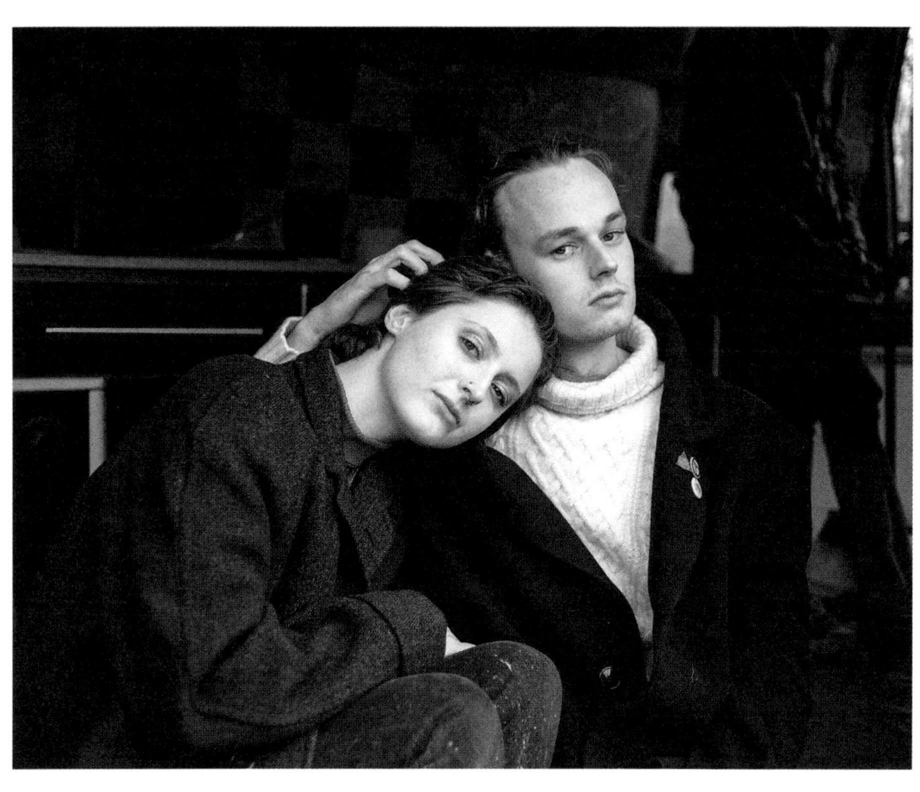

DAISY AND WILL
by Robert Darch
Holsworthy, Devon

Daisy and Will are recent university graduates. I have
been taking images of young people as part of a project
exploring the anxieties and fears around Brexit.

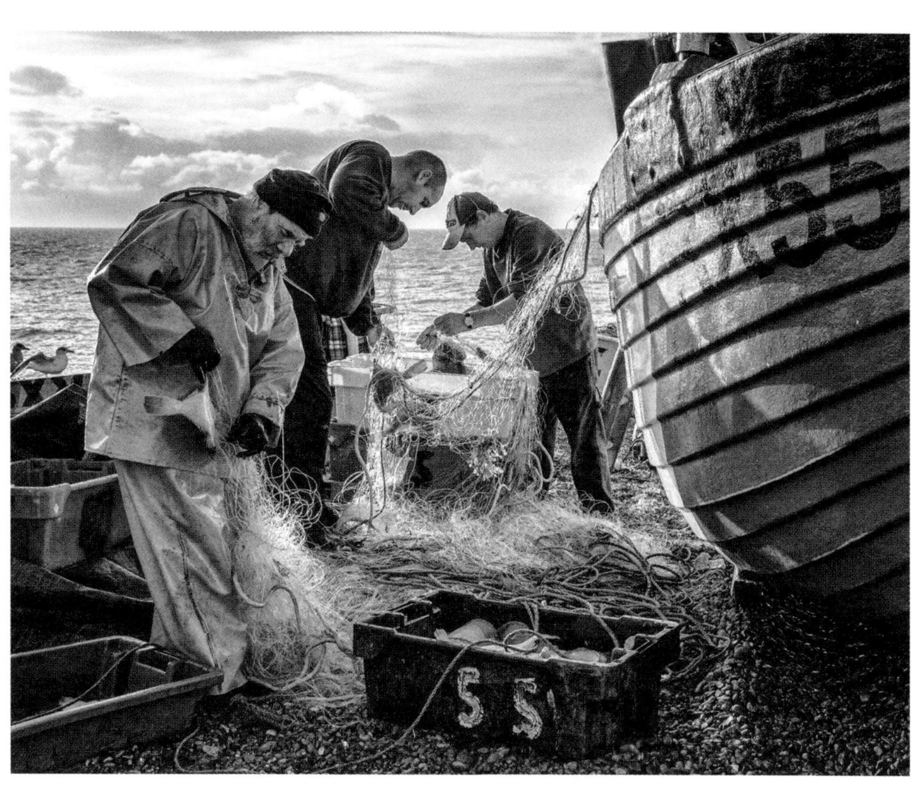

CLEANING THE NETS
by Ann Chown
Hastings, East Sussex

Pete, Simon and Lawrence are from a long line of
fishermen. They have worked at the Stade, home of the
UK's largest beach-based fishing fleet, for many years.

ELLIE
by Ioana Marinca
London

Ellie and I met in a restaurant. I was on a second date
that hadn't started very well; Ellie was our friendly waitress
who turned things around. Her shaved head and arm tattoos
caught my attention so I asked her if she would sit for
a portrait. We stayed in touch and a couple of months
later made some pictures together.

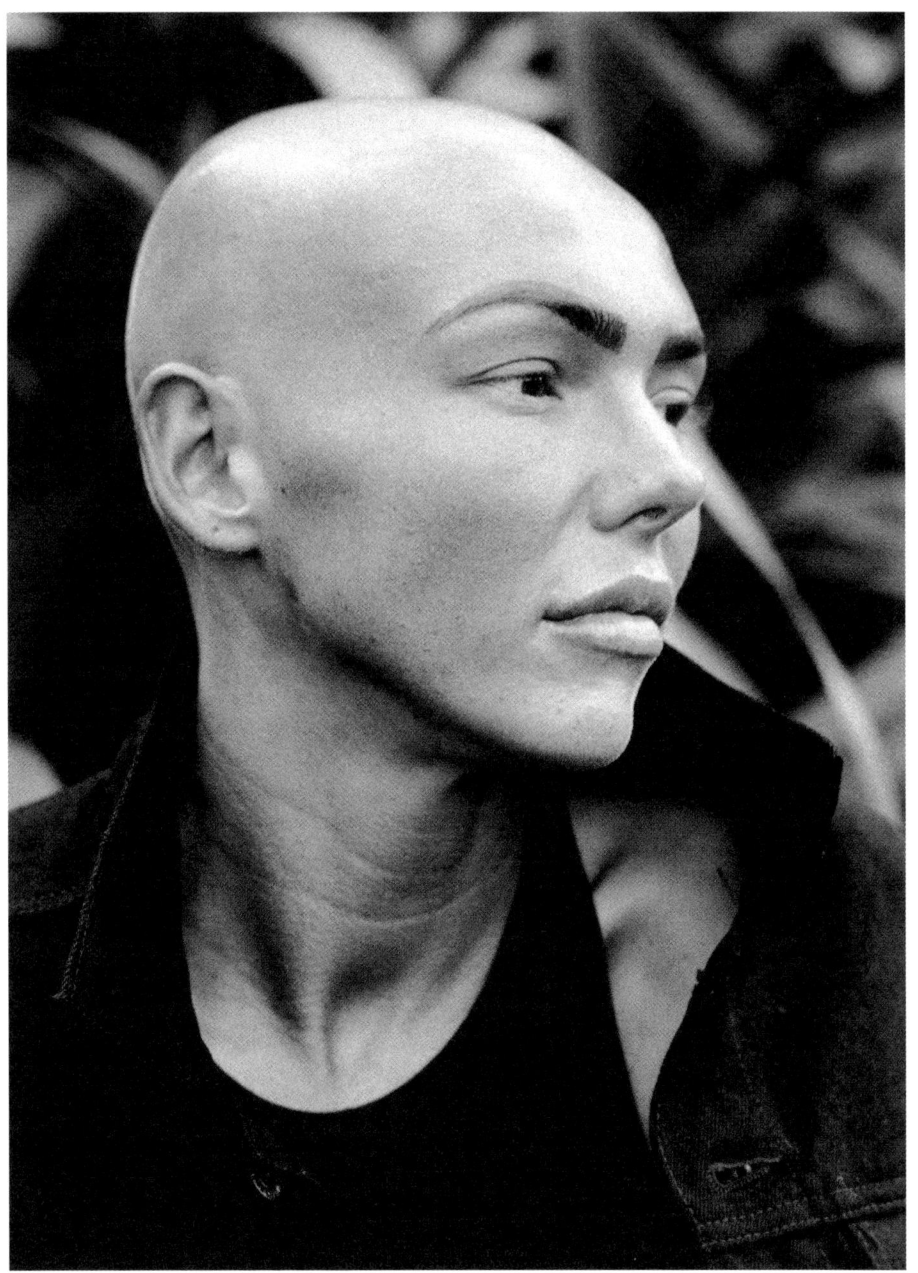

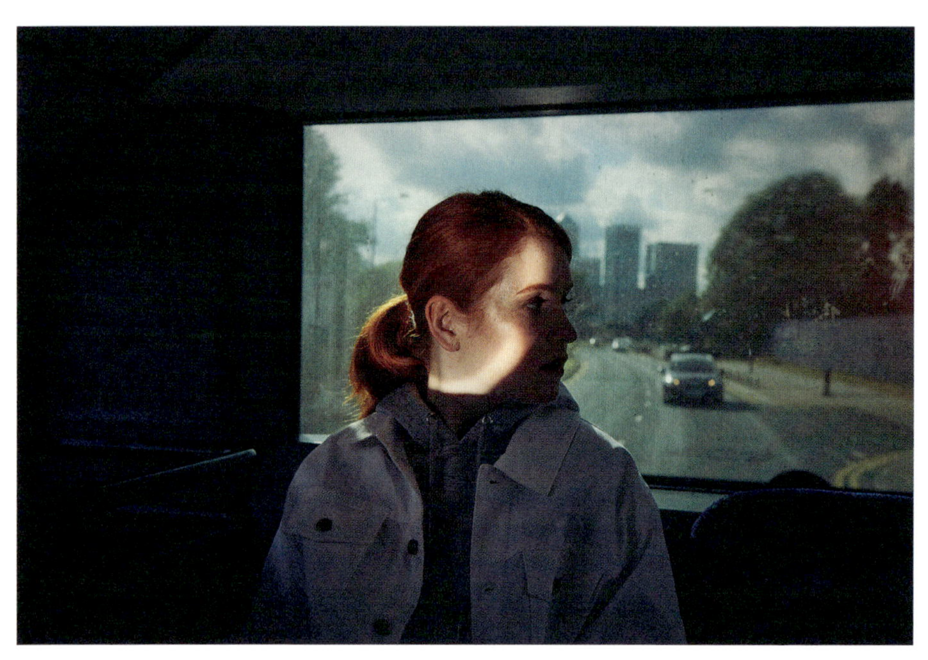

KATIE
by William Green
London

I asked Katie to pose for me while we were travelling on
a regular bus route she takes. Light is really important in
my work so I sometimes use mirrors, pieces of glass or
reflectors to direct the light and add atmosphere.

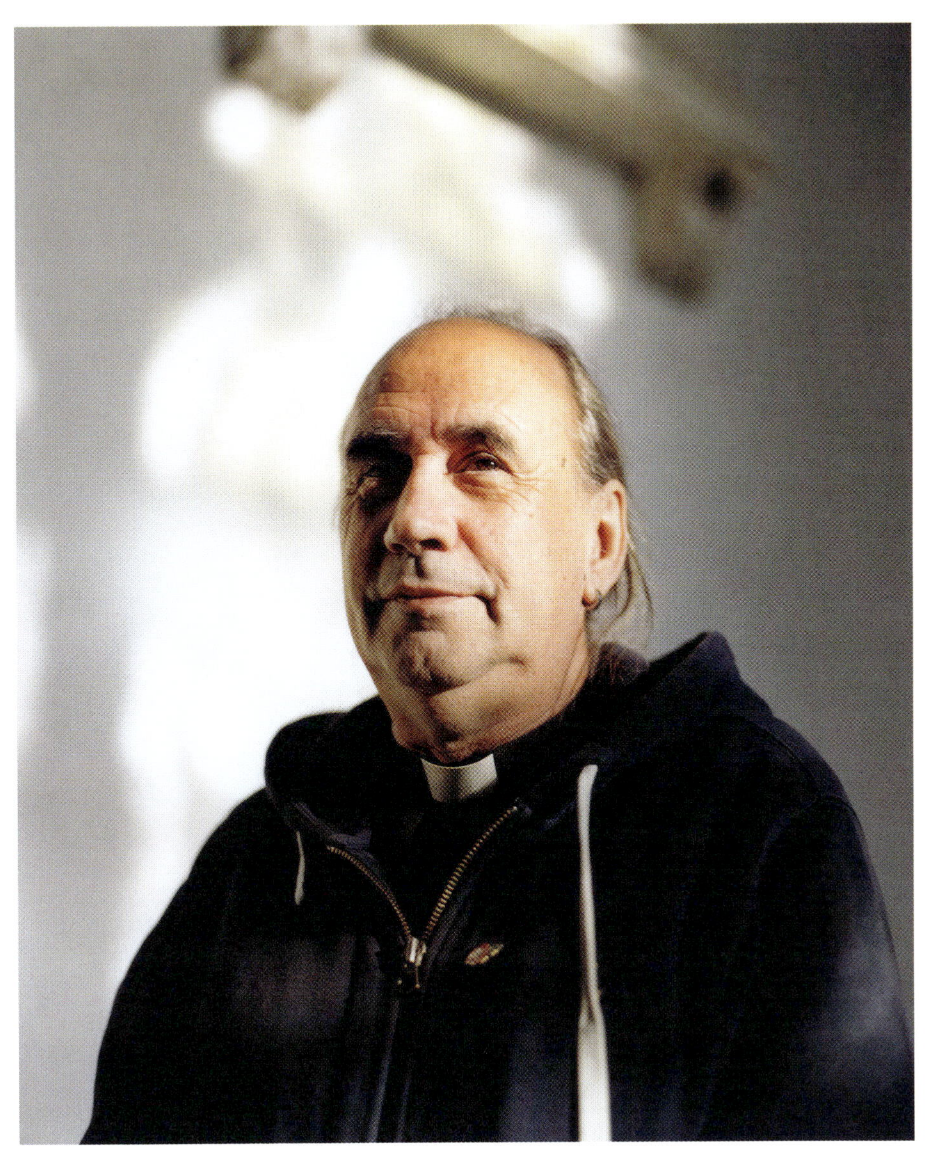

REVEREND MARK HURLEY
by Chi Poon
Swanscombe, Kent

SHAUN RYDER
by Theo McInnes
Salford, Greater Manchester

Former lead singer of the Happy Mondays and UFO
aficionado Shaun Ryder has had a pretty extreme life.
We interviewed him for a magazine and barely talked
about music; we mostly spoke about UFOs and drugs.

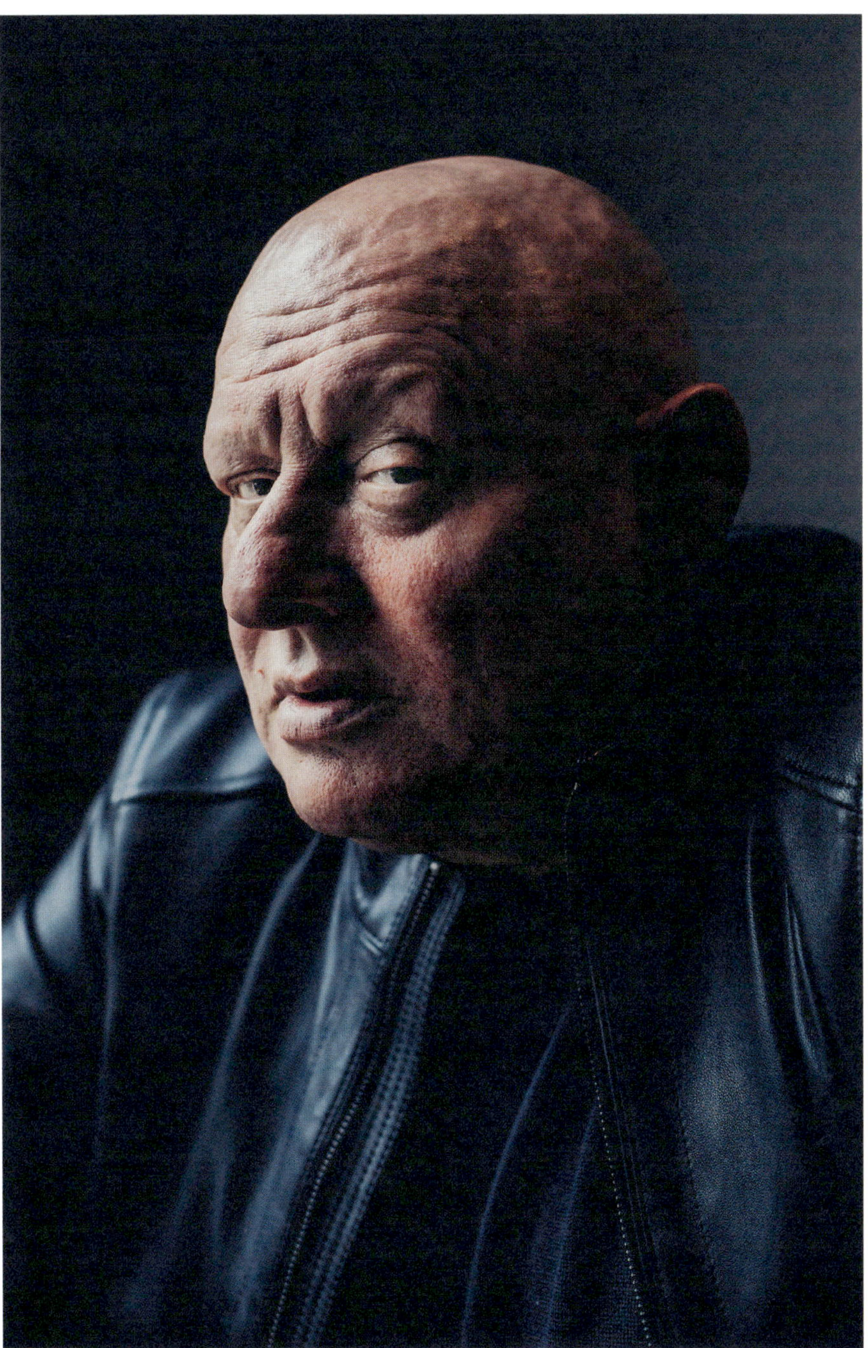

VIDA AS VENUS
by Sarah Weal
London

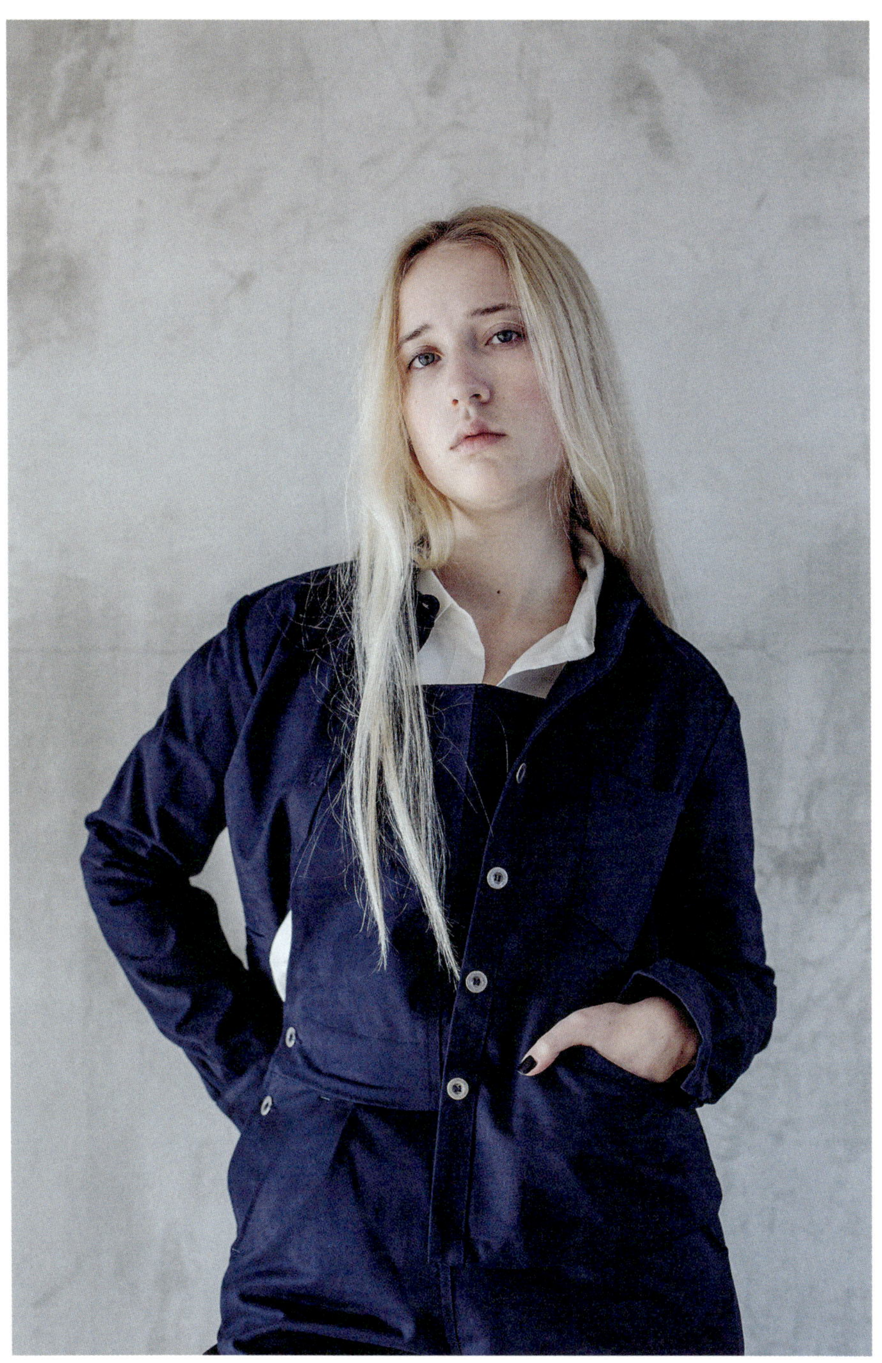

THE FABULOUS MISS K
by Kerry Curl
Norwich, Norfolk

Karen James-Welton, aka The Fabulous Miss K,
is a stylist specialising in vintage. I've photographed
her many times, she's always a good sport.

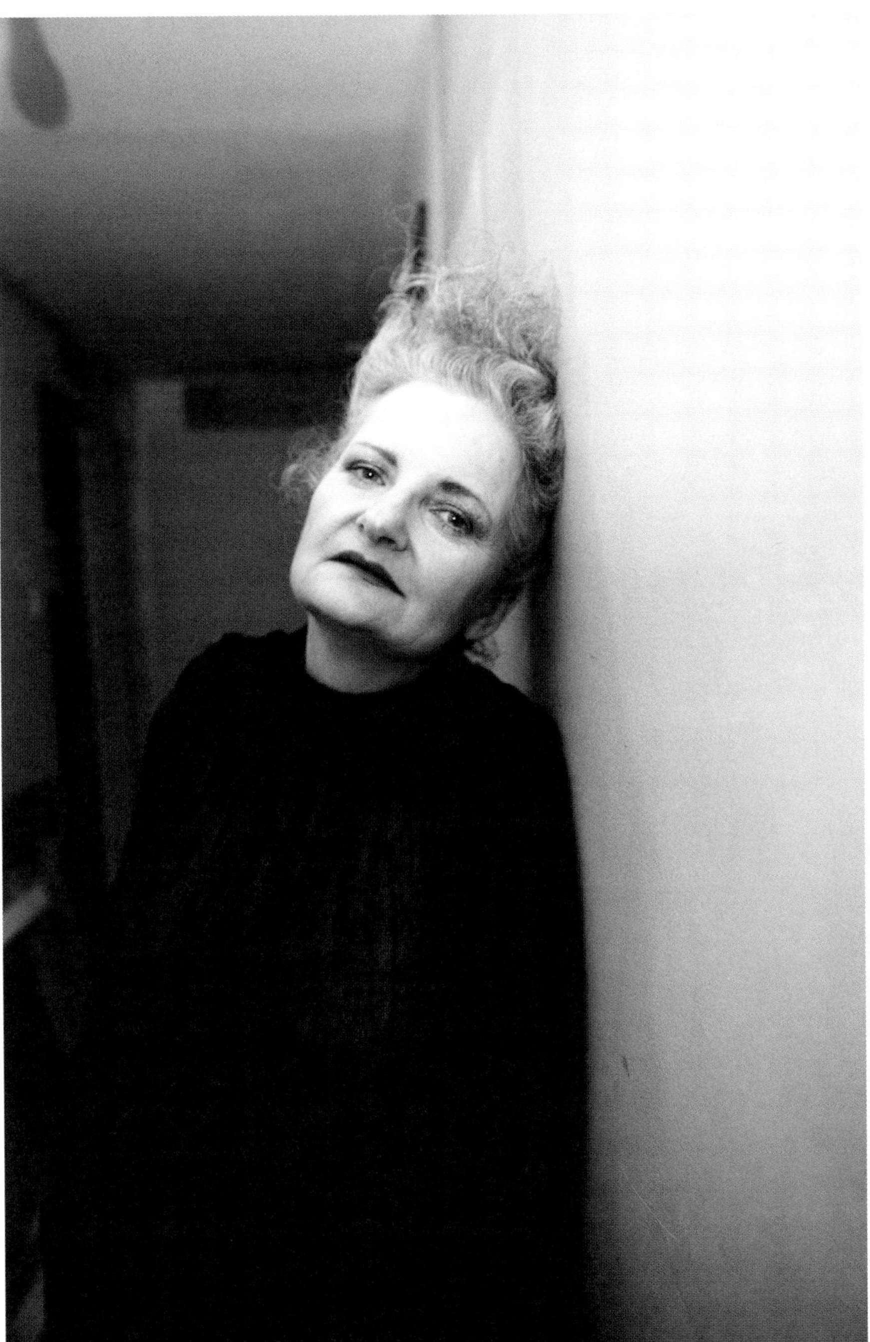

REYNOLD
by Olivia Thompson
London

Reynold is a bodybuilder. He follows an extremely strict
exercise and diet regime involving intense workouts
and periods of fasting.

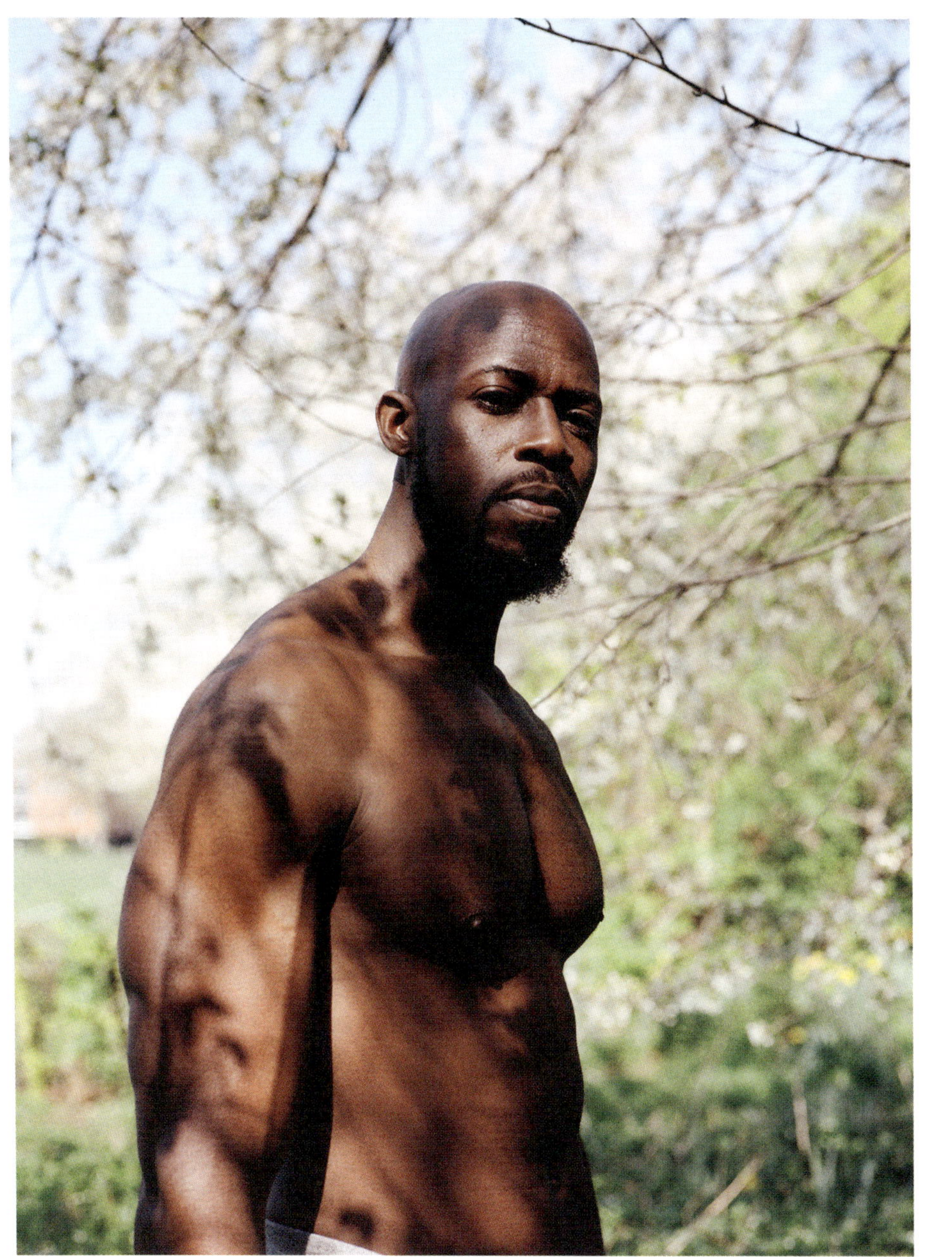

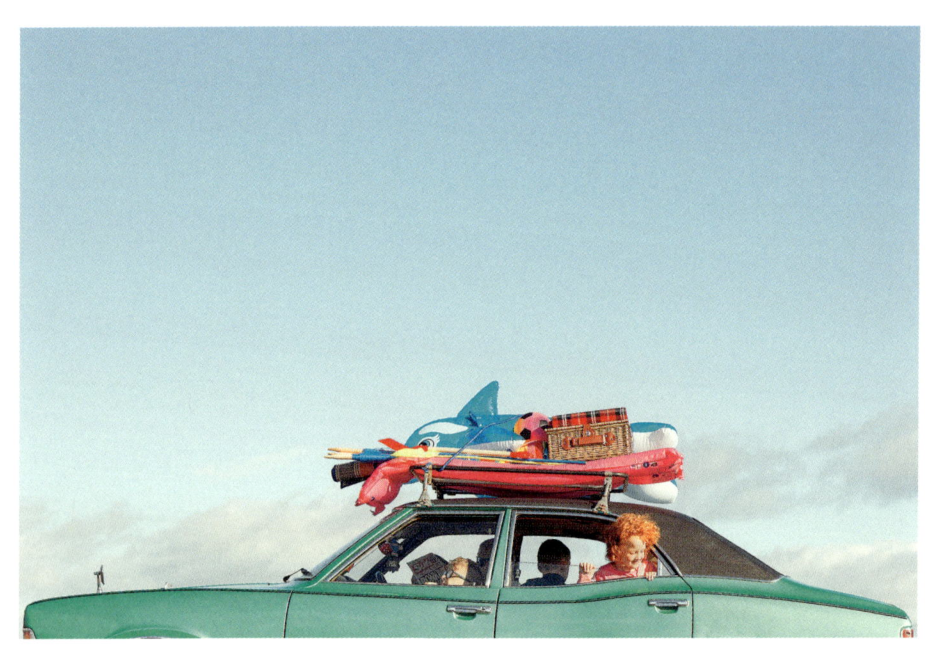

THE HUBBUCKS
by Garrod Kirkwood
Whitley Bay, Tyne and Wear

I joined the Hubbucks on one of their family days out at
the beach. As I shot this scene, I asked them to act like I
wasn't there. The photo reminds me of my own childhood.

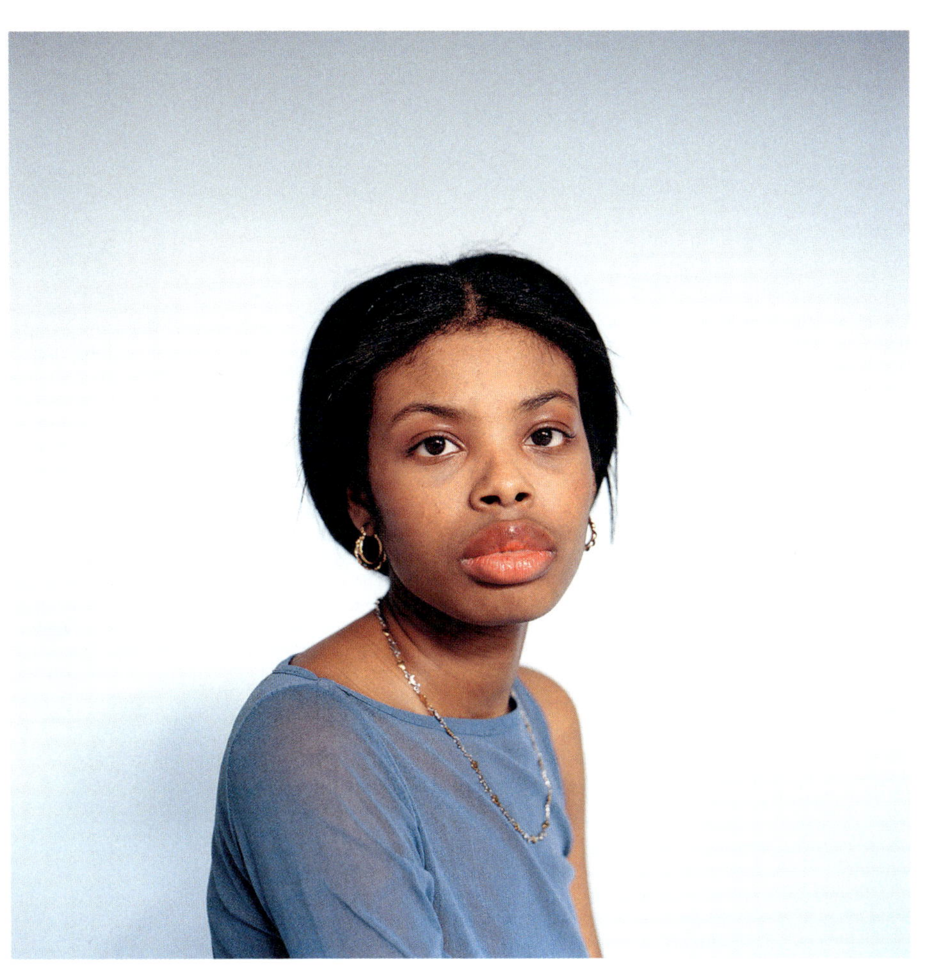

ASHEKA
by Arthur Comely
London

'I got scouted by a model scout when I was 15,
but it wasn't the right time to start modelling because
I was doing my GCSEs. I've wanted to be a model
ever since.' –Asheka

媽媽 (MAMA)
by Naomi Wong
Scunthorpe, North Lincolnshire

My mum has always been stylish and in the 1990s
she owned a fashion boutique with a friend in my native
Hong Kong. She will always be my hero. I am forever
grateful for the love and support she has given my sister
and me as a strong, single mother all these years.

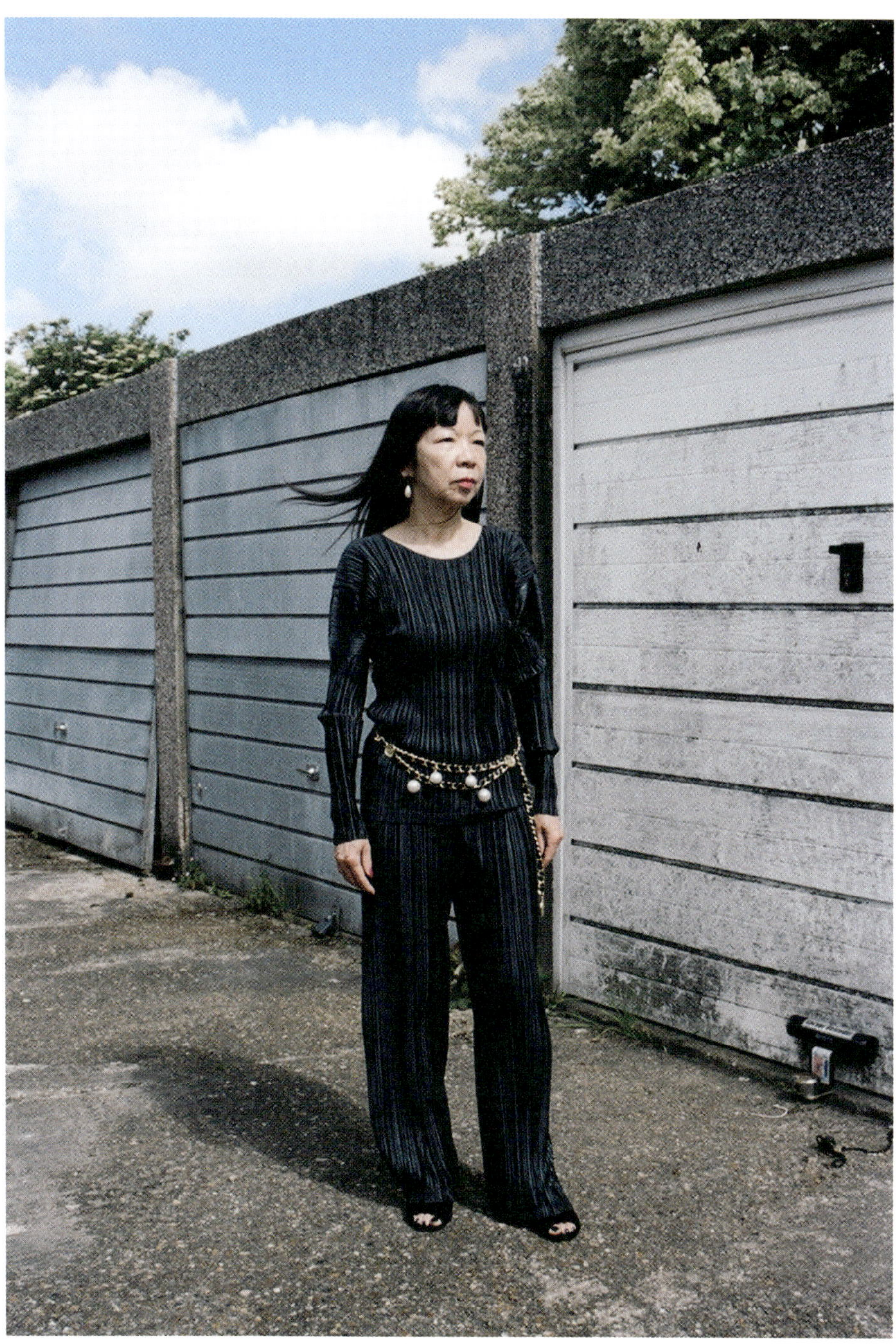

DOUG
by Mark Taylor
Whitley Bay, Tyne and Wear

'I have always swum but only took up sea swimming three
years ago. The pool is good, but cold water, fresh air and
vast skies really make you come alive!' – Doug

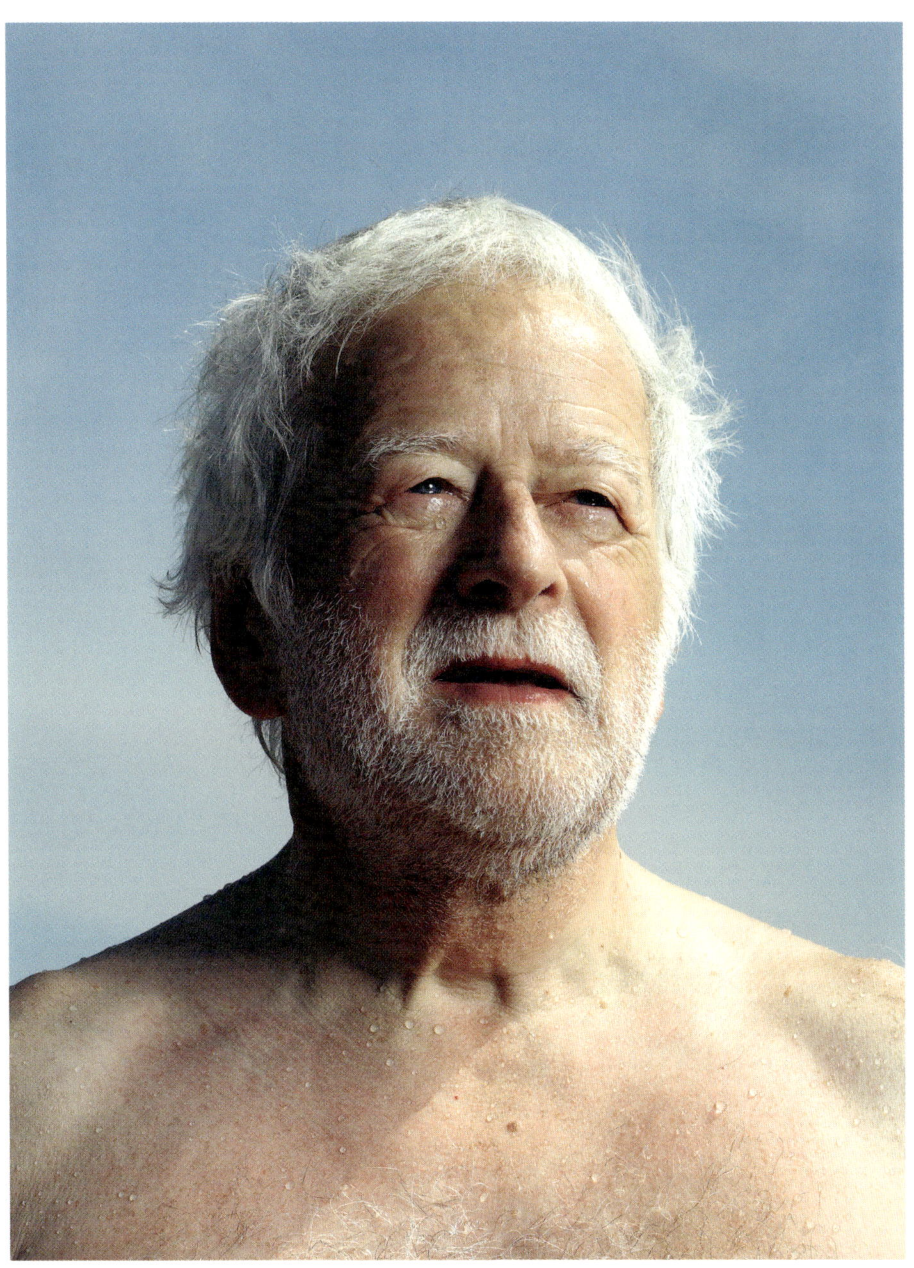

KHADIJAH
by Jay Fenwick
London

Khadijah is full of life and energy. Only seven years old here, she wasn't afraid of anything, not even the camera. We danced, laughed and messed around. Her infectious energy was amazing.

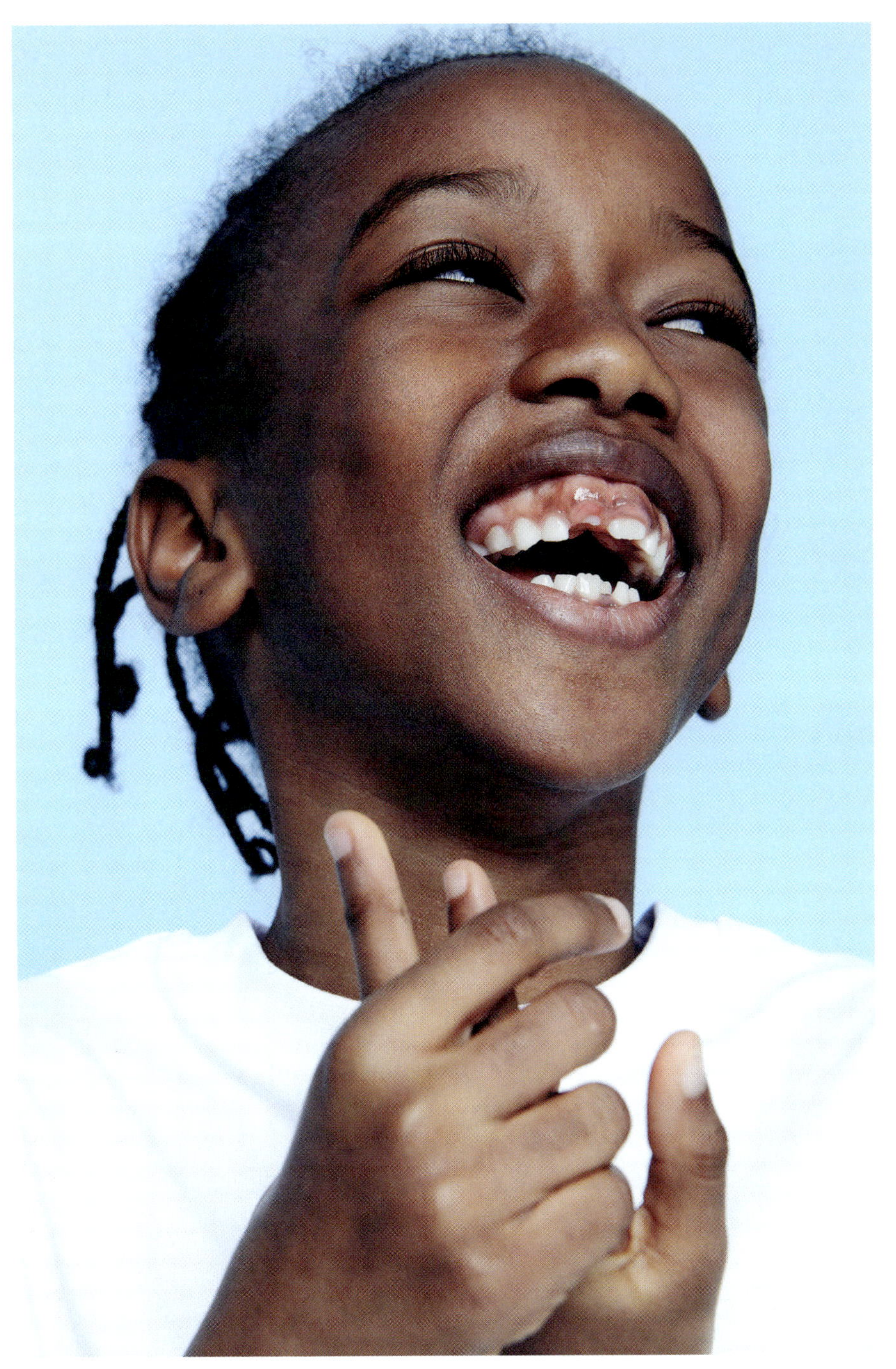

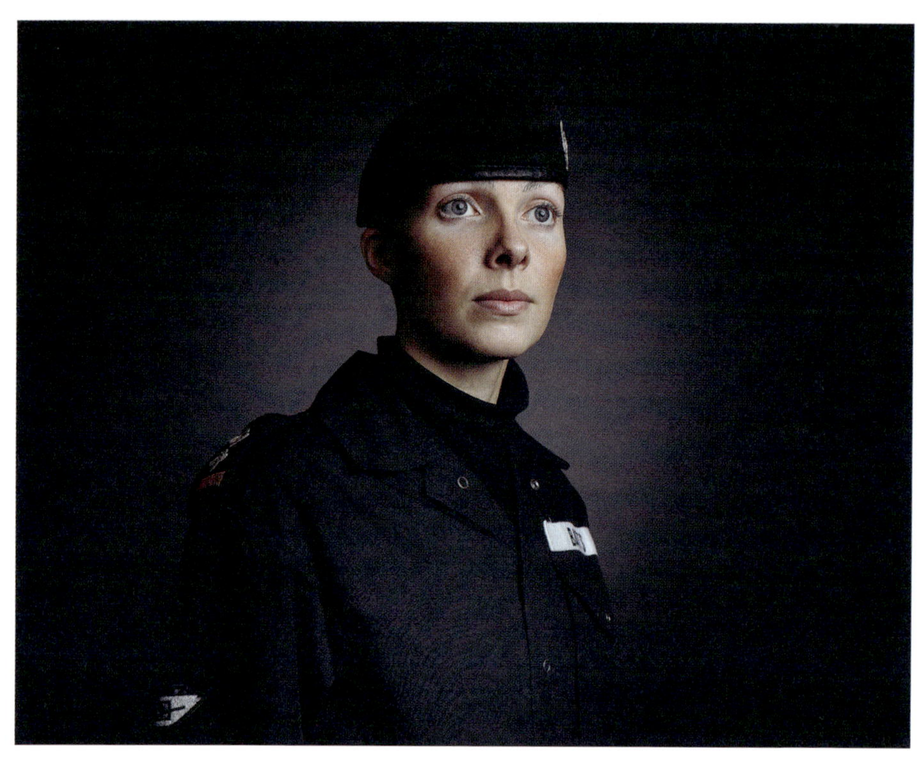

LT BATTS
by Rory Lewis
Tidworth, Hampshire

Lieutenant Sarah Batts is the first female combat officer
and tank commander in British history. Her appointment
came after a long-standing ban on women serving on the
frontline was lifted by the Prime Minister in 2018.

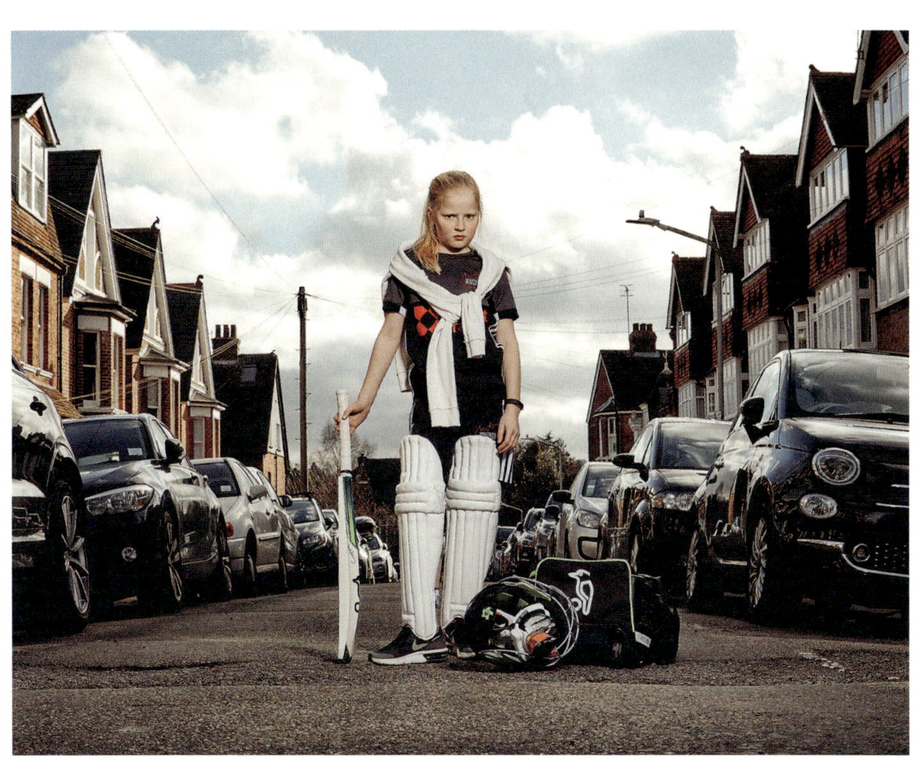

SASKIA WAITING TO LEAVE FOR
CRICKET PRACTICE
by Mark Harrison
Tunbridge Wells, Kent

Saskia, 11, is my neighbour's daughter. Watching my
friends take their girls to cricket practice has made me
appreciate how much more equality there is now
in the UK for young women.

GARY AND ERIN
by Emma Martin
Whitby, North Yorkshire

I took this image during a trip to Whitby Goth Weekend,
a biannual celebration of Gothic and related subcultures.

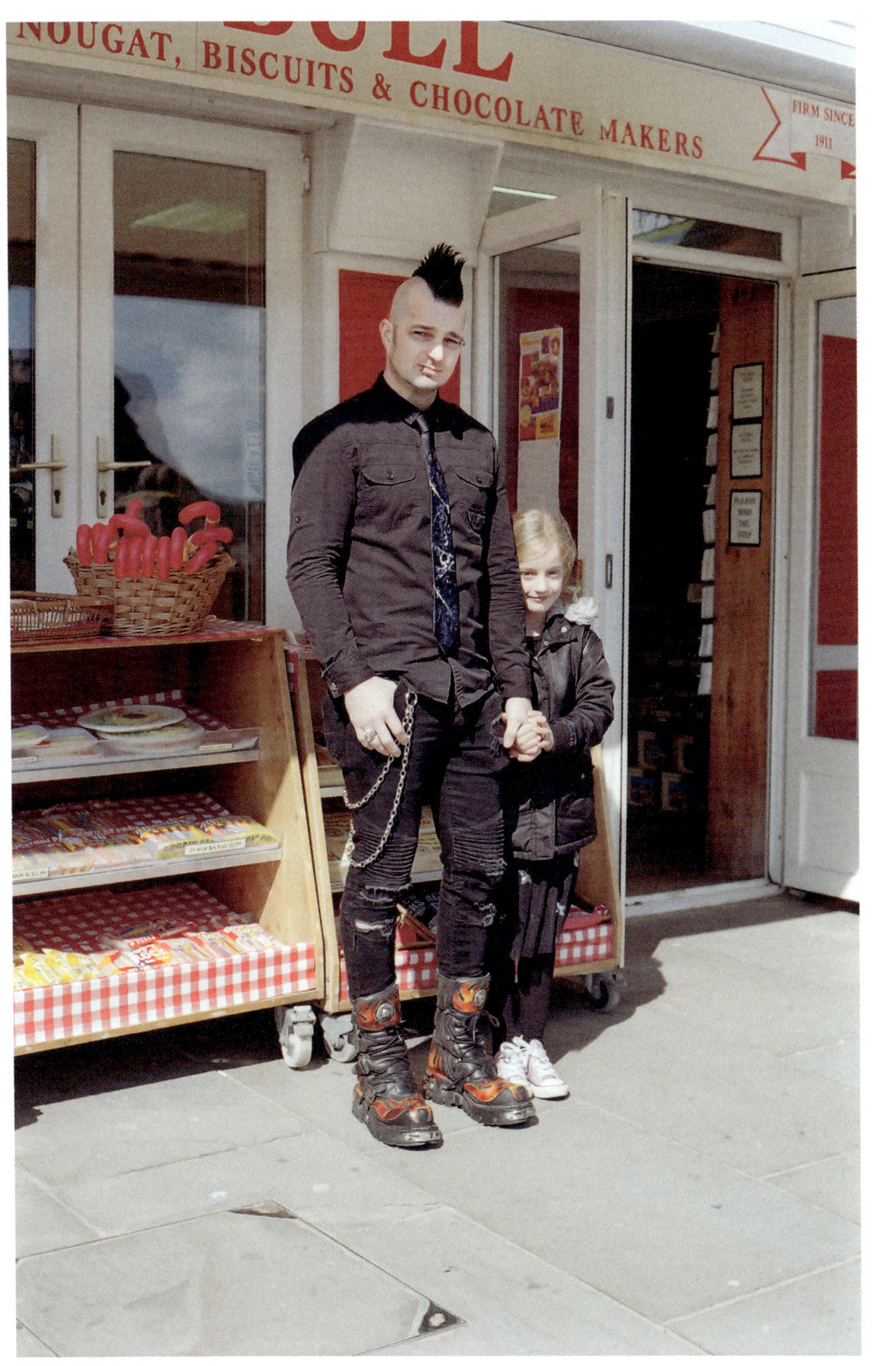
BULL
NOUGAT, BISCUITS & CHOCOLATE MAKERS
FIRM SINCE
1911
PLEASE MIND THE STEP

KASHMALA
by Sandra Mickiewicz
Watford, Hertfordshire

Kashmala had had an accident a few days before our shoot,
which is why she has a bruise under her eye. As I started
to photograph her she became very serious.

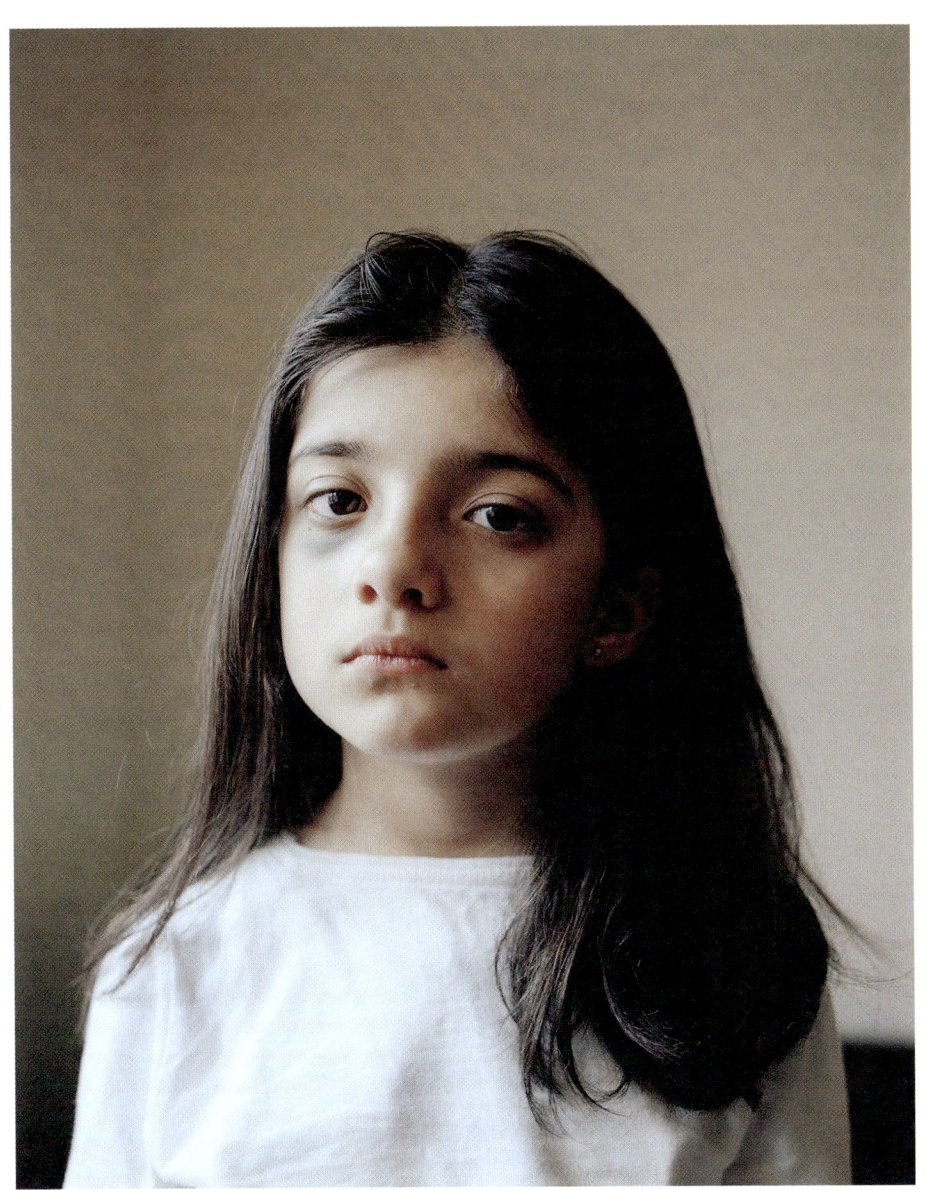

EHA
by Sirli Raitma
London

Originally from Estonia, my mother Eha moved to
London to live with me in 2015. Widowed, suffering
from epilepsy and lacking command of the English
language, she began to suffer from depression. I suggested
making some pictures together, and what started as a bit
of fun has become something of a tonic. My mother is
more confident now and engages more readily
in conversation with strangers.

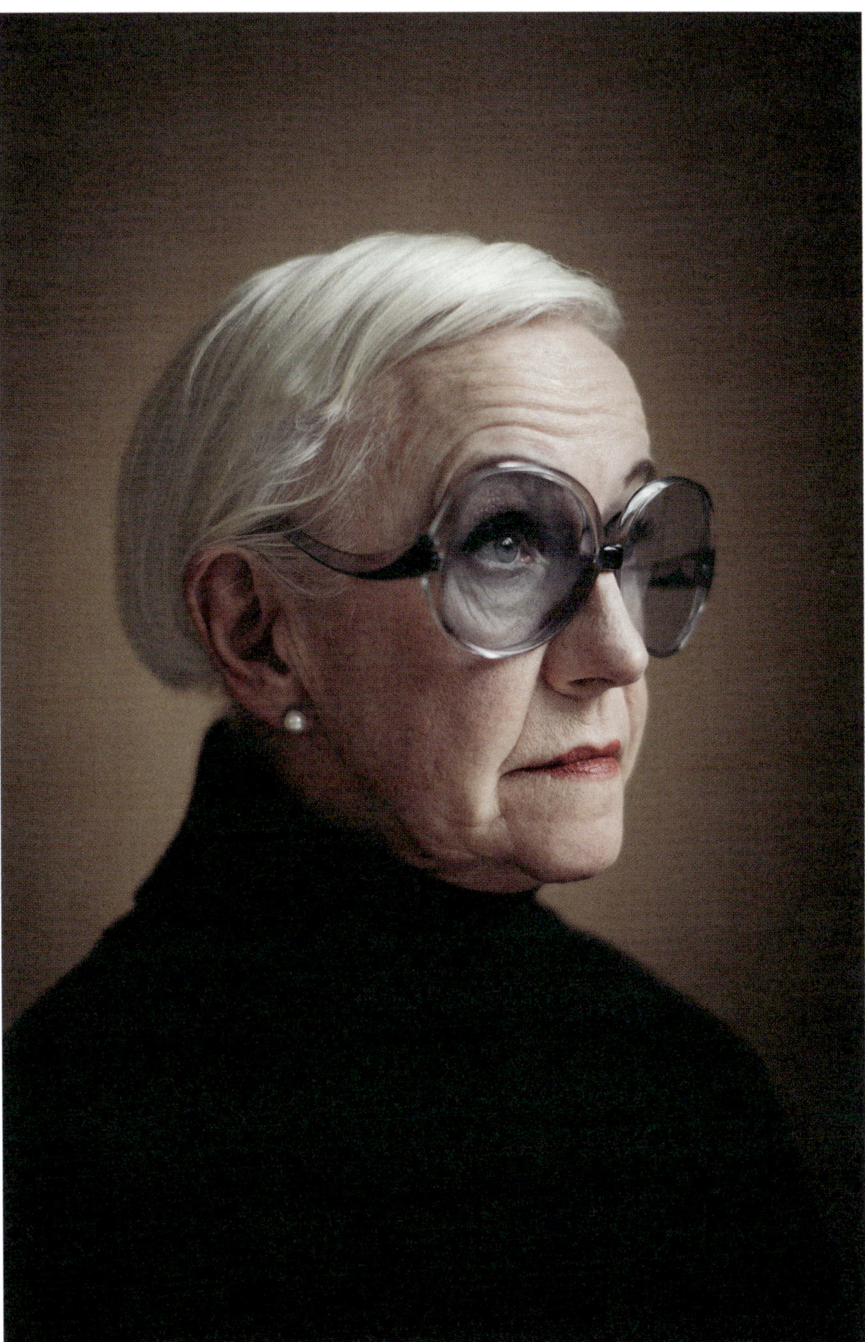

DANNY THE WELD
by Alastair Cook
Dunbar, East Lothian

Danny welds for the fishermen of Dunbar. I took up
residence beside them in 2013. Always the first person
to offer me his company, Danny was kind where others
were gruff, open where others were closed.

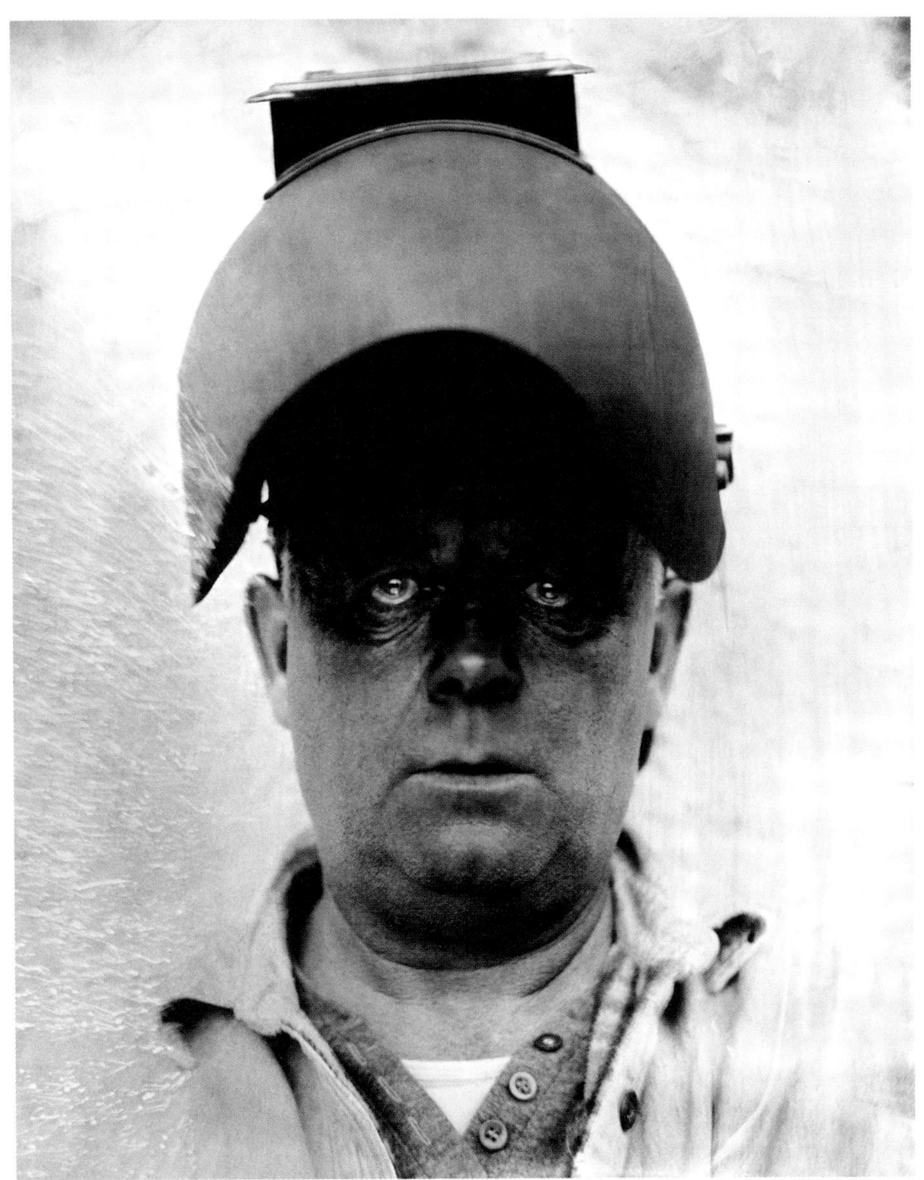

DENZIL
by Olivia Thompson
London

I saw Denzil playing catch with friends after school
in a park. He told me he was going to American football
trials the following day.

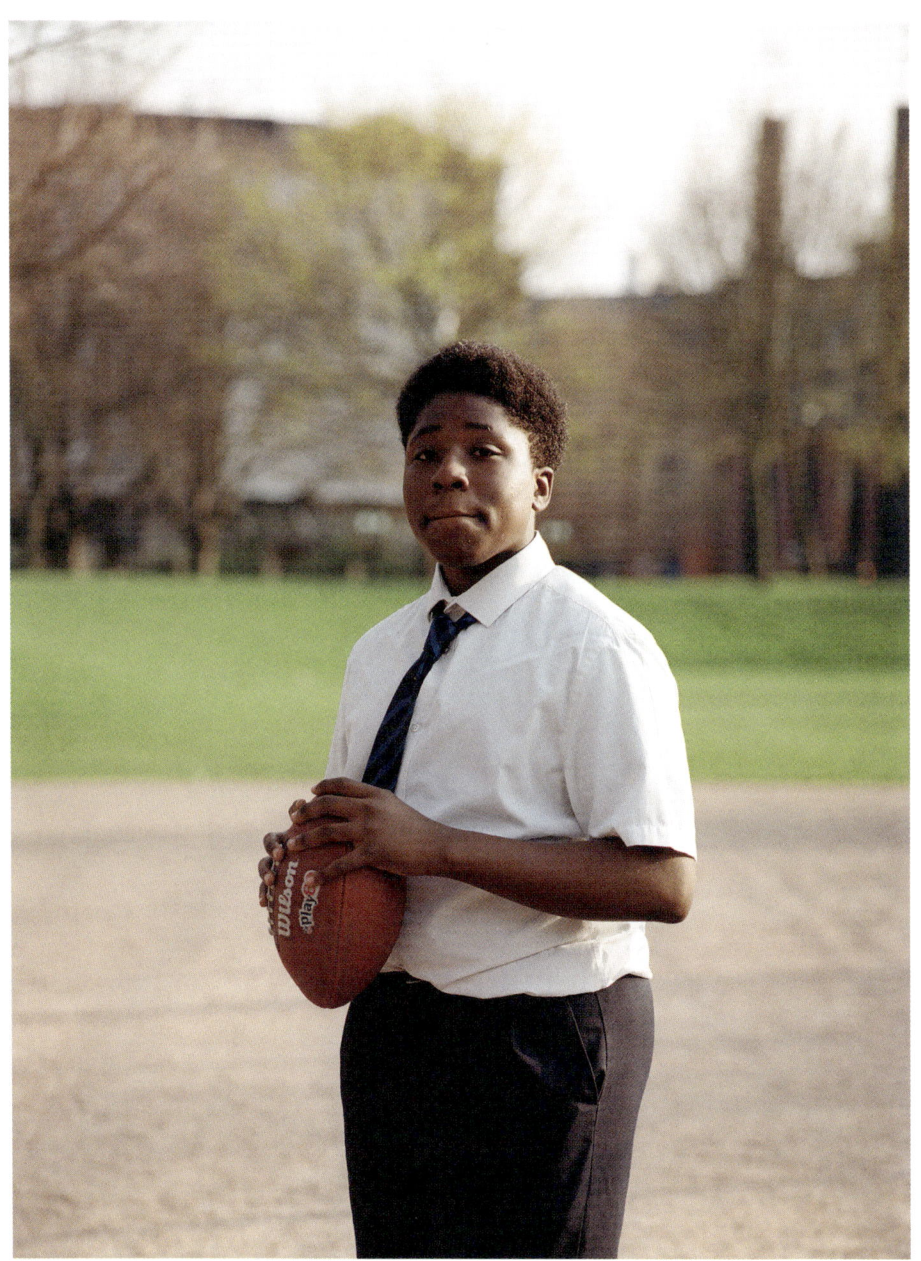

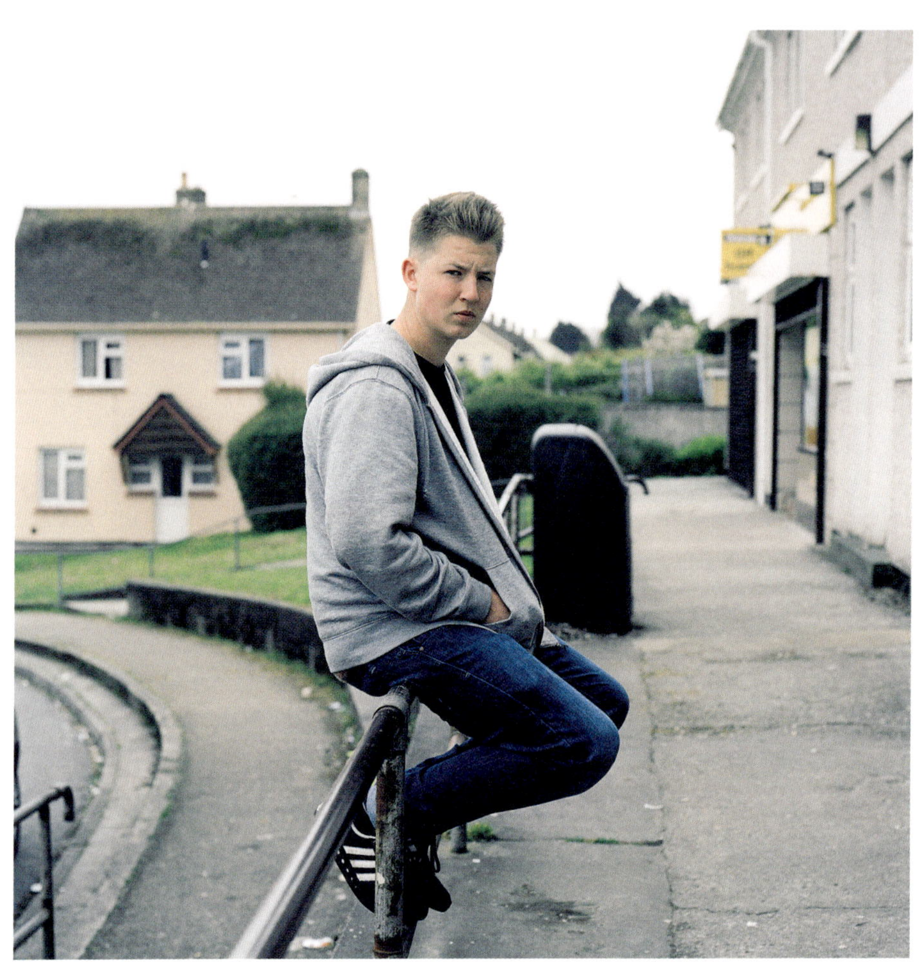

DIAMOND IN THE ROUGH
by Zachary Crawley
Falmouth, Cornwall

I met Aj at Falmouth's Old Hill estate, which has
a colourful reputation. Aj and his friends are aware of
what it means to be associated with the area.

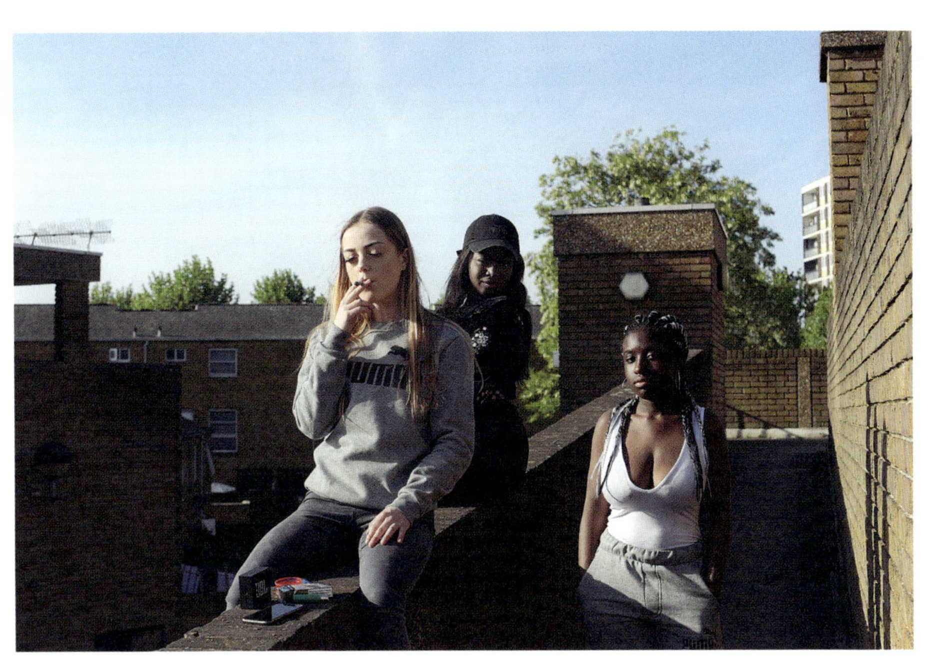

INES, TAMZIN AND MILDRED
by Christian Sinibaldi
London

I was fascinated by the girls' look and attitude.
They call themselves the 'Backshop Bitches'.

GIUMA
by Murray Ballard
Brighton, East Sussex

Giuma runs a garage around the corner from where I live.
When I told him about my idea for a project about jobs
threatened by increasing automation he welcomed
me into his place of work.

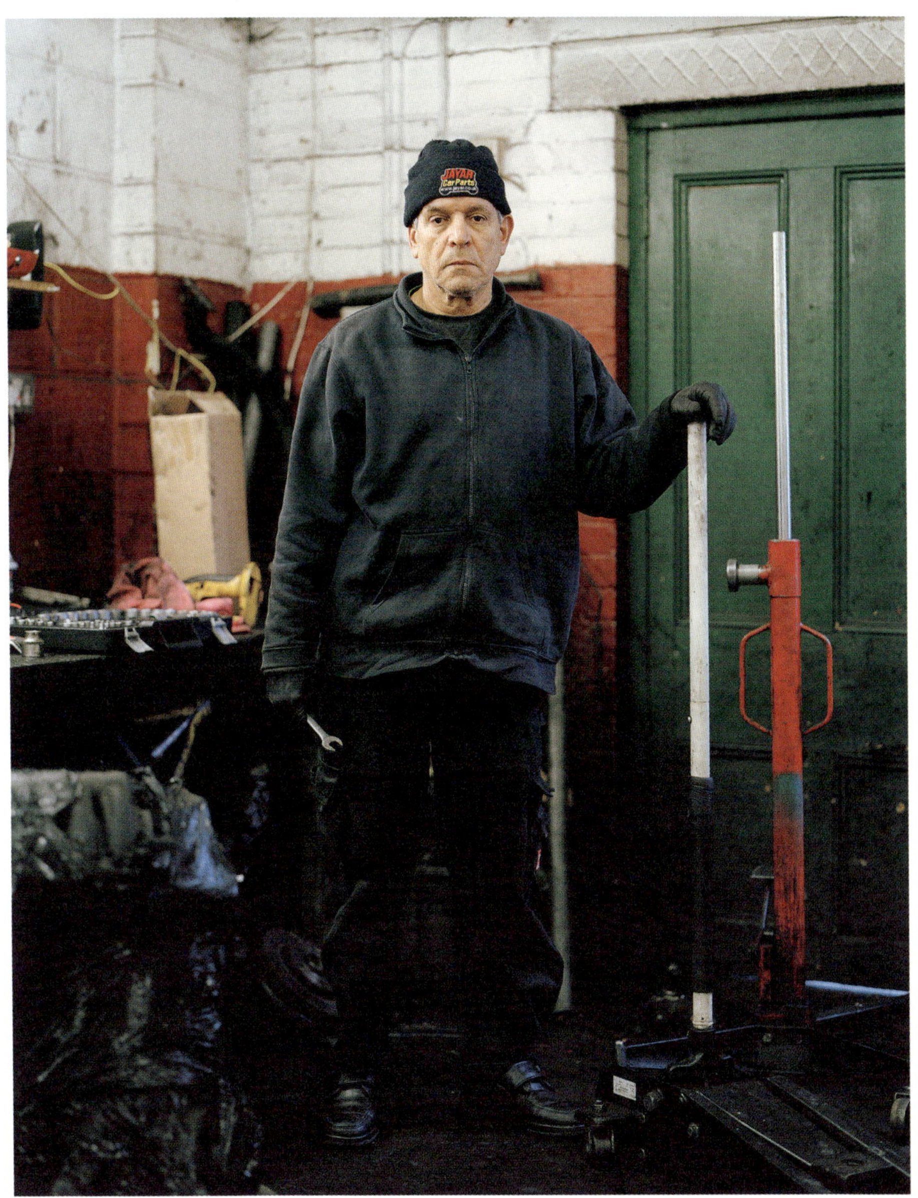

KEVIN
by Sandra Mickiewicz
Jaywick, Essex

Kevin suffers from epilepsy and is unable to work.
He lives in Jaywick, one of the most deprived places to live
in England. I gained the trust of the local community
and made a series of portraits of residents.

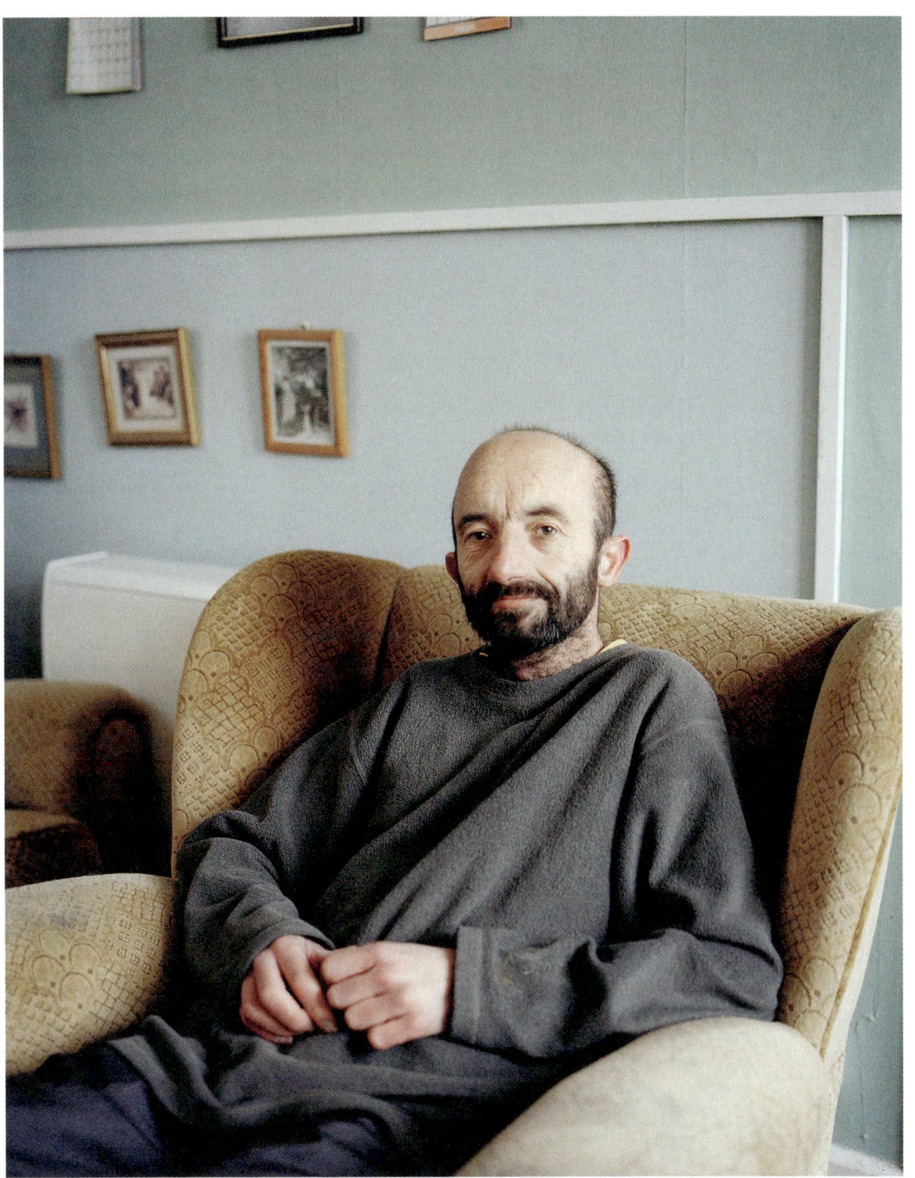

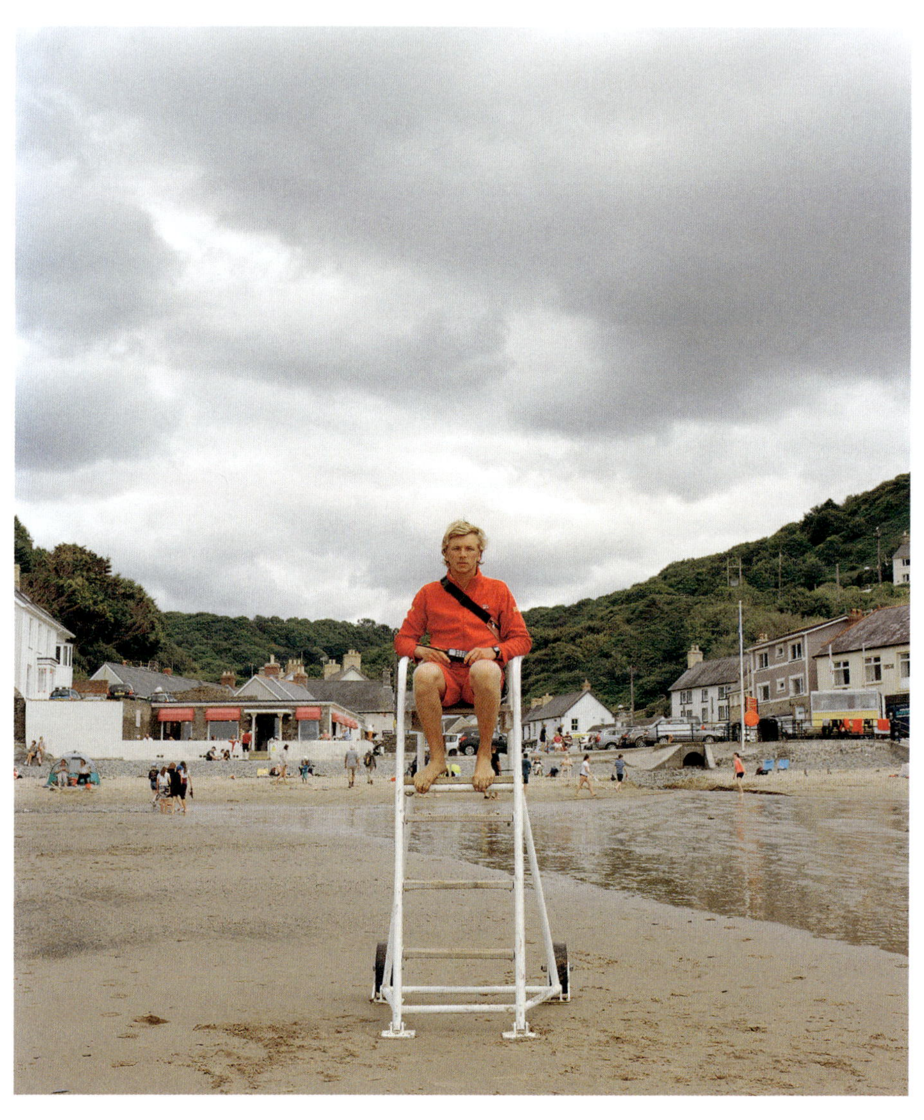

THE WATER'S EDGE
by Leia Morrison
Llangrannog, Ceredigion

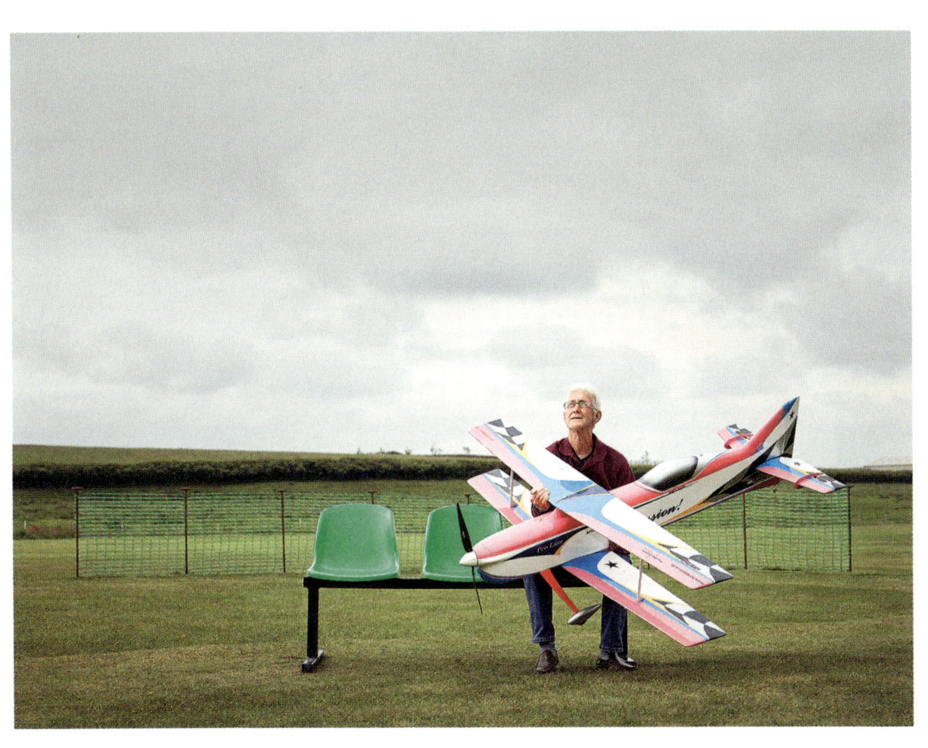

AGES OF US: JIM
by Dylan Collard
Huddersfield, West Yorkshire

'When I'm flying a jet, the adrenalin kick is unbelievable.
It sounds like the real thing, it looks like the real thing,
it's brilliant.' – Jim

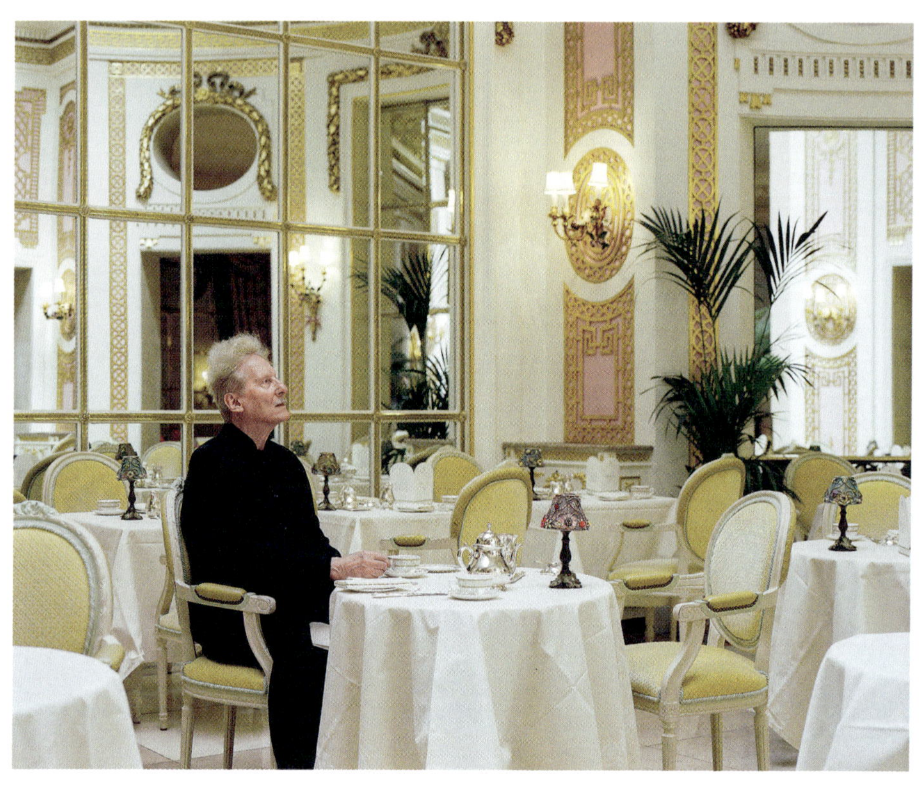

MICHAEL JOSEPH DEAN
by Emile Holba
London

I wanted to make a portrait of my dear friend Michael
to celebrate his 80th birthday. Keen to shoot in a grand
location, we secured The Palm Court at The Ritz.

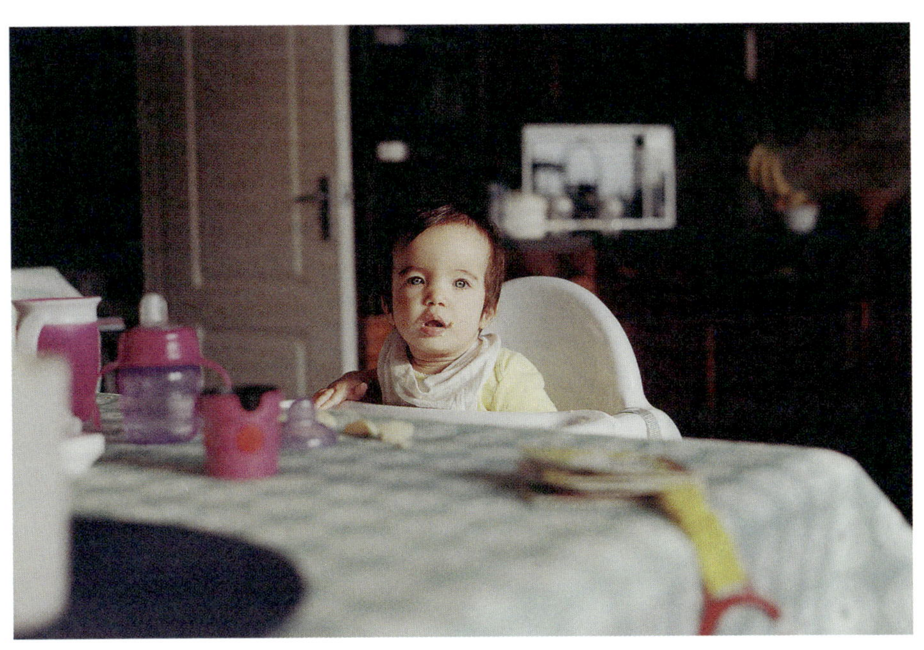

DOTTIE HAVING BREAKFAST
by Matt MacPake
Carlisle, Cumbria

My daughter eating breakfast one summer morning.
Having our first child has resulted in some really difficult
times, but this was one of those moments when, you feel,
everything will be OK.

ANTHONY
by Kate Peters
Orleton, Herefordshire

'My dream is to be successful at what I do,
whether it's barbering or dressage. I try to be
the best I can at both.' – Anthony

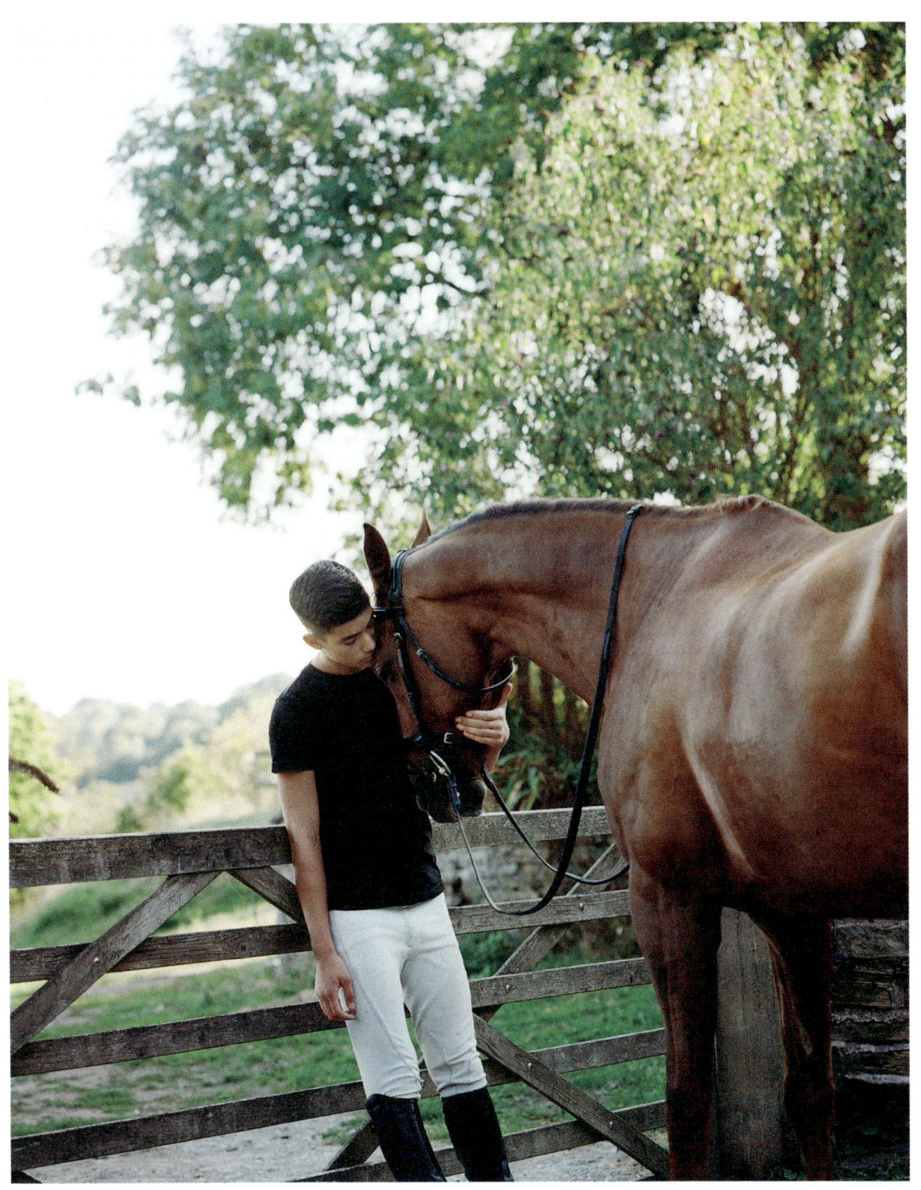

LIKE FATHER, LIKE SON
by Chris Frazer Smith
Cambridge, Cambridgeshire

I grew up in a farming environment in Norfolk where
I spent many hours 'beating' (the process of forcing birds
up into the air) so I felt comfortable photographing these
men during a shoot. It was the son's first time shooting
and the men spoke about the importance of rural skills
that go back decades.

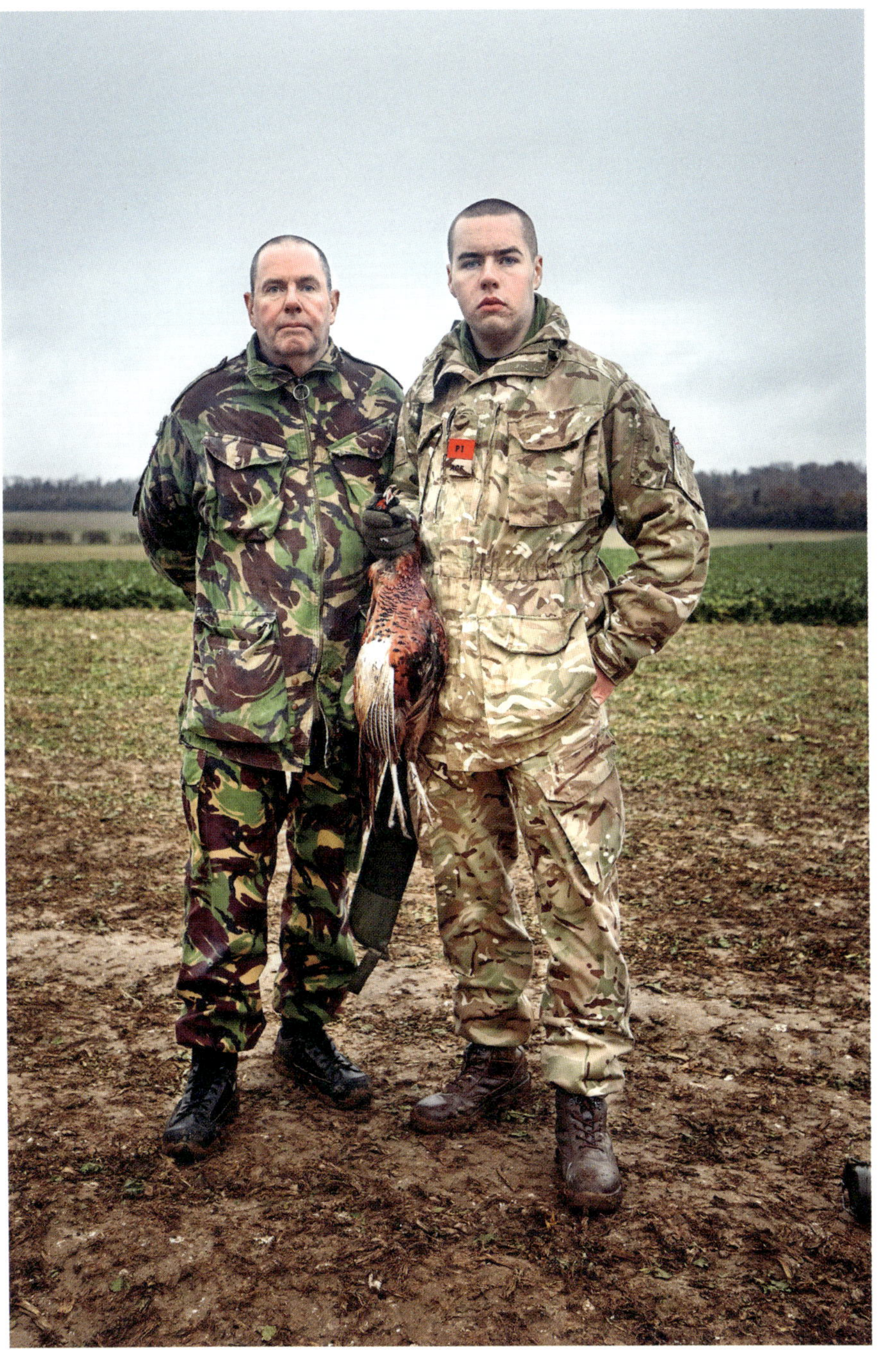

GRANDAD IN THE GARDEN
by Thomas Duffield
Garforth, West Yorkshire

This is my grandad, a retired farmer. After gradually
losing mobility in his left hand, he claimed with great
sincerity and reflection that this ailment is his first
sign of 'becoming an old man'.

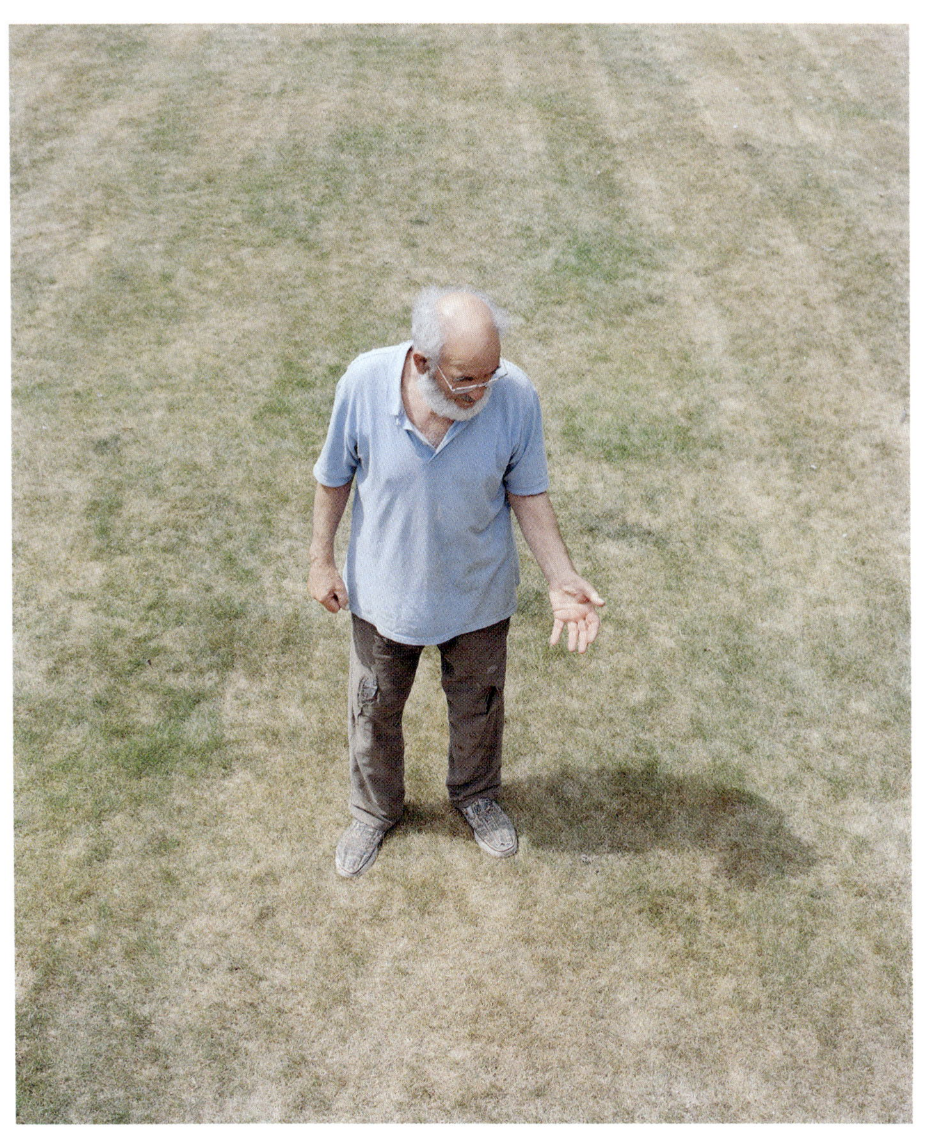

JIM
by Nick Goring
Harrogate, North Yorkshire

Jim was visiting the Harrogate Autumn Flower Show
and found this huge flower in a bin, round the back of
the competition area. He couldn't believe his luck.

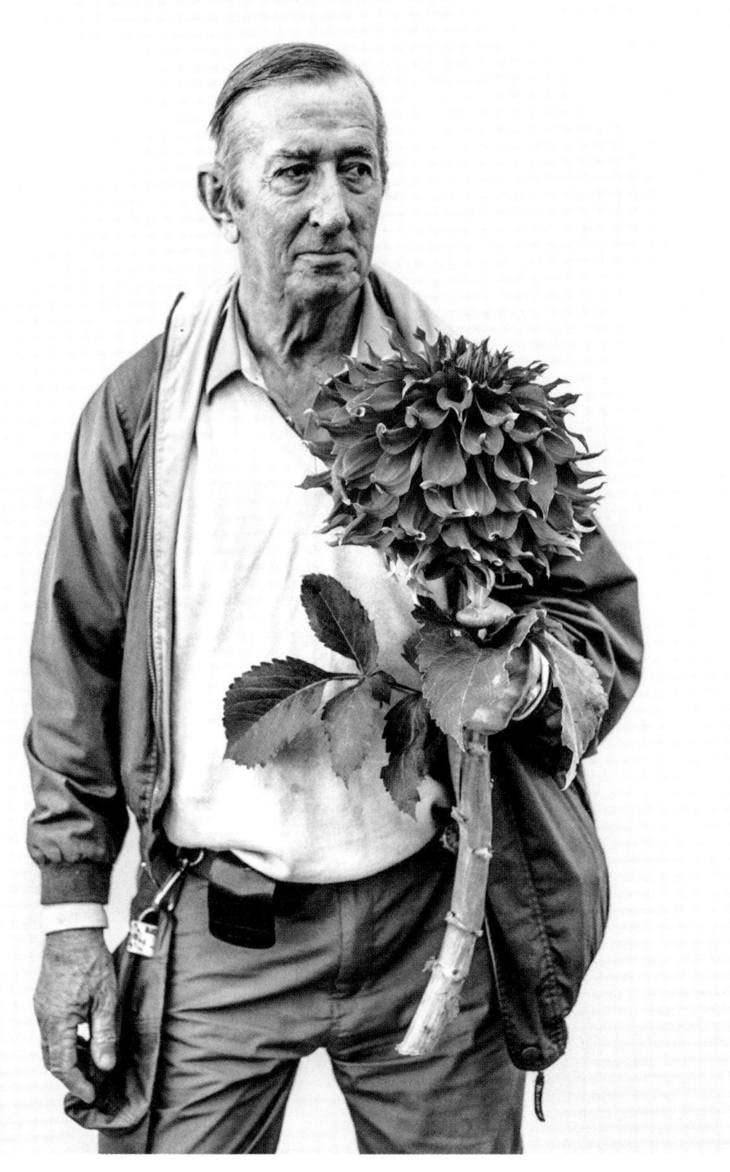

MUNA
by Anna Brooks
London

Muna is an entrepreneur and mum of two from Somalia.
With support from The Entrepreneurial Refugee Network,
she is preparing to launch her new business, a cleaning
service that provides stable employment for
disadvantaged women and refugees.

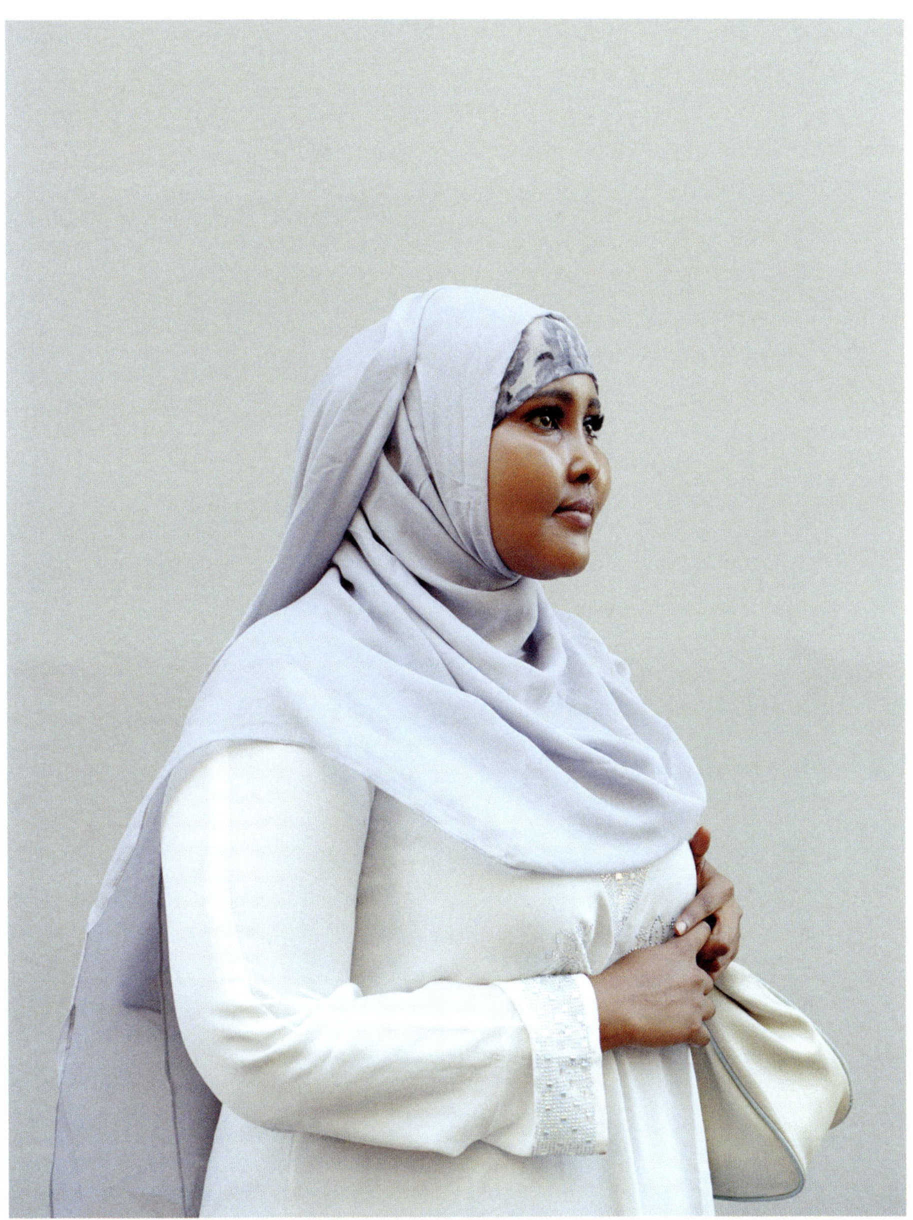

JAYDEN
by Camilla Murray
Shaftesbury, Dorset

Jayden, nine, is my nephew. He is cheeky, kind,
loving and very entertaining.

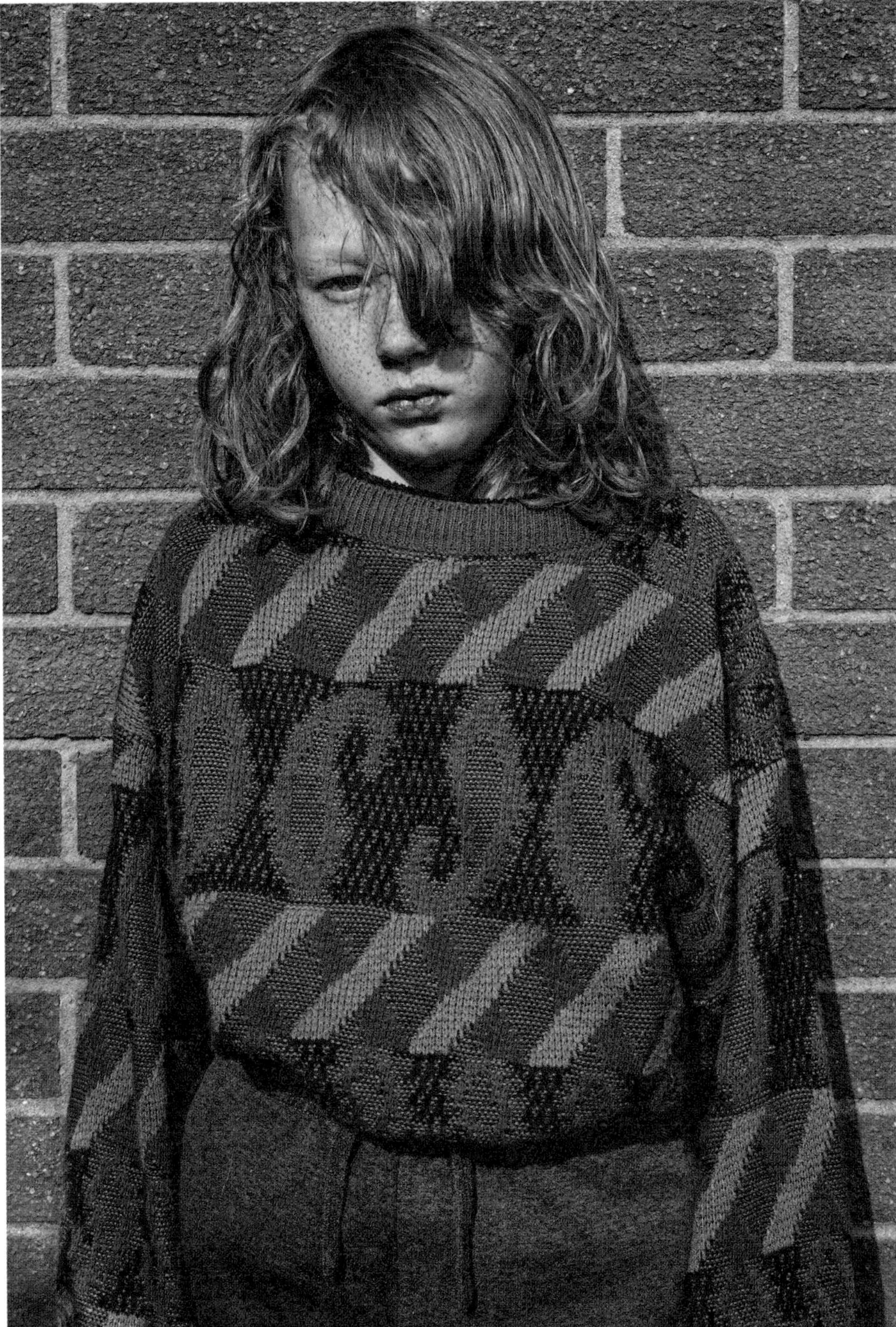

MY MOTHER AND HER HOME
by Thomas Duffield
Garforth, West Yorkshire

For many years my mother Gill raised my sister
and me as a single mum. She also worked two jobs.
Making this portrait was a way of expressing the deep
gratitude I feel towards my mother.

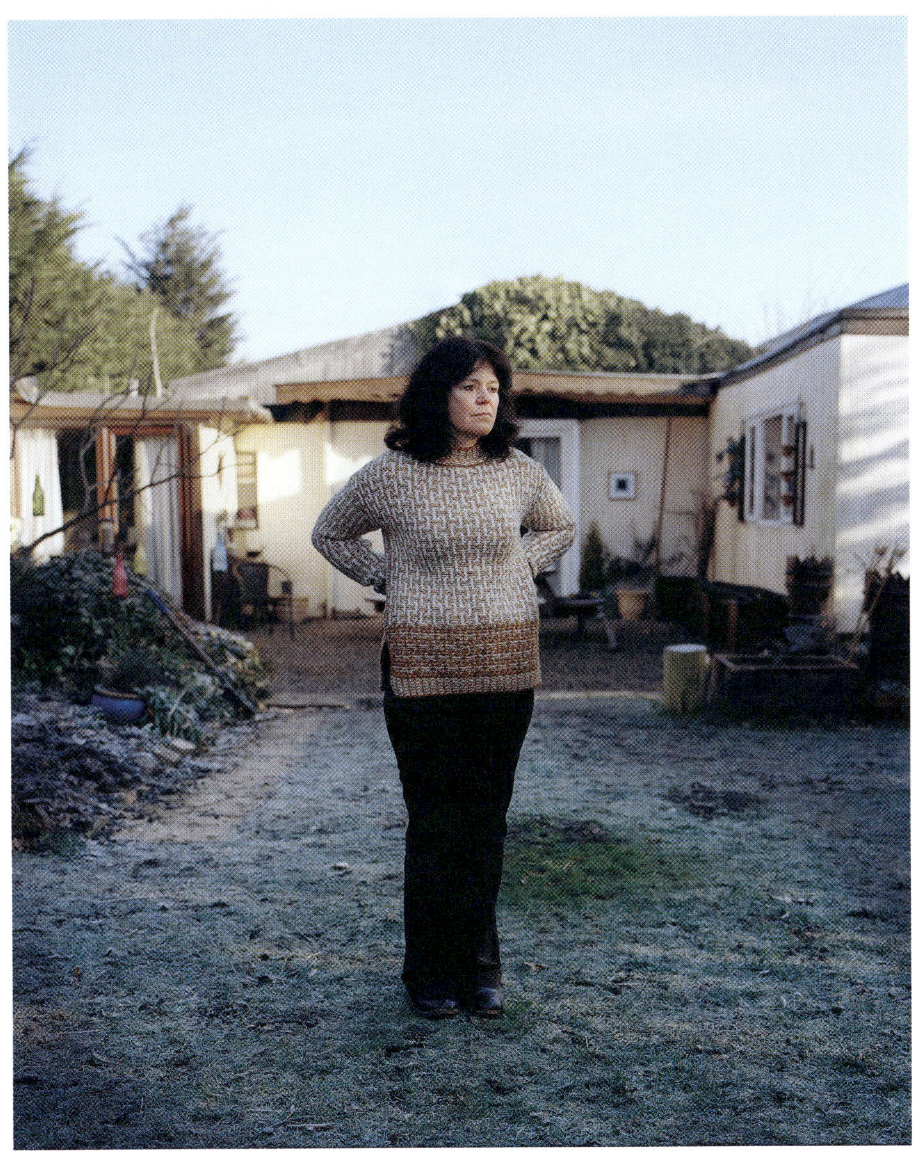

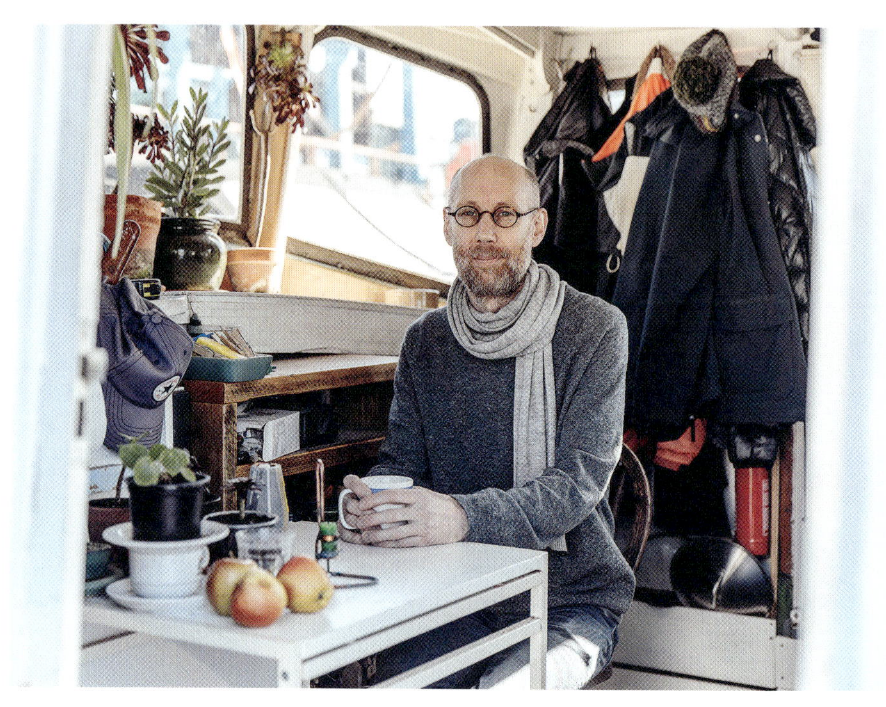

IAN
by Paul Driver
Bristol

I'm intrigued by people and their habitats, particularly
small spaces. There is a big community of people who live
on boats near my workplace. I decided to make portraits
of some of the residents in their floating homes.

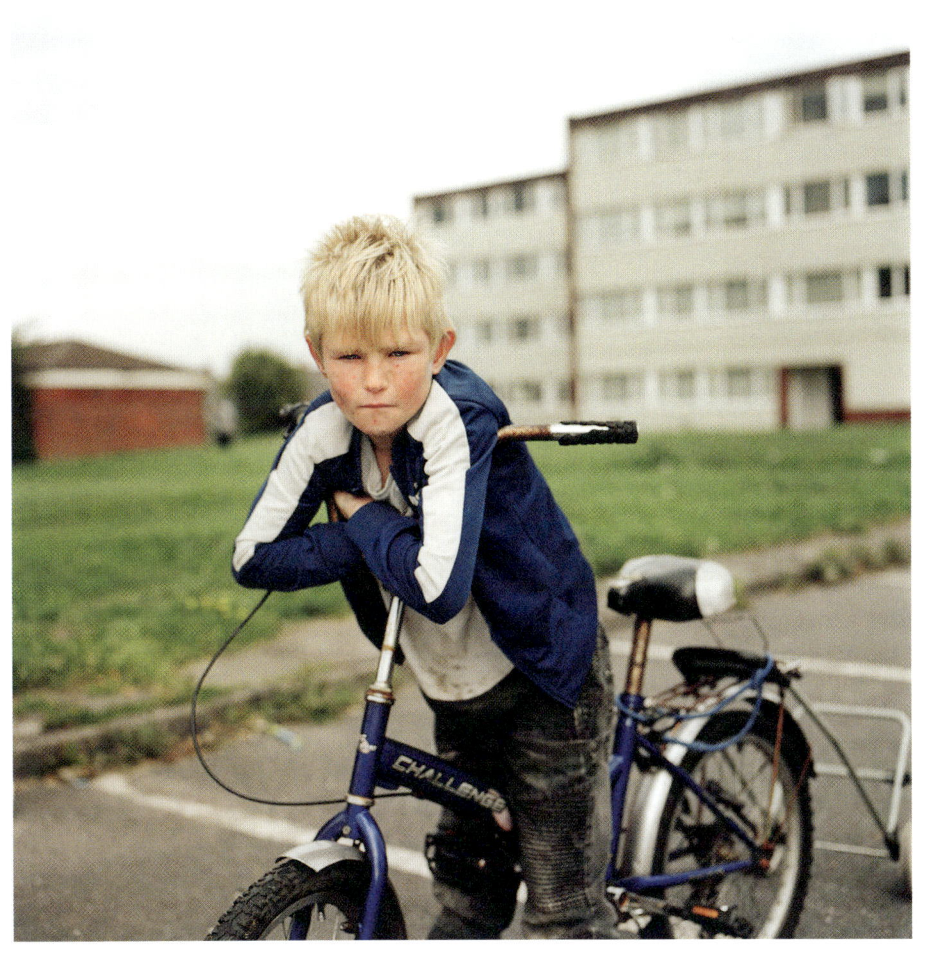

CALLUM
by Laura Pannack
Tipton, West Midlands

I've been exploring what it's like to grow up in Tipton
and what it means to feel 'grown up'. Working with young
people in the area, we have been shooting at their
favourite hangouts.

DOROTHY TYLER MBE
by Katie Hyams
Sanderstead, Surrey

Dorothy Tyler, pictured here at the age of 92, was a
British athlete who competed in two Olympic Games
(1936 and 1948). The first British woman to win
an individual Olympic medal in athletics, she also
set a world record in high jump. Fun and feisty,
Tyler was really happy to be photographed and
shared stories about meeting Hitler and Goebbels.

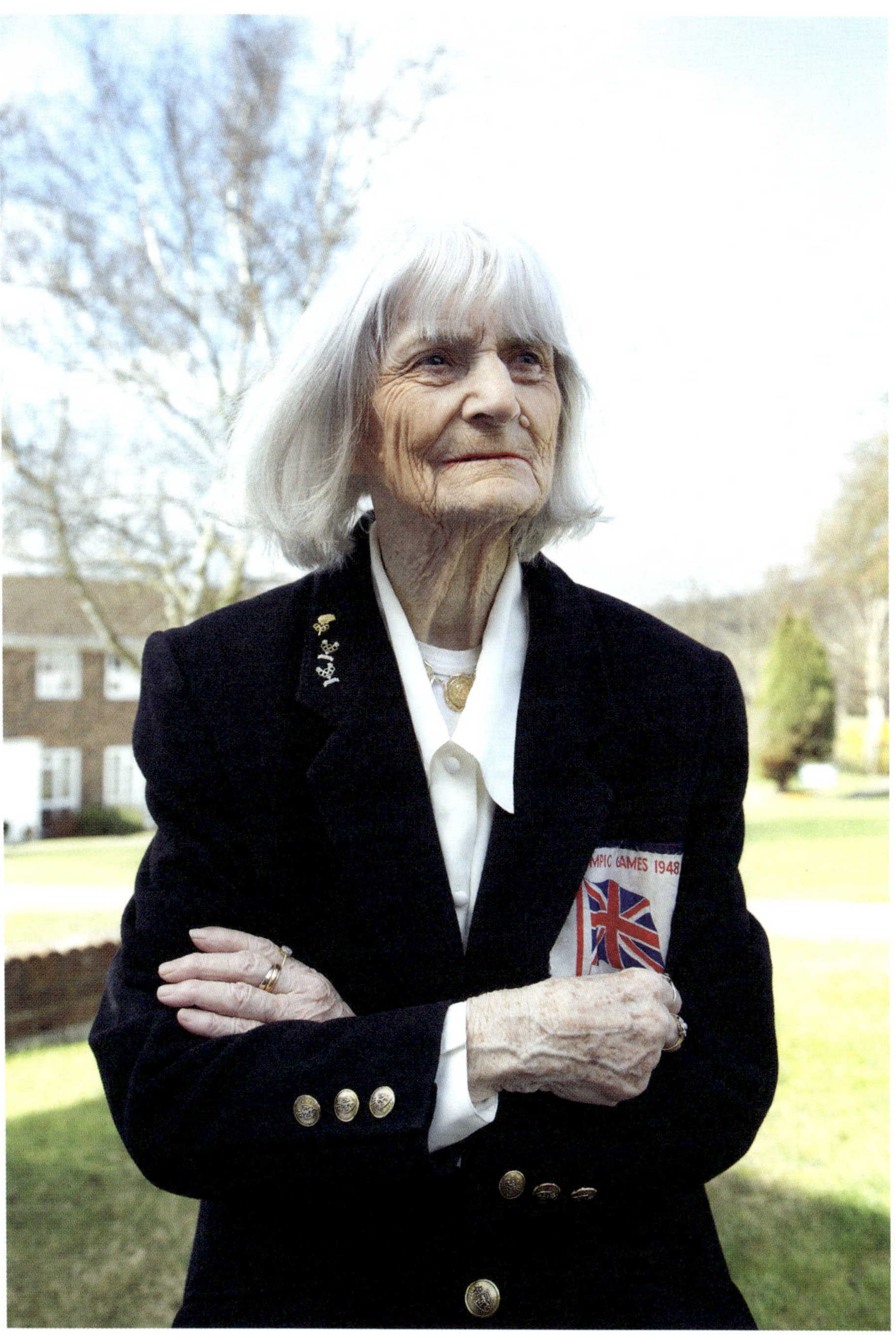
MPIC GAMES 1948

BEX
by Yasmin Elizabeth Gunston
Newquay, Cornwall

I started my project about women after watching the
ITV show, *Love Island*. The women on the show generally
represent just one body type and I wanted to celebrate
all body types.

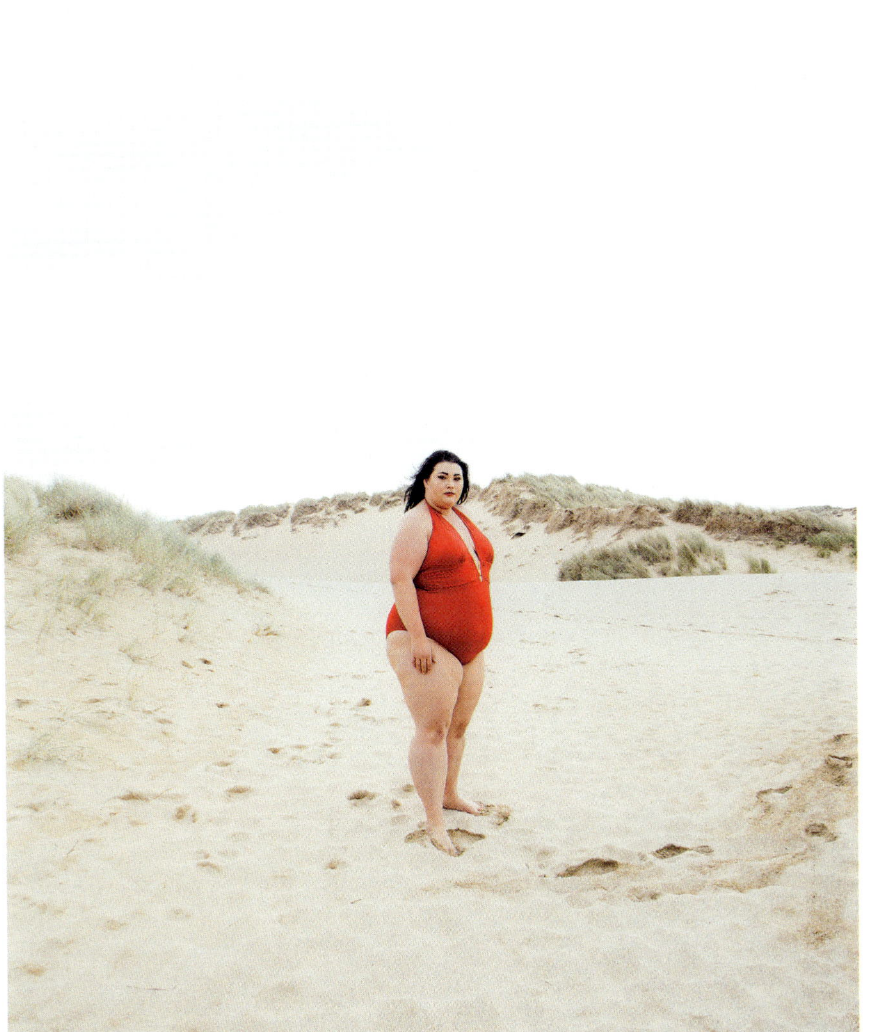

WEE MUCKERS: YOUTH OF BELFAST
by Toby Binder
Belfast, County Antrim

A group of friends gathers at Woodvale Park on the night
of 11th July to celebrate the victory of Protestant King
William of Orange over Catholic King James II at
the Battle of the Boyne in 1690.

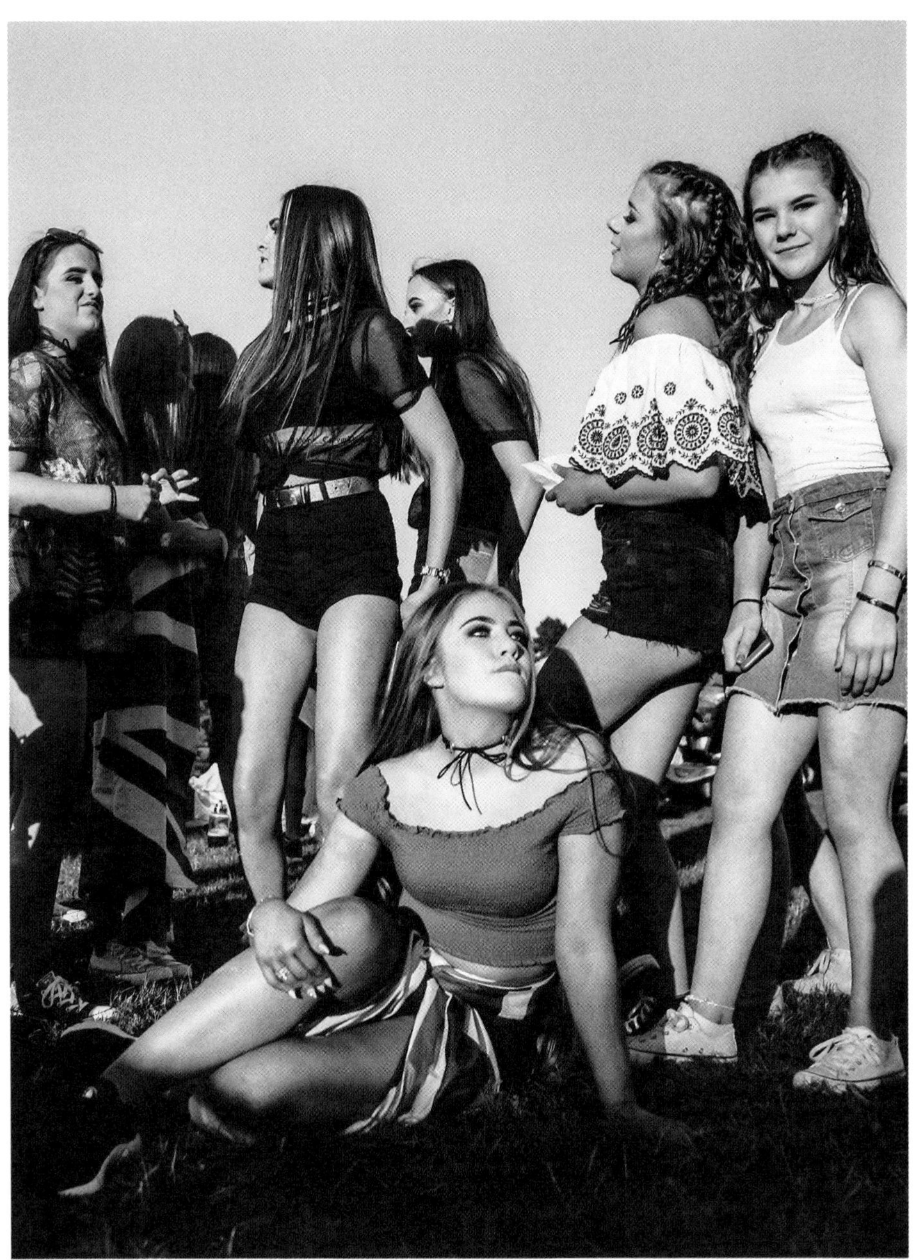

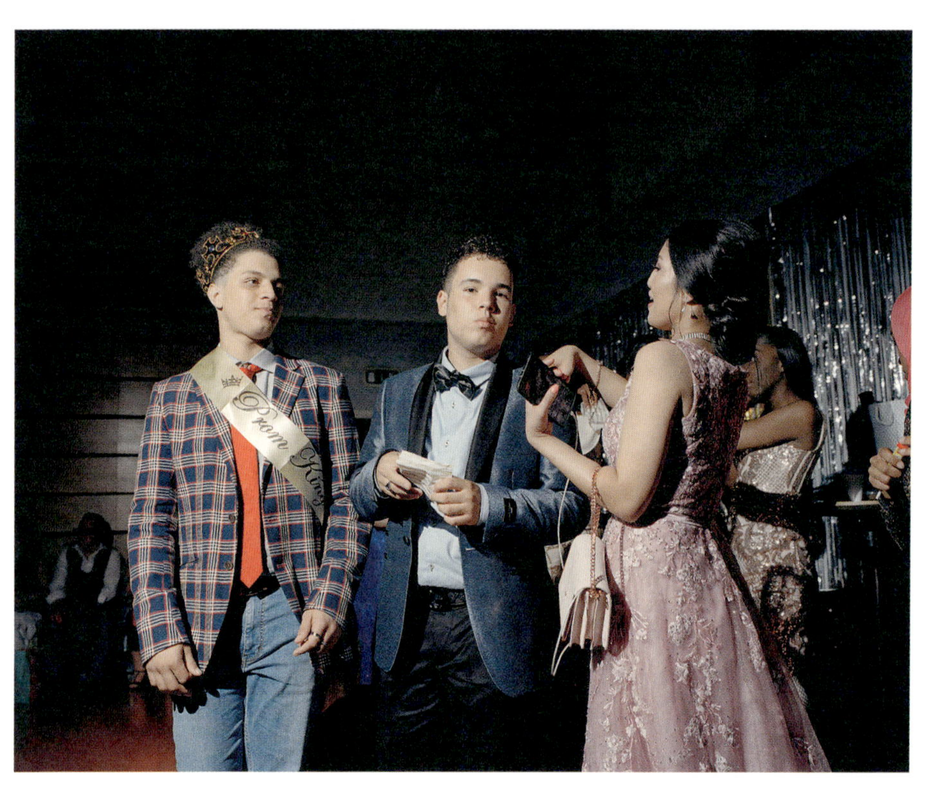

PROM NIGHT
by Lewis Khan
London

I love the mixture of performance and self-consciousness
in this image. There's a tenderness behind the showy façade
that reminds me of being a teenager.

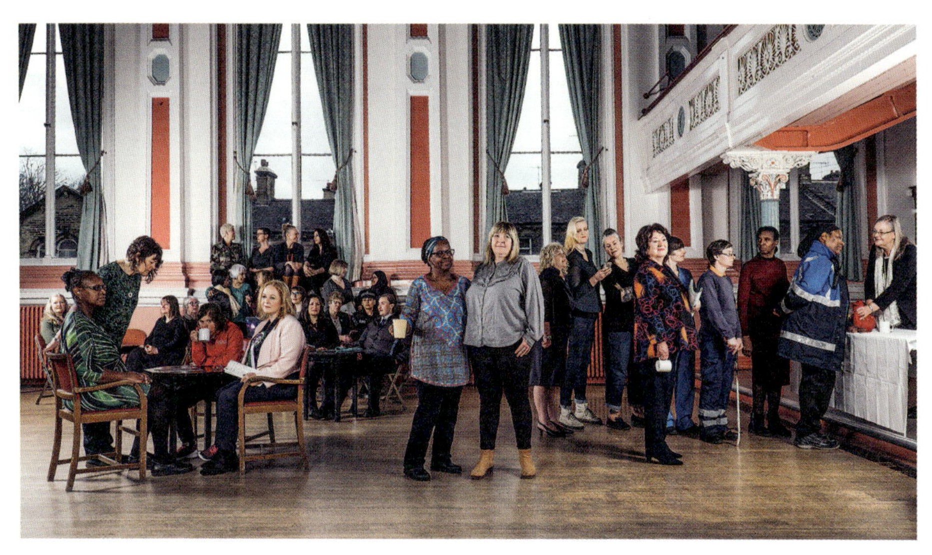

PHOENIX WOMEN, 100 YEARS ON
by Carolyn Mendelsohn
Bradford, West Yorkshire

This image reimagines Flora Lion's 1918 painting *Women's
Canteen at Phoenix Works, Bradford*. Many modern-day
heroines feature, including a bus driver, midwife,
a police officer and local councillor.

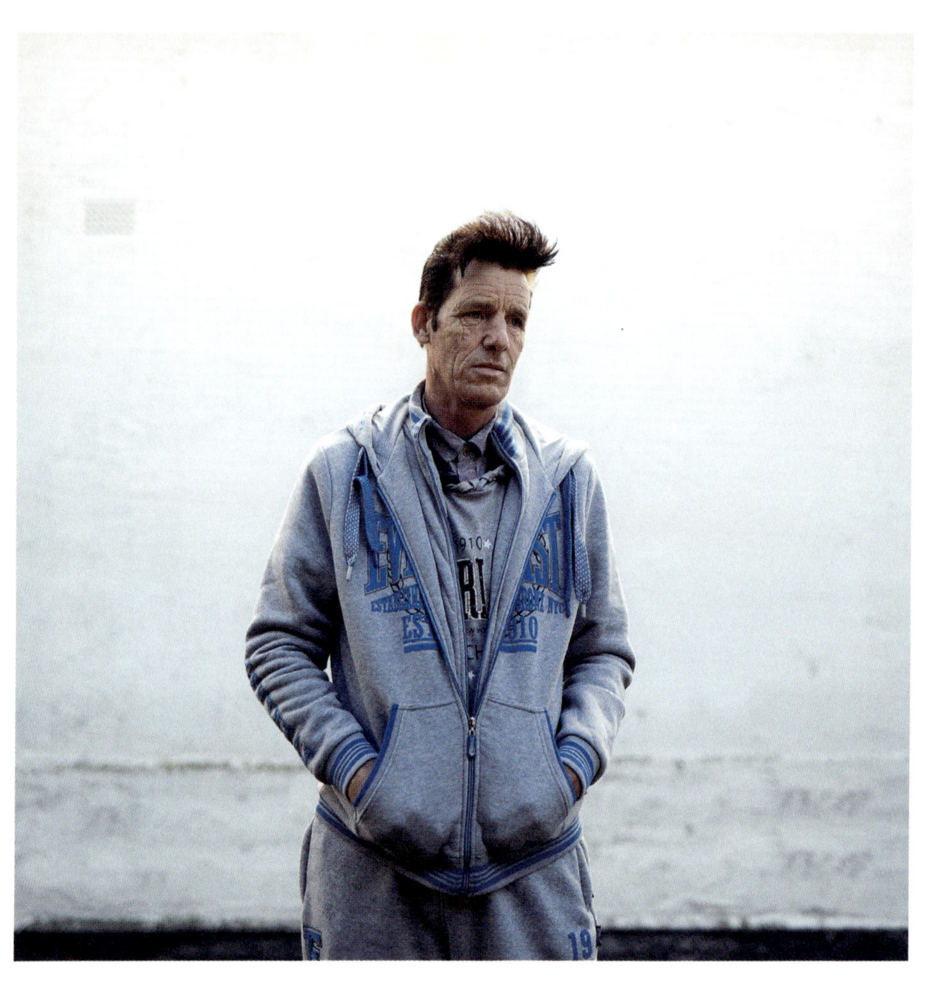

MICHAEL/ELVIS
by Fraser Wright
Richmond, North Yorkshire

Michael has maintained his Elvis-inspired look for years.
He is a familiar face on the Reeth Road social housing estate
and has been known to impersonate the King when asked.

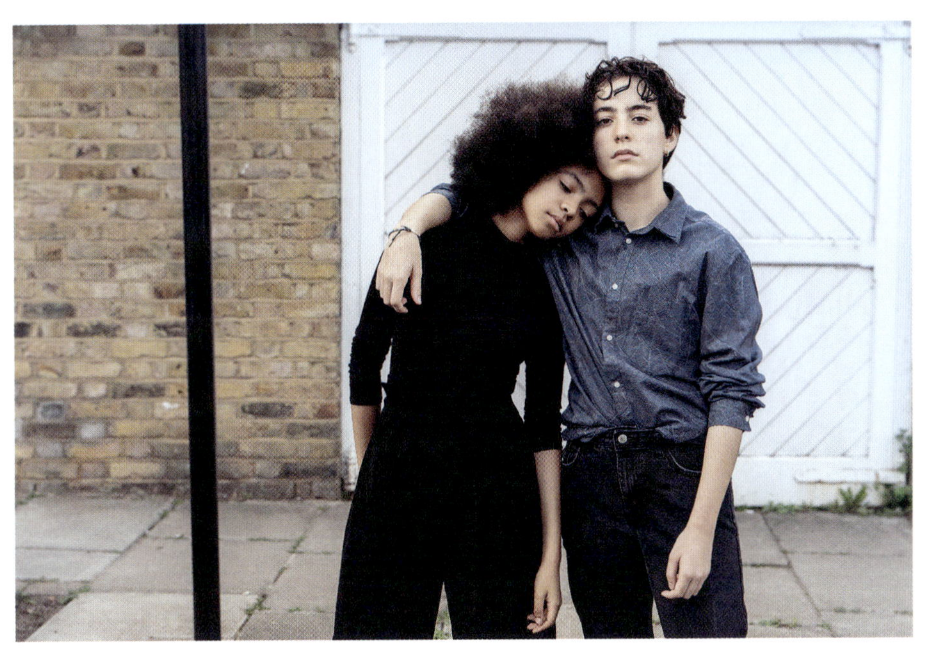

LUCI AND ELIO
by Reme Campos
London

After photographing Luci and Elio, I later discovered
that Elio (right) is transgender. 'I'm most comfortable when
I'm not confined by a set of expectations,' Elio said.

CHRIS BENNETT
by Oliver Mayhall
London

Chris is almost entirely covered in tattoos. He finds
the process of getting a tattoo therapeutic, relaxing and
enjoyable. He doesn't care what other people think
because it makes him happy.

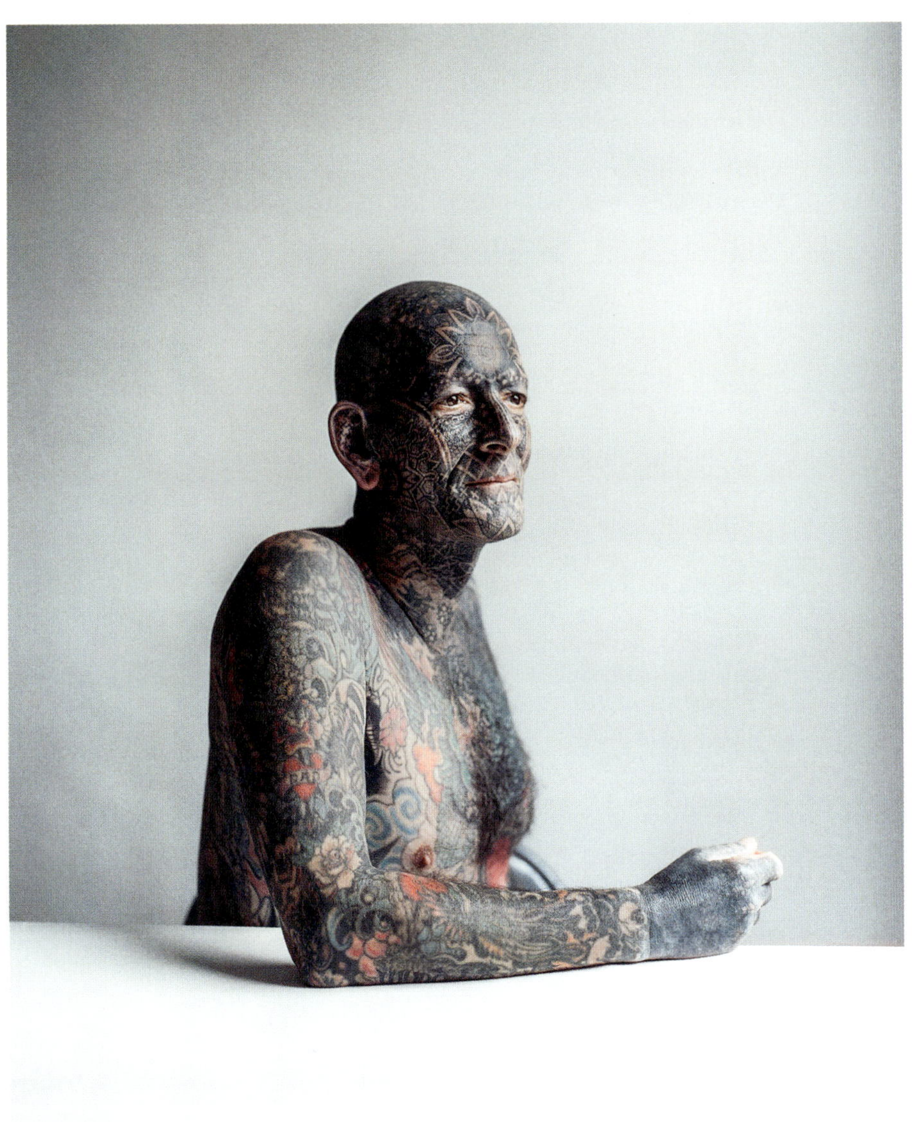

JAKE
by Mary Turner
Houghton-le-Spring, Tyne and Wear

A young cage fighter catches his breath after winning his
first public fight. Although the sport has a bad reputation
it provides a lifeline for some young men in the north east
of England who have grown up in deprived communities.

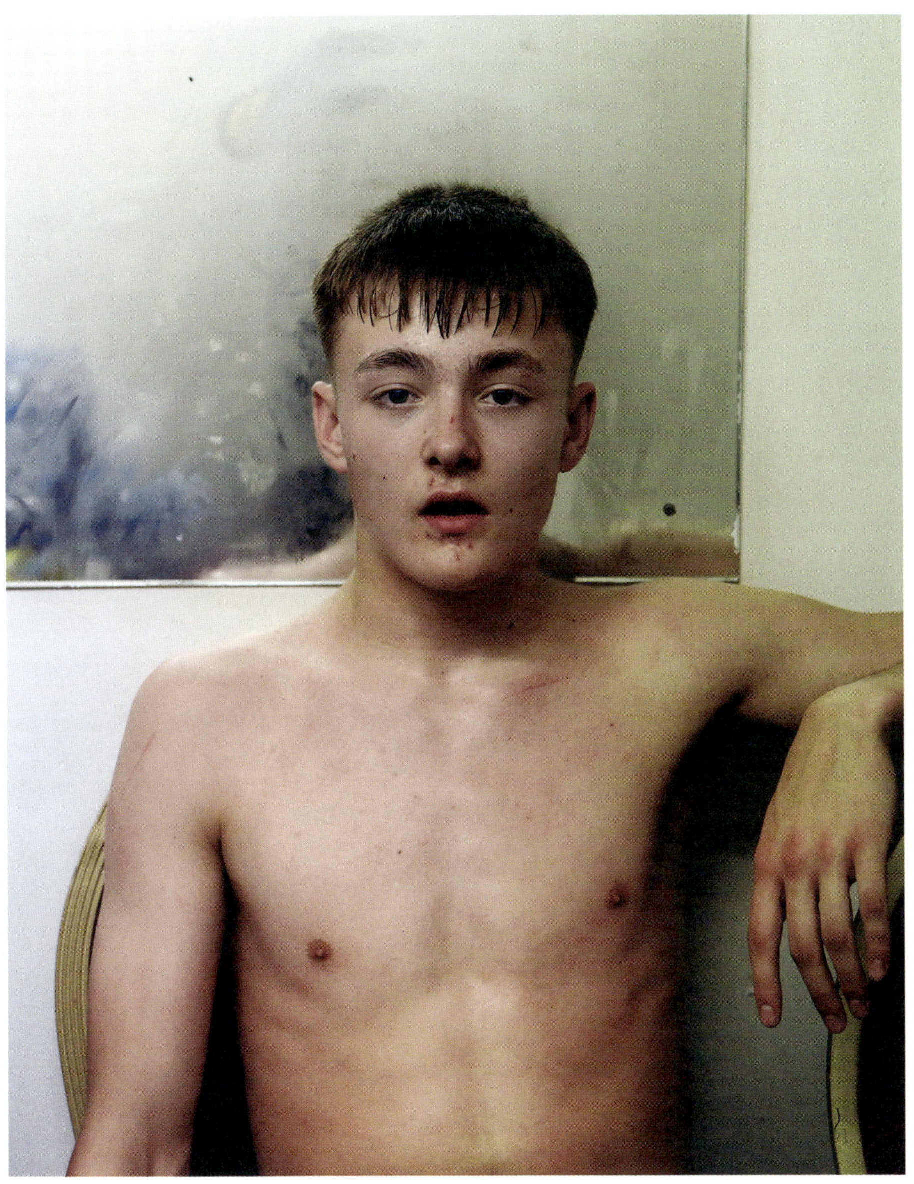

COLE
by Toby Binder
Belfast, County Antrim

I have been documenting the daily lives of teenagers in
British working-class communities for more than a decade.
After the 2016 EU referendum I focused on Belfast. The
problems the teenagers encounter are similar no matter
which side of the Peace Walls they live on.

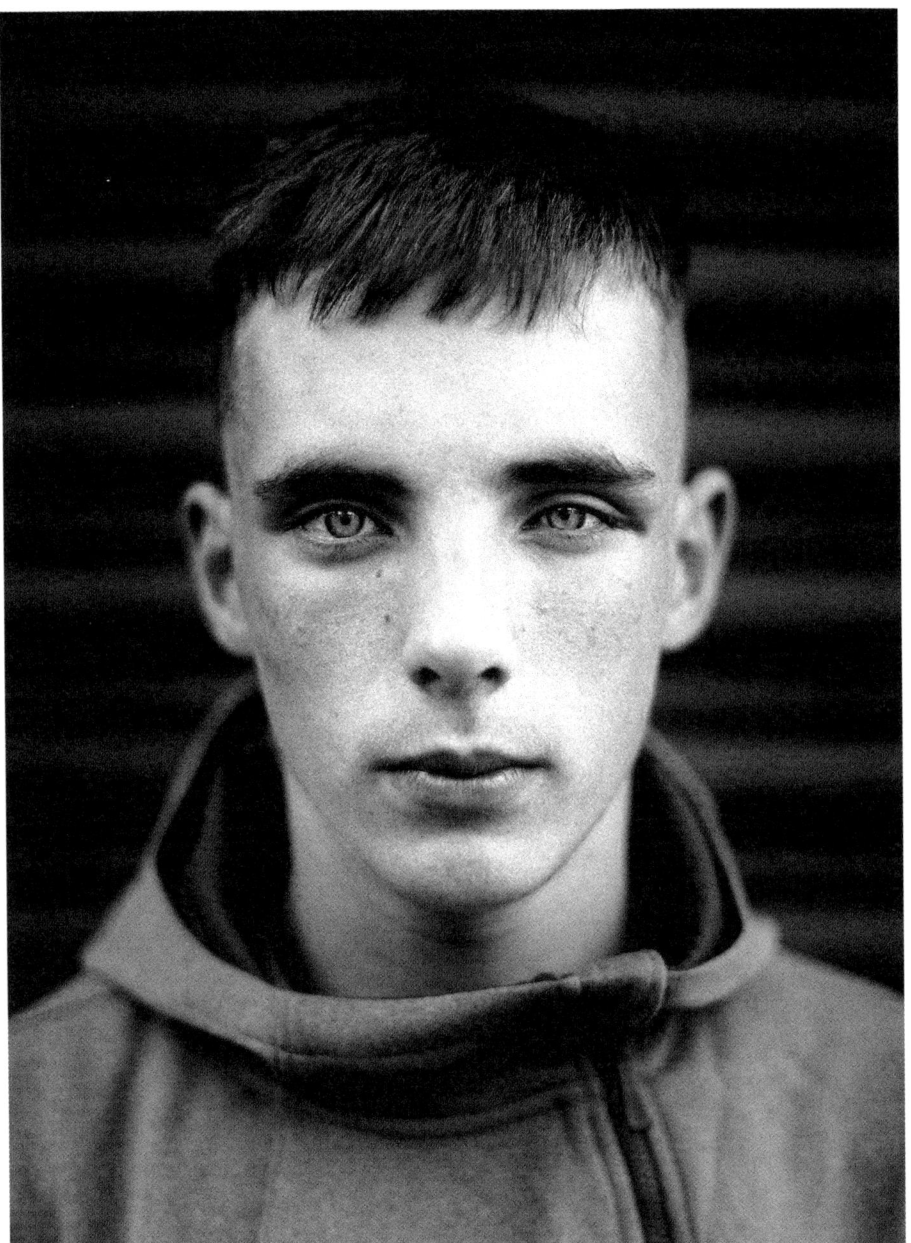

CHUCK
by John Mannell
London

Sometimes you pass someone who has positive energy –
Alex, also known as Chuck, is one such person.
I try to take a photograph of a different person
every day to celebrate the good in people.

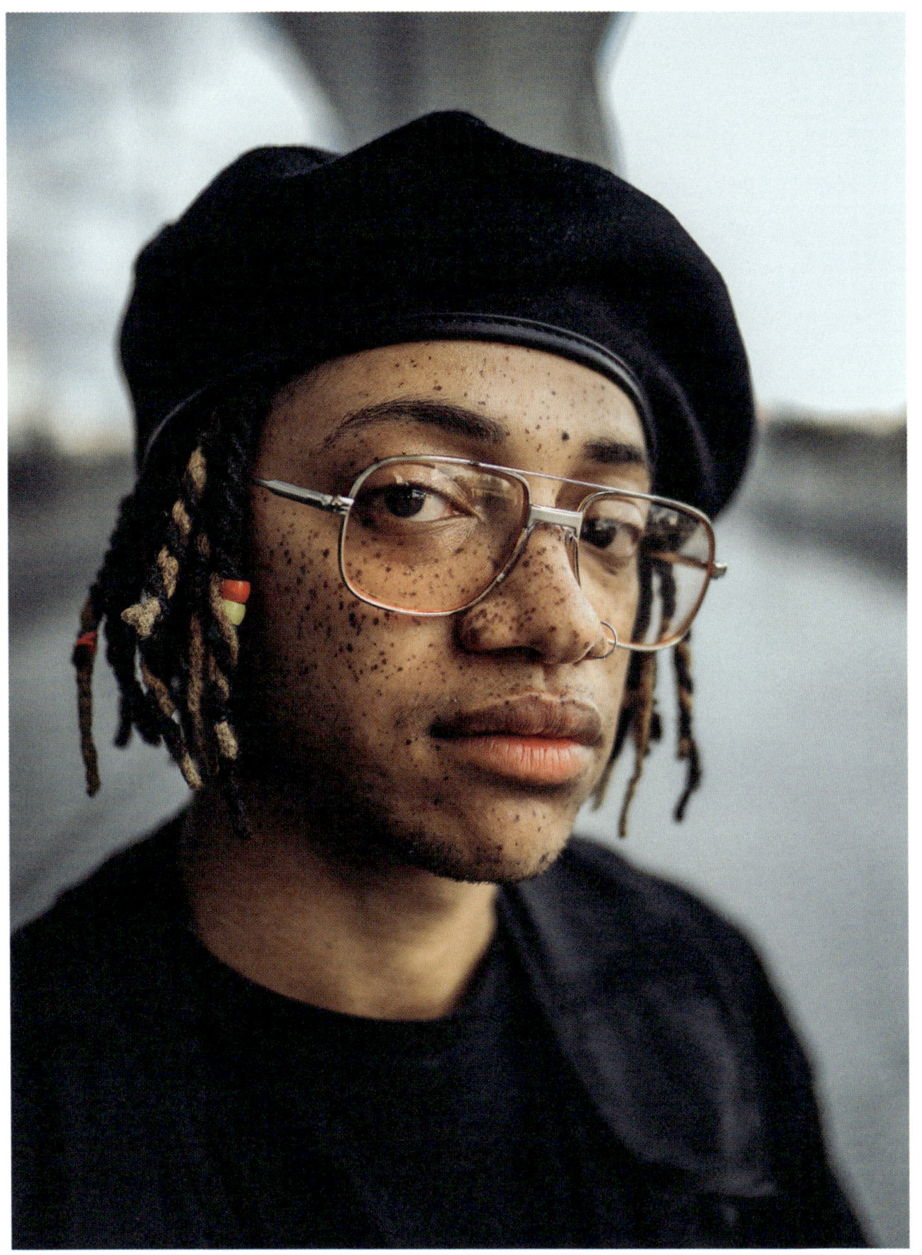

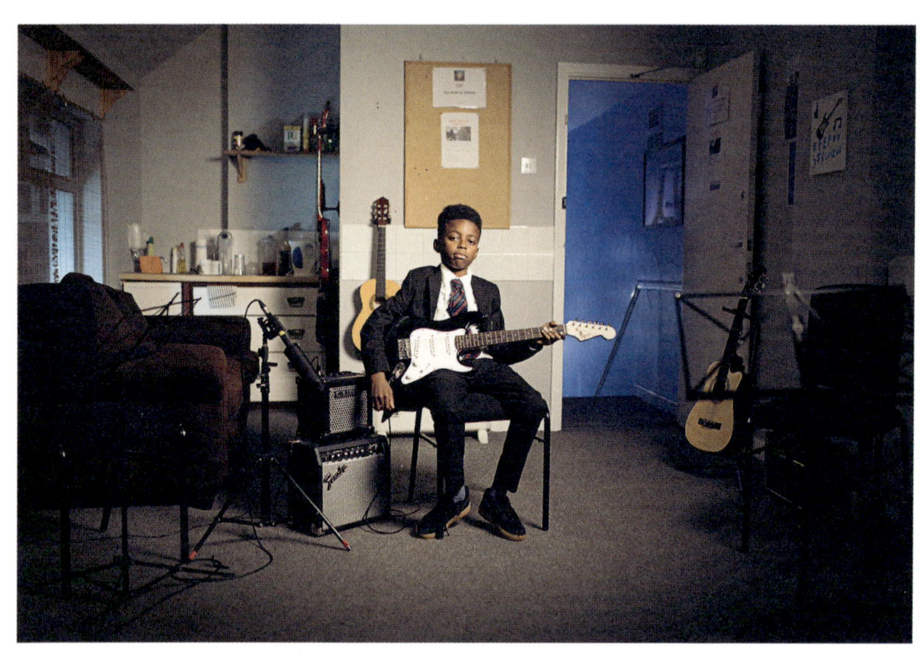

GEMAR AND HIS GUITAR
by Kelvin Murray
London

Gemar is a talented young guitarist. Although he is only
10 years old he has the look and vibe of a blues guitarist
from Chicago. He said: 'For as long as I can remember, I've
loved music. I want to carry on making my own music and
learn to play the piano and violin too.'

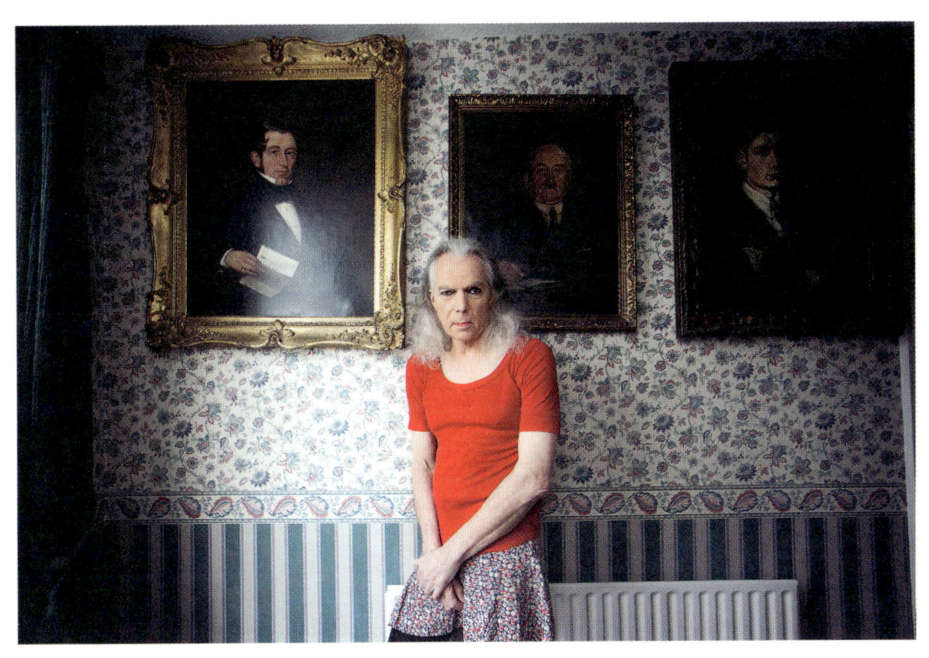

ANDIE AND HER FOREFATHERS
by Chloe Rosser
London

I met Andie at a transgender club. The oil paintings
show her father, grandfather and great-grandfather and
have been passed down through the family. 'I have always
felt they don't really approve of me,' Andie said.

ANN
by Heather McDonough
London

Ann and I have been neighbours for over 25 years.
She was kind enough to take time out from making her
lunch one Sunday to sit for this portrait. I sometimes like
to allude to iconic American paintings in my images and on
this occasion Ann played the part of Whistler's mother.

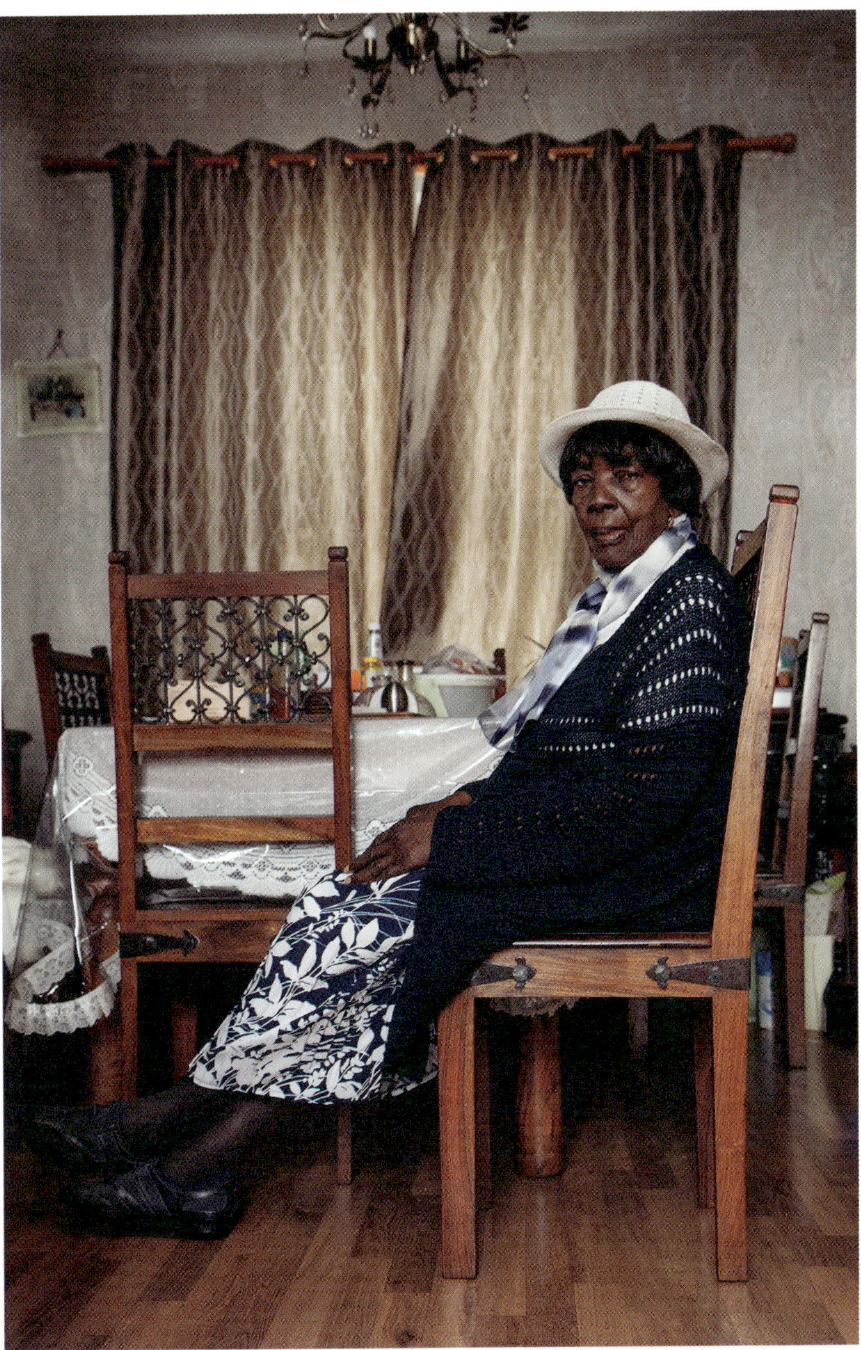

CHARLIE CATTRALL
by Phil Sharp
London

Charlie is an actor and director. We discovered we are
only a few months apart in age and enjoyed talking about
the different paths our lives have taken.

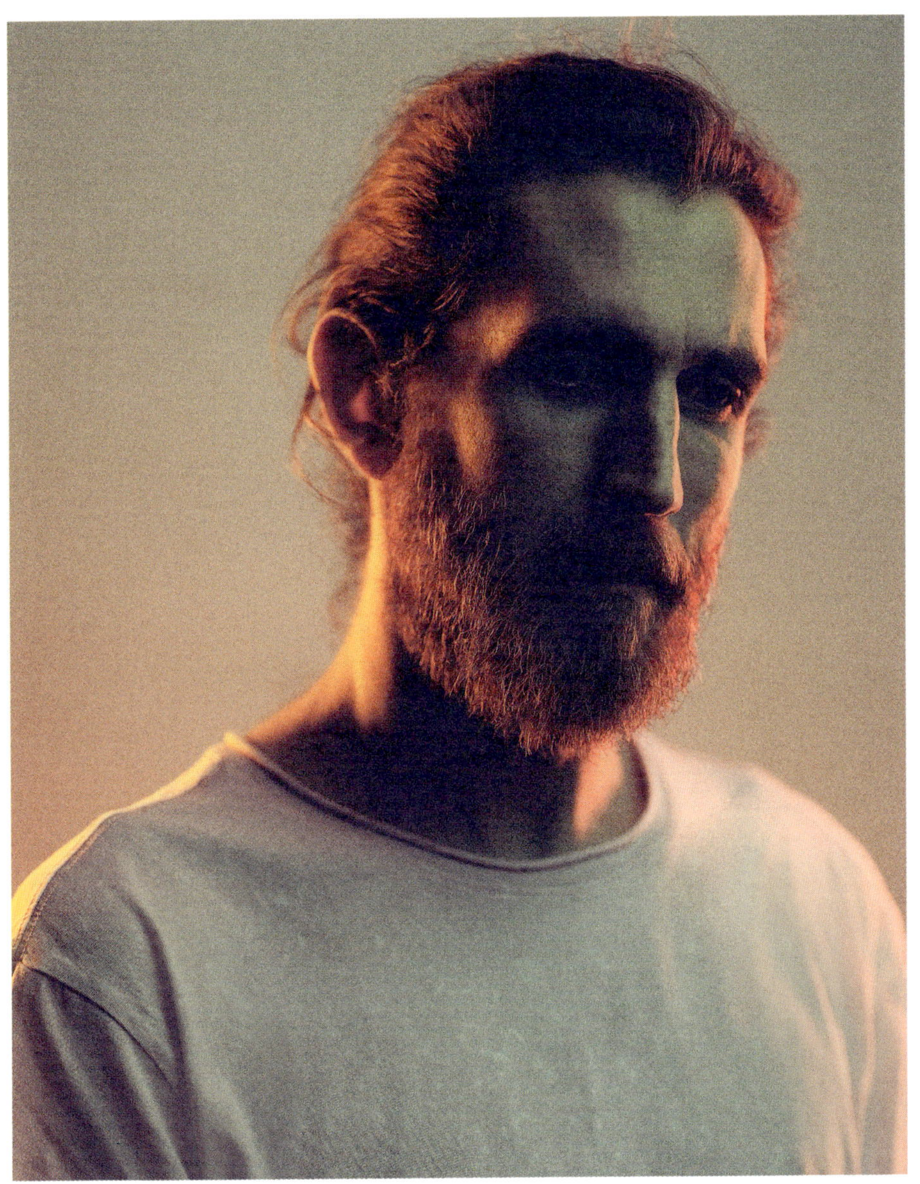

ANTHONY
by Danny North
Donington Park, Leicestershire

Anthony is a Paralympian swimmer. I photographed him
at Download Festival for a long-term project about heavy
metal fans with disabilities. I wanted to research the
connection between the music and how it unites
and empowers its followers.

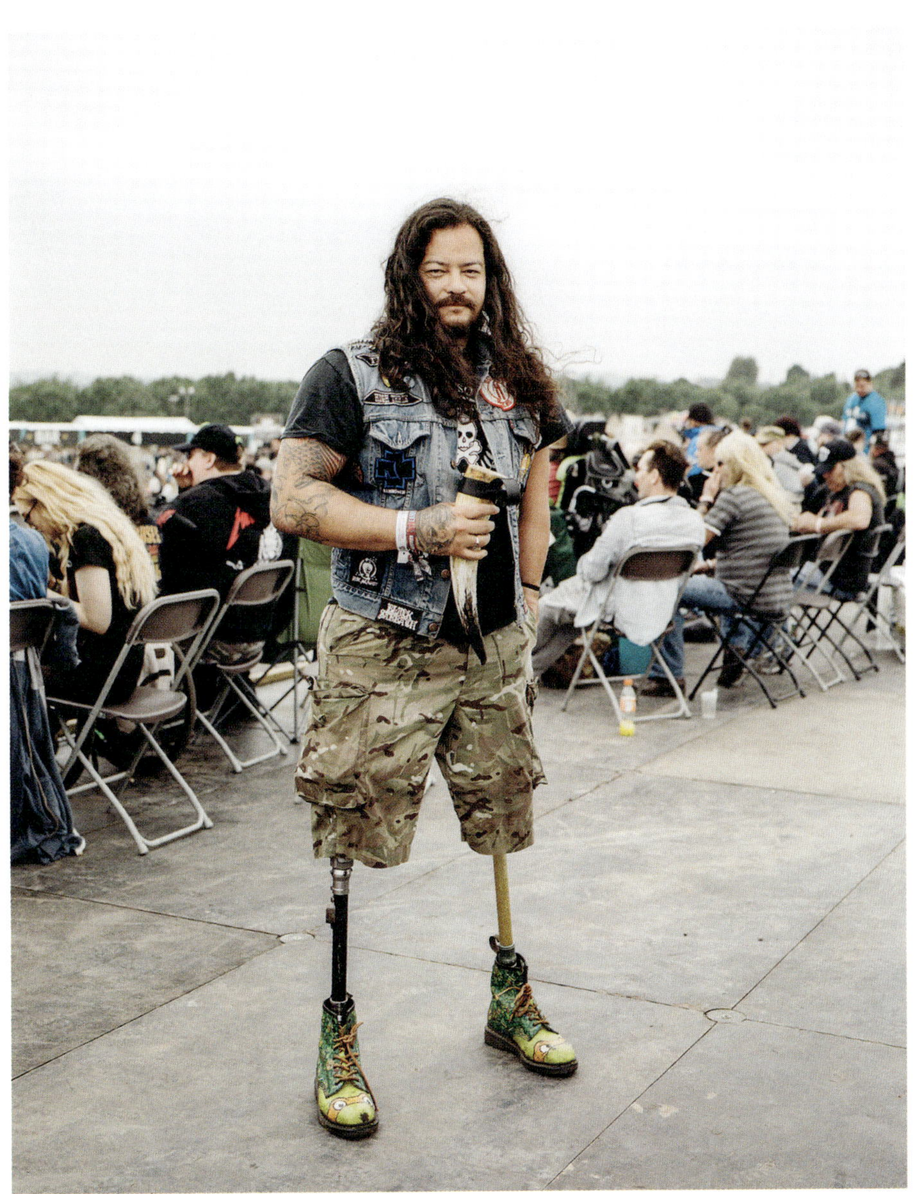

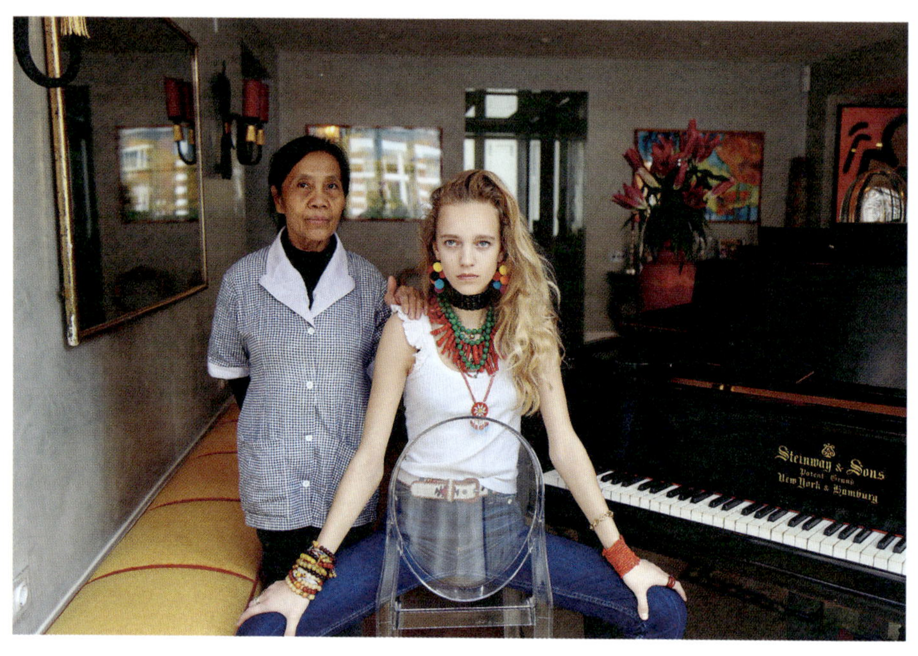

GROWING UP WITH AMY
by Alexandra Adami
London

Our housekeeper Amy and my daughter Allegra have
a close bond. Allegra tried on some of Amy's Indonesian
jewellery and combined it with her own.

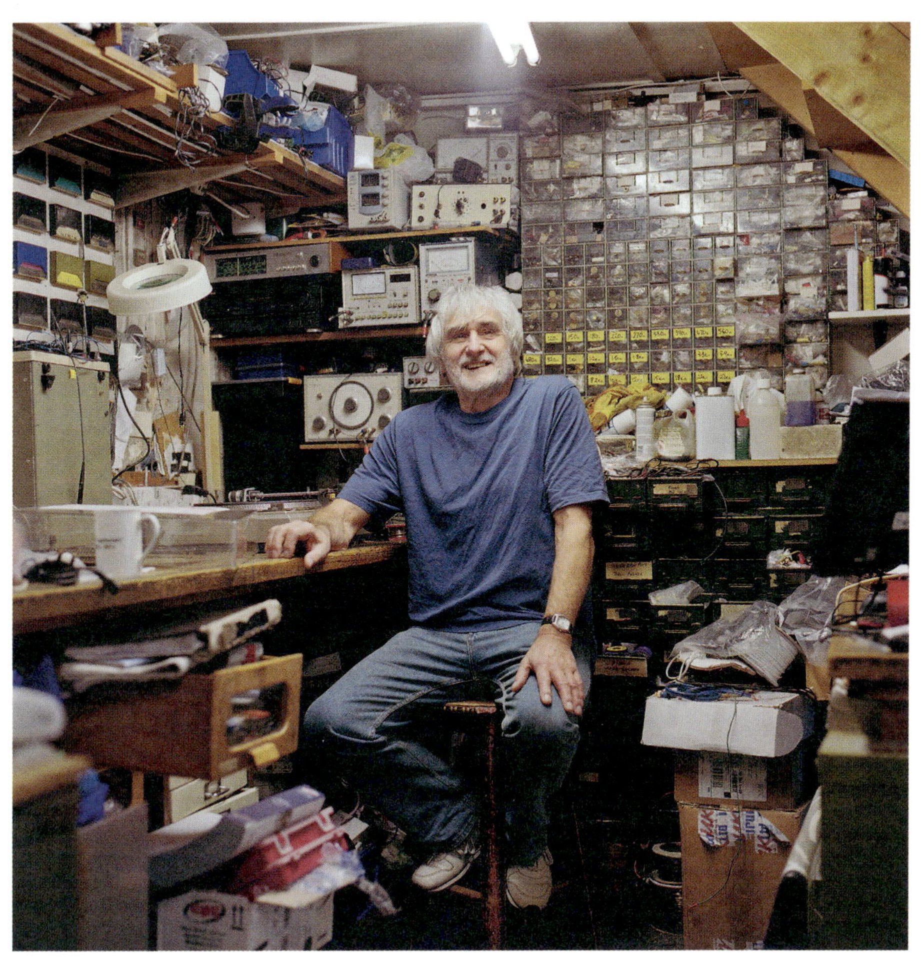

THE REPAIR DEPARTMENT
by Jamie Harriss
London

Seventy-year-old Robin is an engineer. I was taken
by the chaos of his workplace and the sheer volume
of stuff that fills the space. Robin's practical knowledge
and skills are just as dense.

WILFRID AND WILFRID
by Imogen Forte
London

A portrait of the artist Wilfrid Wood at his studio with
a sculpture he made of himself. Wilfrid learnt his craft
working on the television show *Spitting Image*. He uses
pencils and sometimes plasticine to create incredibly
expressive and characterful portraits.

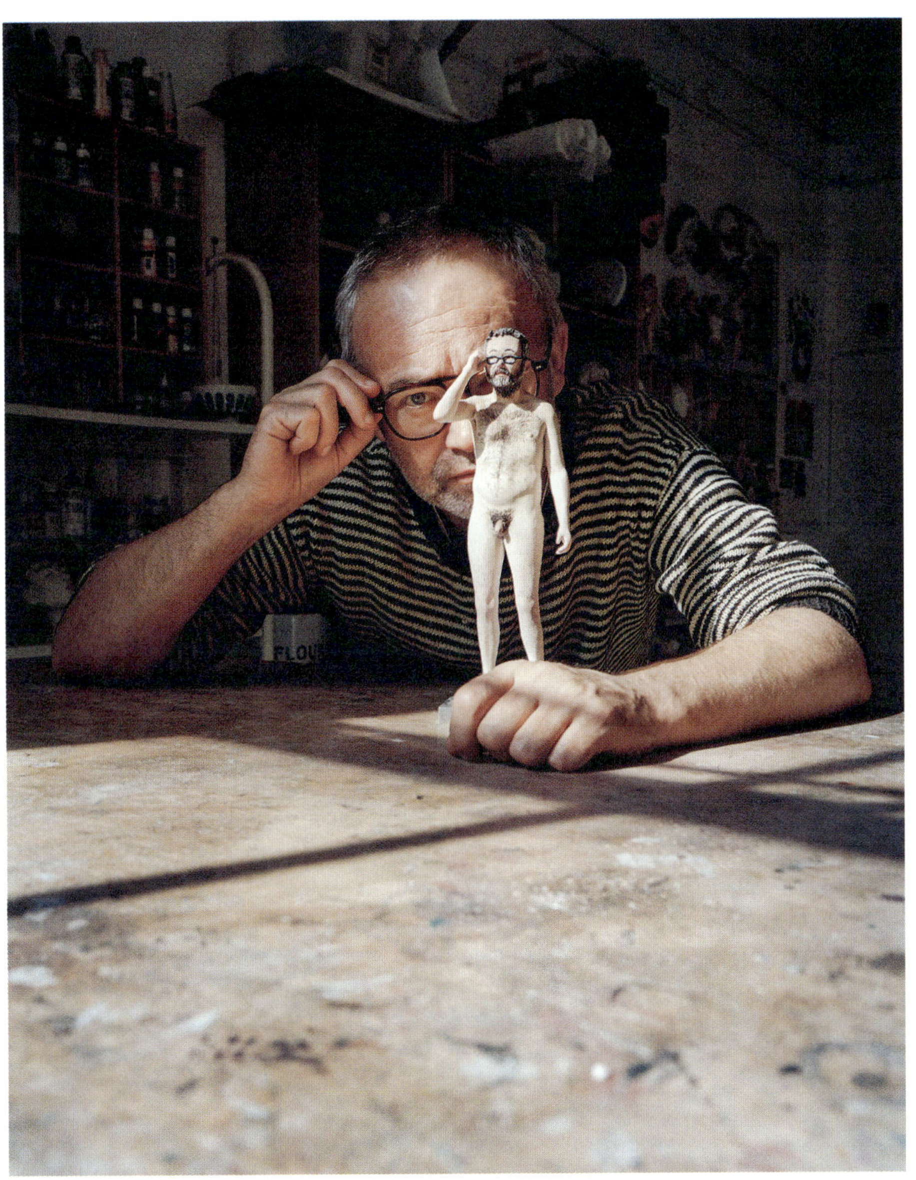

CUMBRIAN WRESTLER
by Leigh Anderson
Ennerdale, Cumbria

Local Cumbrian junior wrestling champion
Matty Hodgson at a country fayre. Matty, who is
dressed in a traditional Westmorland wrestling uniform,
travels all over Cumbria and Northumberland with
his family to compete.

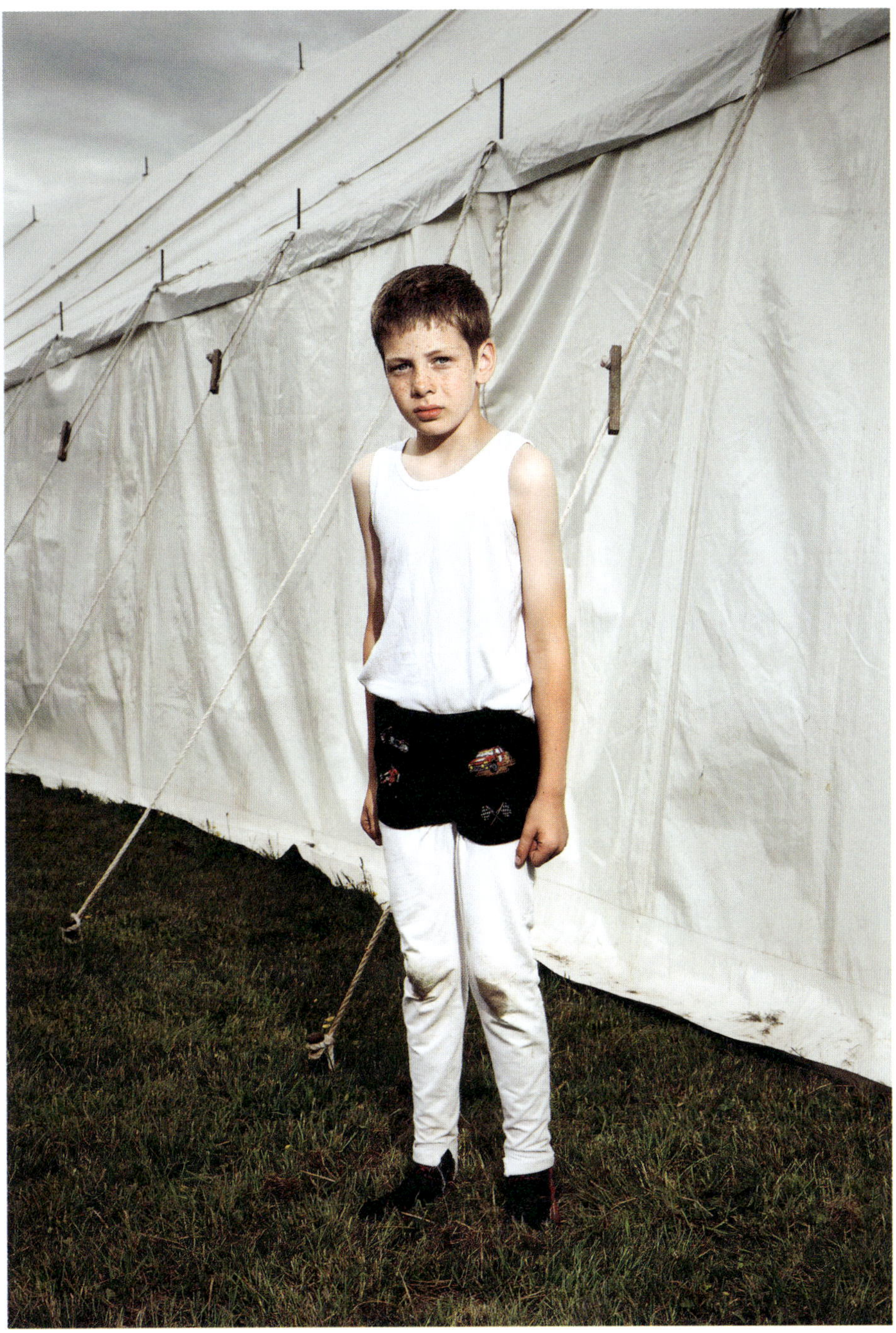

GRACE
by Fiona Bailey
Oswestry, Shropshire

Grace is a student at Derwen College, an incredible
institution for young people with learning difficulties and
disabilities. I photographed her on prom night, a night that
traditionally celebrates the transition into adult life.

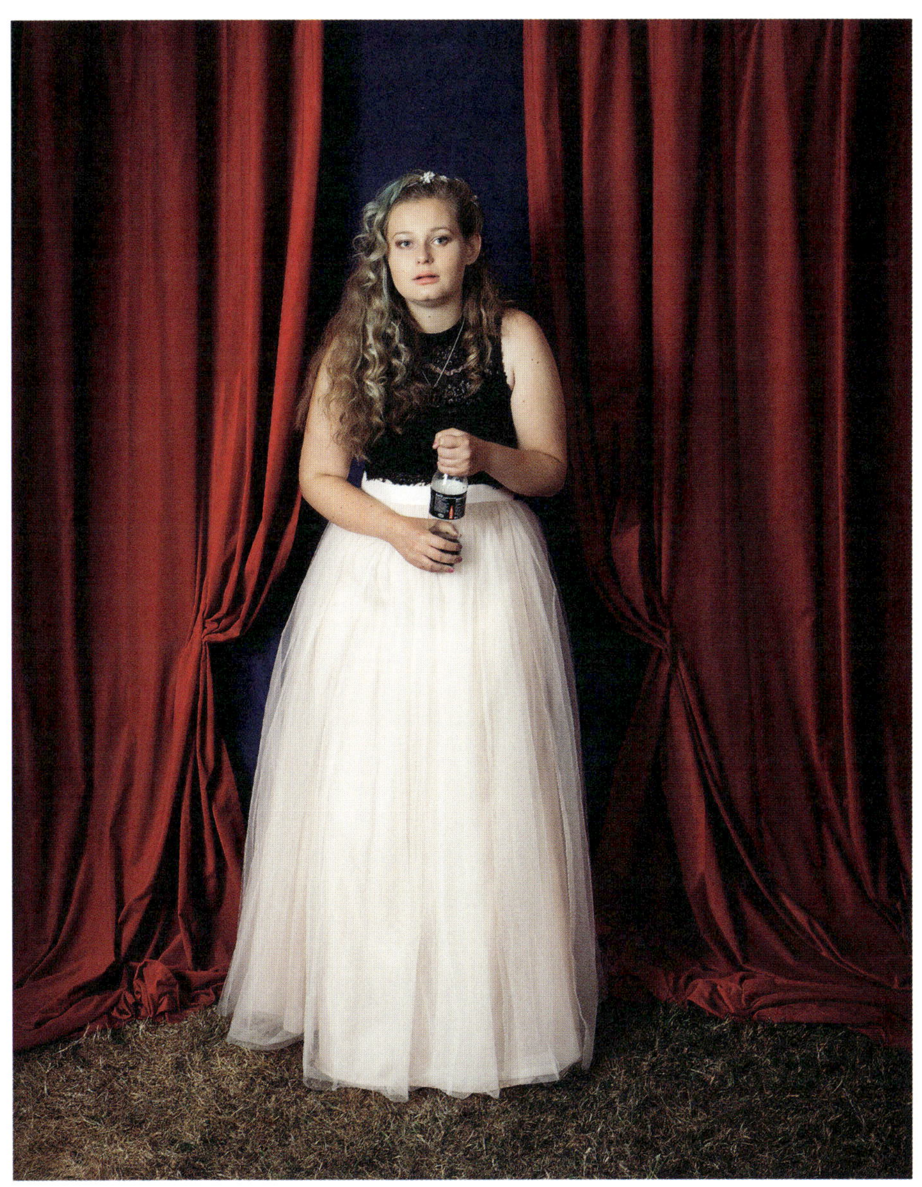

ANNA BURNS
by Charlie Forgham-Bailey
London

I photographed the author Anna Burns a couple of days
after her novel *Milkman* won the 2018 Man Booker Prize.
She was surprisingly chirpy and chatty considering
the gruelling schedule of interviews and appearances
she was doing.

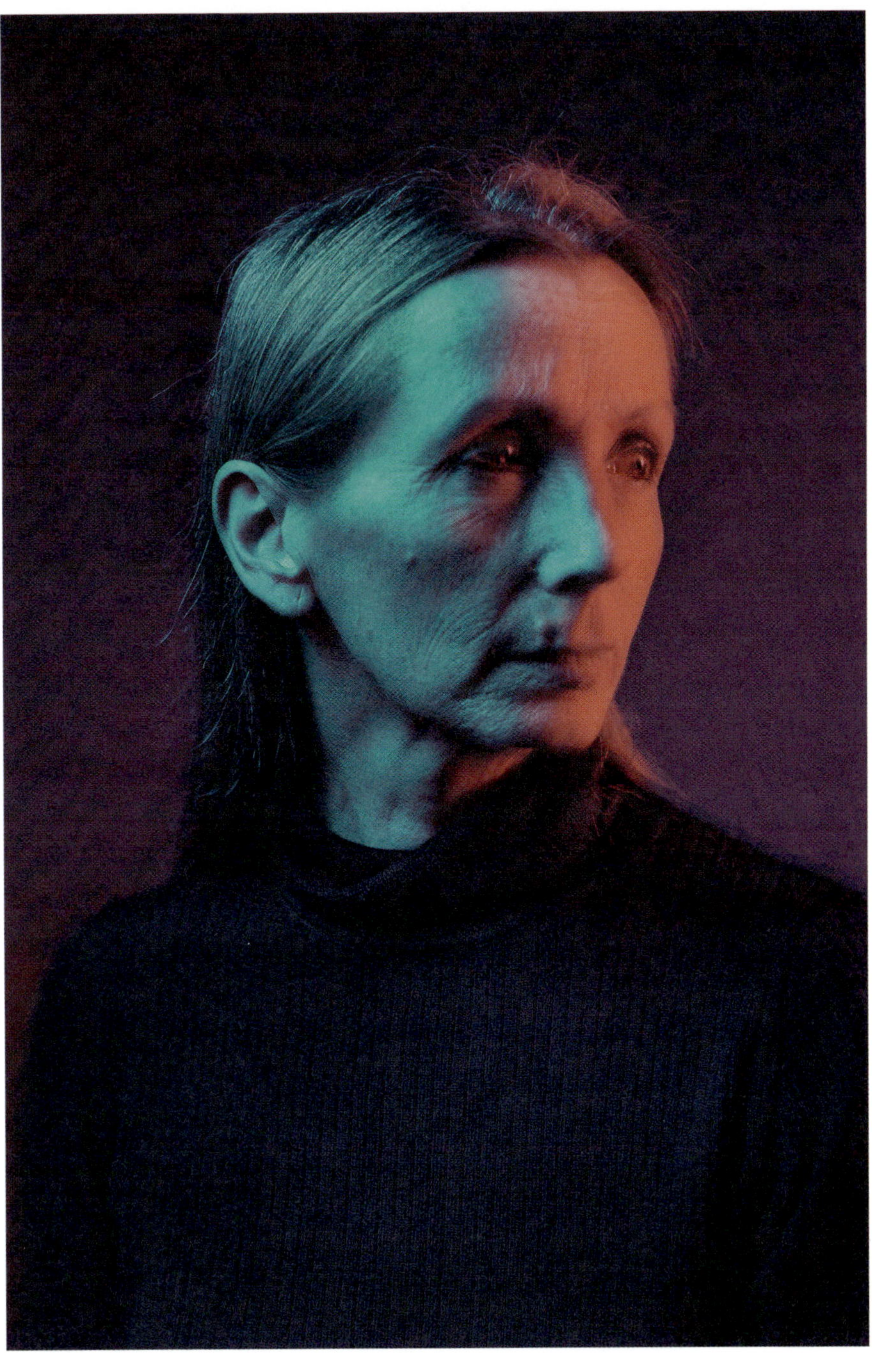

MIKO THE PUP
by Robert Timothy
London

This is Miko dressed up in fetish gear as a puppy.
Making this work about gay men and London's fetish
and BDSM scene is challenging; it takes a lot of explaining
and trust to convince the men I will portray
them sympathetically.

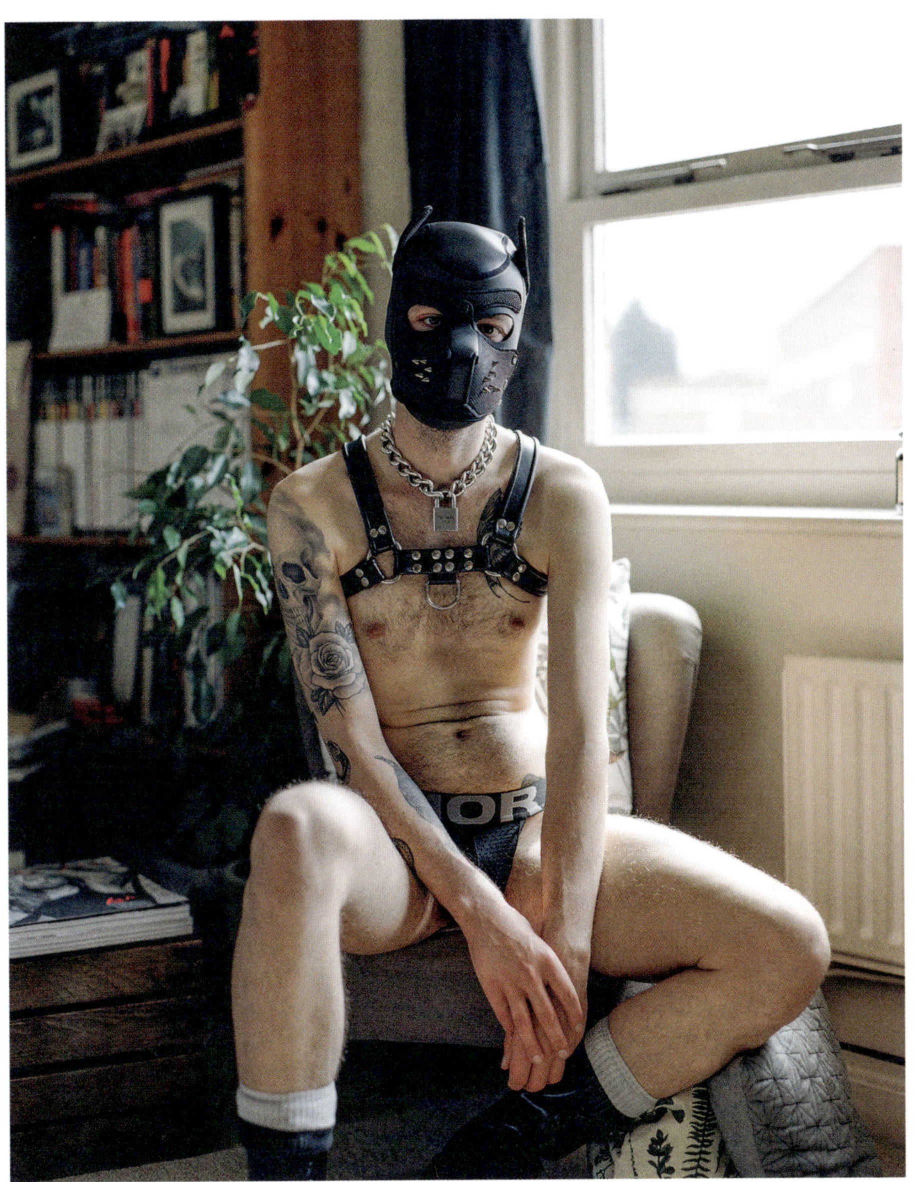

SUFFOLK SKYDANCER
by Harry Hall
Thorndon, Suffolk

This is the 'captain' of the Mid Suffolk Radio Modellers,
a club whose members fly all types of remote control
aircraft. I asked what made a perfect day of flying
and he said: 'Good weather, no wind and
a few digestive biscuits.'

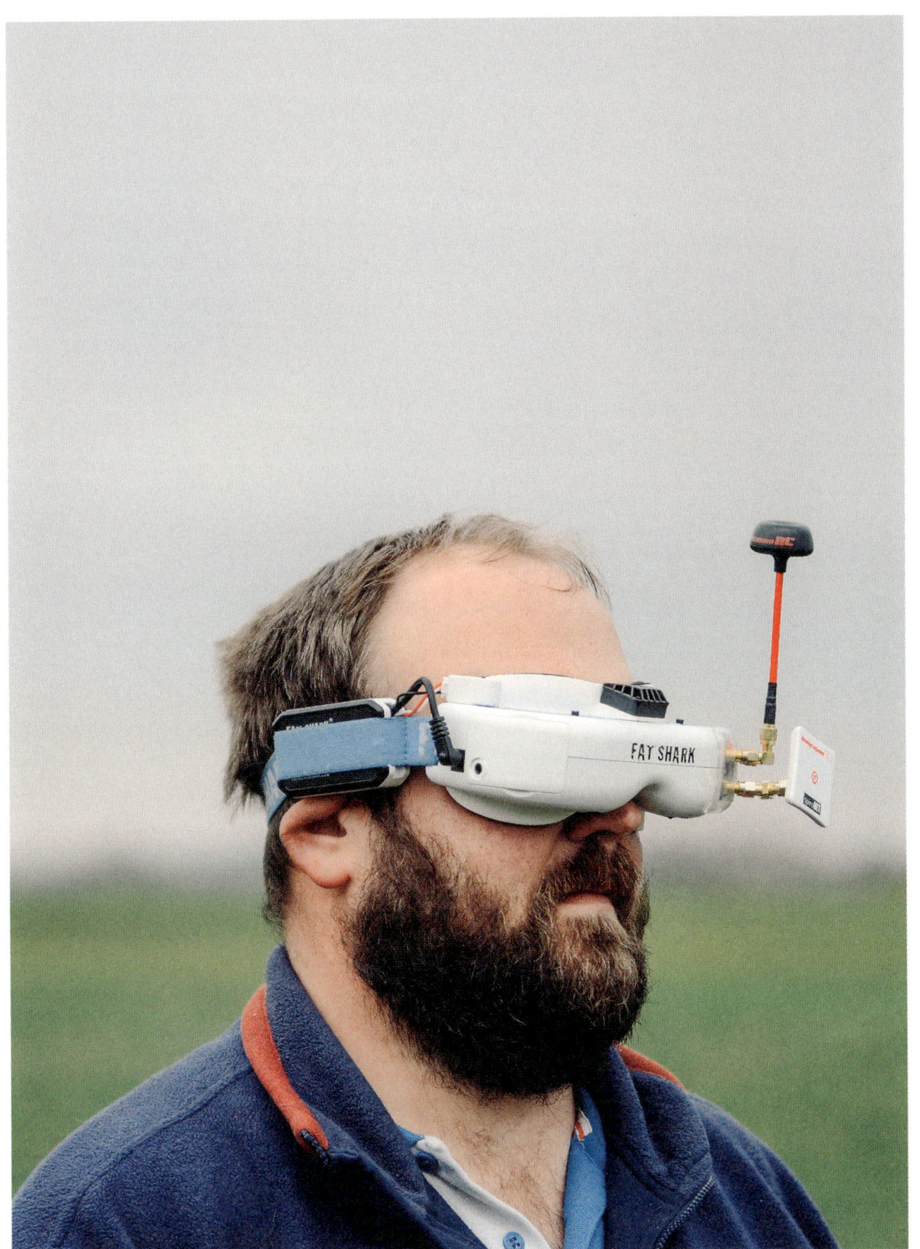

FAT SHARK
RC

COMING UP FOR AIR
by Barry Lewis
London

Julian is an old friend and professional musician and singer.
I was taking some images for his album cover and when
we finished it was time to swim and play!

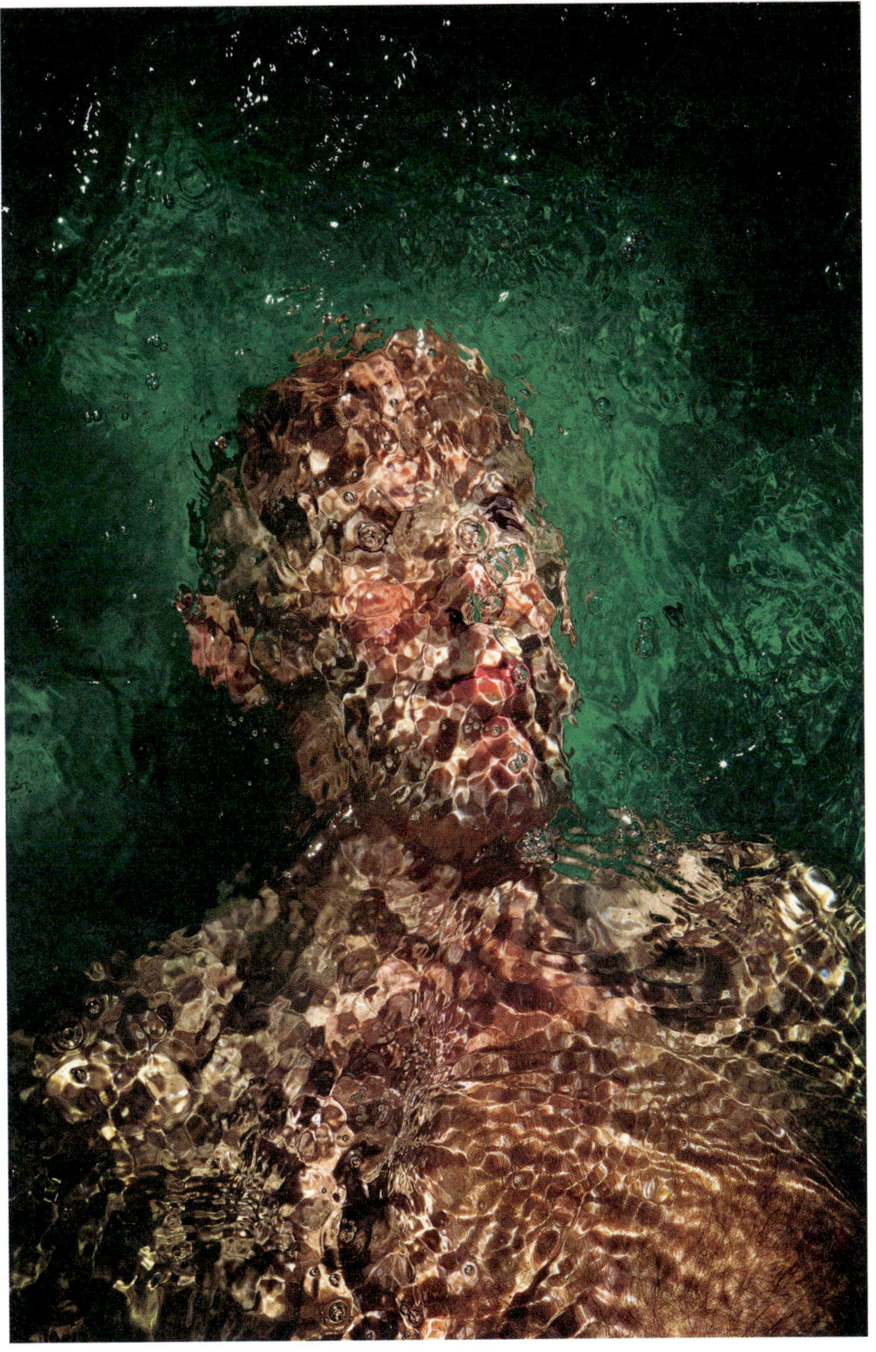

WALKING OFF THAT EDGE
by Joe Horner
Sheffield, South Yorkshire

Ryan had never been to this part of South Yorkshire before
and couldn't help but get as close to the edge as he could
to see how far the drop was.

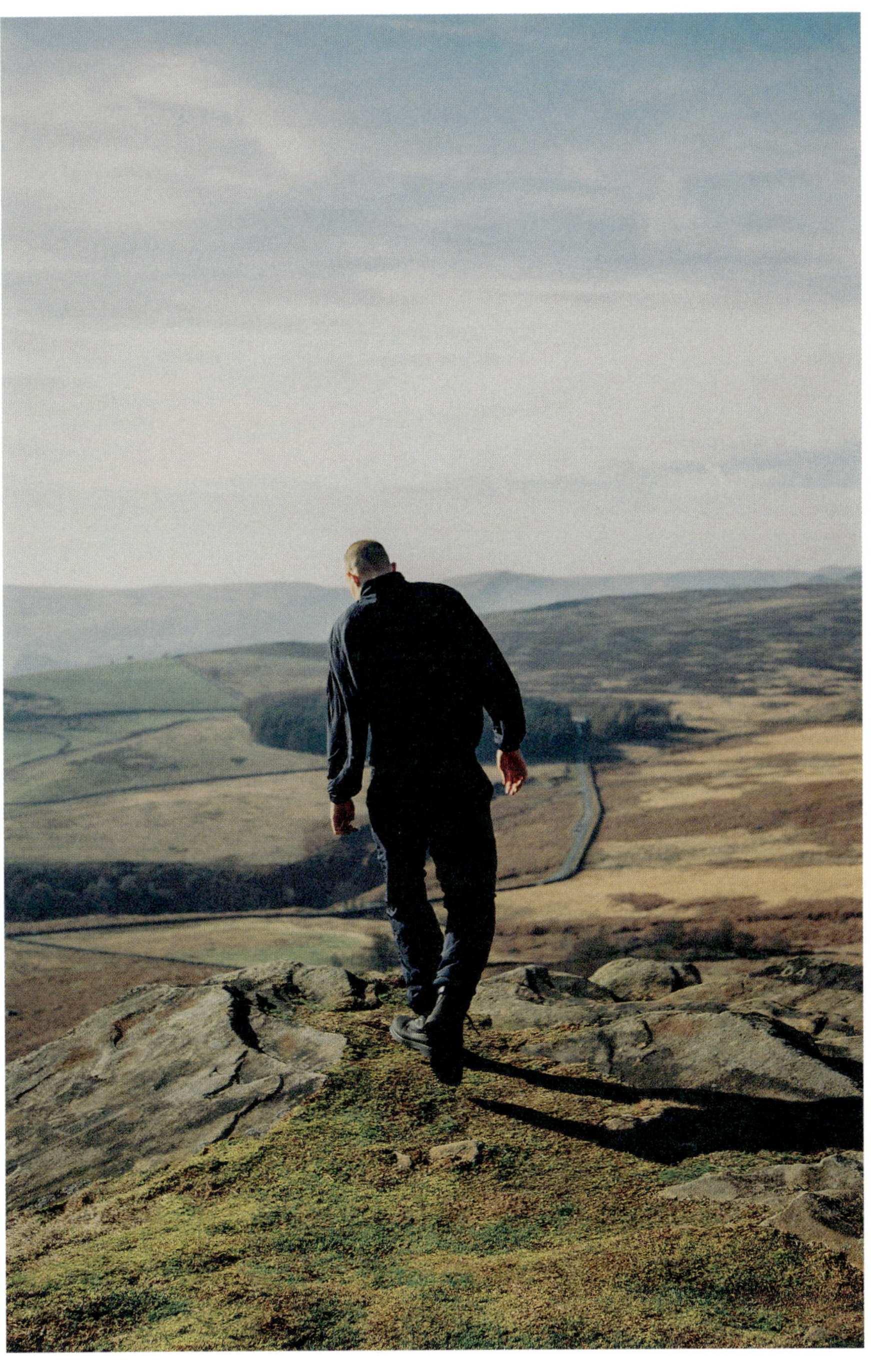

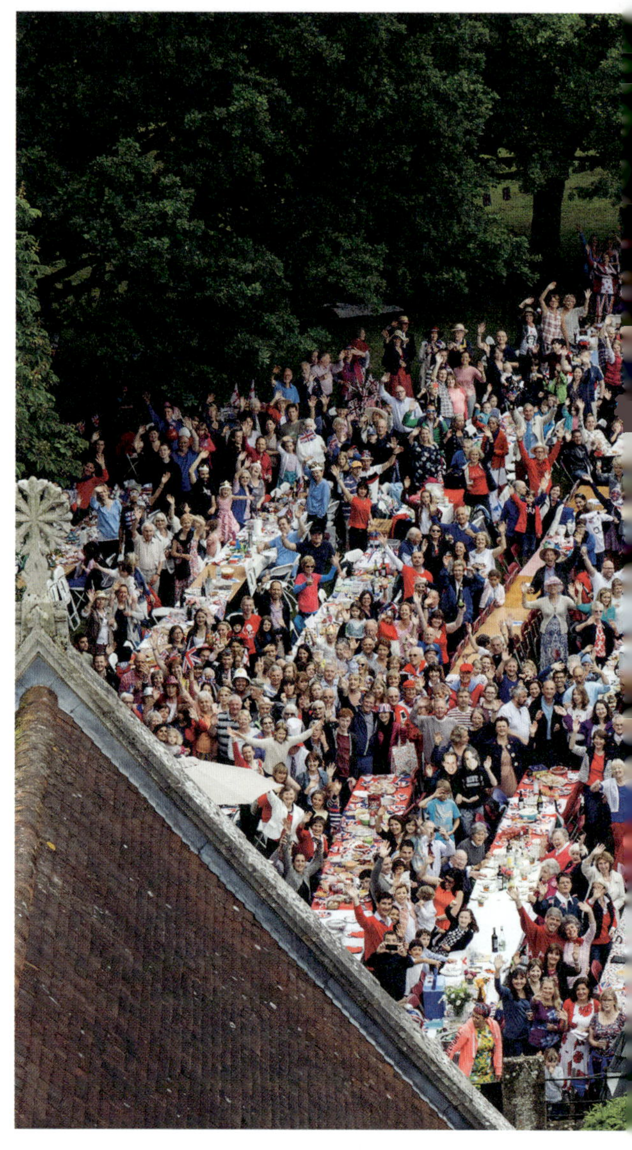

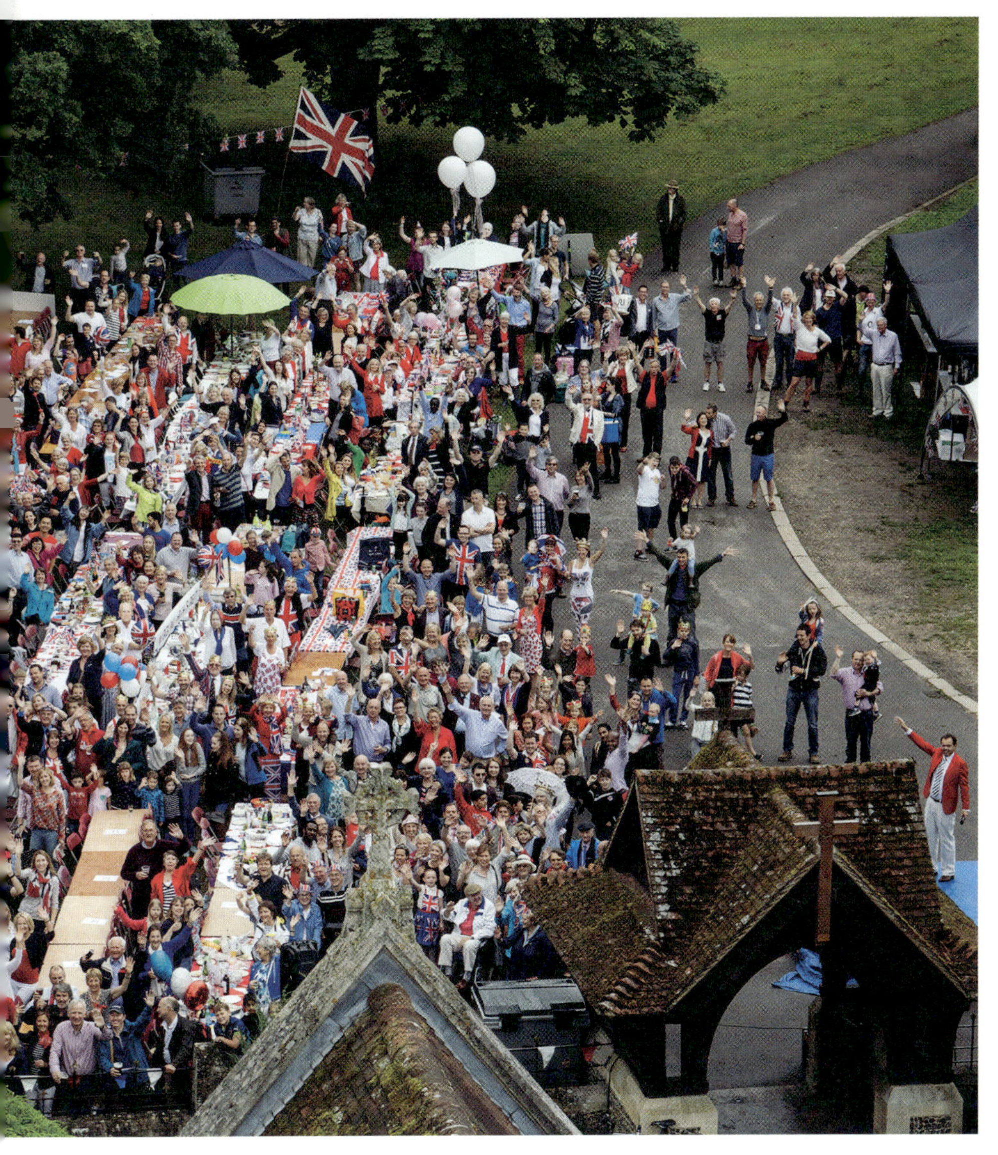

CELEBRATING THE QUEEN'S 90TH BIRTHDAY
by Tim Hodges
Wargrave, Berkshire

331

Index